CASINO MANAGEMENT
A Strategic Approach

Kathryn Hashimoto

East Carolina University

Upper Saddle River, New Jersey
Columbus, Ohio

Library of Congress Cataloging-in-Publication Data

Hashimoto, Kathryn.
  Casino management : a strategic approach / Kathryn Hashimoto.
     p. cm.
  Includes bibliographical references and index.
  ISBN-13: 978-0-13-192672-1
  ISBN-10: 0-13-192672-1
  1. Casinos--Management. I. Title.

  HV6711.H376 2008
  795.068--dc22

                          2007046009

Vice President and Executive Publisher: Vernon R. Anthony
Executive Editor: William Lawrensen
Editorial Assistant: Lara Dimmick
Developmental Editor: Dan Trudden
Project Managers: Jane Bonnell/Kris Roach
Production Coordination: Pine Tree Composition
Art Director: Miguel Ortiz
Cover Designer: Rob Aleman
Cover Images (2): Casino: Julie Cook, Getty Images/Photonica; B/W Vintage: Jon Brenneis, Getty
Images/Time&Life Pictures
Operations Specialist: Deidra Schwartz
Director of Marketing: David Gesell
Marketing Manager: Leigh Ann Sims
Marketing Coordinator: Alicia Dysert
Director, Image Resource Center: Melinda Patelli
Manager, Rights and Permissions: Zina Arabia
Manager, Visual Research: Beth Brenzel
Manager, Cover Visual Research & Permissions: Karen Sanatar
Image Permission Coordinator: Nancy Seise
Poker chip image used with permission by Stephan Aarstol, Sidepot Gaming Company.
This book was set in Jansen by Laserwords. It was printed and bound by R.R. Donnelley & Sons Company.
The cover was printed by R.R. Donnelley & Sons Company.

To the one who inspires and motivates me in my endeavors,
George

and to

Ken Rayes,
my English editor and friend.

Preface

This textbook is entitled *Casino Management: A Strategic Approach*. Unlike other casino books, this textbook's organization focuses on the more traditional theoretical approach of strategic market planning and then places the different aspects of casinos within that framework. It begins by exploring the macroenvironment of casinos and then moves to the most important impacts of these external environments on the consumers and the competition. Once we understand which forces casinos cannot control, we move to the internal control factors of product, price, place, and promotions.

In comparing this book to other casino books (including my first two), there are definite differences in the treatment of topics and in the topics themselves.

Chapter 1

The first chapter explains the organization of the book and gives a general overview and introduction to the subject of casino management.

Chapters 2 and 3

Rather than discussing the pros and cons of gaming, there are separate chapters on economic and social issues. Typically, economic issues are treated as positive, and social issues as negative to gaming. In this book, both the economic and social chapters balance the positives and negatives that casinos bring to a region. This arrangement allows the authors to discuss issues that have not been previously explored in other textbooks.

Chapter 4

Rather than discuss what legislatures do, this chapter discusses why casino managers need to understand politics. Typically, discussions on political and legal environments have been blended in a discussion of different legislation and laws that impact casinos. The main purpose of this chapter is to supply casino managers with the necessary understanding of how governments think when they are formulating casino laws and regulations. Therefore, the perspective in this chapter is unique in that it explores how and why governments do what they do, which is then separated from the legal environment.

Chapter 5

This chapter concerns the legal environment and explores the employment side of the laws and what students need to know about these issues.

Chapter 6

All of the issues in previous chapters come together to determine how and why people make the decision to come to a casino and buy the assortment of available products. This is described as consumer behavior.

Chapter 7

This chapter explores the development of the corporate culture within the casinos, as well as the impact of technology on casino operations. As the United States has become more sophisticated and complex, casino culture has also adapted to blend in with these changes. This chapter reflects several trends that have altered the way casinos do business. Of course, because the technology is rapidly changing and molding the industry, the chapter gives special emphasis not only to technology's impact on culture but also on all the other operations.

Chapter 8

As more people decide to gamble, the competition grows. So this chapter explores the history of gaming in the United States—the circumstances surrounding the development of each type of casino. Typically in other textbooks, this discussion would have a separate chapter on each of the different types of casinos; however, we have placed each type within its historical context to show the rapid growth of competition.

Chapter 9

Once we explore the external factors that impact casinos, we look at the internal controls that casinos use to modify or enhance these impacts: product, price, place, and promotions. This chapter begins a section that discusses standard topics but then explores a whole new realm of ideas. Chapter 9 analyzes the product of the casino—the games and statistics. This is a standard subject, but we place new emphasis on how the probabilities impact the games to make them more profitable.

Chapter 10

This is a second chapter on products which explores the organization of the casino and how it functions.

Chapters 11 and 12

Another new subject—pricing—also includes two traditional subjects—revenue control and comps/credit, which emphasize process.

Chapters 13 and 14

These two chapters cover new subjects on location/transportation and promotion. Chapter 13 explores the issues of geographic location and transportation. Chapter 14 on promotions explores how casinos get their messages to the public. It examines public relations, sales promotions, advertising, and personal selling.

Therefore, Chapters 9 to 14 explore casinos from the inside and look at the different processes they use to create a successful company once a manager understands the outside impact of the macroenvironment.

Chapter 15

Of course, no book would be complete without the requisite chapter on the future of gaming.

Included in These Chapters

The outline of the book places casino management within the traditional business framework of strategic marketing, because it is important for students to realize that casinos are like any other business with the same concerns about the environment, and the same controls. However, the differences in these topics reflect the unique nature of the industry. Students can see the differences in management but also the similarities between casino management and any other hospitality enterprise. When making decisions about gaming, students need to understand that the lessons learned in all their hospitality courses are still important in a casino, but like any industry, special aspects make it more appealing. This book is designed to allow students to see these differences and make their career choices accordingly.

To aid students in their learning, each of the chapters includes:

- Learning objectives
- Chapter outlines
- Key terms
- Review questions
- Internet sites

In addition, many chapters include vignettes. One vignette is covered across three chapters and is actually a trilogy on crisis management. The importance of developing crisis plans for casinos has emerged in light of the recent natural disasters that have occured in the United States. This is a new trend that will have an increasing role in all industries, including casinos.

Other vignettes cover topics and experiences about cultures and countries that focus on a different viewpoint from that of the American casino industry but are still an important part of the industry. In the growing global market, Europe is linked with our past, providing the roots from which we started. Korea is linked with the wave of the future, and the casino industry there will be rapidly expanding. Japan is in limbo, but its pachinko parlors are legendary as a different form of a casino. We have also included a vignette written by a Native American woman expressing in her own words what tribal life was like before and after casinos in the United States. Other vignettes include interviewing a director of surveillance and Harrah's advertising campaign.

Online Instructor's Manual

Also available are an online instructor's manual with PowerPoint presentations as well as a Companion Website which is located at www.prenhall.com/Hashimoto. To access supplementary materials online, instructors need to request an instructor access code. Go to **www.prenhall.com**, click the **Instructor Resource Center** link, and then click **Register Today** for an instructor access code. Within 48 hours after registering you will receive a confirming e-mail including an instructor access code. Once you have received your code, go to the site and log on for full instructions on downloading the materials you wish to use.

I hope you will find that this text broadens the discussion about casinos by placing it into the corporate world setting and exploring new perspectives and topics.

Acknowledgments

Industry Reviewers on Individual Chapters

Elaine Boucha, slot manager, Seven Clans Casino, MN

Roy Brennan, casino shift manager, Palms Casino Resort, NV

Michael Lockhart, games manager, Baccarat Casino, CA

Reece Middleton, executive director, Louisiana Association on Compulsive Gambling

Nicola Mohr, director marketing/advertising, Cadillac Jack's Gaming Resort, SD

Francisco Ravanelli, president, AWCOM, Inc., NV

Steve Romeo, NV

Lisa Stately, table games manager, Seven Clans Casino, MN

Kathy Williams, strategic marketing manager, PA

Lisa Young, special events, Ecker & Kainen, NV

Casinos That Supplied Materials

Linda L. Bordelon, vice president of public relations, Paragon Casino Resort, LA

Valerie DeMatties, external communications coordinator, Harrah's Entertainment, Inc., NV

Rich Westfall Sr., director of marketing, Isle of Capri. MS

Venetian Resort~Hotel~Casino, NV

We would also like to thank the individuals who reviewed this book and offered invaluable comments and suggestions. They are

Bradley Beran, Johnson & Wales — Charlotte Campus; Jack Busch; William D. Frye, Ph.D., CHE, Niagara University; Dr. Francis Kwansa, University of Deleware; Shiang-Lih Chen McCain, Widener University; and Gary Vallen, Northern Arizona University.

Vignette Authors

Marlene Sproul, Coeur d'Alene Native American tribe

Jim O'Brien, Ph.D., director, Emergency Management, Clark County, Nevada

William Thompson, Ph.D., University of Nevada, Las Vegas

Tracy Locke, Harrah's Entertainment Advertising

Contributors

Gary Anders, Arizona State University

Ki-Joon Back, Kansas State University

Bo Bernhard, Ph.D., University of Nevada, Las Vegas, director of Problem Gambling Center, Las Vegas

Peter Collins, University of Salford, England

Steve Durham, The House Advantage, Inc., Tempe, AZ

Robert C. Hannum, University of Denver

Chang Lee, Ph.D., New Mexico State University

Tanya MacLaurin, University of Guelph

Robert A. McMullin, East Stroudsburg University

Marilyn Riley, CTC., Inc. Nova Scotia, Canada

Chris Roberts, University of Massachusetts

Robert Russell, Fraser, Trebilcock, Davis and Dunlap, P.C., Detroit, MI

Jeff L. Voyles, MGM Grand Hotel and Casino, Las Vegas, NV

Dave Waddell, Fraser, Trebilcock, Davis and Dunlap, P.C., Detroit, MI

Ken Rayes, University of New Orleans

Brief Contents

Contents

Chapter 3   Social Environments   39

Chapter 4   Casino Management and Politics   57

Chapter 7   Development of Corporate Culture and Technology   155

Chapter 8   Historical Development Reflects the Changing Competitive Environment   175

PART 4   INTERNAL CONTROL   201

Chapter 9   Product: Games and Statistics   203

Chapter 10   Product: Organization   247

Chapter 11   Pricing: Revenue Control   271

Chapter 12   Pricing: Comps and Credit   303

Chapter 13   Location and Transportation   329

Chapter 14   Promotions   349

PART 5   FUTURE   375

Chapter 15   Future of Gaming   377

Glossary   392

Index   403

PART 1

Introduction

Chapter 1
A Preliminary Exploration

1 A Preliminary Exploration

Kathryn Hashimoto, East Carolina University

Learning Objectives

1. To develop an understanding of the casino environment in order to make informed decisions about questions raised concerning gaming.

2. To present a balanced view of debated issues surrounding gambling so that the reader can be knowledgeable about the casino industry.

3. To provide a brief overview of the history and development of legalized gaming in the United States.

4. To understand the macroenvironment that surrounds a casino and become familiar with the seven external forces that impact the way a casino does business.

Chapter Outline

Introduction

Americans gamble seven times more often than they purchase movie tickets.[1] In 2004, they spent about $29 billion, gambling—more than a 7 percent increase over 2003. In 2004, the commercial casino industry consisted of 445 casinos in 11 states. These commercial casinos provided nearly 350,000 jobs that earned employees more than $12 billion. In addition, state and local economies obtained direct gaming taxes of more than $4.7 billion.[2]

The History of Gambling

Gambling has existed ever since two people first sat together. After all, how do you think two cavemen decided who was going to throw the first rock at that night's expected dinner (that woolly mammoth over there)? Later, in Greek mythology, when a person wanted to make a difficult decision, he/she went to the Oracle to ask for guidance. For example, if a maiden wanted to get married, she would pray at the temple of Aphrodite (the goddess of love) for advice. The high priestess would also pray and ask for a sign. A die or two dice would then be tossed, and the gods would express their wishes through the number that came up. Usually, it was the rich and famous who went to the Oracle. As a result, gambling developed as a pastime for the aristocracy. The rich, who did not have to work, were constantly looking for distractions from the boredom of their lives. Betting relieved that monotony. Later, Romans bet at their arenas on either the Christians or the lions. This behavior seems incomprehensible today, but those were more barbaric times; however, if Martians came to Earth and watched our television programs, news, and movies, would their opinions of us be much different from ours of the Romans?

Gambling occurred more often in Rome at the mineral spas and baths where people came to be healed by soaking in the waters. Betting on cards and dice was convenient and helped to while the time away. In addition, the possibility of winning a bigger fortune by using one's skills and wits was exciting. So, in one location people could get physically well, increase their fortune, and improve their mental faculties by simply going to the baths. As one can see, gambling has been around a long time . . . since the beginning of civilization as a matter of fact, and it has served many different purposes.

Gambling

As an introduction to the study of gambling, we should start with some definitions. According to Webster's dictionary, **gambling** is "to play a game for money; anything involving a like risk or uncertainty."[3] In this book, discussions are restricted to legal forms of gambling performed in a specially designated facility called a *casino* or **house**. Therefore, lotteries, pari-mutuel, sports books, and internet gaming will be peripheral to, but not the central focus of, our discussion.

This brief introduction will ask more questions than it answers. We hope that as the reader develops an understanding about the casino environment, he/she can make an informed decision about the questions raised. We have also attempted to offer a balanced view of any debated issue so that the reader can be knowledgeable about the subject.

Commercial casino operations can be broken down into three categories: land based, riverboat, and Native American. Land-based casinos are built on land, such as those in Las Vegas, (Figure 1–1) Atlantic City, Colorado, South Dakota, and Louisiana. This sounds intuitively obvious, but it distinguishes these casinos from riverboats. Riverboats

Figure 1–1 Do not be fooled. This is not Paris, France, but the front of the Paris Casino Resort in Las Vegas.
Photo courtesy of George G. Fenich.

are found mainly on the Mississippi River, so they run through the middle of America from north to south. Finally, Native American casinos can be land or river based, but they are distinguished by ownership. Native American tribal lands are sovereign entities that are responsible only to the federal government. However, to build a casino, tribes must negotiate with state governments and write a compact (or contract). Therefore, they have different issues than the land-based or riverboat casinos that are controlled by the state governments.

Changing Attitudes Toward Gambling

As Americans discovered a recreational activity in casinos, 26 percent of them over the age of 21 went to a casino, amounting to more than 310 million visits annually.[4] This meant a change in attitude. When the only gambling venue was Las Vegas in 1931, people had to deliberately plan their vacation to gamble. Once Atlantic City opened its doors with bus programs in 1976, people in the area could spend less time reaching a gambling destination—sometimes only a couple of hours. As a result of the bus tours that did all the driving for the customers, the densely populated Northeast corridor was introduced to the idea of gambling. In the 1990s, Steve Wynn, a major player/owner in the gaming industry with many casinos throughout the world, suggested that gambling was an alternative way to spend entertainment dollars. It was a form of recreation, like going to the movies or eating out. It was a short vacation from daily life, a way to have fun and relax and maybe walk away with more than the cost of dinner. As the popularity of casinos has grown, more than 80 percent of adults agree that going to a casino is an acceptable form of entertainment for themselves and others.[5] Fifty-four percent of Americans said that gambling was acceptable for anyone, while 27 percent said that while gambling was not for them, it was an acceptable form of entertainment for others. Only 4 percent of the American population believed that casinos were not acceptable for anyone.

Perhaps this positive attitude partially resulted from the economic impact that communities receive from the casinos. In 2002, across the country, more than $4 billion was received by state and local governments in direct gaming taxes—a $400 million increase over 2001. The federal government's share is less than 18 percent of these taxes; the states keep the rest. Before the casinos, most of these areas were struggling to survive. For example, along the Mississippi River, manufacturing companies left for foreign countries to look for cheaper labor and lower taxes, leaving gaping holes in the economic development of many states. Young people were also leaving the region to seek employment. Riverboat casinos employed 92,000 people in these states in 2002. However, even more important, the riverboats paid, on average, an effective tax rate of 23 percent. These rates varied from a high of 36.4 percent in Illinois to a low of 12.2 percent in Mississippi.[6]

Many people do not realize that casinos pay taxes and fees far in excess of other industries. The level of riverboat casino taxes was particularly notorious during 2002, as state and municipal governments, short of funds, raised the tax rates to cover funding shortfalls for schools, road construction, and infrastructure improvements. Also, every state increased taxes from their 2001 rates at least 1 percent (in the case of Nevada) to 20 percent (in Illinois). In addition, casinos have other financial obligations above these taxes. For example, Atlantic City casinos pay an additional 1.25 percent to the Casino Reinvestment Development Authority (CRDA) for civic improvements. On average, community investment obligations provide more than $32 million in annual funding for host communities. In contrast, because of their sovereignty, Native American casinos do not have to pay taxes to local and state governments. However, many tribes offer concessions to taxes in exchange for a reasonable negotiation with the states. According to AGA (2005) survey, more than 11 percent of the gambling dollars in the United States is spent at the 281 Native American gaming operations in 32 states.

Nationwide, in 2002, commercial casinos directly provided more than 350,000 jobs and paid approximately $11 billion in wages. Also in 2002, a total of 247 of Nevada's largest casino resorts directly employed 205,000 people and spent a capital investment of $29 billion. On the other side of the country during this same time, the 12 Atlantic City casinos directly employed 205,000 people while spending $7.5 billion in capital investments.[7] Two of the largest growth markets in the United States for casinos were Missouri (18 percent) and Indiana (16 percent).[8]

On the other side of the tables are the patrons. Compared to the average American adult, a typical casino customer in 2002 would be a little more educated and more likely to

Figure 1–2 Going to a casino for a trip or vacation has become an acceptable option for many people.
Courtesy of Isle of Capri Casino Resort.

hold a white-collar job, which translates into a higher income. Attitudes toward gaming are becoming more positive, with people from the Northeast appearing to give the strongest support. Also, men are more likely than women to approve of gambling, but by a very small margin.[9] According to the 2003 Harrah's survey, gamblers are an active, financially sound, but aggressive group of people. They are more likely than the average person to engage in a wide variety of vacation and outdoor experiences and are three times more likely than the average person to take a trip to a resort. (See Figure 1–2.) Gamblers are also more likely than the average person to eat out (7.6 versus 6.6 times each month). More than half of casino players go out for entertainment at least twice a week, while more than a third of the nongamblers reported that they had not gone out during the past week. Financially, gamblers tend to save more money and consider themselves to be knowledgeable about investing. As a result, they are generally more active financial managers of their money.[10]

The Social Acceptance of Gambling

Betting and gambling have always been a part of American history, but it is not usually discussed in the history books. In America, the level of the social acceptance of gambling has run in a cyclical pattern. Some might say that we can never get rid of gambling because it is in our blood. For example, in order for the Puritans to have enough money to obtain the ships and food necessary for the trip to the New World, they ran a lottery. Luckily, the organizers were run out of town on a rail before they spent all the money, and there was just enough to fund the voyage. In addition, who would be crazy enough to give up everything they knew to try their luck in an untamed wilderness? Only a gambler! Therefore, some have theorized that America was settled by people with a betting spirit. Later, lotteries helped fund Jamestown when money was needed to build roads and lights. When Charity Hospital in Louisiana needed funding to maintain its work with the poor, it created a lottery. The organizers got too greedy. As a result, a public outcry about the graft and corruption forced officials to take a stand. However, this lottery was so large that it took federal marshals to close it down.

Unfortunately, as gambling opportunities increased, some people wanted to get more than their fair share of gambling money, and crime rates increased. Some also could not control their desire for more and more excitement, and they wagered their entire fortunes on the turn of a card or a throw of the dice. Addiction and suicide rates increased as broken men wagered the family estate and women sold their bodies to pay for their gambling debts. As the negative impacts of gambling grew, the social outcry became louder and louder, until finally public pressure became so great that the government mandated that gambling stop. This cycle of gambling behavior has been demonstrated throughout history.

Because gambling brings in cash quickly with little time lag, it is a very appealing revenue source. Also, citizens who become upset when other taxes are raised do not in general have the same concerns with gambling taxes. Whenever the federal and state governments spend more money than is brought in with taxes, they contemplate legalizing gambling. When casinos are developed, jobs are available, taxes are paid, and people spend money. Lifestyles for citizens improve. In addition, the infrastructure of the town is paid for by these taxes.

Beginning especially in 1976 when Atlantic City, New Jersey opened its doors, the rationale for legalized gambling exemplified a return to the classic theme. Governments in the 1990s were strapped for cash. Some towns had even gone bankrupt, an unheard of concept before the 1980s. Even today, as the population ages, more people are retiring every year, with fewer young people to support the system. Therefore, social programs need more money to operate. In terms of "real" income, people have less disposable income than in previous generations, but the desire to gamble is still very much alive. State lotteries are a classic example of people's willingness to spend money to gamble and not complain, even though at least 50 percent of the revenues from the lotteries are kept by the state. America is in the midst of gambling fever, and gambling's social acceptance is on the rise. But how will the United States handle this new wave?

As the gambling industry evaluates its future, it works with governments and other organizations to prevent the cycle from reoccurring. Casinos have funded many different projects to find solutions to these issues. The 2002 survey by the **American Gaming Association (AGA)** revealed that Americans have noticed the efforts of the commercial casino industry to promote **responsible gambling**. Nearly two-thirds of Americans have said that they think the gaming industry is doing a good job of eliminating illegal and underage gambling, compared with much lower approval levels for other industries dealing with illegal or underage use of their products.[11]

As one studies casino development, many questions arise. Casinos are purported to improve the economic condition of the communities that host them. For example, the Native Americans who build casinos quite often then have money to build homes, hospitals, and schools. In Tunica, Mississippi, where casinos were legalized in 1990, everyone who wants to work can. There are more than enough jobs to go around, and the pay level is high. On the other hand, skeptics point to Atlantic City and say that things have not changed in that town. However, since 1978, the casinos there have given a percentage of their revenues to the city for redevelopment to improve city conditions. Should the casinos be required to fund forms of urban renewal such as this? Is this fair? Are other businesses required to do the same? Is it the casinos' problem that social conditions have not changed?

External Forces

To begin a discussion about gambling, one must understand the macroenvironment that surrounds a casino. This text explores six of the **external forces** that cannot be controlled by the industry but have great impact on the way a casino does business. These forces are: the economic environment, the social environment, the political and legal environments, consumer behavior, development of corporate culture and technology, and the changing competitive environment.

The Economic Environment

Whenever the debate to legalize gambling appears, one of the positive effects of gambling that is usually cited is the improvement of the economic environment. Unemployment decreases as jobs are created. More jobs mean more taxes to improve living conditions. As people spend their newly created wages, spin-off developments of banks, grocery stores, drug stores, and so on are needed to take care of the local residents.

The Social Environment

On the other side of the debate on legalizing gambling is gambling's perceived effects on the social environment, such as a rise in crime, addiction, and underage gambling. These concerns have often brought gambling down. Can these perceived effects be controlled? Can the casinos create programs that will satisfy the public's desire to keep problems at a minimum? It is the people themselves who must decide whether gambling is an unethical, immoral activity, or an activity like any other. Gaming can be one of many recreational alternatives for a Friday night or a possible vacation destination choice. People are heavily influenced by the rhetoric of legislatures and pressure groups that focus their attention on the aspects of the industry that support only their position.

The Political and Legal Environments

Today, it is the political and legal environments that control the regulations and laws that govern what a casino can and cannot do. They make decisions on employment law for hiring and firing personnel. They mandate elements of a casino's design, square footage limits and usage, and the extent of allowable amenities. Ultimately, government makes the decision to allow gaming and then controls the process.

Consumer Behavior

Each of the environments just listed impacts casinos directly as managers strive to mediate the negative effects and enhance the positive ones. However, the external forces also change the way that people buy products or services or choose to spend their time. If the economy is good, I may have extra money to spend on gambling because I am confident about my job. On the other hand, I may not go to the casino because in my social environment, my friends believe that gambling promotes addiction and crime. Also, the political and legal environments regulate whether I can gamble or go to a casino.

The Development of Corporate Culture and Technology

The culture of the United States as it developed into a nation is reflected in the casino industry. Several trends started in the past and adapted to the changes leading to the present. Originally, in European cultures, the rich were the ones who gambled. However, in the new country of America, anyone rich or poor could gamble. Wealthy plantation owners mingled with trappers and explorers on riverboats and in casinos. This trend generated a mass consumer movement to the casinos. Today, like the United States itself, with its big cars, large houses, and gigantic grocery stores, casinos have also become immense. However, in the beginning, the bars that housed the gambling tables were small, and their surveillance and management were simple—one man and one gun.

The external environments were good to casinos and as casinos grew in size, corporations were needed to run their operations. Management teams took over the one-man controls (Figure 1–3). Technological advances created a new way to make management

Figure 1–3 Corporations and group decision making took over the one-man operations.

decisions and control all the different operations. As a result, technology revolutionized the way casinos did business. This sections explores the impact of American culture and especially technology on the organizational culture within casinos from a historical perspective.

The Changing Competitive Environment Reflected by Historical Development

Gaming grew with America's increasing population. America's history reflects gaming's changing attitudes and altering competitive environments. In modern times, Las Vegas and the state of Nevada had a monopoly on gaming. It was the only place that legally legislated gaming. Once Atlantic City opened its doors, the casinos began to service the massive population along the Eastern coast. There was plenty of room for both. Atlantic City was positioned as a day-trip area, whereas Las Vegas was more a vacation or long weekend location for many. However, as the Midwest began to lose manufacturing plants, hopeful legislators began to cast their eyes on the lucrative gaming profits. All along the Mississippi River, states began to explore the option of casino riverboats. Almost at the same time, Native American tribes explored their options to run casinos on the reservations. These developments created a rapidly increasing competitive environment for competent employees and for customers. This growth pattern forced casinos to develop better human resource packages that motivated employees to show better service-oriented behaviors toward the guests. In addition, changing marketing practices increasingly focused on how to keep guests happy and how to lure new gamblers to the tables and slots. With a gambling venue within driving distance for most of the American population, casinos had to develop strategies to lure locals from their normal recreational activities.

Ultimately, it is the people's buying behavior that will determine whether the casinos will survive. The people will make a decision to legislate for or against gambling. The consumers will then decide whether they will gamble often enough and with enough money to allow the casinos to survive. As more casinos are allowed to operate and spread throughout the United States, the questions include the following: Are there enough people to gamble in all the different types of gambling establishments? Will the competitive environment be too much for all the casinos? How many casinos will survive when the dust settles?

Internal Environments

Once one understands the seven external forces that mold the casinos, one needs to examine what is happening inside the casinos. In this section, we look at the five **internal forces** that mold the casinos: product, organization, pricing, location and transportation, and promotions.

Product

First, it is necessary to understand the casino product. How does the casino make money? How do the laws of probabilities affect the rules and profitability of the games? Because the product of casinos is money, more controls, including security and surveillance, are needed to keep employees and patrons alike in check so that the casino can be run honestly.

Organization

We also need to understand how the layers of the organization change to meet the needs for security and what this change means for the power structure in traditional hotels, restaurants, and casino resorts.

Pricing

Pricing in casino resorts is different from that in a traditional hotel or restaurant. There are different objectives in filling casino hotels than traditional hotels: What is the appropriate room price for a gambler? How does a casino price its product? Where do the familiar comps and credits fit in?

Location and Transportation

Like most hospitality operations, a casino's location is set once the building is in place. How does location impact buying decisions? How do you get people from one place to another in the casino property? What channels (agents) do customers use when going to a casino?

Promotions

Finally, what is the message the casino wants to send? What promotions does it use? How does it create a synergistic effect in uniting all the different types of promotions so that customers do not get confused?

Other Questions

These questions concerning the external and internal forces affecting casinos are the ones that all people must ask if they are interested in the gaming environment. Casino gaming operators face other serious questions, both about their business and about the environment in which they operate. Should a new casino in Iowa be more of a destination area like Las Vegas or a day trip like Atlantic City? What kind of people should the casino attract? Should a casino hotel use the hotel as an amenity? Traditionally, hotel operations have been used to keep customers at the casino. Should the hotel or food service operate as a profit center in its own right? In examining the broader perspective, government regulators are developing rules for casinos to protect the area's social environment, but should regulations be tough, like in Atlantic City, to prevent problems before they arise? Or should regulations be used to create a good environment for casinos to flourish, and crack down only when trouble occurs? Is the objective of gambling to promote tourism and generate income from people outside the town or state, or are casinos another business and entertainment center for townspeople? If the objective is tourism (that is—drawing outsiders into town), what happens if every town has its own casino?

Casinos have had to answer all kinds of social questions about the impact of gambling. Do casinos create addicts? Does a person addicted to gambling have a personality that is prone to addictive behaviors? Is there something about the sport of gaming that creates the addiction? An interesting historical analysis suggests that Americans are still pioneers at heart. The settlers on the frontiers were people who took risks and won. This kind of mentality is still respected in America. For example, stockbroking is considered to be a good profession. However, is the rise of gambling fever Main Street's way of reflecting Wall Street's obsession with short-term speculation, instead of long-term investment? What is the difference between gambling in a casino and gambling on the stock market?

The chapters of this book bring you both sides of the issues to provoke thought. The organization of this book is based on a strategic environmental scanning of gambling. It begins with external factors that influence the way gambling develops, such as the economy and the social, cultural, legal, political, and technological environments. Each of these factors is explored to show how it influences and structures casinos. Once it is understood how the outside world alters casinos, it is possible to look at the product, price, place, and promotions to show how these internal factors have developed and how management decision making has adapted to the outside pressures. The last chapter explores possible routes the future might take. When you have finished this book, you should be able to evaluate casinos and decide for yourself where you stand on issues that concern them. In addition, as you explore your future career options, you can objectively think about casino management as a career choice and make an informed decision.

key terms

Gambling	Responsible gambling
House	External forces
American Gaming Association (AGA)	Internal Forces

review questions

1. Into which three categories are commercial casino operations broken down?

2. What percentage of adults agrees that going to a casino is an acceptable form of entertainment for themselves and others? What is believed to be the reason for this?

3. What is the difference between an external and an internal force?

4. What are the six external forces affecting the gaming industry?

5. What are the five internal forces that mold a casino?

internet sites

American Gaming Association
   www.americangaming.org

History (Official City of Las Vegas Web Site)
   www.lasvegasnevada.gov/FactsStatistics/history.htm

endnotes

1. E.M. Christiansen "The Gross Annual Wager of the United States: 2002." http://www.cca-i.com. Accessed December 15, 2005.

2. "AGA State of the States 2005: The AGA Survey of Casino Entertainment." http://www.americangaming.org. Accessed September 20, 2006.

3. "Webster's New Universal Unabridged Dictionary." (1983) New York: Simon & Schuster.

4. Harrah's Survey 04: Profile of the American Casino Gambler. Harrah's Entertainment.

5. "AGA State of the States 2005: The AGA Survey of Casino Entertainment." http://www.americangaming.org. Accessed September 20, 2006.

6. E.M. Christiansen "The Gross Annual Wager of the United States: 2002." http://www.cca-i.com. Accessed December 15, 2005.

7. Ibid.

8. "2003 State of the States, the AGA survey of Casino Entertainment." http://www.aga.org. Accessed February 10, 2004.

9. "AGA State of the States 2005: The AGA Survey of Casino Entertainment." http://www.americangaming.org. Accessed September 20, 2006.

10. (Harrah's Survey 2003: Profile of the American Casino Gambler, http://www.harrahs.com. Accessed February 10, 2004.

11. "2003 State of the States, the AGA survey of Casino Entertainment." http://www.aga.org. Accessed February 10, 2004.

PART 2

External Environments

2 Economic Environments

Gary Anders, Arizona State University

Kathryn Hashimoto, East Carolina University

Learning Objectives

1. To describe the conflicting assessments of the impacts of casino gambling on local economies.

2. To provide an overview of the current research on the economic impact of casinos.

3. To understand the underlying causes of different impacts and to provide an appreciation of the policy issues related to government support for the expansion of commercial gaming.

Chapter Outline

Introduction

The Blind Men and the Elephant

There is a fable about some blind men who were given an opportunity to touch an elephant. Afterward, they compared their experiences. For the blind man who touched the tail, the elephant was like a snake. For the one who touched the elephant's side, it was like a wall. For the one who touched the ear, it was like a fan. For the one who touched the leg, it was like a tree trunk, and so on. To a large degree, this story captures many of the differences that researchers and consultants have regarding how commercial gambling affects the social and economic texture of communities.

Gambling is an economic activity that has spawned considerable debate from both proponents and critics. Some see only the positive aspects of gambling, such as the job creation that comes from casinos and related businesses, the taxes that casinos generate for local communities, and the enhancements of choice that gambling generates by giving consumers additional recreational options. For others, gambling is seen as providing few benefits and is responsible for producing significant externalities in the form of crime, compulsive gambling, and social problems that have to be paid for by taxpayers and local communities. For example, Simmons found that while gambling creates jobs in related industries, for the most part, casinos divert consumer expenditure from other businesses.[1] Furthermore she asserts that the jobs created by casino development are lower-paying positions. Given the possibility of market saturation from increased numbers of casinos, she argues that casinos are not a sound economic development alternative for many local communities seeking to generate increased tax revenues. As with many complicated issues, the truth is likely a combination of both positions. Given the size of the industry, there is a need to better understand the overall impact of casinos on the economy.

As lessons are learned from long-term jurisdictions such as Las Vegas and Atlantic City, more communities are looking to casinos to be part of an overall entertainment and recreation product. Casinos bring in fast cash to start urban renewal and bring in new tourists, but then the challenge is for planners to build other attractions to keep people in town and to have them return. Diversification is the name of the game. To

Figure 2–1 Casinos are seen as a gondola of a hot air balloon that spills bags of gold wherever they go.

attract new tourists and keep others coming back often, a region needs many different attractions. Las Vegas is at the forefront of this concept. Rather than drawing people solely for gambling, Las Vegas is promoting itself as a tourist destination with nearby attractions such as the Grand Canyon and the Hoover Dam. Other attractions include art museums, Broadway-type shows, and reproductions of the wonders of the world. It has been suggested that anything that draws people to the major cities of the world can be duplicated in Las Vegas without the expense and hassles of world travel. As a result, gaming revenues as a percentage of total revenues have been declining in Las Vegas for the past 20 years. In fact, a little more than half of the total revenues in Las Vegas in 2002 were from gaming. Therefore, the economic impact of a casino has many different facets.

Background Information

Multipliers are used to determine the total impact of each dollar of direct spending on the local economy. For example, a dollar is spent by a tourist at a local store (direct). Then the store owner pays his/her employee with part of that dollar (indirect). The employee uses the dollar to buy groceries (indirect). The grocery store sends that dollar to its corporate offices. That means the original dollar has been circulated through the local economy two times. The higher the number of times of circulation, the better the economic worth of the transaction. Generally the multiplier is around two.

The term **leakage** refers to the phenomenon that occurs when parts of that dollar are exported outside the local economy—for example, when the dollar is sent to the corporate offices. When casinos are locally owned, the money tends to stay within the local economy longer, and the money benefits the local community with more investments, which results in a higher multiplier. However, it is more likely that the casino is owned by an outside corporation that siphons most of the money out of the community and back to its home offices. This results in a lower multiplier and more leakage. Therefore, depending on the type of ownership, casinos can have a stronger or weaker economic impact on the local economy.

A question regarding leakage arises for states that do not have casinos and whose citizens simply drive across the border to a state that does. The question is whether a non–casino state does better economically if its citizens stay home to gamble. Would a state lose more money if the leakage occurred from a local casino or from the export of money going to an out-of-state casino?

Another aspect of leakage relates to the customer base. Clients from outside the local community bring fresh money, which fuels the economy, and the money that is exported to the corporate offices has less impact. However, if the client base consists mostly of locals, residents, then casinos may take local money and export it, immediately decreasing the economic impact and increasing the leakage rate. For example in Illinois, around 58 percent of the players are locals, which means that the casinos are taking money that could be spent locally and exporting it outside the community. Grinols and Omorov (1996) explain that only when gambling is able to tap outside markets will the casinos have a positive economic impact; otherwise, gambling results in inefficient transfers from one business to another.[2] This results in less money available for local development.

Positive Economic Impact

Employment—Direct

One of the major reasons for allowing casinos into a jurisdiction is the direct economic impact of jobs. In 2002, Nevada had 247 large casino resorts that directly employed 205,000 people. At the same time in New Jersey, the 12 casinos there employed around

46,000, and riverboat jurisdictions employed another 92,000. These jobs are important in regions that previously had high unemployment rates. Atlantic City had been the seaside resort of choice until regions such as Florida lured the tourists away. Legalizing casinos was the way for communities to pull themselves out of economic chaos and bring them back to solvency. There is even an additional 1.25 percent CRDA tax for a redevelopment fund for Atlantic City. Another example is along the Mississippi River, where manufacturing plants had thrived and people could always rely on the factory for a job. However, with tight economic times, companies began to look overseas to cut costs, and the factories disappeared, leaving high unemployment rates. Riverboats were legalized to lower the jobless rates and bring economic development and wages back to the region.

A study by Thomas Garrett, using monthly employment data from the Bureau of Labor Statistics for six counties (two in Mississippi, two in Illinois, one in Iowa, and one in Missouri), found that in three of the four rural counties, the opening of a casino did increase household employment. However, in the case of urban counties, Garrett found that it was much harder to detect a significant impact of casinos on either household employment or payroll.[3] Using a regression model based on annual employment for eight industry sectors in 10 states from 1991–2004, Anders and Somavarapu (2005) found that measures of casino gambling (i.e., number of machines, number of tables, and gambling revenue) are positively correlated with changes in employment for some sectors, such as in food and drinking establishments and accommodations, but negatively correlated with employment changes in other sectors such as science and technology, management, and arts).[4] Based on this, Anders and Somavarapu argued that those casinos may not have a significant positive effect on higher-paying jobs because of the types of jobs created and possible job losses that occur because of the competition with other sectors of the economy.

The benefits of casino gaming are evident in the increases in job opportunities in numerous states. According to a survey by the American Gaming Association, more than 25,000 new jobs have been created in the American commercial casino industry.[5] In 1999, the states with the most substantial levels of gaming job creation were Nevada

Figure 2–2 The Greektown Casino's neon sign in front of the Renaissance Center in Detroit, Michigan, portrays the image of a casino that creates direct and indirect employment to its locale.

(16,371), Michigan (4,895), and Mississippi (4,635) (Figure 2–2). Overall, as of fiscal year 2000, the industry provided approximately 356,860 commercial casino jobs and 151,688 tribal casino jobs.[6]

Employment—Indirect

While the direct employment opportunities are easy to see, the indirect employment opportunities are less obvious. When casinos are legislated, commissions are formed to oversee the operations, and they, in turn, set up special task forces for enforcement. As a casino moves forward, construction workers are needed to build the casino, but improvements in infrastructure require other occupations as well. As these employees work on the job, services such as restaurants, banking, and housing develop to satisfy their quality-of-life needs. These new services require space, and more construction ensues. The number of indirect job opportunities spirals upward as various community needs are created because of the growing population.

In addition, both Native American tribes and the National Indian Gaming Association, an industry lobby, argue that decreases in unemployment and a reduction in the number of families dependent upon welfare also save state's money. They point to the thousands of jobs created by casinos and the added purchasing power afforded to their employees and tribal members as a result of gambling. At the same time, Native American casinos are said to have been responsible for improved health care, substance abuse programs, educational scholarships, and improved housing stock and infrastructure in reservation communities.[7] However, opponents can point out that unlike commercial gambling casinos, tribal casinos do not pay taxes to states, and unless there is a formal revenue-sharing arrangement, the tribes keep almost all of the revenue that they generate.

An interesting case study exists in the gambling capital of the world, Las Vegas. Few would dispute that the community of Las Vegas represents a "how-to" model of sorts—a city in which gaming has contributed to substantial population and economic growth. In large part due to its reputation as a "job mecca," Las Vegas has become the fastest-growing metropolitan city in the United States, with a population that reached 1.56 million in 2000.[8] This was a 7.8 percent increase from 1990, when the population was 852,737. According to forecasts by Schwer and Riddel, Las Vegas's population growth rate will remain significantly higher than the average growth rate in the nation, and the overall population of Las Vegas is expected to reach 2.6 million in 2035.[9] Las Vegas also appears to have experienced a shorter and less severe economic downturn post-9/11, despite its status as a tourist locale. Therefore, there is strong evidence to suggest that casinos create jobs directly and indirectly.

Taxes

The difference between tribal casinos and privately owned gambling establishments may also have significantly different fiscal impacts. Siegel and Anders found that the opening of Native American casinos results in an increasing loss of public-sector revenues resulting from reduced lottery revenues.[10] However, the main concern with Native American casinos is the sovereignty issue. As mentioned earlier, *sovereignty* refers to the fact that Native American tribes are technically independent nations and are not responsible to the state for anything. Therefore, the state cannot mandate a tax structure or collect taxes. However, the state and tribe must negotiate a compact, or contract, specifying responsibilities on both sides. Depending upon the agreement between tribes and states, the level of revenue sharing from tribally owned casinos could range from 0 percent to 25 percent of net revenues. For example, Popp and Stehwien found that as the number of Native American casinos increased, the taxable gross receipts in New Mexico decreased substantially.[11] Unless the total economic stimulus from gaming results in increased sales taxes, the expenditure diversion from the taxable economy could result in a net reduction of state revenues.

States with commercial gambling casinos are likely to have a much more positive fiscal impact because states directly tax casinos' revenues. In addition, some states with riverboat casinos apply additional charges, such as admission fees. For more underdeveloped states such as Mississippi, the additional tax revenues that come from casinos have made a major impact on the resource base of local communities. These revenues help support additional public services and programs as well as contribute resources for education, health care, and housing assistance. Still, it is important to point out that when casinos draw from other forms of gambling such as horse and dog tracks and state lotteries, the tax revenues from casinos are displacing other sources of tax and state revenue so that the total impact is lessened.

As a result of the income and expenditure multipliers of gambling activities, jobs that are created in the casino stimulate the creation of additional jobs primarily in the service sectors. Because employees in the casinos and related businesses pay state income taxes and sales taxes on their purchases of goods and services, states further benefit from additional tax revenues. Likewise, when casinos create jobs in economically depressed communities, the demand for public assistance is reduced. Thus, the total fiscal impact of casinos depends upon the types of jobs and wages that are created.

Adequate levels of employment are important in raising the standard of living. However, taxes are equally important for federal, state, and local governments. There are personal income taxes; corporate income taxes; and, when people buy goods with their higher wages, sales taxes. These taxes are fairly standard; however, there are added taxes when newfound money can be generated. For example, people buy houses and businesses, and the price of property and property taxes increase as the competition for land goes up. New businesses and retail stores open and everyone pays taxes on their products. New companies need licenses and more employees; so many additional taxes are paid to the federal, state, and local governments. This means more money in the budget for infrastructure and social needs, such as schools and senior housing. For example, in 2002, the economic growth of the casino industry in Nevada represented a capital investment of $29 billion, and the gaming privilege tax collections, that is the tax imposed on the privilege of conducting gambling, totaled $712 or 20.5 percent of the total tax collections. Riverboat taxes provided $32 million in annual funding for their host communities. This is partially because the casino industry pays one of the highest corporate tax rates in the country. From 2001 to 2002, these high tax rates ranged from a 12 percent increase in Nevada to a 20 percent increase in Illinois. In 2000, Illinois had the highest tax rate of the states: 35 percent on adjusted gross receipts of more than $100 million. In 2002, the tax was 50 percent and on wins of more than $250 million, it was 70 percent. All but one of the nine licensees in Illinois had revenues of more than $100 million, and three had revenues exceeding $250 million.

Spin-off Development

As casinos begin to operate, they buy goods and services from the surrounding areas. Therefore, more businesses grow or develop to meet the increasing demands for products from the casino. Many businesses will spring up to satisfy the higher incomes of the new employees. New hospitality services, such as hotels, restaurants, and rental cars, begin construction to meet the needs of the tourists, locals, and corporations. With new businesses, there are more suppliers, both in gaming and hospitality, that need hospitality services.

In terms of land use, there are three major areas of development and redevelopment of land. The first is the new development of virgin land (property that has never been developed). As the prime areas are taken, developers look for the second area of development: new locations to build office buildings, stores, malls, service businesses, and houses. However, much of this development will ultimately take the form of the third area of development: redevelopment for reuse, adaptive reuse, or blighted areas.

According to a 1997 Arthur Andersen report, the introduction of casinos leads to growth in almost all other areas: retail sales, commercial and housing construction, and restaurants. This study also argues that casinos are responsible for increased taxes, employment growth, and reductions in the number of families on welfare.[12]

Negative Economic Impact

Increased land use has been cited as having a positive impact on the local economy. However, it can also have a negative impact. Many positive aspects of gaming also have a negative side. Walker and Barnett's critique of the literature provides a fairly comprehensive list of the accepted social costs of compulsive gambling, including bailout costs, unrecoverable loans, strain on public services, unpaid debts, bankruptcies, industry **cannibalization**, and higher insurance premiums resulting from fraud caused by pathological gamblers.[13] All of these factors are externalized onto the public. While this text contains a chapter on the social concerns of gambling, there is also an economic impact of those concerns, which is discussed here.

The demand for land and the high property taxes paid by casinos increase land values, which result in higher taxes for nearby property owners. This may create an environment that is hostile to small businesses that cannot afford the high taxes. Therefore, more small businesses may leave or go bankrupt, which changes the character of the community. The research on whether or not the opening of casinos results in higher bankruptcy rates in local communities is mixed. For example, a study by the National Opinion Research Center (NORC) conducted for the National Gambling Impact Study Commission based on a sample of 100 countries from 1980–1987 found that there was no significant increase in the rates of personal bankruptcy.[14] In April 2000, at the request of Representative Frank Wolf, the General Accounting Office presented its study of the impacts of gambling in the United States. This study, which focused mainly on Atlantic City, found that there was no direct effect between gambling and the incidence of personal bankruptcies.[15]

On the other hand, a study by Nelson et al. (2000) using eight cities in counties where there was casino gambling found that there was an increase in personal bankruptcies.[16]

Similarly, Barron, et al. (2002) using data for more than 3,000 U.S. counties for the period from 1993 to 1999 found that the proximity of a gambling casino appeared to result in higher bankruptcy rates.[17] However, a 2004 study by Thalheimer and Ali that included broader measures of casino access, including to Native American casinos, found that there was not a significant relationship between pari-mutuel and casino gambling and the rise in the number of personal bankruptcies.[18] No doubt there will be additional research to explore this issue, but at the present time the preponderance of the evidence suggests that while bankruptcies are prevalent among problem gamblers, on a national scale, there does not appear to be a strong correlation between the growth of casino gambling and the rise of personal bankruptcies.

In terms of crime, opponents cite the cost for additional police and security in many jurisdictions. However, in New Orleans, Harrah's pays the city extra taxes for the privilege of having those extra safety measures. Some of the costs of increased crimes are due to the increased numbers of visitors and employees in the area. The casino money also increases the temptation for politicians and other people in power to be persuaded to sway laws. Therefore, additional special law enforcement is needed to address these issues. Other additional security costs relate to maintaining vigilance to make sure the mob influence in casinos is minimal. The first jurisdiction to legalize gambling, Las Vegas, had major problems with the mob running operations; so especially in Atlantic City, strict regulations were designed to keep the mob out of gambling.

Another concern is the creation of pathological gamblers. For example in 1996, Grinols and Omorov estimated that pathological gamblers create social costs of between $110 and $340 per adult per year.[19] Because of the increase in problem gamblers and the increased demand for police and fire protection, social services, and infrastructure that results from a casino opening, local governments also face related increased monetary costs. To some degree, these costs are offset by the revenues received from casinos, but they are also diminished by revenue displacement. For example, if someone gambles at a casino instead of buying lottery tickets, then the state gains from the tax on casino revenues but loses from the reduced lottery sales. There is enough information to know whether the current tax rates provide for a large enough share of gaming revenues to cover both the displacement and the public sector's cost of gaming. Some states such as California are encountering unanticipated fiscal drains from Native American casinos and are attempting to increase their revenue-sharing agreements with tribes. Thus, it is arguable that expanded gambling may exacerbate the current state deficits and possibly lead to cuts in important programs. Certainly these costs and issues need to be taken into consideration when measuring the impact of casinos.

Summary

The existing literature presents a mixed set of results concerning gambling's perceived impacts. On one hand, proponents of gambling argue that gambling increases local tax revenues, creates new jobs, and stimulates economies through induced consumption and employment multipliers. Critics of gambling find that gambling displaces existing expenditures as a result of transfers from existing businesses to casinos. Critics of gambling are also concerned about the social costs associated with pathological gambling that increase both public and private costs.

Several factors will significantly increase or reduce the positive impacts of casinos. First, to a certain extent, the economic benefits of casinos depend upon whether gambling revenues are exported to other states, or whether opening local casinos encourages residents to gamble locally. For maximum benefits to a local economy, casinos should bring in new money rather than displacing existing consumer expenditures. For example, when Illinois opened its own casinos, it captured some of the gambling revenue that was being spent by its residents in Missouri. Likewise, Illinois gamblers now substitute gambling at local casinos for trips to Las Vegas or Atlantic City, which increases the economic contribution to their state.

Second, a major issue is where the money spent on gaming comes from. If some portion of the gaming dollars comes from the customer's savings, or substitutions for other types of entertainment, then the displacement effect would be small. Although we do not have enough specific household information on gamblers, the existing literature indicates that a very large segment of the gambling market comes from lower-income brackets where the marginal propensity to consume is high and saving is conversely low.[20]

Third, the calculation of the net economic impact should take into consideration the reduced revenue from all forms of gaming, including state lotteries and horse and dog racing. If a portion of money spent at the casino comes from one of these activity sectors, then it diminishes sales and incomes there and causes substitution effects that reduce the casino's overall economic benefits. Thus, it is misleading to postulate any positive economic impacts of casinos without considering the corresponding diversion of taxable spending.

Fourth, because there are different tax rates in different states, it is possible that the revenue generation from casinos can vary substantially. At some future time, governments may attempt to institute an optimal tax that balances the gains to the state against the costs of providing increased services.

Fifth, most of the economic impact studies written to support the adoption of casinos typically use expenditure and employment multipliers that demonstrate that casinos benefit regional economics through direct purchases and employment or through indirect **multiplier effects**.[21]

The Future of Commercial Gaming

Given the favorable public attitudes toward legalized gambling, the near future will likely see a continued expansion in new gaming markets. This will eventually raise the possibility of market satiation. Unless the growth of casinos is met with an increase in the demand for gambling, then, as with other industries, the overcapitalization will result in reduced profitability. As we look at the growth of online gambling, it is possible to see a new competitive alternative that could significantly affect the demand for casinos. Already the internet gambling industry is estimated at more than $5 billion and growing rapidly. Given the ease and convenience of this form of gambling, it is certain to become a serious competitor of casinos. While there are ongoing public policy efforts to extend regulatory control, there are also significant challenges because of the low cost of establishing these websites in offshore locations.

key terms

Regression analysis	Multiplier effects
Leakage	Cannibalization

review questions

1. Which types of employment are created from the construction and operation of a casino?

2. What impacts do local communities experience from the establishment of a casino?

3. How strong is the evidence that increased casino gambling increases the number of personal bankruptcies?

4. What is the difference in the impact on states from Native American tribal casinos and other types of casinos?

5. How are restaurants, businesses, and hotels affected by increased competition from casinos?

6. How does casino gambling affect communities (i.e., crime, increased problem gambling, personal bankruptcies, traffic congestion, increased demands on social services)?

7. How does gambling lead to a redistribution of income from lower-income groups?

8. What effect does the creation of a new casino have on the prevalence of problem gambling?

9. What is the relationship between the revenue collected by governments and the expenditures that accompany the adoption of casinos?

internet sites

American Gaming Association
   http://www.americangaming.org/

European Association for the Study of Gambling
   http://www.easg.org/

International Gambling Studies
   http://www.tandf.co.uk/journals/titles/14459795.asp

Journal of Gambling Studies
   http://www.springeronline.com/sgw/cda/frontpage/0,11855,5-10126-70-
   35680327detailsPage%253DcontentItemPage%2526contentItemId%253D143
   597%2526CIPageCounter%253DCI_FOR_AUTHORS_AND_EDITORS_
   PAGE1,00.html

National Gambling Impact Study Commission
    http://www.ngisc.gov/

National Indian Gaming Association
    http://www.indiangaming.org/

The University of Nevada, Reno, Institute for the Study of Gambling and Commercial Gaming
    http://www.unr.edu/gaming/index.asp

endnotes

1. Simmons, L. (2000). High stakes casinos and controversies. *Journal of Community Practice*, 7(2), 47–69.

2. Grinols, E. and Omorov, J.D. (1996). Who loses when casinos win? *Illinois Business Review*, 53(1), 7–11.

3. Garrett, T.A. (2003). *Casino gambling in America*, St. Louis: Federal Reserve Bank of St. Louis.

4. Anders, G.C. and Somavarapu, S. (2005). *The employment impacts of commercial gambling*, unpublished working paper.

5. American Gaming Association, *AGA State of the States*. http://www.americangaming.org/survey2002/summary/summary.html Accessed on February 13, 2005.

6. Ibid.

7. National Indian Gaming Association, *Indian Gaming Facts*. http://www.indiangaming.org/members/casinos.shtml Accessed on February 13, 2005.

8. US Census Bureau, *Fact Finder*, factfinder **census**.gov. Accessed on February 13, 2005.

9. Schwer, R. and Riddel, M. 2002. Clark County Demographics Summary Population Forecasts: Longterm Projections for Clark County, Nevada 2002–2035. The Center of Business and Economic Research, UNLV. February 6, 2002. Executive Summary on Clark County Website. URL: http://www.co.clark.nv.us/Comprehensive_planning/Advanced/Demographics/PopulationForecasts/2035ForecastandSummary.htm

10. Siegel, D. and Anders, G. C. (2001). The impact of Indian casinos on state lotteries: A case study of Arizona, *Public Finance Review*, 29(2), March, 139–147.

11. Popp, A. V. and Stehwien, C. (2002). Indian casino gambling and state revenue: Some further evidence. *Public Finance Review*, 30(4), 320–330.

12. Arthur Andersen. (1997). Economic impacts of casino gambling in the United States. A study conducted for the American Gaming Association.

13. Walker, D. and Barnett, A. H. (1999). The social costs of gambling: An economic perspective. *Journal of Gambling Studies*, 15(3), Fall, 181–212.

14. National Opinion Research Center. (1999). Gambling impact and behavior study: Report to the National Gambling Impact Study Commission.

15. United States General Accounting Office. (2000). Impact of gambling, GAO/GGD 00–78 http://www.gao.gov/new.items/gg00078.pdf. Accessed on June 2004.

16. Nelson, M. W., Stitt, B. G., & Giacopassi, D. (2000). Casino gambling and bankruptcy in new U.S. casino jurisdictions. *Journal of Socioeconomics*, 29(3), 247–261.

17. Barron, J., Staten, M., & Wilshusen, S. (2002). The impact of casino gambling on personal bankruptcy filing rates, *Contemporary Economic Policy*, 20(4), 440–455.

18. Thalheimer, R. & Ali, M.M. (2004) The relationship of pari-mutuel wagering and casino gaming to personal bankruptcy *Contemporary Economic Policy* 22 (3), 420–432.

19. Grinols, E., & Omorov, J.D. (1996). Who loses when casinos win? *Illinois Business Review*, 53(1), 7–11.

20. Borg, M., Mason, P., & Shapiro, S. (1990). An economic comparison of gambling behavior in Atlantic City and Las Vegas. *Public Finance Quarterly*, 18(2), 291–312.

21. Rose, A. (2001). The regional economic impacts of casino gambling. In M. I. Lahr and R. E. Miller eds. *Regional Science Perspectives in Economic Analysis*, Elsevier Science. pp. 345–378.

Vignette
Crisis Management for Casinos—A Test Case

Jim O'Brien

Part One - The Scenario

Road to Crisis

For the past several months, law enforcement officials have monitored the movements of a religious extremist group. A number of state and federal law enforcement agencies conducted a raid on November 30, 2005, near Toledo, Ohio. Items seized included weapons, a large cache of explosives, and communications equipment. Also seized during the raid were computer-generated maps and images of various high-population areas in several cities, including a number of casinos in Las Vegas, Nevada. Decryption of a computer disk seized in the raid uncovered a vast amount of information concerning scientific and technical publications related to explosive agent manufacturing. The disks contained manuals and diagrams on the construction of improvised explosive devices and a list of explosives and locations where additional explosives were stored. Interrogations and other data confirmed that a series of attacks on selected public- and private-sector targets would occur within the next few weeks.

The president is briefed on the ongoing investigation and based on the potential threat orders that the Homeland Security Advisory System (HSAS) be elevated to "orange." This HSAS level indicates a high risk of specific terrorist attacks.

Initial Response

New Year's Eve begins like all others in Las Vegas. Fireworks are staged at several hotels on the Strip and crowds of people begin to gather for a five-mile-long block party. Live bands are playing and the mood is festive as 250,000 to 300,000 people prepare for an evening of fun and entertainment. Metro officers close off the Strip to vehicular traffic and begin rerouting traffic according to the special event traffic plan. Fireworks begin at midnight, precisely the same time that suicide bombers detonate bombs along the Strip. Confusion and panic cause a rush of partygoers into nearby hotels. Security staffs have considerable difficulty controlling the crowds of people. Significant numbers of injured and/or dead litter the street. City and county first responders rush to their aid. Crowds become unmanageable and hotel security is stretched beyond the breaking point.

Consequence Management

Several hours have passed since the initial explosions. The magnitude of the event begins to unfold with the sunrise. Hundreds of people are injured, many with severe and/or life-threatening injuries. It is clear that many have died, and first responders continue to work to save as many others as possible. First responders request nearby hotels to set up temporary morgues and triage areas. Hotels do their best to comply but still grapple with a multitude of problems. Security staffs begin room-to-room searches for additional weapons of mass destruction (WMDs) as well as a search for missing guests. Casino operations have come to a standstill while the limited number of security officers work overtime to control a very dangerous situation. Casinos find themselves completely unprepared for the magnitude of the event, and management now must come to grips with the enormous loss of lives and revenue and the shortage of available staff.

Recovery

Several days into the event, political figures take center stage with news conferences describing actions taken, recovery plans, information, and offers of assistance. Many impacted areas remain closed to vehicular or pedestrian traffic because of the collection of crime scene data. Federal financial assistance is offered to state and local jurisdictions. The National Guard is called in to assist local law enforcement in protecting the very large crime scene. Casinos continue

determining the status of guests and offer assistance. First responders are getting their first break in days, and hotel properties have been burdened with the task of laying off nonessential personnel. Casino properties struggle with massive cancellations and the closure of major portions of the Strip. Federal officials have already begun the arduous task of collecting all available evidence to prosecute those responsible.

3 Social Environments

Ki-Joon Back, Kansas State University

Bo Bernhard, University of Nevada, Las Vegas

Learning Objectives

1. To introduce the social benefits as well as many of the costs of casino gaming.

2. To describe some of the benefits of casino gaming at both the community and individual levels.

3. To provide an understanding of the dynamic of these benefits and how they are linked to public perceptions.

4. To provide a historical perspective in understanding the problems associated with today's gaming industry.

Chapter Outline

Introduction

This chapter discusses some of the social benefits and **social costs** of casino gaming. As noted by a wide variety of researchers, these kinds of assessments are plagued by any number of conceptual challenges.[1] For instance, it is not always easy to separate social impacts from economic impacts: employment provides both economic and social benefits, and we cannot easily determine where one stops and the other starts. Likewise, crime can be considered both an economic and a social cost—and economists would further note that crime can also provide benefits to the criminal (in other words, crime *can* pay). Further complicating assessments of the social impacts of casino gaming is the fact that impacts are often intangible and qualitative. As Besham and White (2002) note, quantifying benefits from any form of entertainment can be difficult.[2]

Despite these challenges, policy makers and gaming operators need to incorporate cost-and-benefit analyses into their decisions. In this section, we address some of the theoretical and empirical questions that have emerged from these debates.

Social Benefits

Benefits at the Community Level

A good deal of research has attempted to assess the social benefits and costs of casino gaming.[3] Although most of these studies have focused primarily on the negative consequences of casino gaming for the community, several studies have also examined its benefits.

The most obvious benefit at the community level is increasing population size resulting from the increased number of employment opportunities and the improvement of infrastructures provided by casino gaming. As a result of these factors, Las Vegas is the fastest-growing metropolitan city in the United States.

Besides Las Vegas, many casino communities have experienced various forms of benefits. In the literature on Native American casinos, studies on communities in Minnesota and Wisconsin reported a variety of social benefits from casino gaming. For instance, five years after the Ho-Chunk's casino opened in 1992, the social benefits were dramatic: the numbers of welfare, income maintenance program, and medical assistance recipients among tribe members dropped by 52 percent, 38 percent, and 43 percent respectively.[4] The numbers were even more impressive for the Oneida nation, which saw a 72 percent reduction in its assisted welfare program. Potawatomi nations, meanwhile, received an average of $3 million per year from its casino industry, and this money has been used to support a variety of local nonprofit organizations.[5]

Hsu (1999) critically reviewed the literature on the positive impacts of gaming in Native American casino communities.[6] This study revealed that the impacts included health benefits through the construction of a medical center,[7] educational benefits through the building of schools,[8] and cultural benefits through the founding of a museum.[9] Taken together, these social benefits can enable Native American tribal members to exert less pressure on social programs and to support their own social service amenities, through education and jobs for tribal members.

Furthermore, many casino companies provide social benefits by supporting community programs. For instance, Harrah's management team teaches classes at several local community colleges in North Carolina, thereby providing preemployment training to area residents.[10] In Atlantic City, about $170 million in gaming tax revenue was used to provide benefits for senior citizens; most of these funds helped defray medical and utility costs.[11] These figures were actually much greater than the amount predicted by the city before casino gambling was legalized.

Benefits at the Individual Level

Casinos are wildly popular places, and visitor counts appear to be increasing each year. Casinos provide self-contained, vibrant, partylike atmospheres that allow for a break from routine. Some suggest that casino gaming provides stress relief from tensions brought on by everyday life.[12] Rosecrance argues that gamblers may view the social world of the casino as an intimate place where they may feel free to "play" with a sense of security and confidence.[13] This theory is supported by an American Gaming Association survey,[14] which indicated that the majority of casino customers go to casinos primarily for fun and entertainment. This study also suggested that for many casino customers, casino gambling is a valuable social activity that they engage in with their spouse, family, and/or friends.

In the future, the benefits of responsible gambling may well become more apparent—much as we have recently discovered that responsible drinking may actually have health benefits. If we suspect that laughter or having fun has real health benefits, for example, and we know that the majority of gamblers are, in fact, having fun, it is reasonable to explore whether health benefits can be correlated with certain gambling behaviors. In addition, more research needs to be conducted on the potential for cognitive benefits associated with gambling. For instance, it may well be that certain types of gambling can help maintain cognitive faculties that tend to decline with age—much as completing crossword puzzles or other problem-solving activities can.

However, it should be noted that whatever the actual benefits of casino gambling, the public perceptions of social benefits are not always stable. Although a study by Giacopassi and Stitt (1999) showed that the majority of respondents favored the casino in their community and believed that it enhanced their quality of life, several longitudinal studies found significant differences in the residents' perceptions after the casino opened.[15] Roehl (1999) compared Nevada residents' attitudes about the impacts of gaming in 1975 and 1992 and found significant decreases in perceptions of the benefits associated with casino gambling.[16] Shifts in social perceptions are even more evident in Back and Lee's (2004) four-year-longitudinal study of the benefits of casino gambling in Korea.[17] Prior to the casino's opening, respondents reported favorable perceptions of the casino's impact on the local quality of life, community camaraderie and pride, and improvements in education. After the casino's opening, residents' perceptions of the levels of these perceived benefits dropped significantly. The major reason for the significant drop in perceived social benefits was the social costs, including those associated with problem gamblers. This trend indicates that those interested in studying the benefits of casinos need to understand the oft-related issue of costs, which will be covered in the next section.

Hence, it appears that we can learn a handful of lessons from this examination of the social benefits of casino gambling. Clearly, the benefits are real and have been demonstrated in a variety of studies. These benefits exist on both the community and individual levels. At the same time, the sociological phenomena associated with public *perceptions* of these benefits are dynamic. Finally, it appears that the issues of benefits are linked in the public's mind with the issues of costs, and hence an understanding of both is necessary when conducting these sorts of analyses.

Social Costs

Gambling: The Downside

This section reviews a series of problems commonly associated with gambling. It is interesting that relatively few of society's complaints about the downsides of gambling have endured over the years. The morality issue is no longer as resonant as it once was, as more and more people have come to see gambling as something other than the sinful act that preachers used to condemn. Indeed, sin *itself* has transformed, as Las Vegas, the gaming capital of the world, arguably illustrates: after all, if "Sin City" is the most popular place to visit in all of America, how can the city's most prominent behaviors be considered at all "deviant" anymore? Furthermore, the issue of greed—of "getting something for nothing" from the gambling act—seems no longer to upset as many cultural critics and economic conservatives as it once did.

The one gambling problem that has most visibly endured is known, appropriately enough, as **problem gambling**.[18] In gaming jurisdiction after gaming jurisdiction, legislators and regulators want to know what gaming operators plan to do about problem gambling, as well as the other problems that go along with it (e.g., crimes committed by those who develop problems, family/work problems that result from it, and financial damage resulting from excessive gambling). Gaming operators and organizations, for their part, are wary of being grouped with businesses that have neglected the problems associated with their products (most notably, the tobacco industry), and many have set out to take a proactive stance. Antigaming organizations, meanwhile, insist that problem gambling represents a major—perhaps *the* major—challenge to the well-being of communities that choose to embrace gaming.

Amid all of this are the problem gamblers themselves, a group that has been around for some time, but that only recently has attracted any substantial research attention.

Figure 3–1

Most people have some perception of what a gambling problem is, but few individuals on either side of this issue have spent substantial amounts of time with problem gamblers themselves. Who are these individuals who seemingly cannot stop gambling? In this section, we address the complexities of this issue.

Yesterday: Historical Problems

> Why am I really such an irresponsible infant? . . . I lost everything I had then . . . I walked out of the Casino, and suddenly discovered that I still had one gulden in my waistcoat pocket. Well, that'll pay for my dinner at least, I said to myself. But after I had taken a hundred steps or so, I changed my mind and went back to the roulette table. . . .
>
> Tomorrow, tomorrow, it will all be over!
>
> —*Final lines from Fyodor Dostoevsky's The Gambler*

Dostoevsky's words remind us of his literary skill, but behind them lies an interesting tale: Dostoevsky wrote his classic *The Gambler* in a matter of weeks, purportedly to cover debts resulting from his own gambling problem. We can see, then, that the history of gambling problems is a long one—older indeed than the modern-day casino industry, and probably as old as the act of gambling itself.

Historically, people who gamble too much have not always received the kindest of social receptions. Consider the period before many of our current entertainment options existed—before television, video games, the internet, or slot machines—when churches represented not only the moral center of their home communities, but also the primary source of social contact and entertainment for those who lived there. Religious institutions were then the central definers of public life, and these moral—not medical—experts were the ones who identified those who gambled problematically. Sermons such this one (delivered by Samuel Hopkins on "The Evils of Gambling") both shaped and reflected the social environment of the day:

> Let the gambler suffer... Lay upon him the biting lash of public odium... Let the gambler know that he is watched, and marked; and that... he is loathed. Let the man who dares to furnish a resort for the gambler know that he is counted a traitor to his duty, a murderer of all that is fair, and precious, and beloved among us. Let the voice of united, incensed remonstrance be heard—heard till the ears of the guilty tingle.[19]

Moral institutions thus contributed substantially to the problems that excessive gamblers experienced in that time (and they continue to haunt the lives of problem gamblers today in the form of social stigmas). This history is especially ironic given that today, moral institutions have often voiced some of the harshest criticisms of the gaming industry—ostensibly on *behalf* of problem gamblers.[20]

Some important lessons of history, then, are that gambling problems have been around for a long time, these problems are complex, and they are global. We need to keep these historical matters in mind when contemplating the best course of action in dealing with gambling problems today and in the future.

Today: Current Problems

Problem Gambling

How do we define problem gambling today? How does one know if someone has a gambling problem? These are legitimate questions, and to some degree, they continue to challenge even the finest of researchers who devote their careers to examining these issues. These questions should be kept in mind when contemplating the obligations of casino employees, who should not be asked to diagnose a sensitive problem that even established mental health professionals have difficulty identifying. Because problem gambling can be considered a more "invisible" affliction than, say, alcoholism (which can be seen and smelled more easily), special care should be taken with any efforts to assist these individuals in a gaming environment. While diagnosing a gambling problem should be left to the professionals, employees should know how to help those who indicate that they have a problem (for instance, by directing them to telephone help lines run by professionals trained to provide assistance).

Today, the field of studying problem gambling is still very young—perhaps where the field of studying alcoholism was a generation ago. Despite its youth, however, clinicians and researchers have made substantial strides in their understanding of what, exactly, this "problem" represents.

The American Psychiatric Association publishes a large volume on mental illnesses entitled the <u>Diagnostic and Statistical Manual of Mental Disorders</u> (DSM). This volume has included **pathological gambling** (the official psychological term for problem gambling) since 1980, when it was first introduced thanks to the tireless advocacy of the "founding father" of problem gambling treatment, Dr. Robert Custer. Originally based upon the clinical experiences of Dr. Custer, the DSM criteria have evolved into a list of ten items, and an individual who satisfies five of the criteria is diagnosed with pathological gambling.

There appear to be two types of problem gamblers, and while these groups are not necessarily mutually exclusive, they can provide a useful analytical framework. The first type is the classic **action problem gambler**, who gambles to achieve a rush that ultimately proves problematic. This individual develops a destructive affinity for the excitement of the game and seeks a "high" from it. He or she tends to be associated with action-oriented games such as craps or sports wagering. The second type is the so-called **escape problem gambler**, who gambles not so much to feel great, but rather to feel nothing.[21] He/she wishes to anesthetize or "escape" from problems through gambling, a behavior that should be discouraged.

Gambling and Crime

One of the most often cited problems associated with gambling is crime. Several studies have suggested that correlations exist between pathological problem gamblers and a variety of offenses, including fraud, stealing, embezzlement, forgery, and robbery.[22] According to one study, criminal behaviors among adolescent gamblers may be more prevalent than among adult gamblers because young people in general have limited access to the finances needed to gamble.[23]

We should point out, though, that while crime has been associated with gambling since Samuel Hopkins's day, these claims are rarely supported by strong empirical evidence linking crime directly to gambling.[24] Let us be clear, though: any activity that generates an increase in traffic will lead to an absolute increase in criminal activity. This does not mean, however, that any one individual's chances of being victimized necessarily increases when a casino is built. All in all, care should be taken in any environment that is crowded or that attracts a variety of tourists, and it appears that casinos are no different.

Gambling and Age

Another problem that concerns many today is youth gambling. According to a 2003 study, approximately 80 percent of youth ages 12 to 17 had gambled in the past 12 months.[25] Shaffer (1998) found that the top four games of choice among adolescent gamblers were non–casino card games (40 percent), games of skill (32 percent), sports gambling (31 percent), and the lottery (30 percent).[26] According to a 2000 study by Derevensky and Gupta[27], 4 percent to 7 percent of youths in their sample were classified as pathological gamblers, and 9 percent to 14 percent exhibited criteria that qualified them for the "at-risk" category.

Of course, many adolescents engage in risky behaviors that do not endure over time; nevertheless, youth gambling is a serious enough problem that a number of gaming companies have incorporated youth gambling policies into their responsible gaming programs. These policies are designed to keep underage gamblers away from gaming properties and to educate minors about the perils of underage gambling.

Figure 3–2

At the other end of the age spectrum, McNeilly and Burke's (2000) study found that 2.7 percent of the seniors they surveyed could be categorized as pathological gamblers.[28] Another 5.5 percent exhibited some gambling problems. However most seniors do not have problems. When it came to their gambling activities, the most commonly cited motivational factors were to relax and have fun, to get away for the day, to pass the time, to relieve boredom, and to meet new people. Playing the slots gives them some excitement in their lives and it gives them something to look forward to. They have something to talk about with almost everyone now, especially their kids and grandkids; most people have a story about gambling, so it is a great conversation generator. Other external motivation factors are inexpensive meals, free transportation, discount coupons, slot clubs, dance clubs, or discount prescription offers.

The major negative consequences of problem gambling behaviors among retired senior citizens were gambling away a pension and experiencing depression. However, when New York City wanted to 'protect' its elderly from gambling, its efforts were met with a hostile attitude. Some responded by saying "I have lived through the Great Depression and a couple of world wars. I think I can handle my own money by now."

There is a tendency to **infantilize** older adults by insisting that they engage in certain recreational activities and not others—and gambling is often cited as a less than desirable recreation for this group. One might wonder whether this value judgment is linked to moral and historical objections to the act of gambling. For better or worse, in many communities senior citizens lack access to a wide variety of recreational activities aside from gambling. Precisely because gambling appears to be so popular with older adults, and because this can be an economically vulnerable population, casinos have a responsibility to encourage seniors to gamble responsibly and not problematically.

Tomorrow: Future Problems

The gaming location of tomorrow may well pose new challenges for those interested in promoting the downside of gaming. The rapid and dynamic developments associated with internet gaming concern those who think that problems with escapism may actually be exacerbated in the home (after all, gambling locations contain any number of distractions that can redirect the player's attention). The news is not all bad on internet gaming, though: data on gambling patterns can be easily collected with every gambling transaction, and this transparency allows researchers greater access to more sophisticated information about how people gamble and how they develop problems.

This brings us to an important point: in the future, research will play a vital role in helping us demystify the nuances of gambling problems, and the gaming industry thus far has been active in encouraging and supporting research (contrast this with the tobacco industry, which actively worked to *conceal* research on the downside of smoking). Research may well allow us to identify (through biochemical means, perhaps) those at risk for developing gambling problems, and health professionals can act accordingly to address this issue. On the supply side, studies that examine the safety of gambling products—much as automobile companies test the safety of theirs—can inform business decisions on how to construct a safer gambling locale. A reasonable goal may be to help problem gamblers—without interfering with the gambling experience of the vast majority of healthy recreational gamblers.

What is certain, though, is that problem gamblers have been around for some time, and they are not going to be cured anytime soon. As a result, gaming leaders will need to continue to learn about the downside of the products they provide, and they will need to continue to take a proactive stance to help assist those customers who develop problems. Long-term sustainability in any industry requires long-term thinking. The problems created by problem gamblers far overwhelm any short-term benefits that casinos may gain from their destructive play.

Conclusion

Before we conclude, it should be pointed out that no product has ever been invented that has not hurt some of its customers some of the time: cars maim, pillows smother, and bits of steaks get lodged in windpipes (to say nothing of what they leave lodged in our arteries). Even Disneyland, the "happiest place on earth," has seen innocent attendees killed by relatively tame amusement rides. When viewed in this light, the question becomes not "Will this product harm anyone?" but rather "How much harm is acceptable, and what can we do to reduce the risks?" On the former question, a consensus has not yet been reached, but on the latter one, gaming industry professionals have taken a series of steps to help alleviate problem gamblers' suffering. The American Gaming Association, for instance, has developed a code of conduct with a series of guidelines designed to encourage responsible gaming.

Gambling is meant to be fun and entertaining for players. When gambling is not fun anymore, chances are something may be wrong. Researchers, mental health professionals, problem gambling organizations, and the casino industry have a responsibility—to the problem gamblers themselves—to avoid bickering unnecessarily and to unite with a common goal of reducing the costs associated with gambling. Communities may avoid many of the problems associated with problem gamblers by encouraging public education campaigns, by supporting quality treatment, and by helping casino employees better understand these afflictions. Dr. Robert Custer, the founder of the problem gambling field, was fond of citing an interesting analogy. In a sense, he claimed, operating a casino can be similar to operating a ski slope—the majority of customers will have a fun time, but a handful will be seriously hurt. This does not mean that we condemn ski slopes, but it does mean that ski slopes and those who operate them have a special obligation to help take care of those who fall.

key terms

Social cost	Action problem gambler
Problem gambling	Escape problem gambler
Pathological gambling	Infantilize

review questions

1. List three social benefits found in studies conducted on gaming in Native American communities.

2. What is the major benefit of gaming at the community level? At the individual level?

3. What are the two primary reasons the majority of casino customers cite for going to casinos?

4. How can communities avoid many of the problems associated with problem gamblers?

5. What is the rapid and dynamic development in non–casino gaming that concerns those who think that a problem with gambling is escapism?

internet sites

University of Nevada, Reno, Institute for the Study of Gambling
    http:/ /www. unr. edu/ gaming/ index. asp

National Council on Problem Gambling
    http:/ /www. ncpgambling. org

Illinois Institute for Addiction Recovery
    http:/ /www. addictionrecov. org

endnotes

1. Oh, H.M. (1999). Social impacts of casino gaming: The case of Las Vegas. *In* Legalized Casino Gaming in the United States, C. Hsu, ed., pp. 177–199. New York: The Haworth Hospitality Press.

2. Besham, P., & White, K. (2002). *Gambling with Our Future? The Costs and Benefits of Legalized Gambling*. [Electronic Version]. The Fraser Institute Digital Publication.

3. Besham, P., & White, K. (2002). *Gambling with Our Future? The Costs and Benefits of Legalized Gambling*. [Electronic Version]. The Fraser Institute Digital Publication; Blaszczynski, A.P. & Silove, D. (1996). Pathological Gambling: Forensic Issues. *Australian and New Zealand Journal of Psychiatry*, 30(3), 358–369; Lesieur, H.R. & Anderson, C. (1995). *Results of a Survey of Gamblers anonymous Members in Illinois*. Illinois Council on Problem and Compulsive Gambling; Lueders, B. (1994). Buffaloed: Casino cowboys take Indians for a ride. *Progressive*,

58(8), 30–33; Nowlen, C., (2004). Casinos bring benefits: In other places around state. [Electronic Version]. The Capital Times; Schwarz, J., & Linder, A. (1992). Inpatient treatment of male pathological gamblers in Germany. *Journal of Gambling Studies*, 8, 93–109.

4. Nowlen, C., (2004). Casinos bring benefits: In other places around state. [Electronic Version]. The Capital Times.

5. Ibid.

6. Hsu, C. (1999). Social impacts of Native American casino gaming. In Legalized Casino Gaming in the United States, C. Hsu, ed., pp. 221–231. New York: The Haworth Hospitality Press.

7. Stepheson, J. (1996). For some American Indians, casino profits are a good bet for improving health care. *Journal of the American Medical Association*, 275(23), 1783–1785.

8. Segal, D. (1992). Dance with sharks: Why the Indian gaming experiment's gone bust. *Washington Monthly*, 24(3), 26–30.

9. Lueders, B. (1994). Buffaloed: Casino cowboys take Indians for a ride. *Progressive*, 58(8), 30–33.

10. (Harrah's Casino, 2000). http://www.harrahs.com/harrahs-corporate/about-us.html. Accessed July 15, 2000.

11. American Gaming Association (2000). *State of the States: The AGA Survey of Casino Entertainment*. [Electronic Version]. Washington, D.C. http://www.americangaming.org/survey/index.cfm. Accessed July 15, 2000.

12. Besham, P., and White, K. (2002). *Gambling with Our Future? The Costs and Benefits of Legalized Gambling*. [Electronic Version]. The Fraser Institute Digital Publication.

13. Rosecrance, J. (1998). Gambling without Guilt: The Legitimization of an American Pastime. Pacific Grove, CA: Brooks/Cole.

14. American Gaming Association (2000). *State of the States: The AGA Survey of Casino Entertainment*. [Electronic Version]. Washington, D.C. http://www.americangaming.org/survey/index.cfm. Accessed July 15, 2000.

15. Giacopassi, D. & Stitt, B.G. (1999). Assessing the impacts of casino gambling on crime in Mississippi. *American Journal of Criminal Justice*, 18, 117–131.

16. Roehl, W. (1999). Quality of life issues in a casino destination. *Journal of Business Research*, 44, 223–229.

17. Back, K.J., & Lee, C.K. (2004). Korean casino impact study. *In* C. Hsu (Eds.) *Asian-Pacific Casino Industry*. New York, Haworth.

18. Because an extraordinarily wide variety of words have been invoked to describe these phenomena, and because it is the term most commonly used in everyday conversation, "problem gambling: will be used throughout this discussion.

19. Hopkins, S. (1835). *The Evils of Gambling: A Sermon*. Monteplier, VT: E.P. Walton and Son 15, 17–18.

20. Bernhard, B. (2002). From Sin to Sickness: A Sociological History of Problem Gambling. Unpublished doctoral dissertation, University of Nevada, Las Vegas.

21. See Jacobs, D. F. 91987) Evidence for a common dissociative-like reaction among addicts. *Journal of Gambling Behavior* 4:27–37; Shaffer, H. J., Hall, M. N., Walsh, J. S., & Vander Bilt, J. (1995). The psychosocial consequences of gambling, In R. Tarnnenwald (Ed.). *Casino development: How would casinos affect New England's Economy?* Boston: Federal Reserve Bank of Boston, 130–141.

22. Blaszczynski, A.P. & Silove, D. (1996). Pathological gambling: Forensic issues. *Australian and New Zealand Journal of Psychiatry*, 30 (3), 358–369; Lesieur, H.R., and Anderson, C. (1995). *Results of a Survey of Gamblers anonymous Members in Illinois*. Illinois Council on Problem and Compulsive Gambling; Schwarz, J., and Linder, A. (1992). Inpatient treatment of male pathological gamblers in Germany. *Journal of Gambling Studies*, 8, 93–109.

23. Schwarz, J. & Linder, A. (1992). Inpatient treatment of male pathological gamblers in Germany. *Journal of Gambling Studies*, 8, 93–109.

24. Miller, W.J. & Schwartz, M.D. (1998). Casino gambling and street crime. *The Annals of the American Academy of Political and Social Science*. 556, 124–137.

25. Derevensky, J.L, Gupta, R., Dickson, L., Hardoon, K., & Deguire, A.E. (2003). Understanding youth gambling problems: A conceptual framework. *In D. Romer (Ed.), Reducing Adolescent Risk*. California: Sage. 115–120.

26. Shaffer, H. J. (1998). *Testimony: On the study & treatment of disordered gambling*. National Gambling Impact Study Commission. http://govinfo.library.unt.edu/ngisc/reports/finrpt.html. Accessed July 15, 2000.

27. Derevensky, J. L. & Gupta, R. (2000). *Youth gambling: A clinical and research perspective. E-gambling*. http://www.camh.net/egambling/issue2/feature/. Accessed July 15, 2000.

28. McNeilly, D. P. & Burke, W. J. (2000). Late life gambling: The attitudes and behaviors of older adults. *Journal of Gambling Studies*, 16(4), 393–415.

references

Abott, D. A., Cramer, S. L., and Sherrets, S. D. (1995). Pathological gambling and the family: Practice implications. *Families in Society*, 76 (4), 213–219.

American Psychiatric Association. (1994). *Diagnostic and Statistical Manual of Mental Disorders*, Fourth Edition. Washington, DC: American Psychiatric Association.

Cohen and Wolfe (1999). The 1999 Industry Report: A profile of America's Casino Gaming Industry. Prepared for the American Gaming Association.

Fisher, S. (1991). Governmental response to juvenile fruit machine gambling in the U.K.: Where do we go from here? *Journal of Gambling Studies*, 7(3), 217–247.

Gupta, R., and Derevensky, J. L. (1997). Familial and social influences on juvenile gambling behavior. *Journal of Gambling Studies*, 13(3), 179–192.

Harrah's Casino. (2002). Effects on families and other quality of life issues. [Electronic Version].

McClearly, R., and Chew, K. (1998). Suicide and gambling: An analysis of suicide rates in U.S. counties and metropolitan areas: A report to the American Gaming Association. University of California Irvine: Department of Environmental Analysis & Design School of Ecology.

Schwer, R. K., and Riddel, M. (2002). Population forecasts: Long-term projections for Clark County, Nevada 2002–2035. Las Vegas: Advanced Planning Division—Clark County Demographics Summary.

Vignette

Crisis Management for Casinos—A Test Case

Jim O'Brien

Part Two - Recommendations for Dealing with the Crisis

Recommendation 1: Security chiefs from each casino must be individually notified by local law enforcement. The call-down list should be proceduralized and documented to ensure that each casino is notified and prepared. It is insufficient to rely upon word of mouth to ensure that security is aware of the threat.

Recommendation 2: Casino security chiefs, in conjunction with local and federal law enforcement, should prepare a comprehensive set of actions and procedures for each HSAS level. Since many of these procedures exist at larger casinos, the casino security chiefs should review these existing procedures and prepare them as generically as possible. They should offer those procedures to each property and suggest they be included into each casino's security plan.

Recommendation 3: Additional training elements should include the incident command system (ICS), the use and different types of personal protective equipment (PPE), and the detection of all types of WMD (i.e., chemical, biological, or radiological) agents. Setting aside litigation issues, it is through this training that both private and public first responder teams can work together and exercise protocols.

Recommendation 4: Provide a common radio frequency/channel and protocols to improve communication between county/city first responders and hotel security staff.

Recommendation 5: Develop, update, and/or expand MOUs between casinos to reflect the resources needed to mitigate a high-explosive weapon of mass destruction. Coordinate with neighboring and sister properties to share resources, including but not limited to security personnel during a terrorist event. Ensure that county emergency management officials are consulted during development of any cooperative agreement and appropriately reflect knowledge of mutual aid agreements in response planning.

Recommendation 6: Each hotel/casino property should establish a crisis communication center (CMC). An operational CMC is essential as the focal point for the transmittal of critical information and rumor control. It establishes the necessary protocols and ensures that the proper resources are communicated to the decision maker.

Recommendation 7: Conduct an annual functional exercise of the CMC, ICP, and EOC. Bottlenecks in communication between casinos and first responders, as well as between casinos themselves, can be alleviated through annual exercises involving CMCs, ICPs, and the county EOC. Exercising middle to upper management ensures that properties can act quickly to mitigate a response to a terrorist event.

Recommendation 8: Casinos should strongly consider and embrace all opportunities to exercise with local, state, and federal authorities. It is through these exercises that upper casino management can better understand the multijurisdictional efforts at mitigating the effects of terrorism. Casinos would better understand their need to document and account for the use of supplies, personnel, and/or other casino resources required in a coordinated response. Individual properties would better understand the role of government and the resources available to them.

Recommendation 9: Develop a casino recovery plan, similar in scope to the local city/county disaster recovery plan. Assistance can be obtained in preparing these documents from city/county emergency planners or consultants familiar with emergency planning and preparedness.

Recommendation 10: Develop a county disaster contingency plan to use private industry first responders as disaster workers at impacted properties.

4 Casino Management and Politics

Peter Collins, University of Salford

Learning Objectives

1. To provide the necessary understanding of how governments think when they are formulating casino laws and regulations.

2. To discuss aspects of the casino industry regulated by the government.

3. To understand in some detail the vital nature of the arguments and the dynamics of the debate between those who are for and against casinos in their communities.

Chapter Outline

Introduction

Why Casino Managers Need to Understand Politics

More than in any other industry, casino profits depend on governmental decisions. This means that casino managers have a vital interest in seeing casinos not only from their own point of view as suppliers of a service, and from their customers' view as consumers of that service, but they must also be able to see casinos from the point of view of government—the politicians and civil servants who authorize and regulate them. The main purpose of this chapter is to supply present and future casino managers with the necessary understanding of how governments think when they are formulating casino laws and regulations.

Casino managers need to be able to identify politicians' principal concerns about casinos so they can design, develop, and operate their projects in ways that meet the needs of government and encourage governments to treat them in ways that are commercially helpful. They also need to know how governments think, so that they can influence that thinking by addressing their lobbying efforts accordingly. Therefore, casino owners need to demonstrate to politicians how they can achieve their political objectives in ways that are at least consonant with the interests of the casino owners themselves.

Is the Casino Industry Treated Differently from Other Industries by Governments?

How Casinos Make Money

In the commercial gambling[1] industry, casinos sometimes make their profits by charging a fee for the services they provide, such as when they impose a charge for participating in a poker game or take a percentage of each pot. More commonly, they make their profits by arranging for players to play against the **House**—the casino company—on games in which the odds favor the house. In this way casino customers pay for the pleasure they get by losing money in the long run, and casino companies pay for the capital and operating costs of building and running a casino out of this money.

It should be stressed that there is nothing underhanded in the fact that casinos make money by offering only games in which the odds favor the house. After all, everyone knows that this is how casinos are paid for the services they provide. In the long run, although the customers are sure to lose, in the short run, individual customers can and do win (and sometimes win big). What makes the playing of games for money fun for many people is precisely the prospect of winning, and the roller-coaster excitement that comes from not knowing whether you are going to win or lose. Therefore, it should also be stressed that the essential commodity that casinos are selling is fun. Casinos are built and make substantial profits because they provide people with a lot of enjoyment that they are willing to pay for. As such, and apart from the fact that customers pay by losing money, the casino industry is like any other industry that exists primarily to provide people with pleasure or enjoyment.

How the Casino Industry Is Unique

Although we have seen how the casino industry is similar to others, the casino business also differs from almost all others that provide pleasure and entertainment. The selling of gambling opportunities is different from selling bars of chocolate, seats in a movie theatre, or meals in a restaurant. For reasons to be considered later, in all jurisdictions where casinos are legal, they are subject to a far greater degree of government regulation than other service industries that compete for the public's **discretionary income**. Some aspects of the casino industry that are commonly regulated are

- The number of casinos in a given jurisdiction
- Where they may be located
- Who may and may not operate them
- Who may and may not play at them
- The age at which people may gamble
- The kind of gambling products that may be offered
- What other entertainment may be offered
- The technical standards for gambling apparatus
- The hours that the casinos may operate
- The security and surveillance they must provide
- The records they must keep for their regulators

- How they may and may not market themselves and their products
- The procedures they must follow to prevent money laundering
- The forms of consumer protection that must be available
- What steps they take to discourage people from becoming problem gamblers and what help is available for those who do develop problems

These regulations mean that there is never a purely free market in the supply of gambling services: the supply is always to some extent restricted, and so is competition among suppliers. This has the important consequence that suppliers can charge more for gambling services (especially by offering the players worse odds) than they would be able to under unrestricted competition. This is why governments often require casinos to pay taxes, usually called **gambling privilege taxes**. These taxes are over and above all the other income, consumption, and property taxes that any business has to pay.

Why Is the Casino Industry Treated Differently from the Rest of the Entertainment Industry by Governments?

Democracy and Public Opinion

The main reason why governments, especially democratic governments, subject casinos to a high degree of regulation is in response to public opinion. The main strength of a democratic system of government is precisely that it compels politicians to conform their conduct to what is regarded as desirable or at least acceptable by a reasonably large body of public opinion. This is because in a democracy, if politicians' actions make them unpopular, they will lose what they most want to keep, their jobs. Besides, politicians like to be popular and have a reputation for effectiveness in protecting and promoting the interests of the community as a whole. This is why members of governments are anxious about how the decisions they make will play in the court of public opinion, not just at election times, but constantly. More particularly, they are concerned how they will appear in the media to their constituents. In relation to casinos, this means that the most fundamental need of government is to ensure that if it legalizes casinos, it is done in such a way that the casinos will enjoy broad and sustained popular approval. Electorates

Figure 4–1 Eugene Bertelsen of Richland, Iowa, exits after filling out his primary ballot in the old one-room Wisner School.

will need to be persuaded that for the most part, it was and remains a good idea for legal casinos to operate in their communities. They will consequently judge casinos on whether they think that casinos on the whole make their communities either better or worse (Figure 4–1).

However, and contrary to what is sometimes suggested, economic considerations are not the only—and perhaps not even the most important—factors that weigh on electorates when they cast their votes. There is also a moral and psychological dimension to the popular perceptions of politicians. This means that politicians need to persuade voters not only that they will be effective in promoting their constituents' interests, but also that they are decent human beings. This is not just a matter of politicians having a reputation for a reasonable degree of integrity and clean living, they must also be associated with policies that cause their constituents to believe that their communities occupy the moral high ground. It is this factor that makes gambling legislation controversial with voters and consequently makes wise politicians devise their policies toward them with great care. The fact is, gambling is an activity about which people have moral views that they do not have about other goods and services purchased for enjoyment. Many once regarded the theatre and more recently the movies as morally dangerous, if not downright wicked. Consequently, those forms of entertainment were strictly regulated in terms of what could and could not be shown. Similarly, some people object to going to bars on moral grounds, though not many would favor a return to the infamous days of prohibition.

Because of some people's moral or religious convictions, gambling is still thought of as a vice. But many others, who would not describe necessarily gambling as a vice, feel uneasy about it and would have misgivings if there were a great deal of it taking place in their communities. Other people take the opposite view, that there is nothing wrong with gambling, that going to a casino is no different from going to the movies, and that in any case, it is none of the government's business how people enjoy themselves.

The result is that the debate about casinos, both before and after they are built, tends to consist of arguments between two opposing camps, which we may call, for convenience, the *permissivists* and the *protectivists*. Out of this conflict there usually emerges a kind of democratic consensus on which politicians can base policy. It should be emphasized, however, that this consensus, when it tolerates the authorization of a limited number of highly regulated casinos, remains fragile and unstable and can quite easily shift back in the direction of prohibition. Casino managements have a very important role in trying to influence public opinion in this area. It is, therefore, vital that they understand in some detail the nature of the arguments and the dynamics of this debate.

The Permissive View

In the democratic jurisdictions that consider how much casino gambling the law should permit and what additional regulations should be applied, opinions will typically differ among politicians and members of the general public. At one end of the spectrum are the **permissivists**—champions of a permissive libertarian position that stress the role of government as restricted to only preventing citizens from harming others. This philosophy promotes that government should not be concerned with preventing people from doing things that may be harmful to themselves, nor compelling them to do things that others think would be good for them—even if the others are right.

In practice, those who take a libertarian view of casinos are likely to see nothing wrong with casino gambling and will think that the operations of casinos should, as are restaurants and the cinema, be left to the free market. In their view, to condemn going to a casino as immoral is archaic. It is like condemning going to the theatre as immoral— something that was practiced and preached by Puritans, and which led to practices (now considered ridiculous) such as a prohibition on burying actors in hallowed ground.

However, for libertarians, a much more important point of principle is involved than the question of whether casinos are in fact bad for people. Libertarians espouse the principle that even if there is something morally undesirable or harmful about going to a casino, adults should be free to decide for themselves how they will spend their own time and money on entertainment—even if they sometimes make choices that are foolish or that others disapprove of.

Moreover, such people are likely to be staunch defenders of individual freedom, not only in the private domain but also in commercial transactions. They will, consequently, often believe that people should be free to invest their own time, talents, energies, and resources in trying to make a profit by supplying the public with goods and services that the public wants. Consequently, libertarians believe that if people want to spend money gambling at casinos and others are willing to invest their time, energy, and capital supplying these customers, then the number of casinos and how they operate ought to be determined by market forces. These forces would include the normal economic transactions between willing buyers and sellers, with government intervening only to prevent the illegitimate use of force or fraud by either party.

The Protectivist View

At the other end of the spectrum are the **protectivists**—people who will be vehemently opposed to casino gambling and think that it should be banned in the same way and for the same reasons that dangerous narcotics are. Sometimes, these people believe that all gambling is immoral, and/or they object to it on religious grounds, and/or they think that casinos will disfigure communities and harm individuals. Moreover, they deny the basic libertarian principle of limiting government activities. Instead, they believe that governments ought to enforce the moral rules that are accepted by the majority of the community. They may also believe that governments must enforce adherence to particular moral and religious rules that they deem to be essential to spiritual well-being.

It would be wrong to represent that all those who oppose the liberalization of gambling laws are necessarily driven by such powerful and passionate religious beliefs. Many opponents of liberal gambling laws simply hold that the government has a duty to protect its citizens—especially its most vulnerable citizens—from harming themselves. They believe that this duty is particularly needed when the source of potential harm is an activity that is known to be addictive and, therefore, deprives one of any real choice about its consumption.

For some or all of these reasons, there will be politicians and a significant portion of the electorate who believe that ideally all gambling should be banned, or the less gambling there is and the more difficult it is for the public to participate, the better. These people generally believe that the fewer casinos there are the better; the smaller they are, the better; the more inconveniently located they are, the better; and the more regulatory inhibitions there are, the better.

In governments that are explicitly based on adherence to a particular religious faith, such as some countries with Christian or Islamic majorities, the key question will not be whether gambling harms people, or whether it is a good way of funding public services or attracting tourists, but whether it is contrary to the will of God. For this reason, there are no casinos in Ireland, Brazil, Saudi Arabia, or Indonesia.

In governments with an explicit and constitutionally entrenched separation of church and state (most notably in the United States), it is much harder for the many people who want gambling to be banned to appeal to religious attitudes. This does not, however, alter the fact that many people do find gambling and casinos religiously offensive—just as they do the existence of alcohol and bars, of opium and opium dens, of commercial sex and brothels. And though governments cannot ban gambling on the ground that it contravenes the teachings of particular religions, it also cannot stop people from expressing their hostility to gambling and casinos through the ballot box. Casino managers in the United States should not, therefore, assume that they are constitutionally protected against the passage of laws that promote an antigambling agenda. Nor should they assume that the Constitution affords the same free market protections that are enjoyed by other sectors of the entertainment industry.

The Democratic Consensus

Between these two extremes of permissivism and protectivism, there is a middle position around which public opinion tends to coalesce in democratic societies. The majority view in democracies tends to acknowledge that if people want to be able to gamble at casinos, then they should not be prevented from doing so by the law. On the other hand, the majority view also acknowledges that gambling in general and casino gambling in particular have the capacity for causing a tremendous amount of harm to both individuals and families, as well as being a potential source of an addictive illness that will have negative economic consequences for the wider society. The result of this majority opinion is that a democratic consensus emerges that says, "We will support government authorization for some casino gambling, but not for too much of it."

Precisely how much gambling and how many casinos would constitute "too much" and "too many" is, of course, an open question and a subject for fierce political lobbying by both progambling and antigambling groups. One of the reasons why jurisdictions differ so markedly in their gambling and casino regulations is that the policies that eventually receive majority approval differ considerably on the answer they give to this question.

The democratic consensus in the jurisdictions that do end up authorizing casinos goes further. Typically, jurisdictions stipulate not only that they will permit a limited number of casinos, but also that they will only allow casinos to be built that

- Enhance rather than detract from the general attractiveness of their environment
- Bring various kinds of economic benefits not only to those who like to gamble at casinos but also to the wider community where the casino is located
- Are required by law to do everything realistically possible to ensure that negative social impacts such as crime and excessive gambling do not materialize.

The democratic consensus stipulates that not only will we limit the overall availability of casino gambling opportunities in our jurisdiction, but we will also ensure that those that we do allow are popular with the public. And they will be popular with the public only if they produce substantial economic benefits for their community, and if they are not perceived to be a danger to the individual. In short, the costs of allowing casinos must be kept to a minimum, and the benefits maximized.

How Governments Decide on Policy

The Complexity of Public Opinion

The problems that confront governments in relation to gambling laws are not just the conflicting opinions about the rightness or wrongness of gambling. The fact is that public opinion is a much more ambiguous and complex phenomenon than this. Many

Figure 4–2 Public opinion is very important to the political process. Here, a young man questions a young woman while taking a poll with a clipboard in his hands in front of shops along a sidewalk.

people acknowledge that they are pulled in opposite directions by different considerations on issues such as gambling. People also quite commonly hold views that are mutually contradictory without realizing it. Also, the public is easily swayed by skillful rhetoric or by the partisan representation of dramatic events, and so public opinion is inherently fickle.

Therefore, before we can understand how governments respond to public opinion on the gambling industry and casinos, we need to understand what generally determines government behavior in relation to public opinion (Figure 4–2). In particular, we need to understand what might be described as the "dilemma of democracy."

The Dilemma of Democracy

Democracy broadly requires that governments give people what they want, and what they want are first-rate public services. The public wants to be made secure against outside attack and criminals; therefore, they want first-rate defense forces and top law enforcement agencies. They want to be protected from ill health; therefore, they want excellent health services. They want their children to receive the best possible education; therefore, they want good schools and universities. They want to be able travel easily and in comfort; therefore, they demand high-quality transport systems, and so on and on.

On the other hand, the citizens of a democracy would prefer not to have to pay for any of these public services. Since they realize that this is impossible, they would also prefer that people other than themselves pay for them. Who, after all, would not prefer to be a free rider rather than having to pay full fare? The dilemma, therefore, that confronts governments is how to optimize their popularity by providing services that the public wants while not becoming unpopular by raising the taxes necessary to pay for them.

Effects on Gambling and Casino Policy

Given this background, the principal features of the commercial gaming industry and casinos, which are relevant to government decision making, include the following:

- Gambling is a very popular form of entertainment. The proof is in both the high participation rates when gambling is legal and the large illegal industry that typically flourishes when gambling is prohibited.

- Gambling is a good way of raising taxes from the government's point of view. Not only are gamblers a group that is not widely thought to deserve protection from discriminatory taxation, but many gamblers also do not really notice the tax they are paying, since it is usually built into the odds against them in the games. Gambling taxes are, therefore, comparatively unresented, especially when they are earmarked for popular public interest causes, as they are with lotteries.

- Historically, gambling has been associated with crime, and the public will consequently be nervous that legalizing gambling may lead to increases in crime.

- Gambling may be thought of as an activity that can easily defraud customers.

- Gambling, like drinking alcohol, certainly can become an addiction for a small minority of those who engage in it and, like shopping, can get a rather large minority into heavy debt. These problem gambling issues not only have negative, and sometimes devastating, consequences for those who gamble too much and those close to them, they may also have significant costs for society as a whole (e.g., increased taxation-funded welfare payments).

- Traditionally, gambling has been thought of as a vice that is prohibited or frowned upon by most religions and that some believe has a negative effect on the moral character of the individuals who indulge in it and the communities that permit it.

Therefore, when governments are considering how to regulate gambling, they have to carefully think about

- The difficulties and dangers of having a substantial illegal industry if they prohibit gambling
- The best way of harnessing the authorization of gambling to the funding of public interest projects not otherwise able to be funded from other forms of taxation
- How to prevent an increase in various forms of crime, including fraud, loan-sharking, money-laundering, and so on
- What to do about excessive or problem gambling
- How to gauge and respond to public opinion about the general desirability of permitting different forms of commercial gambling

When all of these considerations are taken together with the overarching moral differences about the morality of gambling, it becomes almost inevitable that all gambling legislation will be controversial. Moreover, controversy is likely to be particularly sharp toward proposals to authorize and regulate casinos. This is because casinos are typically large, highly visible structures in their communities. They also house the most addictive form of gambling associated in the popular imagination with vice and organized crime.

Faced with these difficulties, governments typically try to find as cogently and objectively as possible the best policy to adopt by identifying the pros and cons of proposals and analyzing them in terms of their costs and benefits.

Cost-Benefit Analysis

Whenever governments contemplate introducing any new policy or changing any existing one, they try to weigh the advantages against the disadvantages. They then compare possible advantages with the advantages and disadvantages of the other courses of action they might otherwise take. When this practice is systematically engaged in by governments or firms (and when it involves putting dollar values to all potential costs and benefits), it is called **cost-benefit analysis**. This is always a valuable exercise for governments to undertake, mainly because it generates a degree of objectivity. But there are a number of other features of cost-benefit analysis related to the gambling industry that need to be recognized.

First, companies need to determine in their cost-benefit analysis which group of people will benefit from their policies. Do they want to benefit everyone equally or do they want to mostly benefit the least well off? Do the burdens of their policies fall mostly on the children of the poor, while the benefits accrue mostly to the wealthy; or do their policies lead, through job creation, to a transfer of wealth from the more affluent to the less affluent?

Second, in a cost-benefit analysis, it is often not possible to attach actual dollar amounts to costs and benefits. For example, it seems not merely very difficult but also inappropriate to put numbers to the benefits of living in a free society or to the costs of individual suicides.

Third, politicians must confront the problem of whether to attach more importance to minimizing the negative social impacts of casinos or to maximizing their potential economic benefits. Politicians will sometimes sacrifice concerns for the long-term public good to the short-term objective of quickly raising tax revenues. More commonly perhaps, governments give priority to minimizing the harm that may be caused by liberalizing gambling laws, claiming that taxation and other economic benefits are of secondary importance. These concerns reflect the three main reasons why gambling allegedly needs to be more strictly regulated than other industries and why, therefore, the supply of gambling services cannot be simply left to market forces. These reasons define the three core objectives of gambling regulation:

- Keep crime out of certain areas
- Keep the games honest
- Protect the vulnerable

Figure 4–3 Diversity in gender, race, cultures, age, and so on needs to be analyzed for different political views in order to pull everyone into a common focus.

It should also be noted that decisions by governments to change gambling laws cannot be driven by considerations of social risk versus economic advantage. There are other principles that governments need to take into account when making decisions on the gambling industry, which may conflict with a straightforward cost-benefit analysis. These principles include

- *Issues of local democracy.*   Should small local communities be allowed to decide that they wish to prohibit or restrict the availability of some types of businesses that are not prohibited or restricted by national law?

- *Issues of protecting legitimate existing interests.*   To what extent, if any, will changes in gambling laws damage existing interests? Most commonly, this is a case of preventing people from earning a living in a way that had been legal and who have reasonable expectations that the law would remain the same. Legitimate expectations also need to be weighed when considering how far authorizing new forms of gambling will subject existing industries to new and possibly unfair competition. Governments also need to examine whether new gambling laws create unlevel playing fields for existing suppliers or new entrants.

- *Issues concerning enforceability and respect for law.*   When laws prevent people from engaging in activities that they enjoy and that cause no harm to anyone else, there is always a danger that the law will prove unenforceable and will itself generally undermine respect for law.

- *The principles of good regulation (including proportionality and effectiveness).*   These require that, for example, any measure taken in order to prevent harm to potential gambling addicts should not be excessively onerous for those who gamble harmlessly, and that there should be good reason for believing that these measures will achieve their stated purpose.

- *The principle of consistency.*   This would require that the same principles be applied to all forms of gambling in respect to permissions and restrictions. This principle also argues that games such as lotteries, which generate substantial funds for the state, should not be allowed to advertise in ways that are forbidden to other gambling activities unless relevant differences can be demonstrated.

Governments should consider these principles in addition to the fundamental question already discussed: that of the duty of a democratic government to decide whether to enforce moral rules governing personal choices when it is difficult to demonstrate that they do significant harm.

Minimizing Negative Social Impacts

Keeping Crime Out and Keeping the Games Honest

A great deal of attention is paid by regulators to keeping crime out and keeping the games honest. The reasons are mostly historically related to a time when casinos were illegal and owned and operated by organized criminals. There is also a strong association in the public mind, fostered by popular culture, of illegal activities.

Lawmakers consequently require people who want to work in the gambling industry to undergo abnormally stringent tests of **probity**. Whether this really makes a difference to the propensity of casino owners and employees to engage in crime is uncertain, but at least it is widely perceived as an effective way of keeping crime out of casinos. The public is also thought to believe that if regulators impose strict rules about what games can be played and how, and check on their compliance, it will afford significant protection against cheating.

Similarly, governments impose many regulations on casinos because they fear that they may be used to launder money. These regulations require the reporting of transactions over a certain amount and those deemed to be suspicious. It is again unclear how much real impact these regulations have either in preventing or deterring would-be money launderers from doing business through casinos. Nevertheless, the existence of the rules and procedures provides governments with comfort.

The truth about crime, cheating, and casinos is that commercial casino companies—which are now typically public companies, and, therefore, subject to all of the regulations that entails—have the strongest possible incentive to avoid any activity that could lead to their being accused of breaking the law or defrauding their customers. They would lose their reputation for honesty and, consequently, their customers. This incentive is almost certainly what keeps casinos honest and crime free, far more than any regulatory activity.

There may even be a downside to this regulatory activity; it may supply a motive for the corruption of public officials. Regulations are tolerated with reasonably good grace by casino companies because the very existence of regulations makes it easier to defend the authorization and continued operation of casinos against those who say they should be banned because they promote crime and fraud.

Protecting the Vulnerable: Problem Gambling

Today, when people and politicians talk about limiting the negative social impacts of gambling, they are almost always referring to issues relating to problem gambling. This is the Achilles' heel of the whole gambling industry, especially the casino industry. Those who want to see casinos closed down or severely curtailed almost always rely on the issue of problem gambling to support their case. Antigamblers are not always scrupulous in presenting available evidence in a balanced, impartial, judicious, and scholarly fashion. Moreover, it is reasonably easy to whip up popular hostility to casinos based on emotional appeals, such as telling stories of people losing everything through gambling, resorting to crime to fund their gambling habits, reducing their children to penury, and committing suicide because of gambling debts. These stories make sensational copy and are, therefore, popular with journalists.

In making these claims, antigamblers will often make claims about the dangers of problem gambling that are not warranted by current knowledge. They exaggerate the dangers for propaganda purposes because they really believe that the less legal gambling there is, the better, and that the best way of getting governments to reduce the levels of legalized gambling is to maximize public alarm about problem gambling.

Because worries about problem gambling are so strong and so widespread, most governments believe that if they liberalize gambling laws, they must do so only after satisfying themselves that they have done enough to minimize the dangers of excessive gambling. Furthermore, because those opposed to gambling will continue to maintain that problem gambling is a major social problem at least partly caused by casinos, governments will always be looking for ways to address this problem, or at least be perceived as trying to address it.

Another concern that casino management should remember about problem gambling is that some casinos are more conveniently located than others for players simply to drop in. This level of availability may foster more problem gamblers to visit these casinos more often if they do not have to travel far. Also, some jurisdictions introduce casinos into a community without any accompanying public awareness campaign that alerts people to the dangers of casino gambling. For all of these reasons it is absolutely essential that casino managers take the issue of problem gambling extremely seriously and ensure that they do everything they can to minimize the harm that it causes. Casino managers genuinely recognize that no issue has greater potential for damage than problem gambling. Wise casino managers do not wait to be forced to take necessary steps to deal with this issue; they will be proactive and make sure their commitment to minimizing problem gambling is highly publicized.

The problems of underage gambling usually present less difficulty to casinos than to other suppliers of gambling (such as gambling machines outside of casinos or gambling on the internet). Usually, casinos have a reasonably easy policy to enforce—simply keeping underage people off gaming floors. In addition, they may contribute to gambling education programs that are targeted to children.

The bigger problems arise for casinos with true problem gamblers, those for whom gambling is an addiction quite as devastating as drug addiction. Casinos should pay for messages targeted to problem gamblers to be incorporated into public awareness campaigns in the general media. Obviously, this means that there has to be a helpline in place, and it must be reasonably easy for people with gambling problems to get appropriate professional help. Casinos typically subsidize the availability of such help as part of their funding for responsible gambling programs. Casinos also need to have policies and practices for training staff and developing codes for advertising and marketing to neutralize political attacks on problem gambling.

Moral Damage

A great deal of research has been published on the psychological and material harm caused by problem gambling, much of it unreliable, partisan, and/or inconclusive. There is virtually no empirical work purporting to measure the harmful effects of gambling on the moral character of individuals or communities. We do not know, therefore, whether the availability of commercial gambling tends to make people more greedy, idle, and irrational or whether it makes them less materialistic and more courageous. Nor do we know whether gambling outlets are regarded as either enhancing or detracting from the general attractiveness of their environments.

The issue, however, is not a trivial one. The extent to which the gambling industry is perceived as selling products that exploit people's moral weaknesses or corrupt them or are generally unsavory or somehow "lower the moral tone" of neighbourhoods and communities is an important determinant of the regulatory environment and, therefore, of a casino's profitability.

What this shows is that it is especially important for casino companies to demonstrate that they are good corporate citizens. This means that they should aspire to fit in architecturally with the surrounding community. They should stress the forms of entertainment, other than gambling, that they offer. They should publicize the fact that they want their patrons to gamble responsibly. They should be seen to support local causes and should be regarded as a good local employer. They should also not allow their antigambling opponents uncontested occupation of the moral high ground and should stress that people should be free to decide for themselves how they want to live their lives—not have it decided for them by those who are trying to impose their own moral and religious convictions on others.

Maximizing Economic Benefits

Creation of Wealth

If governments can satisfy themselves that they can control the negative social impacts of casinos and especially that they can persuade their constituents that their proposals will not lead to an epidemic of problem gambling, then they will start working out how to maximize the economic benefits for their community, which they can eventually take credit for. As with any other industry, there are different kinds of economic benefits that may be associated with commercial gambling. The best economic benefits are those that make society richer overall. This can occur by liberalizing gambling laws in two ways.

First, there is **consumer surplus**. This means that if players are able to purchase gambling services more cheaply than before, they will be better off to that extent. In general, the wealth of a community grows as its members are able to buy more and more of the goods and services they want for an increasingly smaller portion of their incomes. This is important in thinking about gambling legislation, because prohibitions or restrictions on supply, which drive the price up, will make consumers worse off; while anything that promotes competition will tend to drive the price down and make consumers better off.

Second, there are **export earnings** and **import substitutions**. In respect to commercial gambling, a jurisdiction benefits economically as people come into the jurisdiction because of gambling and spend money that they otherwise would spend elsewhere. Conversely, jurisdictions benefit through their own residents spending money in local casinos rather than in other jurisdictions. Jurisdictions such as Monte Carlo, Baden Baden, Nevada, Macao, and South Africa's Sun City prospered when gambling was illegal in the vast majority of their neighboring jurisdictions. Legal gambling is now much more widely available, and, therefore, it is much harder to link higher gambling rates to the increased number of tourists who come specifically to gamble. At the same time, more and more jurisdictions are legalizing gambling for defensive purposes—that is, to prevent gambling dollars from going abroad.

Redistribution

A different type of economic benefit from gambling is the redistribution of wealth and income from richer to poorer people. Not everyone agrees that this is a desirable objective of government policy, but many governments do try to use their gambling policy as a way of helping the economically disadvantaged. They do this through policies that tax gamblers more heavily than other consumers and by ensuring that those taxes are used to improve the circumstances of people poorer than those who pay them. Therefore, we see that all governments restrict the supply of gambling in response to various kinds of public anxiety about the harmful consequences of gambling.

This has the important economic consequence that the suppliers enjoy a degree of protection from competition, which they would not enjoy if there were a free market. This means that the price of gambling to consumers can be raised without increased costs, and, therefore, abnormally large profits can be generated. Governments could prevent this profiteering, as it does with other monopolistic industries such as utilities, by regulating the price. They do not do this for gambling because they believe that if gambling is expensive, it will discourage vulnerable poor people from engaging in it, and because they recognize that gambling taxes are relatively unresented. However, governments usually prefer to try to capture a share of these high profits through the taxation and licensing processes. This same rationale is often applied to the taxation of alcohol and tobacco. Of course, all taxation in theory promotes the public interest by funding public services. However, in the case of gambling taxes, taxation policy is usually held to be fair only if its net effect is to redistribute funding from the richer to the poorer.

It should be noted that governments sometimes seek to capture abnormal profits by means of a special tax on gambling, called a gambling privilege tax. Governments sometimes adopt other gambling policies that seek to capture abnormal profits, which are effectively taxation policies under other names. These policies include requiring lotteries to contribute a percentage of a ticket price to a "good causes" fund; auctioning licenses or setting high license fees; prescribing investment in public interest projects; and particularly, in the case of casino developments, awarding licenses on the basis of which one offers the largest economic benefits to the community as a whole.

Some countries, notably Canada, Holland, Sweden, and Austria, seek to minimize the negative social impacts of gambling and to maximize its economic benefits by having gambling industries nationalized. This means that the state has a monopoly on some or all gambling products. The gambling industry may also be directly run by a particular ministry, or the state may appoint the management and be the sole shareholder in a company set up to operate gambling businesses.

Like all monopolies, this strategy is a disadvantage to consumers compared to a competitive system because of pricing and the quality of products. However, this disadvantage is not necessarily greater than other systems that restrict supply and capture abnormal profits through taxation. Also, any small disadvantages to consumers are outweighed by the greater protection afforded them when the state is responsible for the integrity and safety of the games.

Displacement and Employment

Whatever types of economic advantage governments seek from liberalizing gambling laws, they need to be aware of the fact that if customers start spending money on gambling, they will stop spending it on something else. This is called **displacement**. Normally, displacement is a desirable economic phenomenon that signifies progress and makes various products better and cheaper. For example, the fountain pen displaces the quill, the ballpoint displaces the fountain pen, the typewriter (partially) displaces pens, and the word processor displaces the typewriter. At the same time, technology typically makes certain jobs unnecessary and frees up people who were needed in that industry for other kinds of work.

Recently, technological advances have been rapid in the gambling industry. Games based on random number generators, such as dice, cards, and spinning wheels, have been replaced to a significant degree by electronic gambling machines, which have themselves evolved in the diversity of their attractiveness to players. In the near future, not only are electronic machines likely to be replaced by server-based gambling, but all forms of gambling are increasingly becoming remotely available via the internet, interactive television, and the cell phone.

However, from a government's point of view, displacement in general and in the gambling industry may present problems and needs to be carefully considered. This means that governments always need to ask where is the money coming *from* and what this money would be spent on if it were not being used to gamble at the casino. The possible answers to these questions are that it is being spent on illegal gambling, gambling in other jurisdictions, other forms of gambling, leisure and luxury items, or on family necessities. If the answer is illegal gambling, then this is good news for the government. If the answer is other forms of gambling, everything depends on how casinos relate to the government's general policy objectives. If the answer is family necessities, then it constitutes a social problem.

These questions are particularly important in relation to employment issues. From the point of view of consumer satisfaction and consumer surplus, displacement in the gambling industry has no doubt been beneficial. Nevertheless, displacement through technological progress and changes in consumer preferences are naturally unwelcome to shareholders in the industries that are displaced. Additionally, as governments generally try to keep rates of unemployment low, they may not welcome those forms of displacement that lead to a net loss of jobs.

As an example of displacement in the gambling industry, technological developments have been accompanied by a decrease in the number of people who need to be employed in the delivery of gambling services. Electronic gambling machines require no croupiers and very little maintenance compared to table games. More substantially, increases in gambling expenditures on activities that are not labor intensive are likely to displace spending on other leisure activities that are more labor intensive. For both of these reasons, growth in the gambling industry may be expected to lead to a net loss of jobs rather than to an increase.

An important corollary of these issues of displacement for casino policy is that the great majority of customers are going to be residents within the jurisdiction rather than visitors from outside. Although the main economic objective of casino policy is to create economic development and employment in relatively disadvantaged areas, the most benign public policy will have the following characteristics:

- The number of casinos will be limited to a realistic estimate of what the market will require—based on social grounds, and to prevent unnecessary capital expenditure that can instead be captured for the public.
- The casino projects will be located in areas most in need of the kinds of economic benefits that casino projects are best fitted to deliver.
- The licenses will be awarded to whichever project delivers the greatest benefits to the people of the jurisdiction as a whole, especially to the poorest people.

In practice, this will require casino developers to exercise great ingenuity in maximizing the public interest, for example by subsidizing the building of infrastructure, such as conference centers that will be effective in generating new employment.

Implications for Casino Managers

There are five stages in the life of a casino company:

1. Identifying a promising jurisdiction and persuading its government to authorize the building of casinos in a regulatory environment that is conducive to profitability
2. Seeking to secure a license, often through a tendering process
3. Building the project

4. Opening and operating the project

5. Returning to stage one in new jurisdictions

At all stages, an understanding of how government works and an ability to navigate successfully in the political arena are essential to success. The following aspects of this ability are especially worth emphasizing.

First, casino companies need to be able to generate public support for legalizing casino gambling in a jurisdiction. This also (and less obviously) means that casino managers have to be constantly aware, once they are operating their casinos, of the need to do all that they can to *retain* support among the general public and not just from their customers. They must avoid doing anything that might cause the public to change its mind and conclude that it was a mistake to allow casinos into the community.

Failure to succeed in this essentially political process will result at best in profit-damaging regulatory restrictions and increased tax burdens. At worst, it will result in a popular backlash that will lead to the reintroduction of prohibition. What good perception requires is an understanding that casinos typically operate as part of an unofficial public-private partnership in which both parties have an equal interest in profitability and a good public image. Specifically, casino managers need to be sure that the public is generally perceived to be enjoying significant economic benefits from the casino and, perhaps more important, that the casinos are not perceived to be ruining lives and damaging communities.

Second, competition between companies is likely to focus on the competition for licenses in a restricted market, rather than for customers in a free market. In competing for licenses, companies are likely to stress the greater economic benefits, especially the amenities and jobs that will result if a license is awarded to them. Normally, this is a formal process, and companies are required to participate in some sort of tendering process that requires them to accept lower rates of return on capital and/or to outperform their rivals by finding more creative ways of delivering value to the public. At all points in the process, casino managers need to expend much creativity to devise ways to make the political authorities who authorize or regulate licenses happier than their competitors are able to.

Third, once a license has been secured, opportunities to supply gambling services are always restricted to minimize perceived negative social impacts; therefore, competition among suppliers is also limited. This means that much of the energy of managing commercial gambling companies has to be directed to securing and sustaining a favorable regulatory environment. This means that all gambling companies seek

- Maximum freedom and minimum regulation for themselves
- Minimum freedom and maximum regulation (preferably prohibition) for their competitors
- Low gambling privilege taxes

Established casino companies, therefore, devote substantial resources to lobbying against new competition in the face of lobbying from would-be licensees. Competitors are likely to stress the comparative safety of their own products and operations from a problem gambling, negative-impact perspective, and the greater dangers of their competitors' products and operations.

Conclusion

How much profit a casino company makes depends much less than in other businesses upon how good it is at competing for customers. Profit levels depend much more upon how successful casino companies are at persuading politicians to pass laws and impose regulations that serve its interests. Some casino managers may regret this truth, but some may find it challenging. However, the amount of money a company makes in the casino business depends mostly upon how successful the company is at persuading the government to allow it to do what it wants (for example, having unlimited numbers of unlimited-prize gambling machines) and not forcing it to do what it does not (paying very high taxes).

A further twist is that casino profits depend to a very considerable degree upon what governments do and do not allow the casino's competitors to do. The profits of a casino company will be tremendously lowered if other casinos are allowed to operate within its catchment area, and so it competes for its customers' gambling dollars. Profits will also be lower if similar products, notably high-prize electronic gambling machines, can be located in bars, taverns, or arcades that are more convenient to potential customers and have lower operating costs. This is why "slot routes" or machine gambling outside casinos is a major threat to the profitability of casinos. Therefore, casinos must persuade politicians to allow them to do what they want and not force them to do things they do not. Casinos also must try to persuade politicians to forbid their potential competitors from doing what they want, and force those competitors to do things *they* do not want to do.

Obviously, casino management can't make this case explicitly and, like all good businesspeople, have to profess a commitment to free markets and claim that they "welcome competition" (even though like all good businesspeople, they would really rather do without it). They then, however, need to add a "but," explaining why in this particular case, competition should be restricted (in a way that just happens to suit them).

That the management of casino companies behaves in this way in trying to influence the decisions of governments is by no means reprehensible. The fact is that it is the duty of top management in casino companies, as in any other company, is to try to maximize profits for their shareholders in whatever political environment they find themselves. In the political environment in which casinos operate, this kind of behavior is both appropriate and necessary—as is their concern with profits rather than the public interest. If this seems to require that managers in the casinos be distastefully Machiavellian and hypocritical, it is no more so than in most other businesses, and it confronts casino managers with no more serious ethical dilemmas than those confronted by lawyers retained to make the most effective case that they can for their clients, regardless of their guilt or innocence.

The simple fact is that the casino business in most jurisdictions is still controversial, which means that it is also highly sensitive politically. Casino managers consequently need to learn how to protect and promote their interests in the political domain at least as much as in the commercial domain.

key terms

House
Discretionary Income
Cost-benefit analysis
Gambling privilege taxes
Probity
Permissivist

Protectivist
Consumer surplus
Displacement
Export earnings
Import substitutions

review questions

1. What is the essential commodity that casinos are selling?

2. List five aspects of the casino industry that are commonly regulated.

3. What is the strongest possible incentive for casinos to avoid any activity that could lead to being accused of breaking the law or defrauding their customers?

4. When people and politicians talk about limiting the negative social impacts of gambling, what are they almost always referring to?

5. What are the main reasons that casinos should conduct public awareness campaigns?

6. What can casino companies do to demonstrate that they are good corporate citizens?

7. What principles do governments need to take into account that may conflict with a straightforward cost-benefit analysis?

8. What are the five stages in the life of a casino company?

9. List the three core objectives of gambling regulation.

internet sites

eGambling
http://www.camh.net/egambling/

Casino City Times
http://www.casinocitytimes.com/

Pechanga (Native American Casino News Site)
http://www.pechanga.net

endnotes

1. This chapter does not follow the custom of calling all forms of gambling *gaming* nor of using the term *gaming* as opposed to *gambling* to describe the playing of the types of games for money that are played in casinos. The two words are etymologically identical, but to

eschew the more natural and commonplace word *gambling* in favor of *gaming* seems to involve a deliberate attempt to mislead by trying to suggest that the gaming that takes place in casinos is somehow *not* gambling—which of course it is. Furthermore, the attempt to suggest falsely that gaming is different from gambling suggests that the industry thinks that there is something shameful about its activities that it needs to try to hide. Since this fools no one, it is bad public relations, which in turn gives ammunition to the enemies of the gambling industry.

Vignette
Crisis Management for Casinos—A Test Case

Jim O'Brien

Part Three - Questions to Consider For Each Module of Crisis Management

Module 1—Warning

1. Would coordination with local law enforcement be done at this time?

2. What factors would support a decision to alert and/or preposition selected response assets? How many assets? Would you request external assistance based on a credible threat?

3. Does your facility have a "New Year's Eve Contingency Plan"? Does it include pre-event coordination with area emergency response agencies? Is it coordinated in-house with other departments? What are the unique roles and responsibilities in the plan?

4. Are there unique considerations for properties adjacent to casinos that have fireworks to consider before and during the fireworks display?

5. How do you prepare your department with other in-house departments? With other casinos? With local emergency response?

6. Is casino security part of the local emergency response planning for the New Year's Eve event? Are casino contingency plans shared with the local community? Are there physical barriers or traffic routing that impacts casinos?

7. What type of casino security support would you request and from whom? What would be the advantages of having a pooled asset capability for your facility?

8. What does the elevation of the HSAS mean for your casino? What activities does this elevated threat level prompt? What is casino security's role when the HSAS level is elevated? How does it relate to other casinos? To local emergency response departments?

9. What intelligence would you expect to receive from law enforcement organizations concerning the threat? From which agencies would you pursue data?

10. How would you expect to be informed of the FBI's determination of a credible threat? With whom (inside and outside the casino) would this information be shared?

11. Specifically, what interagency coordination is necessary at this point? Is intercasino coordination and sharing of security resources a viable alternate resource?

12. Do your disaster contingency plans address WMD threats? How does the fact that there is a credible threat of a terrorist attack affect your planning? What actions would you take at your level?

13. What refresher training could be implemented for your staff prior to a special event? Is the current level of WMD/terrorist training adequate? What PPE is available for first responders in view of a significant threat?

14. What public affairs guidance will be provided to your personnel? Would information derived from FBI intelligence be relayed to casino employees?

15. What plans do you currently have that would need to be reviewed for potential implementation?

16. Would special events be given any specific emphasis? Which, if any, special areas or company assets would your interest be focused on at this point?

17. Would the medical community be alerted to take any preliminary action because of the known threat? What plans would need to be reviewed for potential implementation?

Module 2A—Initial Response

1. What local capabilities exist to identify an explosive ordnance device (EOD)? What detection equipment do you have to assist in this process? Where would additional capabilities be acquired?

2. What will be the primary means of coordination at the incident scene? Who is in charge? What are the primary objectives of the casino's security at this point?

3. How are you communicating with public safety incident command, 911 dispatch, medical treatment centers, or hospitals?

4. What in-house operator protocols are in place for this type of incident? What mutual-aid resources could be activated through the dispatch center?

5. How would operators meet the staffing and operational requirements of the casino during this event? Do you have a callback plan to meet needs such as this? Do you have communications interoperability capabilities with other federal, state, county, and local agencies that may be involved in this incident?

6. What actions would be taken to protect the public at this point? Who would perform the functions? How would you notify the public?

7. What capability do you have to support or secure a crime scene investigation and collect or preserve evidence? How would the contaminated environment affect these efforts? Will crime scene and rescue procedures interfere with each other? What concerns do investigation and evidentiary requirements present for response efforts, if any?

8. How would suspicion of a secondary or additional attack or explosive device affect initial response activities? What steps would be taken if an actual secondary explosive device were found?

9. What level of response would you activate? Where would additional units be staged? How would transportation issues for officers be handled?

10. What other security concerns would you have as a result of this incident?

11. What actions would be taken for traffic and access control for the casino in or near the affected area? Who would perform the functions? How would you notify the public?

12. How would the short-term or long-term closure of Las Vegas Boulevard affect casino operations? How would it affect evacuation of guests registering or checking out? Have traffic contingency plans have been coordinated with local law enforcement?

13. Do you have a triage system in place that can accommodate this type and number of injuries?

14. Are communications systems adequate if commercial and cellular systems experience overload? Does a backup communications plan exist for the casino?

15. If another explosion were to occur at another casino (off-Strip), what would be the impact of community services available to respond? What assistance could be made available from other casinos?

16. Are there lockdown or emergency shutdown procedures/capabilities in place to prevent the surge of nonregistered public from entering your property?

17. How would casinos communicate with one another? What information or resources could be made available and shared by unaffected casinos to affected casinos?

Module 2B—Response

1. How will the casino coordinate its efforts with local/area emergency response team resources? Will interoperability be a problem?

2. Explain the coordination between casinos and the bomb squad conducting a sweep for secondary devices on casino properties.

3. What are your plans to rotate security staff? Are there sufficient assets available for sustained operations? Can other nonaffected casino staff be utilized to augment casino security that is impacted by the disaster?

4. How do you maintain crime scene security? How long would you maintain crime scene security? What protocols will be used for contact with contaminated victims?

5. How will casino security coordinate with law enforcement agencies in charge of the crime scene processing?

6. What procedures are being followed to identify and track guests who have become casualties? Do existing plans address guest/victim tracking?

7. What procedures are in place to handle stress management for security and staff? What procedures are in place to handle logistical and administrative support for security and staff?

8. What is your media strategy at this time? What plans are in place to establish or coordinate with a joint information center (JIC)? How would they be implemented?

9. How far ahead are you looking/planning? What contingencies would be made to address the possibility of additional attacks?

Module 3—Recovery and Restoration

1. What are the short-term and long-term effects of a prolonged decrease in tourism resulting from a terrorist attack in Las Vegas? What is the impact on other future scheduled special events?

2. Will casino security and staff require any long-term medical monitoring? Who will be responsible for this function? Is the current disaster contingency plan adequate for incidents of this magnitude or severity?

3. Who will determine decontamination methods for the site and declare the area "safe"? Will long-term monitoring be required?

4. What critical incident stress support would you consider for casino security and general staff? How long would you need to use these assets? Are sufficient assets locally available?

5. What process will be followed to reconstitute the local response capability?

6. How will crime scene investigation requirements be managed and coordinated during the long term?

7. What materials would the FBI require for evidence and what procedures would be followed for their transfer?

8. What procedures will be taken to ensure that all medical facilities have been fully decontaminated? Who will fund these actions for public and private institutions?

9. How will medical monitoring of victims and workers be accomplished? Who will maintain these records, and for how long?

10. How will personal effects of deceased hotel guests be handled, and who will maintain chain of custody?

11. What public health information should be provided to security, staff, and guests during the long term? Do current plans and procedures address the long-term health information needs related to WMD events?

12. How would it be determined that an emergency situation no longer exists? At what point would emergency operations stand down and staff be released? Who makes this determination?

13. Are current record-keeping requirements adequate for an event of this magnitude during the short term and long term?

14. Who determines that the previously contaminated (biohazard) areas or the structural integrity of the damaged facilities is safe for reentry? What long-term site remediation support is needed and can be expected from federal, state, or regional sources?

15. Who will pay for cleanup and decontamination? Will regional agencies be involved in the disposal of contaminated material?

5 Legal Environments

Robert R. Russell, Gaming Analyst, and David Waddell, Attorney:
Fraser, Trebilcock, Davis & Dunlap, P.C.

Learning Objectives

1. To introduce the commercial and tribal regulations of the casino gaming industry.

2. To provide practical information that will give a baseline reference for a career in the industry.

3. To gain an awareness that the rules and regulations governing this industry vary in each jurisdiction.

4. To encourage additional learning about the laws and regulations that govern this ever-expanding industry.

5. To provide an understanding of the federal regulations that govern the casino industry.

6. To understand the interrelationship between tribal casino regulations and the state in which the casino exists.

Chapter Outline

Selecting the Casino Industry as a Career Choice—a Life Decision

Which industry has expanded its employee base by 85 percent in the past decade? Which industry has expanded the number of states that allow it to operate? The answer is the casino gaming industry—11 states now allow commercial casino gaming, and 29 states now authorize Native American casino-style gaming. The gaming industry directly employs more than 700,000 individuals who are either managers or will some-day have the opportunity to be a manager (Figure 5–1).

According to the federal government's 1999 National Gaming Impact Study Commission Report, the revenues from legal wagering grew nearly 1,600 percent from 1979 to 1997. The gaming industry is a major component of the American leisure industry, and there are many new professional career opportunities associated with it. However, people new to the industry and individuals interested in joining the industry often underestimate the extremely strict governmental and legal regulations that govern this ever-expanding industry.

For example, in Detroit, Michigan, it is impossible to work as a dealer if you stole a pack of gum when you were 18 and the arrest resulted in a theft-related misdemeanor conviction.[1] Also, in Indiana, a supplier licensee and his or her key management personnel

Figure 5–1 Becoming a dealer requires many security checks. If you want to be promoted up the ladder, even more legal checks and licenses will be needed.

are prohibited from making any political contributions to a candidate running for office, whether it is a state or local office.[2] This prohibition also extends to any candidate's committee, a regular party committee, or a committee organized by the legislative caucus of the state general assembly or the senate.

Consequently, for those who select the casino gaming industry as a career, it is imperative to understand at the start that personal integrity and history are key factors to your success. If you cannot be licensed because of your past, then no matter how talented you are, or how connected you are, you are prohibited from working in the industry. With this said, the gaming industry has made thousands of people very successful and has enabled many to reach significant professional goals. For example, Punam Mathur, vice president of corporate diversity and community affairs at the MGM Mirage, says that she was attracted to the gaming industry because "the industry places people first—both employees and customers."[3] Ms. Mathur also said that "the industry's rapid growth means that there are many opportunities for employees to learn and grow. Plus, there is such rich diversity in the types of jobs and careers that the industry offers employees."

The following sections highlight the commercial and tribal regulations of the casino gaming industry. In addition, they provide practical information that will serve as a baseline reference for a career in the industry. Although this chapter highlights a number of legal areas that impact the industry, it is important to note that the rules and regulations governing this industry vary in each jurisdiction. Thus, we hope that the information contained in this chapter will encourage you to learn more about the laws and regulations that govern various jurisdictions. This overview is not designed for legal professionals, but rather for the average individual interested in gaining a general understanding of the regulations that govern this industry.[4]

Personal Perspectives: A Gaming Industry Professional's View of Legal Compliance

Anyone who has held a key position with the casino industry will tell you that your personal history is of great interest to the regulators who oversee the company's operation. These same individuals will also likely concur that the success of the gaming industry up to this point has been built on the strict regulations that govern the casino industry in the United States. Therefore, before examining the details of industry regulations, let's take a practical look into the importance of regulatory compliance.

We asked several casino industry executives the following questions:[5]

- From your personal perspective, what are the potential problems for not complying with casino laws and regulations?
- What advice do you have for young professionals looking at the casino industry as a career choice?
- Why should they value compliance with the laws and regulations?

Here are some of their responses:

- Saul Leonard, president and CEO of Los Angeles–based Saul F. Leonard Company, who has more than 40 years of experience consulting for casino operators, financial institutions, and regulators and is a featured lecturer at national and international tradeshows:

  The casino industry has finally earned the respect and backing of most of the business and financial community. It is now considered a "legitimate" business as well as being legalized. This growth is the result of the stringent investigation of key personnel by governmental authorities prior to licensing and the excellent internal controls established within the industry. Young professionals in this industry should understand the necessity of doing everything possible to enhance the reputation of the casino industry. This is the only way the industry can continue to grow and provide the greatest opportunities for those who make it their career choice.[6]

- Thomas Shepherd III, shareholder, Watkins Ludlam Winter & Stennis, who has developed a successful law practice representing casino operators and suppliers in the state of Mississippi:

  The potential problems to the individual for not complying with gaming regulations range from the obvious (fines, suspension, revocation of a gaming work permit or finding of suitability, etc.) to the not-so-obvious (poor reputation within the industry, difficulty in receiving recommendations from peers and co-workers for promotions and/or other employment). Failure to comply is one thing, and it can be overcome with the passage of time and an unblemished record for a long period after an initial problem. Willful failure to follow regulations may result in a permanent ban from the industry. To the young professional considering the gaming industry as a career choice, remember that your reputation is the most important asset you have. You can spend a lifetime building it, and only one bad decision can ruin it. Compliance with all gaming regulations, not just the letter of the regulations, but the spirit, can ensure a long-lasting reputation for honesty and integrity with the regulators and with your peers.

- Roger Gros, editor and co-publisher of *Global Gaming Business* magazine, who began his career in the industry as a dealer in Atlantic City, New Jersey, and used this experience to eventually establish the industry's most comprehensive trade publication:

  Before the advent of gaming in New Jersey, the casino industry was considered a racket, not a legitimate business. Once New Jersey proved you can introduce gaming to be an important revenue source for the state while controlling and regulating it, gaming became an industry that started to attract talented people who may have gone into another field at another time. The only thing, however, that continues to separate the industry from the racket is integrity, brought by fair and even-handed regulations. That integrity is crucial to the acceptance in the community of the casino business.

- John Hawkins, director of slot operations, Potawatomi Bingo Casino, who began his career in Reno, Nevada, and has worked in Iowa, Michigan, and, most recently, Wisconsin for a Native American casino operation:

  Federal, state, local, and tribal laws govern Native American casino gaming. Most regulations have some type of penalty for infractions. The first issue in my career where I saw a large fine levied against a casino was in Iowa for the underage gaming infractions. The regulations called for a $10,000 fine for the first infraction, and the largest I saw was $250,000.

My advice to young people entering the industry and why they should value compliance with the laws and regulations is for them to understand the reputation that gaming historically held and what is being done to combat that reputation. I have worked old Nevada and I have worked the expanding markets. It is very important for gaming to stay free from corruption to continue the exponential growth that it has seen in the past 25 years.

• Tom Nelson, co-founder of Gaming Regulatory Consultants and former deputy director of licensing and compliance for the Michigan Gaming Control Board:

Consequences for noncompliance can range from stern warnings to license revocation. Casino laws and regulations have evolved from, and are based on, often bitter experience with serious problems. Licensees that ignore, or even worse, flout these conventions face the wrath of the regulators. Fortunately,

Figure 5–2

most sensible regulators take a graduated approach to noncompliance matters and reserve the harshest sanctions for repeat or flagrant offenders. My advice, however, to anyone choosing to enter this industry is not to rely too heavily on the kindness of the regulator. There is a very apt saying that all gaming professionals should have emblazoned above their door, which is "Compliance before commerce." Strict adherence to this simple precept can save them, and their enterprise, a world of grief.

In summary, all of these industry professionals concur that it is *extremely important* that you value the rules and regulations of the industry (Figure 5–2). We hope that these statements will give you a foundation for the information provided in the rest of this chapter.

Overview of the Layers of Gaming Regulations: Federal, State, and Tribal Laws

There are numerous forms of legalized gaming,[7] and each form has its own unique set of regulations that governs its operation. However, for purposes of this chapter, we are going to examine legalized commercial casino gaming and Native American gaming.

For our purposes, **commercial casino gaming** is defined as a "casino that operates in a state that has made it legal to operate casinos in accordance with certain rules and regulations established in that particular state." Therefore, New Jersey casinos are commercial casinos, as they operate in New Jersey under laws created as a result of New Jersey voters approving the establishment of the industry in the late 1970s. Other commercial casino jurisdictions are Michigan, Colorado, Mississippi, Louisiana, Indiana, Illinois, Iowa, Missouri, South Dakota, and Nevada.

Native American casino gaming is gaming that became statutorily authorized by the U.S. Congress in 1988 when it enacted the **Indian Gaming Regulatory Act**. This federal law outlines procedures whereby federally recognized Indian tribes can operate casino gaming. The law divides the types of gaming that Native American tribes can operate into Class I, Class II, and Class III gaming. Class III gaming is synonymous with Las Vegas–style house-backed gaming. We discuss the specifics of Native American gaming later in this chapter. The important thing to remember at this point is that Native American gaming is gaming that is regulated by the involved sovereign tribe, with federal government oversight, and in certain situations, some limited state oversight.

The foundation of the casino gaming industry is the establishment of state laws legalizing the operation of the industry. Most of the regulations discussed in this chapter are based on state law. Remember, each state has its own set of laws that do not cross over to another state. This is why in the state of New York, you pay a five-cent deposit on each bottle or can of carbonated beverage, but in neighboring Pennsylvania, you can purchase the very same beverage without paying the deposit. This same situation is true for the regulations that govern the commercial casino industry. Although the core concepts of the regulation of commercial casino gaming are similar in many states, the manner in which each state accomplishes the end goal is different.

Federal Regulations

Federal law is extremely important when it comes to the casino industry, although it is important to remember that most of the daily operational regulations of the commercial or Native American casinos are controlled by state or tribal law. These include rules concerning licensing owners, suppliers, and employees; placement of ATM machines; purchasing requirements; contract requirements; requirements to report certain events; gift giving; transferring ownership interest; debt transactions; excluding patrons; placement of slot machines and table games; authorization of games; minimum payout percentages; check cashing; location of surveillance systems; handling of casino chips; issuing of casino credit; and patron dispute procedures. Federal laws generally assist states in the enforcement of their gaming laws. Generally, for many federal law provisions, a particular gambling business is illegal only if it violates a state or local law.

We now review four important federal laws: the Gambling Devices Act (15 U.S.C. 1171-1178), the Bank Secrecy Act (31 U.S.C. 5311-5330), the Indian Gaming Regulatory Act (25 U.S.C 2701-2721), and the U.S. Patriot Act.

The Gambling Devices Act

Although state law typically governs whether a particular type of gaming device is authorized or prohibited in that state, the **Gambling Devices Act** establishes procedures for manufacturing and shipping gaming equipment in interstate commerce throughout the

United States. The act prevents the shipment of gaming devices into jurisdictions where the machines are not legal under state law. The act also requires that manufacturers and distributors of gambling devices[8] keep detailed records of machines they sell or service. There are harsh penalties for individuals or businesses that do not comply with the Gambling Devices Act,[9] including fines of up to $5,000 and imprisonment of up to two years.[10]

The Bank Secrecy Act

The Currency and Foreign Transactions Reporting Act, also known as the **Bank Secrecy Act** (BSA) or Title 31, was established in 1970 to fight money laundering and other crimes involving currency. The act was initially created with an exclusive focus on banking institutions and required reports to be filed on anyone who completed a cash transaction involving $10,000 or more. However, in 1985, the law was amended to include commercial casinos, and, in 1996, it was further amended to include Native American casinos. As the casino industry was brought under the BSA, additional "suspicious activity" reporting requirements were put in place. The Department of Treasury is charged with enforcing the BSA, and it has created the Financial Crimes Enforcement Network (FinCEN).[11] FinCEN has worked to maximize the sharing of information among law enforcement agencies and its other partners in the regulatory and financial communities.

The U.S. Patriot Act

The **U.S. Patriot Act**, Section 314(b), permits financial institutions, upon providing notice to the U.S. Department of the Treasury, to share information with one another to identify and report to the federal government any activities that may involve money laundering or terrorist activity.

The Indian Gaming Regulatory Act (IGRA)

The Indian Gaming Regulatory Act (IGRA) was enacted in 1988 to establish a balance between tribal sovereignty and the interests of state governments. The act established regulatory procedures by which tribes could operate gaming activities for their economic benefit. The act divides Indian gaming into three classes. Class I gaming generally includes social and traditional games and is within the exclusive jurisdiction of Indian tribes. Class II includes bingo and games similar to bingo that can be operated by a tribe if it is located in a state that permits that type of gaming for any purpose by any person or entity, and if it is authorized by tribal resolution or ordinance. Class III gaming includes all types of gaming that are neither Class I nor Class II gaming. In other words, Class III gaming is Las Vegas–style gambling. Class III gaming must occur only in a state that permits that particular type of gaming for any purpose by any person or entity and must also be authorized by tribal resolution or ordinance. In addition, there must be a compact negotiated between the tribe and the state that defines how the Class III gaming will be conducted. This act also created the National Indian Gaming Commission[12] to oversee Indian gaming.

State Regulations

The first step in regulating the commercial casino industry is legalizing the industry in a particular state. There are several ways in which a jurisdiction can legalize casino gaming. Whether it occurs by a vote of the people on a state or regional ballot or via an enacted piece of legislation, the end result is that once a state authorizes casino gaming, the state legislative and executive branches of government are required to establish regulations under which the industry can operate.

The legalization of the casino gaming industry outside of Nevada occurred for two basic reasons. Primarily, legalized gambling was a way for state governments to raise additional revenue for state programs. Consequently, states that allow casino gaming have a direct financial relationship to the money generated by these businesses, as there is most often an additional business tax levied on the industry. This tax is commonly referred to as a **wagering tax** or a fee assessed by the state on gaming revenue generated by the casino operator. The wagering tax is often levied on the gross revenue of a casino's operation.

The second reason that states often legalize the casino gaming industry is to provide entertainment value to its residents. Thus, in addition to the collection of tax revenue, the state government has an interest in assuring that the industry operates fairly and the patrons to the state's casinos are given a fair wagering opportunity.

Structure of a State Gaming Control Board

In a state that authorizes the industry, the commonly accepted model of casino gaming regulation is the formation of a new state agency to oversee the integrity of the industry's operation. This agency is most often referred to as a *gaming control board or gaming control commission*. The size and scope of authority given to this regulatory body varies by jurisdiction. For example, in Nevada, the state has both the Nevada Gaming Commission and the State Gaming Control Board that comprise a two-tiered system charged with regulating the Nevada gaming industry.[13] The board deals with the day-to-day regulator and licensing activities of the industry, while the commission has the final authority on licensing matters, with the ability to approve, restrict, limit, condition, deny, revoke, or suspend any gaming license.

In Michigan, the State Gaming Control Board is a single-tiered system that is charged with licensing casino employees, suppliers, and operators. The Michigan board is composed of five volunteer members who are appointed by the governor. This five-member board has complete authority over all commercial casino gaming that occurs in Michigan, which is currently limited to three locations in Detroit.

In both Nevada and Michigan, the core duties of the state regulating entities are conducted by staff members. Each state differs in the total number of employees who work for the regulating agency. In Michigan, for the three Detroit casinos, there is a total staff of 98. In addition, state regulating entities typically work with other state agencies, such as the police, treasury, attorney general and tourism departments.

To provide additional information about the state commercial gaming boards, Table 5–1 includes the name, contact information, and website for the 11 state commercial gaming boards.

Duties of a State Gaming Control Board or Commission

States and tribal gaming commissions that authorize casino gaming often give extremely broad duties and powers to the gaming control board. These include

- Investigating applicants and determining whether they are eligible and suitable to receive a license to own a casino, work in a casino, or supply the casino with goods or services

Table 5–1   Jurisdictional contact information

Jurisdiction	Contact Information	Website
Nevada	**Gaming Commission** 1919 E. College Parkway Carson City, NV 89706 (775) 684-7750	http://gaming.nv.gov
	Gaming Control Board 555 E. Washington Ave., Suite 2600 Las Vegas, NV 89101 (702) 486-2000	
Michigan	**Michigan Gaming Control Board** 1500 Abbott Road, Suite 400 East Lansing, MI 48823 (517) 241-0040	www.michigan.gov/mgcb
New Jersey	**New Jersey Casino Control Commission** Tennessee Avenue & Boardwalk Atlantic City, NJ 08401 (609) 441-3799	www.state.nj.us/casinos/
	New Jersey Division of Gaming Enforcement 1300 Atlantic Avenue Atlantic City, NJ 08401 (609) 441-7464	www.state.nj.us/lps/ge
Illinois	**Illinois Gaming Board** 160 N. LaSalle, Suite 300 Chicago, IL 60601 (312) 814-4700	www.igb.state.il.us
Indiana	**Indiana Gaming Commission** Suite 950, South Tower 115 W. Washington Street Indianapolis, IN 46204-3409 (317) 233-0046	www.ai.org/gaming
Colorado	**Colorado Division of Gaming** 1881 Pierce Street, Suite 112 Lakewood, CO 80214-1496 (313) 205-1355	www.revenue.state.co.us/gaming/home.asp
Louisiana	**Louisiana Gaming Control Board** 9100 Bluebonnet Centre Blvd. Suite 500 Baton Rouge, LA 70809 (225) 295-8450	www.dps.state.la.us/lgcb
Mississippi	**Mississippi Gaming Commission** 620 North Street, Suite 200 Jackson, MS 39202 (601) 576-3800	www.mgc.state.ms.us
Missouri	**Missouri Gaming Commission** PO Box 1847 3417 Knipp Drive Jefferson City, MO 65102-1847 (573) 526-4080	www.mgc.dps.mo.gov
Iowa	**Iowa Racing & Gaming Commission** 717 East Court, Suite B Des Moines, IA 50309 (515) 281-7352	www.state.ia.us/irgc/
Pennsylvania	**Pennsylvania Gaming Control Board** PO Box 69060 Harrisburg, PA 17106 (717) 346-8300	www.pgcb.state.pa.us/

- Supervising casino gambling operations in the state
- Entering the premises of a casino operator or supplier in order to investigate the licensee
- Investigating alleged violations of the gaming regulations
- Adopting standards for licensing electronic gambling manufacturers
- Requiring that all financial documents related to the operation be made available
- Inspecting and testing all gaming-related products used in casino operations

- Requiring licensees to file annual reports on their responsible-gaming education activities
- Imposing fines or revoking licenses that are in violation of the gaming regulations.

It is not uncommon for state laws and gaming control board regulations to surpass 200–300 pages. Consequently, it is impossible to give a complete summary of typical gaming regulations in this chapter. The list of nine duties just outlined will give you an understanding of the enormous scope of these regulations. For more information, the second edition of *The Michigan Gaming Law Legal Resource Book*, authored by the Fraser, Trebilcock, Davis & Dunlap, P.C. law firm in Michigan, is a good microanalysis of the Michigan regulatory structure. Also, the third edition of the *Nevada Gaming Law* publication, authored by the law firm of Lionel Sawyer & Collins, is a good resource for individuals wishing to learn more about the details of the Nevada regulatory process.

State Selection of Casino Operators

Once a particular state has decided to legalize commercial casino gambling, the state must then decide which industry model it will develop. This is often decided within the legislation or law that legalized the industry, but not always. It may also be modified once the industry is initially authorized.

The two most common models of casino markets are (1) free markets and (2) limited licenses. In either case, the casino operator must go through an application process in order to be licensed. We review the licensing process in greater detail later in this chapter. However, in addition to the casino licensing application process, there is also the casino license selection process. The selection process is of more significant interest in a limited license jurisdiction where there are a greater number of applicants than available licenses. In jurisdictions where there are more interested operators than licenses, the jurisdiction will typically conduct a competitive selection process. As you can imagine, the competition for these licenses can be extremely intense, and as a result there are numerous safeguards that governments need to put in place to assure that no one applicant receives an unfair advantage.

At the time this chapter went to print, a dispute was pending in Illinois over the manner in which a tenth casino operator's license was awarded to Isle of Capri. The dispute involved Isle of Capri's $518 million proposal to build a privately operated casino in Rosemont, Illinois. After being successfully selected in March 2004 under the state's competitive selection process, the state's attorney general challenged the selection of Isle of Capri. The attorney general has alleged that the city of Rosemont and the Isle of Capri are ineligible for the tenth license in Rosemont because of alleged ties to organized crime. Thus, the Isle of Capri is in this dispute as a result of alleged financial concerns that apparently the Illinois Gaming Board did not consider a problem. Separately, the Illinois Supreme Court upheld the constitutionality of legislation that designated Rosemont as the location for the state's tenth license.

A separate matter in the state of Michigan's Detroit casino selection process also continued as this chapter went to print. In the Michigan case, a northern Michigan Native American tribe that did not submit a bid for one of the three Detroit casino licenses filed a federal court challenge and was ultimately successful in getting a judgment finding the Detroit selection process unconstitutional because it granted a preference to two groups that had been involved in getting ballot initiatives passed. The tribe argued successfully that by rewarding those who have been involved in the political process with a "preference," the city of Detroit's competitive selection process violated First Amendment rights.

The Illinois and Michigan examples illustrate the controversial nature of the casino license selection process. These situations also illustrate the need for a strict and structured selection process in order to limit any sense of confusion or controversy. As new states look to legalize the casino gaming industry, they should learn from the lessons of Illinois and Michigan.

State Licensing of Casino Operators and the use of Background Investigations

The process of applying for a casino operator license is a difficult and grueling one. Most states that allow private casino gaming require that the license applicant provide reams of paper explaining the history of its business operations. In addition, these applications require personal history disclosures by key persons involved with the applicant's business operation.

The purpose of the license application is to provide the state gaming control board with information on the licensee so that the board and its staff can make a determination as to whether the applicant is "eligible and suitable" to receive a license. License investigations are initiated by the submission of an application but often require hundreds of personal interviews and thousands of hours of investigative time into the integrity and suitability of the applicant. It is not uncommon for a license investigation into a casino operator to take anywhere from 6 to 18 months to complete. As the number of casino operators in the United States has consolidated into a few major conglomerates, the investigative process is becoming easier for expanding jurisdictions. However, as mentioned earlier, each state that authorizes casino gambling has its own unique laws and its own citizens to which it is ultimately accountable. Therefore, although regulators who govern the casino industry share information, they often do not rely on license approvals in another jurisdiction to sway their decisions. Thus, the casino licensing process remains time consuming and tedious.

Following are sample application questions that typically appear on a casino operator's license application:

1. Submit name, birth date, home address, percent of interest in casino operation, title and position for all key persons within your operation. Key persons include anyone who is involved in a key management function, has any ownership interest, or is able to affect the operation of the casino.

2. Submit the name of any affiliate or affiliated company, its address, percent of interest in casino operation, the authorized representative from this entity, and the position held by this individual.

3. Submit the name, date of birth, address, and percent of interest in the casino operation for anyone that holds 5 percent or greater in a publicly traded entity or 1 percent or greater in a privately owned entity.

4. List any licenses held by the applicant. Include the name, address, and telephone of the licensing agency, along with the type of registration and license number.

5. List whether any complaint or other notice of pending disciplinary action from any jurisdiction has been issued to the license applicant.

6. List whether the licensee has ever had any license or certificate issued by any jurisdiction revoked, denied, restricted or suspended, or not renewed. List whether the licensee has ever withdrawn a license application. List whether the license applicant has been assessed and/or paid any fines or penalty fees to any federal, state, local, or city jurisdiction.

7. Has the applicant ever filed, or had filed against it, a proceeding for bankruptcy or been involved in any formal process to adjust, defer, suspend, or otherwise work out payment of a debt. If yes, provide the date of filing, name of court, case number, and disposition.

8. Provide copies of the following documents referenced in question 7: a copy of the approved reorganization plan, final order from court, final statements of assets and liability, list of equity security holders, and details of the license applicant's involvement in the bankruptcy.

9. List whether the license applicant has been served with a complaint, lien, judgment, or other notice filed with any public body regarding the payment of any tax required under federal, state, or local law.

10. List whether the license applicant has ever been subject to a tax audit by any governmental agency.

11. List whether anyone listed under questions 1 and 2 has made a political contribution, loan, gift, or other payment to any candidate, campaign committee, or officeholder elected in this state.

12. List whether the applicant has ever been convicted of a crime or been charged with a crime in this state or any other state.

13. Submit a copy of the applicant's most recent certified financial audit by an independent certified public accountant.

14. Submit copies of any term sheets or written summary on all mergers or acquisitions that have involved the applicant for the past 10 years.

15. List whether the applicant is or has been party to any litigation. If yes, then list the following information: official title or caption of the case, docket or case number, name of court, identity of all parties in the litigation, and nature of claims.

16. Submit a chart showing the corporate organizational structure of the license applicant, including all officers, directors, and managers.

17. Submit a list identifying all committees of the applicant. Include the names of all committee members, their titles, and the committee with which these individuals are affiliated.

18. Submit a flowchart illustrating the fully diluted ownership of the applicant. List all parent, holding, or intermediary companies until the flowchart reflects the stock, partnerships, or ownership interest as being held by a natural person(s) and not another enterprise(s). If the ultimate parent company is publicly traded and no natural person controls more than 5 percent of the publicly traded entity stock, indicate this in a footnote.

19. Submit all material events that have taken place by the company since it was established.

20. Does the applicant have any interest, direct or indirect, in any company outside of the United States?

21. Have any of your key officers, employees, or any third parties acting on behalf of the applicant made any bribes or kickbacks to any employee, company, or organization to obtain favorable treatment?

In addition to submitting an application that answers these questions, regulators typically also require that key employees of the applicant complete a personal disclosure statement and a financial summary statement. Key employees typically include anyone involved in the gaming process or who handle cash in a casino. These applications ask questions similar in scope to those just outlined. Table 5–2 shows sample questions.

State Licensing of Gaming and Nongaming Suppliers

In addition to licensing casino operators and key employees of a casino operation, the states also license suppliers of the industry. Some jurisdictions license only gaming-related suppliers (e.g., slot manufacturers), while other jurisdictions license nongaming

Table 5–2   Basic personal questions

Basic Personal Questions

Job Title/positions held	Date of Marriage
Company Name	Place of Marriage (City, County and State)
Company Address	Spouse's Full Name (Maiden included)
Company Fax	Spouse's Social Security Number
Company Phone	Driver's License Number, State, Year Issued
Last Name	Date of Birth
First Name	Place of Birth (City, County, State, Country)
Middle Name	Home Address
Aliases (Nicknames)	Home Phone
Home Address	Spouse's Employer
Home Phone	Spouse Title
Do you have a safety deposit box? If so include bank name, date opened, and number	Spouse's Work Address
Date Moved into Present Address	Spouse's Work Phone
Job Description	List Previous Marriages (Date of Order, Nature of Action, City, County, and State)
Date of Birth	List the Names and Current Addresses of Previous Spouses (Name, Date of Birth, Address and Phone)
Place of Birth (City, County, State, Country)	Place of Residence Since Age 18
Social Security Number	List employers and positions held since age 18.
Sex	List any business in which you, your spouse, your parent, or your child has equity interest of more than 5 percent.
Eye Color	List all children, including stepchildren and adopted children, and give the following information: name, date of birth, social security number, address, and occupation.
Hair Color	List information for parents and parents-in-law: name, date of birth, social security number, address, and occupation.
Height	List information for brothers and sisters and your spouse's brothers and sisters, including stepbrothers and stepsisters and said persons' spouses: name, date of birth, social security number, address, and occupation.
Weight	List all licensees held.
Complexion	List all schooling completed by applicant, include grade school through graduate school.
Build	Do you own a firearm?
List Scars, Tattoos, Distinguishing Marks	Have you ever served in any armed forces? (Yes or No)
Driver's License Number, State, Year Issued	If yes, what branch?
United States Citizen, Yes – No	Date of entry—active service

(continued)

Table 5–2   Basic personal questions (*Continued*)

Basic Personal Questions

List all political contributions made by you, your spouse, or your child to any party or committee at a local, state, or national level.

Date of separation from military

List all arrests whether or not you were ever convicted, charges were dropped, or never filed, regardless of the outcome. Include ALL arrests (except minor traffic citations, speeding, stop signs, equipment, etc.).

Type of discharge from military

Have any of your relatives, or any of your spouse's relatives, ever been charged with or convicted of any criminal offense?

Rating at separation from military

List five character references who you have known for more than five years. Do not include relatives, present employer, or employees. List the following information for each person: name, date of birth, social security number, address, and occupation.

Serial number while in military

Have you ever had a criminal indictment filed against you in ANY jurisdiction?

While in the military service were you ever arrested for an offense that resulted in summary action, a trial, or special or general court martial? (Yes or No)

Have you ever been detained or questioned by any law enforcement officer?

Do you have, or have you ever had, a substance abuse problem?

Have you ever been a suspect or possible suspect in any crime?

Have you ever been treated, or are you currently being treated, for any substance abuse problem?

Have you ever been convicted of a crime and

Do you have, or have you ever had, any gambling-related problems or debts?

1. Had a conviction "purged" from your record?

2. Been given a "deferred sentence"?

3. Been given "diversion"?

4. Been given a "pardon"?

Have you ever been the subject of a grand jury investigation?

Have you ever been treated for any gambling-related problems?

Has a criminal indictment, information, or complaint ever been returned against you, but for which you were not arrested or in which you were named as an unindicted co-party?

Under federal, state or municipal law, have you ever been delinquent in the payment of any taxes?

Have you ever entered into an agreement with any law enforcement agency or prosecutory agency to cooperate with them in lieu of being prosecuted? (Example: testifying for the prosecution, working as an informant, etc.)

Have you, as an individual, member of a partnership, or owner, director, or officer of a corporation, ever been a party to a lawsuit as either a plaintiff or defendant?

(*continued*)

Table 5-2 Basic personal questions (*Continued*)

Basic Personal Questions	
Have you or your spouse, been a beneficiary, settlor, trustee, grantor, or transferor, to any trust during the past ten (10) years?	Have you, as an individual, member of a partnership, or owner, director, or officer of a corporation, ever been a defendant in any civil lawsuit that was predicated in whole or in part upon conduct that allegedly constituted a crime or crimes?
Within the past ten (10) years, have you or any of your relatives been a public official, an officer, or an employee of any governmental entity?	Within the past five (5) years, have you, or your spouse, filed any insurance claims in excess of $5,000?
List all memberships you have held since the age of 18 in any social, labor, fraternal, union, or veteran's organization. Begin with the most recent and work backwards.	Provide the following information for all motor vehicles, boats, or planes used by you: type, license number, ownership value.

suppliers whose contracts exceed certain dollar thresholds. The licensing process for suppliers is similar to that of casino operators. Therefore, the questions outlined in the previous sections are also asked of industry suppliers and of the key employees of those suppliers.

The gaming industry also requires that the gaming products sold by industry suppliers be tested by governmental or private gaming laboratories. These laboratories test to make sure that the games are random and fair and meet the requirements of the jurisdiction.

Tribal Casino Regulations

The process of the state licensing of casino operators is similar to what the Indian Gaming Regulatory Act requires that Native American tribes institute in connection with the operation of their tribal casinos. The major difference is that a Native American tribe is a sovereign entity, and, as such, its government is responsible for the oversight of its casino operation, and the licensing of key employees and suppliers. Under federal law, it is required that a tribe and state enter into a compact if Class III, Las Vegas–style gaming, is going to occur on the tribe's reservation. Each tribal/state compact is different, but the document outlines certain obligations that the tribe has in operating the Class III facility. In addition, the Indian Gaming Regulatory Act also created the National

Indian Gaming Commission to assist with the oversight and regulation of Native American gaming in the United States. This federal agency's mission is to

> Regulate gaming activities on Indian lands for the purpose of shielding Indian tribes from organized crime and other corrupting influences; to ensure that Indian tribes are the primary beneficiaries of gaming revenue; and to assure that gaming is conducted fairly and honestly by both operators and players.
>
> To achieve these goals, the Commission is authorized to conduct investigations; undertake enforcement actions, including the issuance of notices of violation, assessment of civil fines, and/or issuance of closure orders; conduct background investigations; conduct audits; and review and approve Tribal gaming ordinances.

The agency works very closely with the Native American tribes and the gaming commissions of each tribe.

Conclusion

The goal of this chapter has been to give you an overview of the laws and regulations that govern the casino gaming industry in the United States. As you have learned, the gaming industry is regulated by various state, federal, and tribal agencies. The primary goals of these agencies are to make sure that suitable individuals and entities are involved in the industry, that the games are played fairly, and that the proper tax dollars are paid by the industry.

As recommended at the beginning of this chapter by Ms. Mathur, Mr. Leonard, Mr. Shepherd, Mr. Gros, and Mr. Nelson, should you select the gaming industry for your career, your personal history is extremely important. So, if you are going to proceed with a career in the gaming industry, make sure that you preserve your reputation, because the gaming industry regulations do not allow unsuitable individuals to participate.

The casino gaming industry provides unique opportunities to those who are willing to comply with strict, ongoing, comprehensive regulation. With its explosive growth worldwide, the industry has a lot to offer those with high standards for ethics and personal integrity.

key terms

Commercial casino gaming

Indian Gaming Regulatory Act

Gambling Devices Act

Bank Secrecy Act

U.S. Patriot Act

Wagering tax

review questions

1. What are the obvious and the not-so-obvious potential problems to the individual for not complying with gaming regulations?

2. What are the two basic reasons that the legalization of the casino gaming industry outside of Nevada occurred?

3. What are the five key federal regulations governing the gaming industry?

4. What are the duties of a state gaming control board or commission?

5. What are the differences between the two most common models of casino markets?

6. Who is responsible for regulating the gaming industry in the United States?

7. What is the function of the National Indian Gaming Commission?

internet sites

National Indian Gaming Association
http://www.indiangaming.org

National Indian Gaming Commission
http://www.nigc.gov

Pechanga
http://www.pechanga.net

International Masters of Gaming Law
http://www.gaminglawmasters.com

endnotes

1. MCL 432.208(3)(d)

2. *IC 4;33;10-2.1*

3. "Upward mobility: A fact of life in the casino industry," *Casino Connection*, December 2003.

4. If you are interested in gaining a more legal explanation of the gaming laws in the United States, then the Federal Gambling Law written by Anthony Cabot and Joseph Kelly is suggested. In addition, we also suggest the *Gaming Law Review* for those interested in gaining an in-depth look at laws affecting the gaming industry on an ongoing basis.

5. All quotes are from interviews by the authors.

6. All quotes are from interviews by the authors.

7. Commercial casinos, Native American casinos, bingo, pari-mutuel wagering, charitable games, and lotteries.

8. The term *gambling device* means (1) any so-called slot machine or any other machine or mechanical device, an essential part of which is a drum or reel with insignia thereon, and (a) which when operated may deliver, as the result of the application of an element of chance, any money or property, or (b) by the operation of which a person may become entitled to receive, as the result of the application of an element of chance, any money or property; or (2) any other machine or mechanical device (including, but not limited to, roulette wheels and similar devices) designed and manufactured primarily for use in connection with gambling, and (a) which when operated may deliver, as the result of the application of an element of chance, any money or property, or (b) by the operation of which a person may become entitled to receive, as the result of the application of an element of chance, any money or property; or (3) any subassembly or essential part intended to be used in connection with any such machine or mechanical device, but which is not attached to any such machine or mechanical device as a constituent part.

9. http://www.usdoj.gov/criminal/oeo/gambling/

10. 15 U.S. 1176

11. http://www.fincen.gov/

12. http://www.nigc.gov

13. http://gaming.nv.gov/

Vignette

The European Casino: The Way Things Were Meant to Be?

William Thompson, University of Nevada–Las Vegas

Formal casino gambling has its roots on the European continent. The institution that we call the *casino* had its origins in the seventeenth and eighteenth centuries. Governments gave concessions to private entrepreneurs to operate buildings in which games could be legally played in exchange for a part of the revenues secured by the entrepreneurs. Whereas from time immemorial, players had competed against one another in all sorts of private games, here games were initially structured to pit the player against the casino operators—the "house." These gambling halls were designed to offer playing opportunities to an elite

Figure 5–3 Baden Baden
Photo courtesy of Bill Thompson.
Baden Baden Casino.

class in an atmosphere that allowed them to enjoy relaxation among their peers (Figure 5–3).

The twenty-first century seems to have brought a strong movement that is pushing for the expansion of gambling all around the globe. Given that casino gambling has European origins, it is somewhat ironic that those pushing gambling now almost totally overlook the traditional manner in which casinos have operated over the past three centuries in Europe. Promoters of new casino gambling, including British and European politicians, are quite willing to scrap the European model in favor of the modern model of casinos found in Las Vegas and other American jurisdictions. Almost everywhere, the slot machine is the pervasive form of gambling. Machines are found in urban and seaside parlors, recreational arcades, and in pubs, bars, taverns, and restaurants worldwide. Major moves are being made in the parliaments of Japan and the United Kingdom to have Las Vegas–style casinos in several locations from Tokyo to Osaka, from England and Wales to Scotland.

Before we bury the idea of the "European Casino," we should reflect upon its attributes. Perhaps political leaders who are enthralled with the idea of merely using large open casinos as vehicles for gaining maximum revenues for governments could reflect on the virtues of a different style of operations. Maybe policy makers in my home jurisdiction of Las Vegas could reflect on these virtues as well.

I once visited the casino that operated within the Kurhaus in Wiesbaden, Germany. The casino manager was describing a new casino that had opened in an industrial city a few hours away. With a stiff demeanor he said, "They allow men to come in without ties; they have rows and rows of noisy slot machines; they serve food and drinks at the tables; and they are always so crowded with loud players; it is so awful." Then with a little smile on his face, he added, "Oh, I wish we could be like that."

Actually, the rival casino to which the Wiesbaden manager was referring, the casino at Hohensyburg near Dortmund, was really just a bigger casino, where a separate slot machine room was within the main building, as opposed to being in another building altogether. Men usually had to wear ties, but the dress code was relaxed on weekends, and the facility had a nightclub, again in a separate area. It was crowded simply because it was the only casino near a large city, and the local state government did not enforce a rule against local residents entering the facility.

The traditional casinos of Europe were not as large as those in Las Vegas. The largest may have hundreds of machines, not thousands. Typically, they would have fewer than fifty. Twenty tables would be found in a large casino. The largest casinos such as those in Madrid; Saint Vincent, Italy; and Monte Carlo had playing floors smaller than the ones found on American riverboat casinos. Revenues were but a fraction of revenues found in American casinos. The largest casinos produced gaming wins similar to those of average or small riverboat casinos.

Most traditional European casinos were local monopolies. Governments had vital roles in some facet of the operation. Some governments owned and operated the casinos (Figure 5–4). Some owned the building housing the casino. When the casino was a private operation, it might as well have been a government corporation. Taxes were so high that the government was the greatest financial beneficiary from the operations. For example, casinos in Germany pay a rate on their gross wins as high as 80 percent. In France, the tax rate is on a sliding scale up to 80 percent; in Austria, taxes took 60 percent of the revenues, in Spain 54 percent. Nowhere were tax rates below the typical 20 percent to 30 percent rates in U.S. jurisdictions (the Nevada rate is less than 7 percent).

Still, given the size of the operations, nowhere do governments heavily rely on the taxes for budgetary reasons.

The traditional casinos restricted patron access in many ways: (1) Many would not allow local residents to gamble. (2) All required identification and all registered

Figure 5–4 Santanter Spain Government Casino
Photo courtesy of Bill Thompson.

patron attendance. (3) They enforced dress codes. (4) They permitted players to ban themselves from entering the casinos if they worried about compulsive gambling behaviors. The casinos allowed families to ban individuals from gambling, and the casinos themselves would bar compulsive gamblers. (5) The casinos had limited hours of operation, usually during evening hours. (6) Casinos did not advertise. (7) Credit policies were restrictive; checks were not cashed. (8) Alcoholic beverages were restricted. (9) Complimentaries—drinks, meals, and hotel accommodations—were rare.

The clientele of the traditional European casino was from the local region. The casinos did not rely upon international visitors (Monte Carlo being one exception). Very few had facilities for overnight visitors. The casinos featured table games, and where slot machines were permitted, they were found in separate rooms or even separate buildings. The employees at the casinos spent entire careers at one house. The employees were almost always local nationals. The advent of the European Union has affected that pattern.

The casinos of Europe have traditionally adopted what would be called a "player protection" model of operation. The gamblers in this case are local area elites (some of the casinos do ban residents of the local town), and, therefore, what happens to them during their casino experience becomes known to most patrons. The casino would show a level of care to these players that is well reflected in the statement: "Treat a sheep well, and he gives you wool forever; skin a sheep and you never get anything from him again."

The casinos also follow a community responsibility model. Casinos receive their licenses or concessions for a number of years based upon competitive bidding. The bids include a list of promised obligations toward the community. Casinos agree to finance public parks surrounding their properties; some have art museums for the community, others historical displays. Some financed other community buildings, including church buildings. Several won their licenses with a promise that they would revitalize a historical building that was scheduled for demolition. The casinos offered concert series to town residents. Bands and orchestras played outside the facilities, not inside, as in Las Vegas. They did not play in order to entice players to enter their doors, but rather to improve the quality of life in the towns.

I write about the European casinos in the past tense, because it was in 1986 and 1987 when I toured 140 of their facilities. Since that time I have occasionally visited some of these casinos. I do recognize desires to change, but I wonder about what is being sacrificed with the embracing of the Las Vegas–style as the one dominant model to be emulated. During my tour, I constantly asked about crime, prostitution, and other social maladies considered to be related to casinos in America. Most of the time, the response was an incredulous, "What is it you are asking about?" "We know nothing of these problems." The responses came from casino operators, government regulators, players, and citizens in general.

The traditional European casinos have had a style that would be welcomed by many North American patrons. However, in achieving that style, the casinos must forfeit what most entrepreneurs, governments, and citizens want from casinos—large profits, many jobs, economic development, and tax generation that could support many government programs. Those things do not come with the player protection and community responsibility models of casinos found in Europe.

PART 3

External Environmental Influences

6 Consumer Behavior

Tanya MacLaurin, University of Guelph

Kathryn Hashimoto, East Carolina University

Learning Objectives

1. To provide an overview of the study of consumer behavior in order to understand how people make purchase decisions.

2. To explore the external and internal influences that persuade consumers to look for products and services.

3. To understand how a consumer makes the final decision to purchase.

4. To provide an overview of the five subdisciplines on which the majority of consumer behavior research in the casino gambling field has been based.

5. To explore player demographics to gain insight into who the casino customer is.

Chapter Outline

Introduction to Consumer Behavior: How, Why, Who, What, and Where

I knew a retired couple who were very frugal. They were careful with every penny they spent. I could always find them at home, unless they were grocery shopping on Wednesday, or if Mary was getting her hair done on Friday. One day, their daughter asked them to go to an Atlantic City casino by bus for the day. Although they were not sure they wanted to go, they agreed because it was an anniversary present from their children. They each received $20 in tokens, a free lunch buffet at the casino, and the bus had free food and drink during the trip. Tom gained $20 from the venture because he didn't gamble. Instead, he sat on the boardwalk and then went to the casino to eat his free lunch. Mary lost the $20 at the slot machines, but she was able to spend the day with her daughter. It was a pleasant day for all. Mary's birthday was a few months later. Again the daughter invited them to take the bus, and this time they agreed more readily. Tom played his $20 because it was after all, "found money," and hit for $500.

Five years later, Tom and Mary drive the three hours to Atlantic City because the bus doesn't give them enough time at the casino. They eat on the way in, because they don't want to waste precious gambling time once they arrive. On average, they take $1000 each and go once a month. The money comes from presents for special occasions, their winnings, and Tom's extra work now that he is retired. Why do they go? They say it is exciting, a change from their daily routine, and it gives them a topic of conversation. They can always talk about their Atlantic City visits to anyone. In addition, Mary shows everyone the picture that the casino took when she won $1500.

What aspects of this story concern consumer behavior? Everything. **Consumer behavior** is the study of how, why, who, what, and where people make purchase decisions. It begins on a broad scale by exploring the external influences that persuade a consumer to look for products and services and then studies how these ideas are internally processed. As people mull over ideas, they may decide that a service is necessary to their lives. From this stage, we look over the consumer decision process, which examines how people make their final decisions to buy. In our story, the external influence was Mary's daughter who decided to buy the tickets. Tom and Mary thought about what they had learned about casinos and gambling over the years and tried to reconcile these external ideas with their own values and norms. Their external ideas of casinos were neutral, but the factors that the trip was a gift and that they did not have to spend any money tipped their decision to go. Each of these steps is part of the buyer behaviors.

The "How" of Consumer Behavior in Casino Management: Consumer Behavior Theory

Consumer behavior refers to the study of how a person buys products. However, this is only part of the definition. The study of buying behaviors reflects the totality of consumers' decisions with respect to the acquisition, consumption, and disposition of goods, services, time, and ideas by purchasers over time. For example, consumers who have traditionally traveled to places such as Las Vegas and Reno to gamble now can do so on internet-based casinos. This is an example of consumer behavior modification as a result of new technological advances,—the internet. This phenomenon is sometimes referred to as **disruptive technologies** because they change the status quo of prior established product and service offerings.

Psychological Core: External and Internal Inputs

The study of consumer behavior begins with external forces that a person cannot control, such as culture, social environment, economy, and laws. Culture refers to the typical or expected behaviors, norms, and ideas that characterize a group of people. The cultural environment also affects the motivations of consumers, and the kinds of consumption decisions they make. Consumer culture is influenced by many variables, such as religious affinity, educational level, and peer group recommendations. For example, some religions frown on any type of gambling activities.[1] For some, this relates to the Puritan work ethic that describes work as everything. If you do not work for something, it cannot be good. Therefore, pleasure for its own sake is distrusted. This especially applies to gambling. Under the Puritan work ethic, gambling is not considered work because most people enjoy it.

There is also societal resistance to casino marketing that targets specific demographic groups, such as youth and seniors. Overall, in American culture, norms and values have slowly changed over time from seeing gambling as an evil, immoral activity to seeing it as recreation. Therefore, more people have included going to a casino as part of their social lives, which has been made possible because of the legal and political environments that have changed the laws to adapt to new economic and social conditions. For example, when casinos were first proposed, 58 percent of community leaders were generally positive about the impact of casinos, 18 percent were ambivalent, and 24 percent were negative. However, when asked how casinos have lived up to their expectations, 58 percent said the impact was better than expected, 31 percent remained unchanged, and 9 percent thought it was worse than their original projects.[2] These various external forces impact a person's internal attitudes and values. When a person thinks about gambling, all of these ideas about what other people will think and how they will react are combined with the person's **internal core attitudes**. The psychological make up of an individual filters the external information and blends it with his or her personality. This include initial exposure, motivation, ability, perception, and opportunity to create a judgment.

The Process of Decision Making

There are four stages of the consumer decision-making process: problem recognition, information search, decision making, and postpurchase evaluation. For casino consumers, this process might begin by a friend wanting company when he or she goes to the casino. The invitation might spark a search for further information on the internet, from a travel agent, or from another information source. This would be followed by deciding whether or not to purchase the casino product, and from where (i.e., direct purchase from the casino, travel agent, or electronic commerce). Once the person makes the decision, there is a postpurchase evaluation called **cognitive dissonance**, during which the person asks whether or not it was the right decision. This phase would include conducting further searching for information on the product or experience, and/or evaluating the purchase after the actual casino product has been experienced (the post casino trip). This is a crucial stage for casinos. It is important to know that cognitive

Figure 6–1 On May 26, 1978, people wait in a line 3 blocks long on the boardwalk to get their chance at the gambling tables and slot machines at Resorts International casino.

dissonance (or the after-decision evaluation) will determine whether the patron returns. This is the stage at which the person makes a judgment about the experience and whether it was worth the time and money.

Depending on the person's location, a decision to go to a casino may be a simple choice of recreation or a complex vacation choice. So, how do people make recreation decisions as part of their everyday lives? First, they must decide which recreation activities they would like to spend their money on. A day trip to a casino must compete with all the other activities people engage in during the week. How does gaming fit into daily life? What are the reasons for people choosing gaming when they plan their activities?

Whenever people go out for fun, they must agree on the decision, whether it is to go to a casino or the movies or to dinner. A couple will discuss what movies are playing and whether they want to go see them, whether they want to go out with friends or by themselves to celebrate an occasion, or go to a casino for some excitement. For our example, let us assume that they decide to visit a casino. On the way home after the casino visit, the couple talk about how much they won or lost, and whether they should have left earlier or later. This entire scenario is the consumer decision-making process. The problem recognition stage occurred when the couple first thought about going out; the information search stage began as they thought about where to go; during the decision-making stage, they actually made the decision; and the postpurchase evaluation stage occurred during their discussion as they were coming back home.

The majority of the people who walk into a casino will have a good time, lose some money, and leave without any problem. It is like going out to dinner. Each dining experience depends on the service received that night. If you have a bad experience, you do not go back to that restaurant, or you do not go out to dinner for a while. It is not a continuous experience like other forms of recreation; you plan an evening out. To begin the "meal," you start off with an appetizer (like slots) and then move to the main course (say blackjack). Once you have finished the main activity, you might play a little keno or hit the slots again as a small "dessert" before heading out the door.

As with any service, the client's experience and satisfaction are individual. The virtual reality of the casino is in the mind of the patron. It is important to remember that this virtual reality can be easily altered by a bad experience or an unpleasant dealer. Understanding the consumer decision process helps the marketer decide where to intervene in the process. For example, an advertising campaign should ideally generate excitement and anticipation that the casino is the only activity choice and there is no need for an information search. Therefore, gamblers will go from problem recognition straight through to purchase without any of the steps in between. This is the best possible scenario because it means that we have a brand loyal customer.

In this section, we explored some of the ways that consumers make decisions about casinos. These examples are not true for everyone, but they do provide food for thought. Since gaming has proliferated, there are more possibilities for leisure activity. It used to be that gambling meant going to Las Vegas, which meant a vacation trip or convention. Now with riverboats, Native American casinos, and state-sanctioned land-based operations, day trips are gambling options. Day trips also compete with other forms of recreation. You cannot play golf and spend the whole day at the casino. If you go to the casino at night, you may have chosen gambling over going to the movies. This is a different process than deciding on where to go for a vacation; therefore, different marketing strategies are used. It is important to understand the factors that go into a person's decision-making process. Knowing how people make decisions and what factors they use to judge their experiences is key information to developing a good product that sells.

The "Why" of Consumer Behavior in Casino Management: Perspectives on Gambling Motivation

Humans have always had a gambling streak. Down through the ages, every culture and every social stratum have played games of chance. There is something about the luck of the draw or the throw of the dice that attracts the risk-taking urge. People are drawn to gamble—note the common saying, "Ya wanna bet?" Why do we use that saying in all different types of situations? It has been theorized that since life was a big gamble, primitive humans found a fascination with gambling as divination and primitive justice. To some degree, it made life a little less of a risk. Unpredictable events could be made predictable by throwing a die. This control issue is a powerful motivation for many people.

It has only been since the early 1900s that theorists have tried to answer the question of why people gamble. More people have become interested in gambling behavior as Americans embrace the idea of casinos. For example, the average gambler spent $87.17 in a commercial casino in 2003. Americans spent more in commercial casinos last year than they did on going to amusement parks and the movies combined. In fact, more than 53.4 million Americans visited casinos in 2003, compared with 51.2 million in 2002. That works out to an average of 5.8 casino trips per gambler. Gamblers also make up 26 percent of the U.S. adult population.[3] The majority of consumer behavior research in the casino gambling field has been based on the study of five subdisciplines: economics, sociology, psychoanalytic theory, psychology, and the interdisciplinary nature of work and play leisure.

Economics

Economists believe that people are rational beings. Humans evaluate all the alternatives before making a decision. Therefore, one theory about gambling behavior is that people do not know the probabilities of winning; otherwise, they would not gamble, since the odds are in the casino's favor. A rational person would not deliberately make the choice to gamble knowing that he or she was likely to lose. However, this is too simplistic an explanation, and it does not explain the reality that there are many people who know the odds and still bet.

A possible explanation can be found in Veblen's theory of conspicuous consumption. Historically, it was the rich aristocrats who were allowed to gamble. Gambling was a sign of wealth; therefore, it has been suggested that members of affluent classes gamble to demonstrate their social standing ("I am rich enough to lose all this money"). Another theory revolves around the personality traits of the gambler. People who avoid risk would not gamble; however, if they did, they would underestimate the true probabilities of a loss and overestimate the chance to win. For example, "I have my lucky shirt on today, so I'm sure to hit big." Milton Friedman developed the "utility of wealth" theory. He said that rational people will gamble if they place a high enough value on the chance of achieving wealth. The utility of winning outweighs the misfortune of losing; in other words, a person realizes the true probabilities, but he or she wants the rewards so much that he or she will risk losing. As you can see, economists have tried to explain what draws people to betting.

Sociology

Cotte found that the motives underlying gambling have been studied within many social science disciplines.[4] It is not surprising that sociologists would study gambling because it is concerned with the social rules and processes that bind and separate people not only as individuals, but as members of associations, groups, and institutions. Early sociologists saw gambling as a deviant act, and, therefore, to gamble was rebelling against society, but not a major breach of the social value system. Later sociologists explained that people who were frustrated and rebellious could find in gambling a quasi-acceptable safety valve from the contradictions and stresses of the social value system.

Figure 6–2 Multiethnic group of people plays craps and gambles at blackjack tables at Players Casino, Lake Charles Louisiana.

Therefore, gambling was seen to act as a safety valve for societal tensions. It allowed people to blow off steam and be rebellious, yet still function as a person in society.

In 1951, Bloch claimed that gambling was a retreat from the routine boredom of modern industrial life.[5] It was fun to break the rules and take a chance. It was an opportunity to take on a different role in life, and a great release from the social sanctions that made it easier to go back to routine daily existence. Additional theories suggested that game participants receive temporary satisfaction unavailable in their everyday work environments; people who were not successful at their jobs could be winners at cards. Erving Goffman called gambling a surrogate for risk taking.[6] After working as a dealer in Reno, he suggested that gamblers could show courage, integrity, composure, and other character strengths that could not be demonstrated on the job or in normal life. We admire people who take risks and win; it proves one's superiority and mastery over life. To challenge and overcome an obstacle is a true test of one's strength, skill, endurance or ingenuity. It is part of our heritage as pioneers; thus, we encourage individualism.

In 1977, Ivan Light came up with an unusual twist to the value of numbers gambling among African Americans.[7] Light said that the numbers game was not a deviant activity, but an alternative form of investment. Fundamentally, banks combine savings from depositors to create a fund for loans to improve the community. The numbers game provided the same function for the poor. The numbers game takes the savings from the poor and then returns this money in the form of loans to the community at a high interest rate. Therefore, playing the numbers is a form of forced savings because the money comes back to the poor.

Felicia Campbell devised a theory related to people in nursing homes.[8] She believed that gambling is part of normal human behavior. Furthermore, gambling would provide stimulation to the patients during their days at the nursing home. She advocated the placement of slot machines in nursing homes to improve the people's quality of life. Playing the slots would get people excited and increase adrenaline. As a result, blood flow would increase, which would help circulation. In addition to the health benefits, the nursing home residents would have a reason to get up in the morning and they would have fun during their day. As you can imagine, these suggestions were met with a great deal of controversy.

Psychoanalytic Theory

Psychoanalytic theory is a general term for a psychiatric model that can be applied to the study of gambling. Sigmund Freud, Melanie Klein, and Jacques Lacan the most prominent thinkers within psychoanalytic theory. In the early 1900s, psychiatrists attributed excessive gambling to a person's sex drive. The first known psychoanalytic study of gambling was conducted by H. Von Hattingberg in 1914.[9] After studying one addicted gambling patient, he concluded that the patient suffered from a generalized psychosexual inadequacy. In other words, problem gamblers had not successfully matured past their adolescent stage. Once this diagnosis was made, it became a common thread in gambling motivation. In 1920, Ernst Simmel concluded that the motivation for problem gamblers was the desire to achieve autoerotic gratification, meaning that there is a sexual thrill when a person wins.[10] Gambling thus becomes a replacement for the real thing. Freud agreed with this diagnosis and added that gambling was a self-punishment that stemmed from the Oedipal complex, a stage when young boys have to choose a sexual role model. During this time, they want to eliminate their father, so that they can be the sole person in their mother's life. For people who never matured beyond the Oedipal stage, this conflict leads them to lose everything at the casino in order to punish themselves for their bad thoughts. Robert LaForgue argued that gamblers found pleasure in the pain of losing and that psychic masochism was the reason people gambled.[11] Winning was also thus symbolic for forgiveness.

Psychology

Psychology (from the ancient Greek *psyche* = soul and *logos* = word) is the study of behavior, mind, and thought. The field of psychology has offered many different theories about why people gamble and why they chase after losses. Two of the simplest theories are that (1) life is boring and the excitement of the game confirms that one is alive and (2) people want to win money. The first theory would explain Tom and Mary's experiences from the opening paragraphs of this chapter. The second theory is straight greed, to which we can all relate. Both of these theories are based on universal needs, which may explain why there is no demographic profile or combination of personality characteristics that can isolate potential gamblers.

Applying general psychological theories to gambling offers a series of gambling motives. *Attribution theory* suggests that people attribute their success to themselves, their skill, or their luck. For example, a gambler is on a winning streak or his or her luck is hot tonight. The losses are blamed on something else. Losses occur because the dealer is crooked, a companion has bad karma, the moon is in the wrong phase, or any other reason that comes to mind. Because losses are not the player's fault, it is easy to forget them or write them off as a fluke. It has been suggested that men tend to use this type of attribution more than women. Research indicates that women are more likely to explain winning on outside factors. They might explain winning as "my good fairy was with me" or "the slot machine was ready to hit and I happened by." On the other hand, losing tends to be attributed to a personal failure. "I picked the wrong machine," or "I have a bad luck streak running today." This kind of thinking may explain why males' perceptions of winnings are higher than females' perceptions. Both views tend to be inflated. This attribution of wins and losses allows people to believe that they have some kind of control over their fate. A feeling of control is important to gamblers. Also, younger gamers have more of a feeling of control, which is why they tend to have greater win perceptions than older players. If you listen to people talk about their gambling experiences, they talk about the big win they had, not about how much they played and lost before they won the pot. People keep a running tab of their wins, but few ever keep track of their losses. This little game we play in our minds keeps us feeling like tomorrow is another day to win. The big score is just around the corner.

Behaviorists believe that these mental games are normal, but it is really what people do and how they behave that is important. Given a particular stimulus, people are programmed to respond in the same way each time. This response pattern is based on the person's previous reinforcement to a stimulus. Sam puts a coin in a slot machine, and he is rewarded with a "hit." This sets up a pattern of behavior. People like Sam continue to put coins in the slot so that they can be positively reinforced with a jackpot. Skinner developed schedules of reinforcement to show how animals behave when rewards are programmed.[12] In his experiments, he used a **variable reinforcement schedule**, which means that rewards were given at totally random times. The reaction of the animals to this stimulus-response cycle was predictable. The birds rapidly hit a key without slowing down until they were rewarded. Then they immediately began the cycle again. If you have ever watched people play at two or three machines at a time, you may notice a resemblance to Skinner's experiments.

Interdisciplinary Study of Play and Leisure

Interdisciplinary work integrates concepts across different disciplines. The casino gaming industry is a complex and multifaceted interdisciplinary field. Understanding the needs, wants, and motivations of both casino patrons and nonpatrons is essential for the continued growth and success of this industry. Today, thanks to Steve Wynn, visiting a casino or riverboat is perceived as play and leisure. Casino gaming competes with many other forms of play and leisure activities. Americans made nearly three times as many trips to casinos during 2003 as they did to professional baseball games (310 million trips to casinos versus 106.5 million trips to baseball games).[13] Understanding the leisure preferences of casino patrons can enable the industry to position itself as a viable alternative to other competing forms of leisure activities.

What makes a person pick a casino destination versus Disneyland? When competing with other vacation spots, casinos can compete based on affordable rooms and inexpensive good food. Many locations have great entertainment both on stage and off. Places such as Las Vegas have every type of tourist attraction a person could want: art museums, amusement parks, theatre, cultural events, and shopping. In addition, players take a shot at changing their lives when they sit down at a table or a slot machine. Gambling is the only recreation that could allow a person literally to walk away in a different economic position in life.

Motivation

Motives for gambling can be broadly categorized into three general groups: economic, symbolic, and pleasure seeking. A common-sense answer to what motivates gamblers is the economic motive: gamblers are in it for the money. However, several writers have

Figure 6–3
Courtesy of Isle of Capri
Casino Resort.

suggested that the role of money is usually not central; money simply makes gambling more important. In other words, gamblers view the risk of potentially losing money as acceptable, because the chance of winning additional money is enough incentive to partake in gambling activities.

Some of the symbolic motives for gambling behavior include risk taking, maintaining a symbolic sense of control over one's destiny, and symbolically replacing love or sexual desire. In the West, the lives most people lead lack the opportunity for this action. For many of us, serious risk taking on a daily basis has been eliminated through technological advances and progress. Gambling is a way to be tested, and the motivation is to voluntarily submit to risk and perform under pressure as a symbolic gesture of risk taking. Gambling also allows people to exercise some symbolic sense of control that the social system will not ordinarily permit, and it gives them the freedom to make decisions. Thus, gambling is a way for the underdog to symbolically attack the gambling system without far-reaching implications for the stability of the social system.

Rather than symbolic or economic motives, other gambling researchers have taken a pleasure-seeking stance. These researchers suggested that gambling is pursued for purely pleasurable reasons, including positive reinforcement, self-esteem enhancement, and pure pleasure seeking or play.

These three theories of gambling behavioral decisions provide an excellent framework for casino marketers to consider. Some gambling consumers might be motivated by just one of these three motivational attributes; others might be motivated by a combination of them. Casino marketing activities should feature a broad base of marketing strategies and messages to appeal to the broadest number of motivational attributes affecting gambling consumers' purchase decisions. This can be accomplished by highly segmented and targeted marketing messages or more broad-based marketing messages that might appeal to the greatest number of purchase intentions possible. One of the inherent dangers of broad-based marketing programs is the potential to send conflicting marketing messages unintentionally. This can occur when broadly focused marketing activities appeal to certain subsegments, while simultaneously alienating others.

Casino marketers must stay abreast of overall consumer behavior trends to minimize the possibility of this unintended negative outcome.

The "Who" of Consumer Behavior in Casino Management: Player Demographics

As we said earlier, there is no single demographic or psychographic profile that allows casinos to say "this is who gambles." All kinds of people from all walks of life and all socioeconomic levels gamble. However, we can discuss some generalities about gamblers. More than 53 million American adults (about 26 percent of those 21 and older) made 310 million casino visits in 2003.[14] We also know that

- The median household income of U.S. casino gamblers ($53,204) is 16 percent higher than that of nongamblers ($45,781).
- Americans in upper income brackets have the highest casino gambling participation rates and those in the lowest income brackets have the lowest casino participation rates. Nearly a third (32 percent) of individuals with household incomes of more than $95,000 gambled in a casino in 2003, while only 20 percent of those with annual incomes of less than $35,000 gambled in a casino.
- More than three-quarters of casino players own their homes, compared to 71 percent of nongamblers.
- The typical casino player is about the same age as the typical American: the median age of casino gamblers is 48 versus 46 for the adult U.S. population.
- The age bracket with the highest casino participation rate is the "empty nest" years of 51 to 65 (29 percent).
- Casino players are more likely than the national average to hold white-collar jobs: 44 percent versus 41 percent.

From these demographics, it would appear that there is a relationship between income and financial security and the number of visits and amount of spending by players.

Types

There are three broad types of gamblers: recreational, occupational, and compulsive. **Recreational gamblers** view gambling as a leisure time pursuit. They can be anywhere from "high rollers" (large spenders on gambling activities) to "low rollers" (minimal spenders). This segment regards the gambling experience as another form of recreation within their individual lifestyles. Gambling activities will rank as just one of a possible bundle of other recreational activities, such as shopping, sports, and hobbies. Obviously, this is the largest group, the majority of the people who enter a casino.

On the other hand, **occupational gamblers** believe that their skills will enable them to make money by gambling. They use a rational process with special bank accounts for gambling and file IRS tax returns on their winnings. They spend a great deal of time learning probabilities of games and attend workshops that give mathematical calculations on the newest games. Some professional gamblers are indeed able to live off their winnings; however, this is obviously not a low stress, sustainable employment strategy for most individuals.

Finally, a small percentage of people are **compulsive gamblers**. They may also live by gambling; however, they more likely live *for* gambling, continuing to gamble obsessively even as losses mount. For these bettors, gambling is not a rational process, and, typically, they may steal to support their habit, create family crises, and have high job insecurity.

Casino marketers need to adopt different strategies, channels, and messages for these three segment types of gamblers. For example, recreational gamblers do not generally have a strong loyalty to casino gambling as an activity. To this segment, casino gaming is just one of many recreational opportunity options available to them. When making the casino purchase/nonpurchase decision, this segment would typically weigh the costs and benefits of the casino experience with other forms of recreation. Additional marketing stimulation might be required to secure a commitment to a gaming purchase decision rather than one of the many other discretionary recreational purchase options available for the recreational gambler. The marketing emphasis here is focused on luring these individuals away from competing casinos through initiatives such as loyalty programs, comps, and other recognition and rewards programs and initiatives. These programs also have the added benefit of increasing the average amount spent by customers per casino visit. Recreational gamblers also offer casino marketers the greatest future potential of market expansion, compared to occupational or compulsive gamblers, who usually require less marketing stimulation than recreational gamblers. Casino patrons who are occupational or compulsive gamblers already have a vested interest in the casino industry. Typically, casinos will work with family and friends by barring compulsive gamblers from the property. They also have created programs and work with different groups to get help for these individuals.

Lifestyle—Psychographics

Psychographics describe a consumer's personality, lifestyle, values, and attitudes. Differences in psychographics will, in turn, influence buyer behavior through variables such as the product and service benefits sought, product usage rate, brand loyalty, readiness to buy, and the decision-making process. A common myth is that gamblers tend to be independent, financially unstable, and of a lower social class. However, studies such as Harrah's annual report repeatedly have dispelled long-standing myths about gamblers' lifestyles, socioeconomic status, and level of community involvement.[15]

Figure 6–4 Does your lifestyle include traveling? You can go to New York, New York itself or to Las Vegas to New York, New York Hotel and Casino. Photo courtesy of George G. Fenich.

Casino gamblers tend to be more connected to community groups, particularly volunteer, fraternal, union, and political groups, while nongamblers are more active in religious groups. With very few exceptions, casino gamblers have greater confidence than nongamblers in government, business and other institutions, such as the military, banks/financial institutions, local law enforcement, the U.S. Supreme Court, public schools, organized labor, and the criminal justice system. More than 40 percent of both gamblers and nongamblers think there is too much government regulation of individuals' behaviors. Casino gamblers are also politically active. Surveys have revealed that gamblers are more likely than nongamblers to have contributed money to a political candidate or cause (26 percent versus 19 percent) and to have signed a petition in support of a political candidate or cause (51 percent versus 42 percent) in the past four years. In no category of political activism were nongamblers shown to be more engaged than casino gamblers.[16]

Casino gamblers utilize a variety of financial investment products, are relatively comfortable with their financial standing, and have a greater inclination toward saving and investment than the overall population. For example, gamblers are more likely than nongamblers to have a variety of investments, including savings accounts, life insurance, retirement/pension plans, mutual funds, stocks, real estate, money market accounts, certificates of deposit, bonds, and annuities. Gamblers are more likely to be comfortable with their financial standing as they age; whereas nongamblers are more likely to worry they will not have adequate funds for retirement. When making financial and investment decisions, gamblers are more inclined than nongamblers to seek expert advice and reference a broad array of resources. If presented with a large sum of money, gamblers are more likely to save or invest it, while nongamblers are more inclined to use the money to pay off debt.

Perhaps because of the financial security and involvement in the world around them, two out of three casino gamblers take at least one long vacation trip per year, while less than half of nongamblers do. Casino gamblers like to travel in style and are more likely than nongamblers to book upscale accommodations when they vacation. These data from Harrah's consumer questionnaires would suggest that people who go to a casino are politically and socially involved and financially sound. Because they have the discretionary money to satisfy their wants and needs, they gamble as part of their recreational lifestyles.

Special Case: Casino Poker Players—The World Series of Poker Survey Highlights

As we discuss demographic and psychographic profiles of gamblers, we should examine World Series poker players. This type of play has become a major televised recreational venture. These professionals have played poker for an average of 24 years, while most amateurs have been playing for an average of 23 years. Since gamblers have typically been male, it is not so surprising that 95 percent of professional and 98 percent of amateur players are men. Obviously, money is the primary reason professionals play poker, but only 41 percent of amateurs also say that they play for the money. Thirty-two percent of professionals and 39 percent of amateurs say they play for the challenge. Professionals believe that tournament play is 66 percent skill and 34 percent luck; amateurs believe tournament play is 65 percent skill and 35 percent luck. No Limit Texas Hold 'Em is the favorite game among both professionals and amateurs. However, more than half of World Series of Poker players enjoy playing other table games at the casino. About a quarter also play slots and place bets in the sportsbook.[17]

Special Case: College Students

Since the majority of this textbook's users are postsecondary institution learners, it should be interesting to explore the segment of college students who gamble.[18] The overall prevalence rate for pathological gambling ranged from 4.78 percent to 11.1 percent. The highest rate was in a Las Vegas research study. One explanation for that higher rate may be that the Las Vegas metropolitan area provides more exposure to gambling opportunities than do most other cities. When the motives for college students' gambling were compared with motives for other recreational activities, a couple of important findings emerged. First, recreational student gamblers wanted to be with their friends, and so being with similar people was in the top five motives for both

Figure 6–5 Professional poker players studying their hands at the Normandie Casino in Gardena, California.

recreational and gambling activities. However, pathological student gamblers had dissimilar motives for engaging in recreational and gambling activities. For pathological student gamblers, only the motive of excitement was rated in the top five motives for both recreational and gambling activities. Although gambling can be a highly motivating recreational activity, it does not appear to be the highest motivating recreational activity for either pathological or recreational student gamblers. This finding could serve as a cautionary note for the casino gaming industry. Clearly, respondents in this study perceived gambling to be "just one" of many potential recreational activities available for their discretionary time and income use, and gambling ranked lower than other competing recreational activities in terms of importance.

The "What" of Consumer Behavior in Casino Management: Games

All kinds of people from all walks of life and all socioeconomic levels gamble. However, the reason people play different games tends to be more predictable. According to a study by Lowenhar and Boykin,[19] slots play is exciting and people drop coins to have a good time. It is probably not surprising to know that slot/video poker machines are the most popular game among both men and women, with 66 percent of male and 81 percent of female gamblers reporting they play electronic gaming machines the most often. On the other hand, men prefer table games by a margin of more than two to one to women (20 percent to 8 percent), with blackjack/21 the single most popular table game. Younger adults are most likely to play table games, with 18 percent of 21- to 35-year-olds reporting that they play table games most often. However, people play keno to pass the time while waiting for a meal or something else to happen.

The "Where" of Consumer Behavior in Casino Management: Places

Not surprisingly, the top two U.S. casino markets in revenue for 2004 were Las Vegas and Atlantic City. However, Chicagoland, Ind./Ill., was third, followed by Connecticut; Tunica, Ms; and Detroit [20]. Additionally, the top six casino markets had total gross gaming revenues exceeding $1 billion and were located in different regions of the country. In looking at the broad scope of casino visitations, 35 percent of the visits were in the West, with the North Central part of the country having 25 percent of the visitors. However, the West dropped 3 percent from the previous years, where the other three regions gained 1 percent.

Internet-Based Casinos

Although technology is rapidly changing, baby boomers often resist changing their ways with the times, while younger generations embrace technology because they have grown up "with a mouse surgically attached to their hands." This could present additional marketing challenges for traditional "bricks-and-mortar" casinos, while creating new marketing opportunities for internet-based casinos. Technology is now available to bring real-time electronic casino activities to the display panels of consumers' cell phones. This makes casino gaming activities available 24 hours a day from anywhere on the planet.

Ongoing advances in internet and online technologies, such as the rapid increase in high-speed broadband services, have led to a significant increase in the number of internet-based casinos. The first internet casino was opened in 1995 by Internet Casinos, Inc. (ICI). While it might cost $300 million to build a new resort casino, which employs thousands, ICI's virtual casino was developed for only $1.5 million and employs just 17 individuals.[21] The financial allure is enormous. ICI has received more than 40,000 registrations for its service since its inception and records more than 7 million visits per month at its site. With more than $500 billion spent on legal and illegal gambling in the United States alone in 1993, with more than 90 percent of adults participating in some form of gambling, the market for in-home gambling was estimated to be $49 billion worldwide by 1998.

Pervasive online gambling will probably increase other forms of gambling, including illegal gaming activities. Data have shown that when gambling is legalized, the number of dollars spent by compulsive gamblers on total gambling activities doubles. Rather than diverting funds from other forms of gaming, it simply draws new players into the market. Kindt postulated that once a form of gambling is legalized, the "thrill" is generally lost, and the illegal gamblers must then move their dollars into harder forms of gambling.[22] Potentially, the same might occur once basic casino games become ubiquitous online.

Putting It All Together: Factors Used in Consumer Behavior and Decision Making

On average, the number of rooms used by leisure travelers is steadily increasing, especially in the baby-boomer and Generation X segments, and, better yet, travelers are going back to longer leisure stays. Multigenerational vacationers, for example, require a greater variety of amenities for all age groups. The trend is toward the consumer's inclusion of cultural experiences on trips. However, Generation X leisure travelers are looking for the most "untouched, exotic, authentic, and remote" locations. Intimate atmospheres and personalization in products and service are important to them, so it is difficult to obtain repeat visits. On the other hand, value-added packaged vacations continue to be strong for all leisure travelers. Some gambling destinations, especially Las Vegas, had experienced a significant expansion of smaller, more personalized noncasino hotels. Some guests may prefer staying in noncasino properties to avoid the factory-like mass tourism experience perceived at the mega-gambling resorts. While these guests might still visit the casino properties for gambling, entertainment, or other purchases, the casino hotels still stand to lose a significant portion of the total revenue expenditures (such as rooms, food, and beverages) of these guests.

The current market focus has switched to the higher-yielding upscale gambling market, with an emphasis on supporting upscale services, such as designer label shopping and gourmet restaurants. So, to attract visitors, the purchase channel of choice for the emerging leisure travel segments is the internet. To attract these visitors, a Web site that draws repeat guests with new, unique, and changing offers with value is needed.

Younger generations have a completely different world perspective than Boomers do (Figure 6–6). The average Nintendo user of yesterday is 29 years old today, gets bored easily, and is less "tradition" oriented. Younger consumers have a higher propensity for more intellectually challenging casino table games, while older gamblers are more likely to choose slot machines.

Retirement at age 65 is also coming to an end because of the rise of pension problems and the fact that people are healthier and more active than they used to be. As a result, many people over 65 want to continue to work, and the fact is that the skills of older people are needed in the marketplace. Although this trend could work in favor

Figure 6–6 The Hard Rock Hotel and Casino in Las Vegas caters to the younger gamblers. Courtesy of George G. Fenich.

of casinos because of an expanded labor pool of potential employees, the overall impact could be negative as seniors represent a significant portion of casino consumers.

However, despite all the consumer behavior information and trends, fundamentally, a casino is a casino is a casino. They all have slot machines, video games, and tables. Some have new, different games, but casino floors feel and sound pretty much the same. So, the question is, "Why do consumers pick one casino over another?" Part of the answer is the concept of **players' clubs.** Casinos have developed a way of tracking each player so it can offer comps to get gamblers into the system. However, a player may be a member of more than one casino's players' club. As a result, many different casinos will send their newsletters and coupons to the same person. This creates a consumer who is a smarter, more value-oriented casino comp shopper. For example, two couples were sitting at a table talking during dinner, planning their next trip to the casinos. Sam was talking about the comps for rooms that he and Sue had. Paul agreed that was a good rooms package and much better than he and Ann had. Next, everyone evaluated their food and beverage comps to find the best deals. This planning process went on for most of dinner. If this sounds like the same kind of shopping behavior that you do during a sale or when you use coupons at the grocery stores, it is. With the frequent player programs at all the casinos, the consumer literally can pick and choose the best buys. As a result, consumer loyalty has been lost in favor of economic utility.

How do casinos win customer loyalty? How can they differentiate their house from the other houses on the block? Service. The characteristics that separate a service from a durable good can be classified as the four "I's" of service: intangibility, inseparability, inventory, and inconsistency. The fact that the product is *intangible* means that the consumer has a mental image of the product, but it cannot be substantiated by the five senses. In other words, it cannot be packaged and taken home. *Inseparability* and *inconsistency* refer to the fact that the product cannot be separated from the provider. The line personnel, not management, interact directly with the customer every time. Therefore, the experiences created by the dealer or wait staff become the virtual reality of the casino experience. *Inventory* refers to the fact that once the visit has occurred, it is over. For example, you have 100 slot machines, but only 50 are played tonight. What happens to the other 50? Can you store those 50 and have 150 tomorrow? Of course not;

that is what we mean by the lack of inventory. Therefore the experiences and perceptions created during each visit to the casino are the image of the product. The casino must create positive feelings every visit. One bad experience can alter mental perceptions of the casino.

Every casino has tables, slots, restrooms, and bars. Most have a buffet for a quick bite to eat and a clean room for the night. These are the basic expectations that a person assumes will be met. For example, on one trip we checked into the hotel for the night and went upstairs to unpack before venturing into the casino. The room was clean, but the cigarette smoke odor was so strong we could hardly breathe. Luckily, we were able to get a smoke-free room and we made the switch. What would have happened if the front desk had told us that there were no nonsmoking rooms available? We would have immediately checked out and never returned. On another day, we went to a riverboat to play the slots. It was so crowded that each machine had a waiting line. The casino did not have enough capacity to meet demand that day. We left. What would you do? Would you stand in line waiting for a machine? Would you leave? If you left, would you go back? These illustrations point out the problems when basic expectations are not met. Most of the time, the player moves on to the next casino and never looks back.

Suppose that during this routine stay the staff is friendlier and the operations are more efficient and better run than the casino next door. What value would be added to this experience? For example, an elderly woman freezes at the escalator. Impatient irate people begin to form a line waiting for her to move. What would you do? One quick-thinking security person walked over with a big smile, offered her hand, and asked, "Need Company?" She proceeded to help the woman onto the first step and then rode down with her. As they chatted and laughed, the elderly woman relaxed and got off the escalator without any problem. How would this incident affect the woman's decision the next time? Do you think she will be more likely to go back to the friendly casino with the nice security person?

You may say, "But the comps make the difference." They will change the value added to the experience. This is true to a certain extent. The thing to remember about any type of discounting is that if it is done too often, consumers begin to change their expectations about the value of the product that is offered. For example, if I can get a 2-for-1 coupon every time I go to dinner for the next three months, the value of that dinner will be equated with this half price. When the coupon is no longer available, my perception will be that the price of the product has just doubled. Therefore, I may say that the product is too expensive for the value I am getting.

Have you heard of "green stamps"? Grocers used to give out these stamps each time you made a purchase. The stamps were pasted in a book. When you had enough stamped books, you could redeem them for nongrocery items. But you do not know about green stamps because they are obsolete. Eventually everyone gave stamps, and so the competitive advantage was lost. Green stamps and comps are very much alike.

Conclusion

Knowledge of consumer behaviors is critical for the casino gaming industry to tailor products and services that will appeal to casino gamblers. Conversely, this information will also provide valuable insights on the types of communications, lifestyle values, attitudes, and behaviors that would be viewed negatively by casino gamblers. Knowing what "turns on" and "turns off" the casino gambling consumer is critical for the success of the casino industry. Casino marketers can use this demographic and psychographic information to establish the optimum mix of products and services for casino gamblers. This information also provides insights into the appropriate communication methods and messages that should be used to appeal to the casino gambling market.

Savvy casino industry operators monitor overall consumer behavior trends very carefully for cues in maintaining and developing new marketing and operational strategies. Many consumer behavior trends can be observed from simple observation of emerging societal trends. For example, the current popularity of so-called "reality shows" on television is probably an excellent indicator of a major groundswell of public interest in forms of escapism from the realities of an increasingly complicated world environment. Casino gambling is well positioned to take advantage of this same trend toward escapism as casinos offer respite from the real world. Have you ever tried to find a clock in a casino? The reason that clocks are not found anywhere inside a casino is that operators do not want casino patrons to know what time it is, as perceived time shortages might prompt a patron to finish playing and focus instead on a non–casino-related activity, such as work or family obligations.

This chapter has explored many areas of consumer behavior. We began by looking at a case study of two retired people. How they started gambling and why they continue is an important question for the study of consumer behavior. From the example, we know how they started. It began as a social event with friends and family. Why did they escalate their visits and change their strategies? This takes a little more comprehensive thought. We began to explore different theories of motivation. Why do people gamble? Is it a simple explanation of greed? Or are there other factors that persuade people to bet? Each of the different disciplines had a rationale for gambling. Perhaps it is a combination of all these ideas.

We then explored who gambles, what games do they play, where do they go, and how do they decide and what factors do they use? As strategies are selected to move the casino forward, it is important to understand the reasons people bet. As you understand the client more and more, decisions can be made that focus on the satisfaction of the customer. In satisfying your players, you give them a reason to return.

Understanding consumer behavior is one of the fundamental concepts for success in the casino management industry. Consumer behavior is dynamic and changing. Therefore, keeping abreast of consumer behavior trends is critical for success. Methods of tracking consumer behavior in casino gambling include industry conferences and events; industry trade associations; industry trade publications; the popular press (i.e., *USA Today*, CNN), and specialty sources, such as hospitality, tourism, and marketing industry websites.

Casino marketers must understand the underlying needs, wants, motivations, and aspirations of their patrons. These changes can be affected by many factors, including demographic variables such as age, income, occupation, education level, and place of residency. Changes can also be affected by numerous psychographic factors, such as motivations, aspirations, lifestyle, and beliefs.

Consumers are also faced with an ever-expanding range of choices in their everyday leisure activities. Casino marketers must compete with all other forms of leisure activities, including hobbies, shopping, sports, and other travel-related options. Consumers also face a future with considerably more choices and options within the casino gaming industry. Traditional gambling casinos have now spread to the majority of state and provincial jurisdictions within North America. Additionally, consumers can now also visit online casinos available 24 hours a day to anyone with an internet hookup. For consumers unable to access the internet, new services are rapidly becoming available that use cellular telephones for casino gaming by combining the telephone number keypad and the visual display screen.

Readers of this book represent the future of casino gambling management. You will face an ever-increasing competitive environment in which consumers will be more boldly empowered to choose their casino gambling options from a broad spectrum of traditional casinos plus distribution services, many of which (i.e. Internet, cell phone) could not have been envisioned even 20 years ago. Casino operators who establish superior competencies in the domain of consumer behavior will have a significant competitive advantage over peer operators who lack this critical skill set.

key terms

Consumer behavior	Recreational gamblers
Disruptive technologies	Occupational gamblers
Internal core attitudes	Compulsive gamblers
Cognitive dissonance	Psychographics
Variable reinforcement schedule	Players' club

review questions

1. In the study of consumer behavior, which aspects of purchase decisions are considered?

2. What does the study of consumer behavior begin with?

3. What are the four stages of the consumer decision-making process?

4. The majority of consumer behavior research in the casino gambling field has been based on the study of which five subdisciplines?

5. Why do sociologists study gambling?

6. What are the two simplest theories offered by the field of psychology as to why people gamble and why they chase after losses?

7. Motives for gambling can be broadly categorized into three general groups; what are these three groups?

8. Which income brackets of Americans have the highest casino gambling participation rates, and which income brackets have the lowest?

9. Which segment of gamblers offers casino marketers the greatest future potential of market expansion compared to the other two segments?

10. Why do consumers pick one casino over another?

11. How do casinos win customer loyalty? How can they differentiate their house from the other houses on the block?

12. What is the reason that clocks are not found anywhere inside a casino?

internet sites

PSI CHI: The National Honor Society in Psychology
http://www.psichi.org/pubs/articles/

The New School—Psychoanalytical theory
http://cepa.newschool.edu/~quigleyt/vcs/psychoanalysis.html

DePaul University—Psychographics
http://www.lib.depaul.edu/eresource/subject_search_infotype.asp?TopicID
=49&SubjectID=34

Ontario Problem Gambling Research Center
http://www.gamblingresearch.org/contentdetail.sz?cid=2096&pageid=848

endnotes

1. American Gaming Association (AGA) (2005) *State of the States annual report*. http://www .americangaming.org/survey/index.cfm. Accessed November 10, 2005.
2. Hsu, C. (2000). Residents' support for legalized gaming and perceived impacts of riverboat casinos: Changes in five years. *Journal of Travel Research, 38*(4), 390–396.
3. American Gaming Association's (AGA) (2004) *State of the States annual report*. http://www.americangaming.org/survey/index.cfm. Accessed November 10, 2005.
4. Cotte, J. (1997) Chances, trances, and lots of slots: Gambling motives and consumption experiences. *Journal of Leisure Research, 24*(4), 380–307.
5. Cohen, J. (1988) "Explaining gambling behavior." In Rosecrance, J. ed., *Gambling without Guilt: The Legitimation of an American Pastime*. Pacific Grove: Brooks/Cole Publishing Co.: pp. 53–70.
6. Ibid.
7. Ibid.
8. Ibid.

9. Ibid.

10. Ibid.

11. Ibid.

12. Skinner, B. F. (1969) *Contingencies of Reinforcement; A Theoretical Analysis*. New York: Appleton-Century-Crofts.

13. American Gaming Association's (AGA)(2004) *State of the States annual report*. http://www .americangaming.org/survey/index.cfm. Accessed November 10, 2005.

14. Profile of the American casino gambler: (2004). *Harrah's Survey 2004*. http://www.hotelonline .com/News/PR2004_4th/Oct04_HarrahsSurvey.html, accessed on: November 21, 2005.

15. Ibid.

16. Ibid.

17. Ibid.

18. Platz, L. & Millar, M. (2001). Gambling in the context of other recreational activity: A quantitative comparison of casual and pathological student gamblers. *Journal of Leisure Research*, 33 (4), 383–396.

19. Lowenhar, J. & Boykin, S. (1995) "Casino gaming behavior and the psychology of winning and losing: How gamers overcome persistent failure." In W. Eadington ed. *The Gambling Studies: Proceedings of the Sixth National Conference on Gambling and Risk Taking, Reno*: Institute for the Study of Gambling and Commercial Gaming. pp. 182–205.

20. American Gaming Association's (AGA) (2005) *State of the States annual report*. http://www .americangaming.org/survey/index.cfm. Accessed November 5, 2006.

21. Mayfield, D. (1995). First virtual casino plans spring opening. *The Virginian-Pilot*, March 26, 1995.

22. Kindt, J. W. (1994). The economic impacts of legalized gambling activities, *Drake Law Review* (43), 51, 51–53.

Vignette

Korea

William Thompson, University of Nevada, Las Vegas

Two Koreas: In Politics and Casinos Too

There are two Koreas. Venture north from Seoul on Highways 70 and 1. The Hangang River is on the left. Its banks are lined with razor wire and guard towers for 25 miles to the demilitarized zone. Then go another 25 miles to Panmunjeon, where wire crosses the land with large spiked wheels, and there are many red triangles—the symbols of land mines. Korea is distinctly divided.

There are two Koreas in the political world and in the world of casino gambling, too. One Korea is represented by two very successful casinos in Seoul and in the town of Kohan in Kangwon Province. (Figure 6–7) The other Korea is represented by twelve faltering provincial casinos at Incheon, Pusan, Gyeongju, Mt. Seorak National Park, and on Jeju Island.

The Successful Duo

The two successful casinos of Korea take very different approaches to their operations. The Paradise Walker Hill Casino in Seoul, established in 1968, is not permitted to allow Korean Nationals to gamble. The casino targets foreign high rollers. The average gambler loses an incredible $500 per visit, and gaming revenues exceed $200 million a year. More than 1,100 players come each day to play at the 78 tables and 162 machines. They are served by 860 employees, half of whom work the games.

As the Paradise Walker Hill caters to foreigners, the government gives the casino leeway in its operations. The casino decides the numbers of games and limits, the entrance fee (there is none), dress codes (minimum standards), credit policies (large amounts of credit are given), and complimentary services (top players receive airfare, room, food, beverage, and show tickets). The casino gives free alcoholic drinks to players on the gambling floor, and the facility is open 24 hours everyday.

The most popular game is Sic Bo, but the biggest money game is Baccarat. Slot machines take bets worth as much as $4.50 per machine-pull (5,000 Korean won), and linked machines have progressive jackpots. There is a high stakes table area where a player may propose any amount for a wager—acceptance of the wager is at the discretion of the casino.

The facility attracts premium players from Japan, China, Hong Kong, Taiwan, and the mainland, and their action adds to losses from standard tourists who have suffered from a slack Japanese economy. About 48 percent of the players come from Japan, while 31 percent are Chinese. Most of the other players—21 percent—come from other Asian and Australian venues. The marketing emphasis is on reaching players from Mainland China. The flight to Incheon Airport (which serves Seoul) is only one hour from Shanghai, and two hours from Beijing or Hong Kong. The casino advertises in airline and travel magazines.

Paradise Walker Hill is a large open casino that is very clean and not crowded. It has a hushed elegance typically found in Europe and only in the high stakes areas of the best Las Vegas casinos. Paradise Walker Hill is attached to a Sheraton resort complex with a large convention center, many restaurants, and a showroom. These attractions are outside of the ownership and control of the casino, therefore, the privately owned property company incurs large costs when they give complimentaries. Nonetheless they are very happy with the results they achieve.

The other successful casino is called Kangwon Land (Figure 6–7). From outward appearances it is just another big fancy casino in a large resort complex. The resort meets the standards of many upscale Las Vegas properties, and inside its gaming atmosphere is "Vegas" all the way—and more. The casino lets Koreans gamble, although they must reside outside of Kangwon Province (except for one day a month).

The philosophy behind Kangwon Land developed out of national legislation passed in December 1995 to bring economic development to a depressed area that formerly was a coal-mining center. Officials of the Ministry of Culture and Tourism decided that a casino could be the catalyst for development of tourist attractions such as golf courses and ski runs. But Kangwon Province was isolated, and it would be difficult to draw in foreign gamblers, especially since they would first arrive in Seoul or Pusan. Special permission was thus given to allow Koreans to play.

Figure 6–7 Kangwon Land Resort and Casino, Korea.
Photo courtesy of Bill Thompson.

The national government insisted on being a major partner in the casino project. It owns a 36 percent share, while the province and its local units own 15 percent. In 1999, shares equaling 49 percent equity in the company were sold to the public. A temporary casino opened in October, and funds from the casino were reinvested in the construction of the permanent casino resort, which opened in 2003.

The casino now welcomes 4,500 players a day. Each loses an average of $350 per visit, making the annual win of the casino in excess of $600 million. Almost all of the players are Koreans. The government takes a protective view toward the players. Players register identities, showing addresses as they pass through metal detectors. There is a 5,000 won ($4.50 U.S.) entrance fee. While residents of the Province of Kangwon are banned from daily play (they are allowed to play on one Tuesday each month only—and on that day 7,000 patrons usually enter the doors), just about all of the players have made a treacherous drive of four to five hours from Seoul or Pusan over mostly two-lane twisting mountain roads. They willingly crowd into a facility that is open from 10 a.m. until 6 a.m. the next morning, except on Saturday evening when it remains open all night long.

The casino does not have to advertise. The out-of-town guests are very lucky if they can find a room, as the new facility has only 700 hotel rooms, and the town itself does not have that many other rooms. Many players sleep in their cars when the casino is closed.

Here, unlike at Paradise Walker Hill, no alcohol is permitted in playing areas. The casino has a policy for dealing with problem gamblers. Kangwon Land may be the only casino in the world that has a gambling treatment center *inside*. Players are observed to see if they have compulsive traits. Certain players are approached by casino officials and each may be given a green, yellow, or red card. The green card is for a player who exhibits some warning sign. The player is told about problem gambling and urged to be careful. The yellow card is given to players with more serious evidence of problems, and they are urged to limit their gambling and to seek counseling, which is provided at the treatment center. Red cards go to those with the most serious traits, and are urged to seek counseling and are banned from play at the casino for some period of time. Players also may exclude themselves from play, and there are procedures that allow family members to have someone banned from play.

The casino has 100 tables and 940 slot machines. The tables include roulette wheels, blackjack, Baccarat and mini-Baccarat games, a Big Wheel, and Sic Bo.

Figure 6–8 Kangwon Land Resort and Casino, Korea #2.
Photo courtesy of Bill Thompson.

There are not enough tables or machines as the casino is full during most of its operating time. The lack of table space has been dealt with by a practice not found in Las Vegas or in the other Korean casinos, called back betting. While there are only seven gambling positions at a blackjack table, there may be as many as 21 players. In back betting, two players may stand behind the player seated at the table and may place the maximum bet on that player's hand.

The Kangwon Land board has set the table minimums and maximums, but it is only the maximums that matter. Every play finds the maximum amount being wagered, the equivalent of 100,000 won ($90 U.S.) a play. In a V.I.P. area the maximum limit is 10 million won, or $9,000, per play. And that is the typical amount played each hand. To be admitted to the V.I.P. room, one is designated as a member and must put forth 30 million won as a deposit in cash, the equivalent of $27,000. There is no credit play; however, the players need not carry cash to the casino. They simply go to their bank for bank checks, which they can use to purchase chips—simple enough. The casino has a full service bank branch inside the facility.

Slot machine play is as frantic as the table play. The slots accept a maximum play of only five coins per play—five times $0.45 U.S., or $2.25. This is quite a contrast to the $90 U.S. table players throw on each bet. But the machine players have found a means of increasing action. If they wedge a paper match stick beside the button that indicates maximum amount bet, and they wedge another match stick beside the button that says play, the machine takes off and plays continuously without the player having to do anything but watch. Of course, they have to first insert large amounts of paper bills into the machine. The machine just keeps track of wins and losses with its credit meter. The poker machines, where this is not possible, are popular with $2.25 plays, as each time a player wins, he or she can immediately make a double-or-nothing bet.

The casino attracts 63 percent of its visitors from the Seoul area, and 35 percent from Pusan and other Korean areas outside of Kangwon Province, with less than 2 percent from foreign jurisdictions. The 940 machines win up to $800 a day each, making machine revenue approximately 40 percent of the total gaming take. The casino has instituted an interesting complimentary system. Points are given for amount of play. The points can be exchanged for hotel rooms and at restaurants, spa, shops, and entertainment areas and can also be presented to merchants, motels, and restaurants in Kohan and nearby towns.

There are more than 3,100 employees at the property with 1,000 of them in gaming positions; 60 percent are from the area, and many are former coal miners. The employees from outside, mostly from Seoul or Pusan, live in casino dormitories. The company also gives preference to local providers of goods. Three-quarters of the food is purchased locally, and one-half of construction activity is handled by Kangwon firms.

The complex, which was designed by the architects of the Las Vegas Mandalay Bay Casino Resort, offers more than gambling. There are nine restaurants including a buffet, and a "Fitness" restaurant. An entertainment area features a show by Russian magicians, a 4D Cinema with virtual rides, and a lateral elevator that moves across the bottom of a lake with a "20,000 Leagues Beneath the Sea" show. In 2004, a golf course was opened, and in 2005, skiing will begin on the slopes of a nearby mountain.

The Other Dozen

The other Korean casinos do not deserve many words in a vignette mentioning Paradise Walker Hill and Kangwon Land. They are not even in the minor leagues in comparison. Their trouble is typified by the eight facilities on Jeju Island. Casinos came to the island in the 1970s as a means for economic development. During the 1980s, major hotel complexes were built as the Japanese economy was booming. Then the boom ended and Japanese quit coming to the island in large numbers. The island is a tourist haven—for Korean honeymooners and sightseers exploring caves and walking by waterfalls and golfers. On a visit of the eight casinos over a two-day period, this writer observed exactly five players. Only two tables were open. Several of the casinos had undergone recent management changes, and probably all were available for purchase by anyone. Managers indicated that they had players on weekends, but each would average fewer than 200 players a week. With losses of $200 a visit, the casino win for the year would be at best no more than $2 million. As each casino employed around 120 workers, net profits were somewhere between minimal and nonexistent. Incredibly, three of the casinos were in very luxurious hotels with full occupancies. The eight Jeju casinos and the other four command combined revenues less than 5 percent of those of the two large casinos.

The Jeju solution is simple—the Kangwon Land solution—let Koreans play. The trouble is that the other Korean casinos would demand the same privilege—including Paradise Walker Hill. And there is a wrinkle; Kangwon Land was given its monopoly on having Korean players for five years—until 2008. The real Jeju solution must include closing several facilities. If only one or two of the luxurious hotels had casinos, then maybe a Paradise Walker Hill marketing approach to foreign players could be successful.

7 Development of Corporate Culture and Technology

Kathryn Hashimoto, East Carolina University

Learning Objectives

1. To introduce the four major trends that have spanned American culture and influenced the development of gaming and casinos.

2. To present an overview of the history of gaming and how it evolved from its illegal roots.

3. To discuss the evolution of the corporate culture in the gaming industry.

4. To present the latest technology used in casinos.

Chapter Outline

Introduction

In American history, the gambling spirit is said to be inherent in the culture. It took a special breed of individual to come from England and settle the American wilderness: a gambling person, someone willing to take a risk to improve his or her lot in life. Because settlements were few and far between, many people settled on land far from their neighbors. Because the nearest person could be hundreds of miles away, tools and equipment were needed to lighten the workload. In order to develop the land for cultivation, new types of plows needed to be developed that could easily be fixed and transported through forests to get to their final destinations. The new frontier required a gambling person who could create and improve on previous inventions to meet new challenges. Therefore, technology, culture, and the gambler developed together in the need to succeed and improve life in America. As the New World became more populated, people continued to take risks and invent new things to make their lives easier.

Four major trends have spanned American culture and influenced the development of gaming and casinos: the trend from being an outlaw to being respectable, from being a low-tech culture to being a high-tech culture, from a focus on the individual to a focus on the masses, and from the rise of individual business owners to the rise of team management. Each of these trends started in pioneer days with a bare minimum of technology to build from and developed into the use of sophisticated tools to make a difference.

Trends

From Being an Outlaw to Being Respectable

Historically, gambling has been associated with shysters, con artists, and criminals. For example, in the case of the lottery, con artists have always managed to build a successful lottery system so that they could later abscond with any proceeds. Even in colonial times, gambling was an important fact of everyday life. In order to outfit the voyage of the Mayflower, a lottery was conducted to raise the necessary money. Although the organizers were eventually run out of town on a rail for cheating, enough money was raised to get the expedition started. Later, when infrastructure was needed to develop New England towns, a lottery was created to fund the needed projects. The scoundrels who ran them were eventually found out and the lottery was disbanded. During the Civil War, the Louisiana Lottery was created to help Charity Hospital meet its expenses. As part of the contract, the managers could keep any money that was not needed by the hospital. This was the largest lottery in the United States, infamously known as "the Octopus," because its tentacles of corruption were so widespread. Eventually, sheriffs had to come from Washington to disband the operations for fraud.

Later, as Nevada became the playground for the California elite, Bugsy Siegel was purported to have created the idea of gambling in the desert. Unfortunately, he was also alleged to have gained his fortune by founding "Murder Inc." for the mob. He also used mob money to market and build the first casino in Las Vegas, which failed when the social elite deserted him on opening night because they did not want to be publicly associated with gangsters. While Bugsy met his demise by his own company, the idea of casinos and fun in the desert remained. Since the mob had a great deal of money to spend and launder at the time, Las Vegas casinos were a great investment. As Nevada prospered, so did the gangsters. Thus, the criminal aspect of gambling has long been a part of American culture.

However, in the 1960s, as the story goes, Howard Hughes liked the penthouse suite at one of the casinos so much that he wanted to stay there all the time. Penthouse suites are for high rollers—people who spend large amounts of money gambling. The casino management wanted to throw Hughes out because he did not spend enough in the casino. Finally, one day, a manager probably told him "Look, this is company policy. You can't stay here and live. You have to leave." Now, company policies were things that Howard could understand as a business tycoon. So, he probably told the manager "change the policy." And the corresponding reply was something like "If you're so hot on changing the policy, you try." So, Howard bought the casino and did change the policy. About this time, William Harrah began to buy into the casino/hotel business with other major corporate geniuses. This was the beginning of respectability for casinos (Figure 7–1).

The corporate tycoons began to run the casinos like traditional big business operations. Big business meant automated systems. The new computerized systems improved efficiency and minimized possible discrepancies in transactions, such as illegal manual entries. Auditing also became easier. The Nevada Gaming Commission required that

Figure 7–1 The beginning of respectability and the growth of corporations in the casino industry.

casinos store a minimum of seven years of reports. As you can imagine, these records filled enormous underground vaults. Eventually, all that paper became small CDs with quick backup data files and continuous upload and download capabilities. Now, satellites allow data to be stored elsewhere with multiple collecting sites so that there is no downtime for backups. This allows for an extra level of security in that multiple copies of the data can be stored at different locations. If something were to happen to the data at one site, there would be another backup of the data at one of the other locations. Linked gaming systems now allow accounting and security management systems to be checked by governmental jurisdictions. Regulators can control illegal machine gambling by licensing, regulating, and monitoring machine play. The central computer systems continuously monitor the network to linked terminals, assuring that the wide varieties of games are fair and honest. In fact, the use of technology by governmental agencies to monitor such activities is quickly becoming a necessity due to the large number of activities that need to be monitored and the increased sophistication of illegal activities. These monitoring systems often include basic forms of artificial intelligence in order to help spot illegal activity that may not be easily recognized.

Seeing the money that casinos can generate, Atlantic City began to explore its options. Originally an elegant seaside resort for New York City residents to spend their summers, by the 1960s, increased tourist travel by planes and trains had eroded Atlantic City's clientele. It had become "a slum by the sea." How could the city be revitalized? Gambling came to mind, but there was a deep concern about mob control of the casinos. Whereas Nevada regulations had been laissez faire, New Jersey gaming regulations were more strict. They included an abundance of laws and regulations to make casinos toe the line for respectability. Then, as Native American casinos and riverboats opened, people began to see that casinos were respectable. It was as Steve Wynn who is credited with changing the public perception to, casinos are recreation and entertainment. The high point of respectability was Steve Wynn's award for "1994 Independent Hotelier of the World." Casinos are now so accepted and respectable that casino stocks are traded on Wall Street.

From Low-Tech Culture to High-Tech Culture

Materials

Traditionally, gambling consisted of the easiest accessible materials: dice and cards. For example, craps was a popular street game (Figure 7–2). All a player needed was a pair of dice and money. Dice fit comfortably inside a gentleman's pants pocket. A deck of cards was also easily obtainable. In the Old West, a table and set of chairs were all that were needed to get a game started. Gambling and the Old West were almost synonymous: think of the fabled card shark sitting at a table inside the saloon with his back to the wall, waiting for his prey to appear. There has not been a movie Western made that does not show some form of gambling as entertainment. As a result, many Americans have grown up playing poker of one type or another. The classic Broadway musical of the 1950s, "Guys and Dolls," was based around a craps player as the lead character. In the 1950s and 1960s, a weeknight out with the "guys" often meant playing poker. Low-tech games such as these were easily transportable, and one had only to reach into his or her pocket and a game was ready. After all, when a person was traveling by horse, and his belongings had to fit on a saddle, the practical aspect of gambling was important.

Figure 7–2 The famous Bella Union gambling saloon in Cheyenne when gambling meant card playing and dice because they were easily transportable.

However, as America grew and became more civilized, the games became more sophisticated. Pascal created the laws of probability to learn how to win at cards. Therefore, playing styles became based more on scientific thought, and the rules of the games adhered to those same laws. A good player knew the odds and bet accordingly. The tables became fancier, with specialized layouts, including betting circles. Also, the game rules and winnings became more easily available by being placed directly in front of the player. Table games became high-tech. The simple chip now has a **radio frequency identification devise (RFID)** with a unique derail number for tracking the chip's location. The tables now have slots for player cards, making it easier for the table games personnel to track information. However, with the sophistication of the Web, even casinos have become virtual reality programs. Internet gaming is the newest high-tech option in gambling development.

Machines

In 1875, the Industrial Revolution manifested itself in the gambling industry with new machines in which a person pulled a handle to set reels spinning. It was suggested that these mechanical devices would be good to occupy the women while the men gambled at the tables. By the 1930s, Jennings had developed the first electrically operated jackpot bell machine; now buttons could be pushed and gambling became much easier. In the 1970s, video poker was introduced. This machine was very popular because it gave players decision-making options and more buttons to push. People believed that the more buttons they controlled, the more their skill dominated their luck. Slot machines were also becoming popular.

In the 1980s, the evolution of the stepper slot allowed greater versatility and fewer parts to break down. Microprocessors enabled people to receive "credits" for their wins, therefore resulting in less handling of the actual money and speeding up the play. Although it had been thought that slots were more attractive for women because they were simple to learn, mechanicals (more affectionately called "one-armed bandits") rapidly grew to be the overall favorite over table games. By 1983, Nevada slot revenues actually surpassed table revenues. Many casinos found that slot revenues now comprised 60 percent to 80 percent of the revenues, and the shift to add more slots and fewer table games ensued. The growth of the progressive IGT slot system in 1986 meant that people could win very large jackpots because the slot machines were linked to a central computer, and all bets were pooled into one large collective prize. Gaming machines were so popular that in early 1990, newer, larger denomination machines such as $5, $25, $100, and even $500 entered the market.

Gaming machines are now faster and allow for less failure in operations. The coin acceptance devices have electric sensors to detect fake coins. A computer chip randomly generates a series of random numbers and selects reel spin/stop sequences. In addition, a player liquid crystal display (LCD) computer chip allows diagnostic troubleshooting, bonus modes, and site-specific player information. A **vacuum florescent display (VFD)** displays the game information, attract sequences, and diagnostic errors and also sets up messages. A player switch illuminates when coins are inserted or credits are won.

Another chip records security violations and detects failures or errors. All the critical game data are stored in the random access memory (RAM) with a long-life battery attached so that data are not lost in case of a power failure.

Some of the newest technology prints tickets containing all of a player's credits; the player does not have to carry around loose, heavy coins that can be dropped and lost. This also makes it easier for the casinos because they do not have to store a vast number of rolls of quarters. On riverboat casinos, this is especially helpful because they are concerned about how to balance the weight of the coins on their boats.

Finally, the slot machine data system allows all the information about every slot machine every minute of the day to be gathered and be available for analysis. Individual machines can be checked for cash flow, malfunctions, and security compromises. This technology was attempted in the mid to late 1960s but none of it was successful. Finally in 1973, Electro Module Inc., IBM, and Harvey's Wagon Wheel at Lake Tahoe developed the first viable system. In 1974, Bally's acquired the rights to the slot data system. There are several components to the slot data system. The communicator is attached to the individual slot machine so that it can keep track of the coin flow. In addition, it monitors the machine for tampering, malfunctions, or other problems. Then there is a card reader to identify employees and players. A program displays the slot machine status data to the employees and also instructional and promotional material to the players. The computer interface unit maintains communications between the central computer system and the slot machine. It also protects the system from transient voltages and electronic interferences. As a result, the slot data system functions in six basic areas: security, operations, maintenance, accounting, marketing, and management. With this system in place, consultants or managers can apply new software to evaluate slot placement. These design programs can evaluate patrons, competitive situation marketing plans, facility, and types of games. Then a programmer can design products with each game type, cabinet style, and exact location on a screen with a scaled three dimensional floor plan.

With the advent of computers, casinos have radically changed. Instead of a couple of tables on which to roll dice or play cards, heavy machinery has replaced many tables. Mechanicals have taken over the floor. Computer programs, digitized screens, and cashless payouts dominate the scene. Instead of the quiet bar with a hush in the room at a large bet, bells and whistles bounce off the walls and generate excitement. Computerized gambling machines with their sophisticated microprocessors also allowed new and creative games to be developed. Today, any table game can be played on a video machine, which reduces the number of personnel needed to operate a casino. However, the downside is that these machines require trained, experienced computer programmers to repair any problems, and they are expensive to hire.

Surveillance

America's early history is depicted by the movie Western and John Wayne as cowboy. The scene is tense as the bad guys with the black hats wait in the saloon with the marked deck of cards for some sucker to enter. Up above on the second floor balcony, sits a man on a chair with a shotgun. He protects the owner below. As people enter, the protector

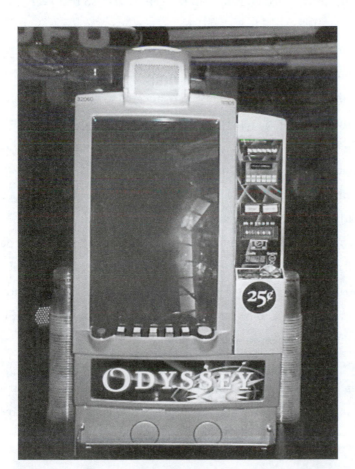

Figure 7–3 The Odyssey with its digital, touch screen functions has dealers that actually chastise you for taking too long between plays. Photo courtesy of George G. Fenich.

stands up and walks slowly back and forth along the railing keeping an eye on trouble-makers. This was the beginning of surveillance from above.

In later developments, as casinos became more sophisticated, the balcony walkway became an intricate grid above the entire floor of the casino. These catwalks allowed surveillance to be hidden from view but able to see everything on the floor. Unfortunately, the viewing required darkness in the catwalk area, so a misstep could send a man crashing through the glass ceiling to the floor below. Catwalks had been in continuous use until the 1990s when hi-tech equipment no longer required this secondary backup.

Another development in casino technology has been the rise of video cameras, which changed the way surveillance was conducted. These hi-tech cameras can focus so well that a surveillance person can see the numbers on a quarter at a table below. These cameras are strategically placed throughout the ceiling area so that every square inch of casino floor space is covered by at least one camera at any given moment. Cameras are hidden by half-circles of smoked glass to prevent a visitor from seeing where the they are pointing. Some of the newest technology has hidden cameras in statues and other places closer to the action. These cameras are connected to recording equipment that stores the floor information as long as necessary to catch cheaters or to prove cases in court (Figure 7–4). This information is stored digitally, which provides higher quality and greater durability than standard videotape.

For a long time, surveillance personnel carefully kept records of cheats to themselves in "black books." However, computer links have changed all that. Now **facial recognition programs** can zoom in on a person, identify him or her, and determine whether surveillance should be concerned. Information on cheats and troublemakers is available globally so that tracking a roulette scam team or a notorious card cheat is easy. This allows surveillance to be aware of cheating teams who might be in the area and to pass on this information to other casinos.

If casino personnel are puzzled, they can contact an independent surveillance team. These teams can link their computers with the casino cameras to see all the action without even being in the same town. The video feed can also be passed on to experts anywhere in the world. If the casino suspects illegal activities but is unsure, it is able to

Figure 7–4 Picture of a surveillance room. Courtesy of Steve Durham, The House Advantage.

share that video feed with an expert on such activities by allowing him or her to view that video feed in real time via a virtual private network established over an Internet connection. Casinos no longer have to have someone with this level of expertise on the property at all times. An expert can be shared with several different casinos, which creates significant cost savings. This allows more eyes and more knowledge to be pooled toward protecting the casino and the customers.

Within the casino, software systems can also integrate with the security environment. They can show total dollars transacted through the games, monitor audits, and display employee transactions. These systems streamline operations by capturing image data, color portraits, and signatures to create identification cards and badges. They also use scans of employees' hands for payroll, for clocking in and out, and for restricting access to certain portions of the casino. This also has some application to the guest, such as access to a hotel room or as identification in a casino for special privileges.

Another topic that is relatively new is radio frequency identification tags (RFIDs). These are used in employee uniforms and on valuable pieces of equipment. This allows items to be tracked. Therefore, RFID tags can be somewhat controversial when they are used to track people, bringing up issues of invasion of privacy. However, they also allow employees to swipe cards at cash registers in the cafeteria, making it easier and quicker to get meals. In addition, the software can facilitate the monitoring of staff levels as well as discriminate between active and former employees. All the specific information about each employee is inputted and stored for instantaneous retrieval when necessary.

From the Focus on the Individual to the Focus on the Masses

Throughout American history, men gambled to pass the time and to make a few dollars. Typically, men were considered to be the gamblers. However, they came with women who had to be entertained. They sometimes disturbed the concentration of the game by asking for money to do other things such as go shopping, find something to eat, or be entertained. Women had to do this at this time because it was believed that "nice girls" did not gamble. Originally it was thought that mechanical devices called "slots" would be the perfect entertainment for these women. While they were using them, they could have free food and drink, and they could spend money. These women were probably the first "low rollers." However, casinos began to realize that low rollers could also contribute to a casino's profitability. As corporations such as McDonald's have learned, having more clients spending fewer dollars equals a few clients spending many dollars. This philosophy meant that rather than all the casinos going after the same 100 **whales** (people with millions to bet), the market opened up to all people more than 21 years of age. The first method to draw low rollers to the casinos was created in Atlantic City—chartered bus programs. Bus companies charge a small amount of money, say $30. The $30 would include the bus ride, drinks, food, and entertainment during the ride, free buffet coupons at the casino, and $20 in slot tokens.

The casinos knew how to attract high rollers and low rollers, but what about the bulk of Middle America? How could casinos identify these people and then track them for "comps" (complimentary or free stuff) in order to get them onto the floor? Computers made this an easy market to attract. To identify this market: Tell people the casino wants to give them 'comps' but needs to know how to reach them to send them the coupons and free offerings. Thus, players clubs were created as a marketing tool.

A newcomer stops by the players' club booth and signs up by giving the casino personal and financial information. In exchange, the player put the player's club card in the slot machine to measure his or her rate of play. Simple. The people voluntarily give the casino important personal information that allows the casino to develop a database of clients, and then people use the club card, which shows the casino exactly how much the player is worth. The players' club card inputs time spent at each machine, how much money was bet, and the overall amount of money spent per visit. This information is necessary for the player rating systems. Now everyone over 21 can be evaluated and tracked for their value to the casino. The information gathered from the players along with other information gathered from other electronic databases allow for an effective marketing campaign to be developed to attract players, especially those considered to be of high value to the casino. Casinos have also integrated this information with their customer relationship management (CRM) systems to become even more sophisticated in providing excellent service to their guests, which in turn will help create life-long customers.

Now that the system within the casino is in place, how do you attract and inform the masses that the casino has all these wonderful opportunities available to them? One way is websites (Figure 7–5). The goal of a website should be to educate and help visitors with their questions. This is important because the number one reason people visit websites is to get information. Within the website, the information should encourage visitors to return frequently to the website for new information, while obtaining their personal data and permission to contact them. The more visits the same person makes to the website, the more opportunities the casino has to learn about his or her wants and desires in food and beverage, social habits, or physical or spectator activities—in other words, his or her demographic and psychographic profile. These facts allow a casino to create offers that are interesting to specific customers. Web visitors are open to information because they actively instigated the contact to know more about the casino. This is an excellent opportunity to obtain permission from the web visitor to increase the level of contact by offering to send a newsletter or emailing them special offers and marketing materials. This request allows visitors to "buy into" the process.

Figure 7–5 Websites make it easy to register for casino promotions, hotel reservations, or even dinner reservations.

On the flip side, every communication must always offer the option to "unsubscribe," so the good will that is created will not be tarnished by the visitor's frustration at receiving materials without any choice. Keep in mind that the objective is to encourage the visitor to obtain more information, not to deliver a sales pitch. This form of website marketing allows casinos to create a database that grows richer in information every day. As more information is known about a specific person, the marketer can divide people into special segments based upon their needs and can tailor offers to match their desires.

Another benefit of these databases is their use to build brand loyalty programs. The objective of these programs is to offer clients a package that will perfectly fit their needs. Because they feel that the casino knows and cares about their wishes, customers become brand loyal. However, one of the biggest concerns of players' club members is that they get offers that are not relevant to them. For example, a member wagered in excess of $10,000 when in Detroit on business; however, the member lived in California. A month later, he received a dinner coupon good for two people. This offer is not going to entice someone from California to venture back to Detroit. He is going to need at least a room and a meal. Another example is a regular tournament player who frequents the local casino and spends $5,000 on an average visit, betting $25 a hand. All the dealers and pit bosses know him on sight. Yet, rather than ask him what he would like as a package, he receives offers for dinner for two. These offers are very standard and very unimaginative. Both men feel that the casino does not care about their business because they did not bother to find out what they each really wanted and needed. As a result, they are not brand loyal customers, but they could have been, given time to explore their needs. Technology is a wonderful tool if used correctly. However, when dealing with people, it still comes back to getting to know the customer and personalizing the offers.

From Individual Business Owners to Team Management

In the United States, the history and evolution of casinos have created two very strong corporate cultures. A **corporate culture** could be described as the personality of an organization. Like a person, a business can be weak or strong, conservative or daring, even stodgy or innovative. Corporate cultures are important because they set the boundaries for behavior by managers and employees. The stronger the culture, the easier it is for employees to know what they should do when the formal rules are not available. In casinos, there are always new situations and problems that must be addressed. A strong corporate culture sets the tone and guidelines for the problem solving and solution.

Individual Owners

When casinos first developed in America, ownership was by a single individual who could lose that enterprise on a toss of the dice. It was the owner's "luck of the draw," not management ability, that determined his or her length of stay. As a result, owners were superstitious and trusted only their own instincts. The "monopoly on brains" syndrome referred to the fact that only the owner could make a great decision. Therefore, the corporate culture was one of "Do as I say; I don't want to know your opinion." Management rested on one person's whim, not management expertise or great management decision-making style. "Dummy up and deal" was the employee's slogan. Fear of management was what kept the employees honest. The individual owners and their traditional cultural practices believed that employees should be constantly reminded that their jobs were a privilege, not a right. They could be taken away at any time. Promotion came to employees who were loyal to management. Employees had to learn the trade from the ground up, starting as a dealer and proving their knowledge and loyalty along the way.

In traditional cultural practices, superstition was as good a factor in making decisions as anything else. For example, women were only considered to be decorations. Furthermore, they were thought to bring bad luck, so they were not perceived as good for business either as good employees or gamblers. If they did appear, sexual harassment was to be expected. After all, what else was a woman good for in a casino? And if she did not want that kind of attention, she would not have walked in the door. African Americans also faced superstitious discrimination. Until the late sixties in Nevada, black employees and entertainers were not allowed to enter the front doors or drink out of cups reserved for the players; it was bad luck. However, the Rat Pack, that famous group of celebrity hipsters led by Frank Sinatra, changed this almost solely with their charisma. Their impressive ability to draw in money whether they were playing or working gave them the clout to alter policies driven by superstition and prejudice. They boycotted any casino in which Sammy Davis Jr., a very popular black entertainer and member of the Rat Pack, was not allowed. Their financial power and influence quickly changed policies.

During this time, employees showed their loyalty by doing whatever they could to help the owner. In some cases, employees were asked to violate rules and regulations in order to favor the house or accommodate a high roller's desires. Even though guests might make unreasonable requests, operators would agree because the customer might take his business elsewhere. For example, at Caesars in Atlantic City, a customer requested that he have a male dealer instead of the woman who was currently at the table. The management complied, even though it knew this was discriminatory. However, it was cheaper to pay the class action suit that followed than to antagonize the player.

Another way to show loyalty was to express extreme concern about the outcome of a game because it would be disloyal to want the customer to win. In addition, the dealer was perceived to be personally responsible for the outcome. After all, it was thought that some people were just "unlucky" and should not deal certain games. Any dealer who lost money had "bad karma" and was instantly fired—no questions asked. However, there were several ways to change bad luck. For example, changing the dice and/or cards would help change the luck of the casino. Changing out an "unlucky" (losing dealer) employee for a different one could also help improve a bad streak. It was rumored that one casino manager was reported to say, "It was a question of mind over matter." So, he would switch dealers with "weak minds" from a losing game. Without any rational decision-making guidelines, superstition and one man's version of common sense ruled the operations.

The Shift to Team Management and Corporate Culture

During the 1960s and 1970s, there was a shift in management styles and decision making. Some say it was Howard Hughes who began the movement. Under his new management style, the casino functioned like any other large corporation. Superstitions were replaced by well-researched facts. Teams of employees replaced the individual owner. The idea that a dealer is responsible for the losses was replaced by probability theory. As a result, the casino made money, and this encouraged other corporate giants such as Baron Hilton to invest in casinos.

These giants of corporate America started a new trend in casino management styles and organizational cultures. The casino was divided into two parts: the casino side and the administration side. The casino side revolved around what happened on the casino floor: the daily grind of securing the casino and tracking the money. The management side handled the marketing, accounting, human resources, and so on. With this split, new emphasis was placed on educational backgrounds, including MBAs. People with no background in gambling began to work on the marketing plans and run the financial enterprise. Computer programs and statistics became the guiding decision makers. For example, the responsibility for comping decisions switched from floor people to computers. When the Old School lost their "comping" privileges to a computer, it was a confusing time. How could a computer know the right people to comp? How could a machine build a rapport with the players so that they would come back? Old-time supervisors issued comps to whomever they pleased; it gave them power. But now, the computer decided.

The Two Cultures Collide

The clash of traditional culture versus the new corporate culture was inevitable. The following sentiments characterize the traditional casino culture: "The guys upstairs don't know the business." "How can an MBA know anything about the way a casino works?" "If he doesn't understand the product, how can he manage it?" "They are just a bunch of kids with degrees but no real experience." "The only real way to learn the business is to start as a dealer and work your way up through the ranks." By the same token, the new corporate culture examined the traditional views and found them lacking. They would say things such as "The traditional managers want to micromanage and keep everything to themselves." "They do not want anyone else to know what is going on." "This way of managing is out of date; they obviously haven't kept up with the times." "It's not necessary to be a dealer to run a company. What does a dealer know about marketing or accounting?" "Formal education is important. It teaches how to manage and oversee operations. It allows a person to step back and see the big picture." These statements reflected the new corporate culture.

Changing times reinforced the new casino corporate culture. However, it was not just the ownership switch that altered the traditional corporate culture. When Las Vegas and Atlantic City found themselves inundated with all kinds of new gaming venues, the competition for employees became intense. Finding trained employees was a big problem. Anyone with any qualifications or experience quickly climbed the corporate ladder, and there was always an enticement of higher wages from the next casino or riverboat. There were too many jobs and not enough workers. As a result, computer management tools became important. For example, gaming management systems united the departments. One system could be used for slot management, patron management, table game systems, cage and credit systems, and integration of all that information into one database.

Conclusion

As American culture evolved, technology and gambling have been integral parts of the development. The American spirit that was willing to take a chance developed into the American creative enterprise that invented newer and better tools to help people cope with their lives. After all, Americans say, "Necessity is the mother of invention," and that is true. An exploration into the intertwining of culture, technology, and gambling suggests that there have been four major trends that have evolved throughout American history. Each one of them has created a unique style of management in casinos, and a highly technical environment in which customers come to relax and be entertained.

key terms

Radio frequency identification device (RFID)
vacuum florescent display (VFD)
facial recognition programs

whales
corporate culture

review questions

1. What is the newest high-tech option in gambling development?

2. What does the "monopoly on brains" syndrome refer to?

internet sites

The Gambling Press
http://www.gamblingpress.com

Bugsy's Club
http://www.bugsysclub.com/club/community/info_seigel

Biometrics (facial recognition programs)
http://www. findbiometrics.com/Pages/face_articles/face_2

references

Daniels, B. C. (1995). *Puritans at Play: Leisure and Recreation in Colonial New England*. New York: St. Martin's Griffin.

Friedman, B. (1982). *Casino Management*. Secaucus: Lyle Stuart, Inc.

Hashimoto, K., Kline, S. F., and Fenich, G. G. (1996). *Casino Management: Past, Present, Future*. Dubuque: Kendall Hunt Publishers.

Hashimoto, K., Kline, S. F., and Fenich, G. G. (1996). *Casino Management for the 90's*. Dubuque: Kendall Hunt Publishers.

Martinez, R. (1995). *Managing Casinos*. New York: Barricade Books.

Thompson, W. N. (2001). *Gambling in America: An Encyclopedia of History, Issues and Society*. Santa Barbara: ABC-CLIO.

8 Historical Development Reflects the Changing Competitive Environment

Robert McMullin, East Stroudsburg University

Learning Objectives

1. To provide an understanding of the historical perspective of gambling.

2. To describe the government's interest in regulating and taxing gaming profits.

3. To facilitate an understanding of the gaming industry's financial contributions to the tourism industry in terms of attractions and job creation.

4. To identify historical periods and specific events that contributed positively or negatively to the gaming industry.

5. To describe the growth and development of gaming industry.

Chapter Outline

Introduction

This chapter explains the growth of gambling from the early colonial period to the present day. Since colonial times, the government has tried to intervene to either ban or tax gambling revenues. However, theories have suggested that Americans are gamblers by nature. In order to cross the Atlantic Ocean to an unknown continent, the Puritans must have been risk takers. Later, as the country spread westward, pioneers gambled their lives on a better world. Reinforcing these theories are the cycles of gambling that have continued to develop over time. There have been several cycles when gambling proliferated in America, but then social problems forced the government to ban it. However, since the 1930s, Nevada started a new wave of gambling across the country that continues to grow. As each new jurisdiction or Native American tribe opens another gambling opportunity, the gaming industry grows; soon competition will start to level out and create an oligopoly. However, the question is, which jurisdictions will be on top when the dust settles? Knowing the history of gambling will allow you to make an educated guess.

Early Settlers and History

The East Coast

Every civilization discovered around the world has been found to have developed gambling devices similar to cards and dice. The desire in humans to bet or stake something of value with the hope of a gain seems to be a strong innate drive. For example, in 1492, games of chance are suspected of having been played on the voyage of Christopher Columbus. Spanish and Portuguese sailors brought dice and cards with them on their expeditions. In leisure moments, they also raced their horses and wagered on the results.

In order to obtain the money for the Mayflower voyage, the Puritans created a lottery. Unfortunately, the organizers stole a great deal of the money, but there was enough for the voyage to get started. Gambling was disdained during the colonial years, presumably because of its immorality. Because of the presumed addictive and sinful nature of gambling, laws were written to forbid citizens to engage in such activities. For example, laws were written and passed by the Puritans of Massachusetts (1628) (Figure 8–1), the Quakers in Pennsylvania (1682), the state of New Hampshire (1721), and the state

Figure 8-1 In Puritans times, gambling was considered a sin.

of New Jersey (1748). Even General George Washington was warned in 1756 to control gambling among his troops in the Virginia Militia.

However, as history has repeatedly demonstrated, government's desire for revenue has encouraged the existence and acceptability of gaming. Even through 1769, the American colonies rejected English lotteries. However, without any tax ordinances to develop the necessary infrastructure for the growing towns, lotteries were used to obtain the necessary funds. This concept was continued by the Continental Congress, which organized a $5 million lottery to finance the American Revolutionary War. Later, lotteries continued to support worthy educational institutions, such as Columbia, Dartmouth, Harvard, Princeton, and Yale. Eventually, the colonies started taxing people and ended the need for lotteries until current times.

The Mississippi River

As America expanded with the Louisiana Purchase in 1803, so did gambling. Laws continued to prohibit gambling, yet society embraced the activity. In 1806, Louisiana established a prohibition against gambling, except in New Orleans. Since New Orleans was the original gaming mecca, this led to an even greater proliferation of gambling in that city. New Orleans licensed and taxed casinos (1815) and donated their proceeds to charity. By 1823, New Orleans' leaders had begun to license the first gambling houses in the country. The Crescent City House (1827) was the first. This "palace of fortune" was ornately furnished and remained open day and night. It was the first to imitate the European casinos with food, drink, and rooms comped to special guests. Gamblers could try their luck at the roulette wheel, roll the dice, or play card games such as faro, monte, poker, and blackjack. During this time, a local gambler imported the game of craps into America for the first time. He played the game incessantly and lost his fortune in the process.[1]

Meanwhile, the Mississippi River offered another gamblers' venue. The river was the country's main transportation route. Therefore, if plantation owners wanted to sell their goods, the Mississippi River was the fastest route from the port to various parts of the Midwest. To while the time away on the voyage down the river, games of chance created some excitement. Scoundrels known as card **sharpers** could choose among hundreds of riverboats leaving from the ports of New Orleans, Vicksburg, St. Louis, and Louisville, to name a few. By the early 1830s, between 1,000 and 1,500 professional gamblers worked the steamboats.

Sometimes a Good Samaritan from among the passengers took on crooked gamblers. A famous story that illustrates this begins one night in 1832, as four men sat at a poker game aboard a Mississippi steamer. One of them, a young man from Natchez, Mississippi, who was coming back from a honeymoon trip to New York, lost heavily. Worse still, he was not playing with his own money. While he had been in New York, he had collected $50,000 from Eastern merchants on behalf of southern planters, and now all but about $5,000 of that sum was gone. As that last amount started to disappear, a group of spectators gathered around to watch the game. Among them, wearing a broad-brimmed hat and a plain black suit was James Bowie, who was the inventor of the bowie knife and later a hero of the Alamo. He immediately recognized a rigged poker game.

When the young man's last dollar was gone, he leaped to his feet and dashed out to the deck, where he attempted to climb over the rail and hurl himself into the river. Bowie, looking like a kindly preacher, helped restrain the desperate loser and led him back to his cabin. Bowie returned to the bar and got into the game with the three gamblers. They played for high stakes, and it was not long before the table was piled high with large-denomination bills. Then Bowie noticed that one of the gamblers was cheating by flicking a card from his sleeve. Almost in a single motion, Bowie pulled an enormous knife from his shirt bottom with one hand and gripped the gambler's wrist with the other. "Show your hand!" he cried. "If it contains more than five cards, I shall kill you!" The gambler made an effort to wiggle free, but Bowie held him like a vice. He twisted the man's wrist, and six cards fell to the table: four aces, a queen, and a jack. "I shall take the pot!" announced Bowie, "with a legitimate poker hand: four kings and a ten." Bowie introduced himself by name and took the $70,000 pot. He returned the $50,000 lost by the honeymooning traveler and received a vow from the traveler to never gamble again.

While the Mississippi River has remained a major route for goods and services to reach the ocean, other forms of transportation have created a very competitive environment. So, as the Midwest settled down and developed into a more civilized and populated area, the forces that created the huge gambling environment began to change. And, as with other colonial governments, gambling was banned.

The West Coast

During the California Gold Rush of the late 1840s, New Orleans was the main port of embarkment for San Francisco, and gambling made its way to the far western frontier. Many gold miners were gamblers by nature, and their appetite was for high risks with big rewards. Gold mining stimulated gambling because it encouraged people's trust in luck and speculation. At the height of the gold rush in late 1849, San Francisco was little more than an assembled outpost of 40,000 newly arrived miners and seamen, who, outside of gambling, found few recreational diversions. The level of competition was high in San Francisco, since there were hundreds of gambling saloons in town.

Gambling and Government

Just as in the time of the early colonies, the 1800s yielded a continued persistence by the government to ban gambling. So, many states took action against gambling because they believed that the growth and development of the professional gambler negatively impacted society. These professionals were blamed for limiting economic growth, interfering with business, endangering the streets, committing numerous crimes, and debasing the morality of the society. The Missouri Territorial Legislature passed its first law against gambling in 1814; Pennsylvania law incorporated a statement that gamblers were "parasites and thieves" in 1847, and the New York Association for the Suppression of Gambling was established in 1851. By 1862, all states except Kentucky and Missouri had banned lotteries.

As the Civil War began, most state legislatures continued to prohibit gambling. In the latter part of the nineteenth century, the federal government outlawed lotteries. The great Louisiana Lottery scandal of 1890 involved corruption and the inability to pay winners, which set the tone for the prohibition of lotteries around the country. More newsworthy corruption was exposed at the close of the century, when in 1892, the New York police superintendent admitted his department was corrupted by gamblers' money. In 1894, the Beach Club Casino was built in Palm Beach, Florida. When it closed after 48 years, it was the longest-running illicit gambling casino in the country. Governments continued to deregulate gaming in their states. However, organized forms of gambling continued to survive in a few places along the Mississippi River.[2]

Baseball and the Mob

In the early twentieth century, organized crime started to develop a great interest in gambling, because it could control the outcome of a waged event through racketeering or other strong-armed techniques. One of the darkest moments in the history of baseball was the fixing of the 1919 World Series by New York gambler Arnold Rothstein. Historians acknowledged that Arnold Rothstein would gamble on the weather if he could "fix" it. Anyone who was watching the betting odds as the 1919 World Series approached must have guessed that something was up. The Chicago White Sox, world champions in 1917 and widely considered one of the best teams baseball had ever seen, were listed as 3-to-1 favorites a few days before the series. As rumors of a fix spread and were denied on the streets and in the papers, more and more money was being bet on the Cincinnati Reds. Suddenly, by the eve of the first game, the odds were in Cincinnati's favor at 8 to 5.

The series opened as a best of nine games in Cincinnati on October 1. In the bottom of the first inning, the first Reds batter came to the plate. Pitcher Eddie Cicotte did something that he only did twice during the entire season—he hit a batter with his pitch. It was a signal that gamblers and players had agreed to indicate that a fix was on. With his second pitch, Cicotte hit Morrie Rath in the back, sending Rath to first base, and a whole new flood of money went on Cincinnati. Any doubts as to Cicotte's resolve to go through with throwing the World Series were put to rest in the fourth inning, when he gave up six hits: four singles, a double, and a triple.

Why would players agree to throw the World Series? The owner of the White Sox, Charles Cominsky, was known as one of the cheapest baseball owners in the league. For example, he refused to clean the player's uniforms. The players refused to pay to clean their uniforms, which started to look awfully dirty, so the team was dubbed the "Black Sox." Charles Cominsky agreed to pay for the cleaning of the dirty uniforms and then billed the players by garnishing part of their World Series earnings. Players like the great "Shoeless" Joe Jackson wanted revenge on Cominsky and a chance to really earn some big money. The Cincinnati Reds ultimately won the World Series 5 to 3.

The Development of Las Vegas, Nevada

As a western state, Nevada experienced the lure and culture of gambling. The activity was legalized in 1869 and then outlawed in 1910. Some say that the demise occurred because of the development of the original downtown red light district, notorious "Block 16." Yet in 1931 the Wide Open Gambling Bill legalized gambling again. However, because of the Great Depression, gaming did not become an important economic factor in Nevada until the end of World War II. Many of the casinos of that period were referred to as **saw dust joints**, because they resembled the old Wild West with cowboys and loose rules.

Figure 8–2 The Flamingo Hotel on the Strip in Las Vegas, Nevada, was Bugsy's casino.

In 1946, Benjamin "Bugsy" Siegel, reputed founder of Murder, Inc., opened the Flamingo Hotel Casino, which became one of the first modern hotel casinos with elegant restaurants, nightclubs, and entertainment (Figure 8–2). Bugsy believed that an elegant casino would attract a more affluent crowd instead of the "saw dust addicts." At that time, the location of the Flamingo was outside of Las Vegas city limits. However, with the massive development in Las Vegas, it is now positioned in the middle of the Las Vegas Strip. During his day, many critics believed that Siegel was foolish to build a casino in the middle of the desert. However, Bugsy is now considered a visionary.

During the construction of the casino, Bugsy was very popular with the Hollywood crowd, which flocked to the upscale resort. However, the initial opening night was a fiasco. There was bad weather, incomplete construction, and the Hollywood stars stayed away. They did not want the notoriety of being seen publicly at a known mob casino. As a result, Siegel asked the mob for more investment money for his project. The reopening was a success, but it was too late for Siegel, who was murdered in Beverly Hills, California, a year later, as a message from organized crime regarding the mismanagement of its funds.

In 1945, the Nevada Legislature passed a gaming revenue tax of 1 percent of all gambling winnings in excess of $300,000. The tax commission was also given power to investigate the backgrounds of individuals seeking licenses. This was a direct response to Siegel's ties to organized crime. Unfortunately, the tax commission was understaffed, and many licenses were granted to individuals with criminal backgrounds. By 1950, Senator Estes Kefauver of Tennessee conducted special Senate hearings regarding gambling operations in Nevada. The outcome of the report largely validated the public's sentiments against gambling and organized crime. But this government intervention did not stop the growing presence of gambling in Nevada.

During the 1950s, expansion in gambling was slow because of its negative image and the difficulty in securing financing for development. So, Jimmy Hoffa, president of the Teamsters, persuaded the Trustees of the Teamsters' Central States Pension Fund to purchase the Sands Hotel and Casino for $10 million. By 1977, Las Vegas casinos held $240 million in Teamsters Pension Fund loans, which was 24 percent of its entire portfolio. With the 1960 election of John F. Kennedy, major controversy developed between organized crime and the federal government. President Kennedy appointed his brother, Robert (Bobby) Kennedy, as attorney general, who promptly declared "war on Nevada." Bobby Kennedy wanted federal agents to raid the casinos and confiscate financial records, but Governor Grant Sawyer was able to cancel the raid. However, other federal organizations such as the Internal Revenue Service, Federal Bureau of Investigation, Bureau of Narcotics, and Department of Labor continued their own investigations into fraudulent business practices.

In 1966, as negative public attention was being drawn to Nevada, recluse Texas millionaire Howard Hughes came to Nevada. He booked a high roller suite at the Desert Inn but did not gamble. Howard Hughes' spokesman, Robert Mayheu, was informed that Hughes had to leave unless he wanted to purchase the Hotel/Casino. On April 1, 1967, Howard Hughes purchased the Desert Inn from a Cleveland mobster, Moe Dalitz, for $13.25 million. With no affiliation with organized crime, Howard Hughes went on a spending spree, and within a year, Hughes had spent $65 million and had acquired 4 of the top 15 hotels on the Las Vegas Strip. The 2,000 hotel rooms he owned represented 20 percent of the total room inventory on the Strip. Because Howard Hughes was a successful businessman, he helped legitimize the gaming industry and took it into a new era of corporate business. As a result of people such as Hughes and Bill Harrah, the **Corporate Gaming Act of 1967** was passed. Later the act was rewritten and passed into law in 1969, which legitimized gaming in the eyes of corporate America. As a result, in 1972, Harrah's was the first solely gaming corporation to be placed on the New York Stock Exchange.

During this transition period, organized crime continued to be involved in casino ownership and management. The mob convinced Allen Glick, a Southern California businessman with a clean criminal record, to become a Las Vegas casino owner. Unable to secure bank loans and naïve to the organized crime element, he turned to the Teamsters' Central States Pension Fund for a $65 million loan in 1973. By 1977, he owed the Pension Fund $156 million. Then, Allen Glick was informed that he was to hire Frank "Lefty" Rosenthal as an advisor for casino operations. Glick opposed the decision but discovered he was not in control of the casino anymore. For Lefty's protection, Anthony "The Ant" Spilatro was hired to watch Frank's back. Spilatro was a mobster's mobster: tough, violent, shrewd, and so crooked that he worked overtime finding ways to rob the casino customers even while they were losing money at the gaming tables.[3] Tony's relationship with Lefty created problems obtaining the much-coveted gaming license necessary to manage a casino. Even though Lefty challenged the decision to deny him a casino license, his house of cards was folding. Tony was having an affair with Lefty's wife Geri. Finally, in the end, Allen Glick divested his casino holdings because of personal threats to his family. Frank Rosenthal had an attempt made on his life but was saved by a custom-built Cadillac that protected him from a bomb. Anthony Spilatro was buried, possibly alive, with his brother, in a cornfield in the Midwest. For the complete story, read Nicholas Pileggi's book entitled *Casino, Love and Horror in Las Vegas*. The movie *Casino* (1995) starring Robert DeNiro, Sharon Stone, and Joe Pesci, is based on this book.

Today Las Vegas is very much a corporate-run enterprise. Its ties to the mob have been minimized, and its new adult entertainment image has arrived. Strategic plans for Las Vegas suggest that with all the money that gambling generates, Las Vegas wants to be the entertainment mecca of the future. In Las Vegas you can go anywhere in the world—for Venice, go to the Venetian Casino Hotel (Figure 8–3); to visit Egypt, the

Figure 8–3 Replicating other attractions around the world is a big job. However, here at the Venetian Hotel Resort and Casino, the singing gondolier gives a great feeling of being in Venice and adds great entertainment value. Photo courtesy of George G. Fenich.

Luxor awaits; or if you want go to Paris, there is the Paris Casino Resort. Why do people want to go to these places? When visiting New York City, people want to see the Coney Island roller coaster, the Stock Exchange, or a Broadway show. However, these also are all in Las Vegas. Because the casinos have so much money available for capital, they believe that they can do a show bigger and better than New York can. What if you want to go to an art museum? The Bellagio in Las Vegas has one. The plan is to develop the best of all kinds of entertainment in Las Vegas so that people will have a "one-stop shopping" experience. Las Vegas is a destination for everyone. Some visitors can go on less expensively, using fun books (coupon books with deep discounts in conjunction with bargain airfare and package deals). Others are VIPs or whales who go first class with the expectation of serious gambling. Many Las Vegas visitors also go for the curiosity of it all.

The Ocean, Emotion, and Promotion

In the early 1900s, Atlantic City, New Jersey was a major tourist destination, luring visitors to the ocean, beach, and boardwalk (Figure 8–4). Because New York City and Philadelphia are close by, many visitors hopped on trains to visit the seaside ocean resorts. Visiting the ocean beaches was the height of fashion, creating an emotional

Figure 8–4 Riding along the board-walk in a rolling chair is the best way to travel in Atlantic City, New Jersey.

high of excitement because of the many promotions that capitalized on the salt air and sunshine. The boardwalk was the center of Atlantic City's attraction, comparable to the present day Las Vegas Strip. Many famous performers visited Atlantic City, including singers and performers such as Frank Sinatra, Sammy Davis Jr., Dean Martin, Jerry Lewis, and Shirley Temple.

Many restaurants, bars, and tourist attractions relied on promotions to lure vacationers to their operations. There were many original Atlantic City promotions such as the animated trademark for roasted peanuts, Mr. Peanut. The Miss America Pageant began in Atlantic City. The Steel Pier was the place to be, with shopping, restaurants, and the original salt-water taffy. However, people also came to see star attractions such as the Traymore Hotel, a first-class resort during Atlantic City's heyday, the prize-fighting kangaroo, and the diving horses. Also, some travelers believed the salty ocean water provided medicinal cures for illnesses. These attractions continued to draw tourists during the roaring 20s. Even during the Great Depression, families took day trips from Philadelphia to enjoy a day at the beach.

Perpetuating the excitement was the draw of illegal gambling, drinking, and late night entertainment. With antigambling sentiment strong in 1908, a group of policemen and detectives raided a gambling joint, capturing an entire ton of paraphernalia. They confiscated roulette wheels, faro layouts, and spindle games. By 1913, gambling devices valued at tens of thousands of dollars had been destroyed.

However, as airline travel became popular in the 1950s and 1960s, the public chose other, further destinations than Atlantic City. Florida became the place for the rich and famous, and Atlantic City experienced a decline in tourism dollars and a physical deterioration of its hotels. Many regarded Atlantic City as the "Slum by the Sea."

Since gaming was gaining notoriety along with the success of lotteries, the state of New Jersey gave residents a chance to vote to allow casino gambling for the entire state (November 5, 1974). When the vote was tallied, the referendum failed. Why?

1. Lack of interest. Not everyone wants to gamble, at least not in his or her own hometown or backyard (leading to the popular acronym **NIMBY**—meaning *not in my b*ack *y*ard).
2. Lack of organization. There was an absence of special interest groups selling the positive virtues of gaming.
3. Lack of money. Funding for marketing and advertising was missing.
4. Lack of strategic marketing.

Consequently, a second referendum was proposed for gaming in Atlantic City only. The reason behind this logic was the need to redevelop Atlantic City into the resort it was early in the century. The mayor of Atlantic City became the chairman of a new group called the Committee to Rebuild Atlantic City (CRAC). This group replaced the negative aspects of the failed referendum and marketed the positive aspects of gaming, such as the benefits that redevelopment would have for labor unions and that the gaming proceeds would aid senior citizens. These issues were addressed, and on Tuesday, November 2, 1976, the voters of the state of New Jersey approved gaming for Atlantic City.[4]

Resorts International opened as Atlantic City's first casino hotel on May 26, 1978. The parking and crowds on the first day were unbelievable, as witnessed by this author, who was home from college and decided to visit Atlantic City that day. During the first year, resorts had revenues of $224.6 million and winnings of $62.8 million. That first year, the state of New Jersey collected $18 million in taxes. Many view Las Vegas as a major destination because tourists go for weekends and vacations. However, because of the size of the nearby population from large metropolitan cities such as New York, Philadelphia, and Baltimore, many Atlantic City visitors travel by charter buses and cars for the day.

Currently, Atlantic City feels the pressure of competition from the Native American casinos in Connecticut. The **racino** in Delaware, along with the future adoption of racinos in Pennsylvania and New York State also contribute to the financial pressure on the Atlantic City casinos. Since the 1970s, Atlantic City has improved many urban areas, built a new convention center, upgraded the highway infrastructures, and also built a baseball stadium named the "Sandcastle" for a semi-pro team named the "Surf." Recent upgrades to the Atlantic City casino industry include new themes such as the Sands motif with history from the original Sands Hotel in Las Vegas and the Quarter at the Tropicana, which resembles Havana, Cuba. Atlantic City also recently added its newest casino (number 13) named "Borgata" (2003). New shopping districts such as the new Steel Pier and parking garages have updated the boardwalk. The completion of the tunnel between the Atlantic City Expressway and the Marina will encourage further development in the Marina area, especially since the Transportation Center will tie all of the different modes of travel together into one drop-off and pick-up area for all the casinos, thereby helping eliminate major traffic problems.

The Native Americans Get Their Chance

Ever since the early settlers arrived, Native Americans have been moved from their lands and eventually placed on reservations. However since the 1830s, federal law has upheld that Indian tribes have powers of self-government over their lands, and that state governments have little or no say within the boundaries of the tribal reservations. The U.S. Congress is the only **plenary power** to place limits on what was bestowed on Native American tribes as sovereign rights. The issue of sovereignty later became a major issue when the casinos began to make money. The sole power to administer laws also means that anything that happens on the reservation stays on the reservation. For example, the reservations have their own police forces, and state troopers cannot enter tribal lands without permission. Sovereignty also means that the states cannot tax anything on the reservation. This was helpful when lotteries were making a comeback during the 1960s and 1970s. Religious groups also began offering bingo to their communities. So, tribes began to offer bingo to raise revenues to enhance their low federal support payments. This was no new device for the Native American tribes; games of chance have long been a part of their ancestral heritage. Anthropologists suggest that gambling was an important means of wealth redistribution within Indian communities. The traditional gambling games of native tribes consisted of dice games, guessing games, and card games, as well as wagers placed on the outcome of horse races, foot races, and other athletic contests between villages and tribes.

Separated from their traditional hunting grounds and their way of life, the Native Americans languished on the reservation and many were forced to leave in order to survive. By 1988, when the **Indian Gaming Regulatory Act (IGRA)** was passed, the people left on the reservation were living in relentless poverty. The alcoholism rate was higher than the rate for the general population; the suicide rate was 95 percent higher; and the unemployment rate was twice the national average. When the tribes applied for federal help, Secretary of the Interior James Watt was reported to say "Stop asking the Great White Father for money and start your own business!" Gaming was selected by many tribes as that business. To attract players, the tribes offered higher cash prizes than state law allowed for other bingo operators, such as charities and churches. As a result, the states moved to shut down the tribes' operations in the historic case of *Seminole Tribe v. Butterworth* (1979). The tribe sued in federal district court because Florida's regulatory power had no power over the Seminole tribe's bingo hall. Judgment was in favor of the tribes as long as a particular form of gaming was not criminally prohibited in the state. Since the state did allow other groups to operate bingo hall games, it had to leave the

Seminoles' bingo operation alone. Then, in the case of *Cabazon Band of Mission Indians v. California* (1987), the Supreme Court approved the lower court's reasoning.

However, states feared that Native American gaming would become an unregulated magnet for organized crime and that the tribes would not bear any of the social costs of gambling. Consequently, Congress used its plenary power to pass IGRA, which provided a regulatory framework for Indian gaming, consisting of three classes of gaming. The first level, Class I, consisted of traditional tribal games, and the tribal council maintained control over them. The second level, Class II, was bingo, which was regulated by the tribe and the federal Indian Gaming Commission. For the third level, Class III, which is casino gaming, IGRA requires that a compact (contract) be made between the tribes and the state governments. This part of the act is extremely important because it means that the state can bargain for a percentage of the casino winnings that they are not allowed to tax because the tribes are sovereign nations. (Remember the previous discussion?). However, the tribes can seek federal intervention if the states are not negotiating in good faith. The financial impact of Native American gaming has been immense. In 1988, tribal gaming earned $288 million. By 2003, the figure was $16.2 billion. That's a growth rate of about 5500 percent. Those tribal casinos employ more than 400,000 people, and roughly 75 percent of those jobs are held by non–Native Americans.[5]

However, those numbers do not reflect some of the problems that the tribes faced. First of all, in the beginning, no American banks would touch the new venture proposal of the tribes. They were considered to be a bad risk. Eventually, other sources were found; for example, the Pequots of Foxwoods Casinos finally found a Malaysian investment group to finance it's venture. Another problem was that the educational level for most of the reservation members was less than the sixth grade. As a result, outsiders were offered management contracts to run the new casinos. Because there were few educated tribal members, many of the first management contracts had clauses that robbed the tribes of much of the profits. When the money started to roll in, some tribes managed funds while building schools and housing and improving health care, which opened the doors for personal and future success. Many tribes began dividing up the profits among each of the tribal members. Major problems occurred with this. Exactly who *was* a tribal member? Many tribes had not developed a sophisticated or specific definition.

Figure 8–5 Foxwoods Resort Casino, Ledyard, Connecticut.

As a result, people claiming tribal bloodlines arrived at the reservation demanding their fair share. In addition, the automatic dividing of the profits created motivational problems for young people. Why become educated if one is destined to have money without any effort? Finally, not all casinos had the financial success of Foxwoods. Like any business, some fail and some are small business ventures that sustain the owners but do not make them rich. In addition, it is important to remember that not all tribes have casinos. Many have voted against building casinos for ethical and moral reasons.

The Return of "Maverick"

Just as Native Americans regained their ancestral heritage, riverboat gambling returned to its historical roots. As with Atlantic City, the Midwest was also in a state of economic depression. In the early 1980s, several major farm equipment manufacturers had closed their factories. Mayors of cities in the Midwest talked on national television about handling 25 percent unemployment rates. As these politicians searched for answers, gambling, with its quick, large profit margins, came up for discussion. The concept was appealing because it would lock gaming into small areas of the state next to the Mississippi River. This meant that gambling was not in the backyards of residents. (Remember NIMBY concept from

Figure 8–6 Riverboat on the mighty Mississippi River.
Photo courtesy of George G. Fenich.

Atlantic City?) Only a small area would be affected, but its economic benefits would impact the whole state's financial structure.

Iowa was the first state to introduce a riverboat casino on April 1, 1991. Passengers who embarked on a short cruise were limited to a maximum $5 bet with a maximum loss of $200 per trip. The major concern was to not encourage gambling addiction. Because the riverboats were unhappy with the restrictions in Iowa, they looked for alternative docks. The politicians had forgotten that a riverboat that is required to sail can easily move its home base to other locations. With the large profit potential of riverboat gambling, cities along the Mississippi quickly jumped on the bandwagon and abandoned the tight betting restrictions. Illinois followed in September 1991, Mississippi in August 1992, Louisiana in October 1993, Missouri in May 1994, and Indiana in December 1995. With the increase in competition, many locations eliminated the sailing requirements and allowed 24-hour dockside gambling. Amenities were basic, dining options were limited, and there were no on-property hotels.

As the riverboat jurisdictions expanded in the early 1990s, people became excited about the new gaming markets that were opening. As a result, Wall Street investors opened their pocketbooks. That all changed when in 1993, gaming began to be voted down in many potential jurisdictions. In addition, Mississippi and Louisiana riverboats were having problems with the increased competition, and riverboats began to shut down. The increased competition forced the cities and states to evaluate their regulations. Many of the cities agreed to develop land-based structures and improve infrastructure in order to allow better access to the riverboats. For example, Tunica County, Mississippi, built a new highway from Memphis that circumvented the old country roads. However, state governments were not only driven by consumer demands. The tax rates for riverboats are the highest of any industry. In the beginning, 20 percent to 25 percent tax rates were the norm. Now, the highest tax rate is a sliding scale correlating profits to taxes, with 70 percent as the top tax bracket. Riverboat gaming has become a major player in this country's casino industry. The only question that remains is how well they will fare against competition from the next trend in gambling expansion.

Mega Resorts and the Future of Gaming

By 1989, lotteries had become commonplace. Native American casinos were in their development stage along with riverboats. The next phase of casino development was about to change the gaming market. In answer to the competitive environment, Las Vegas created the mega resort as the newest casino attraction—all the dining, entertainment, spas, shopping, lodging, and casino action under one roof. History points to the opening of Steve Wynn's Mirage Hotel Resort Casino in November 1989 as one of the first of these mega casinos. Wynn developed the tropical-themed Mirage with the formerly exclusive Siegfried & Roy Show, "The Secret Garden of Siegfried & Roy," which featured six rare animals, a dolphin habitat with a 1.5 million gallon pool, a 20,000-gallon saltwater aquarium display at the check-in area, a royal white tiger habitat, and a simulated volcano that periodically erupted. Besides these attractions, the Mirage has 3,044 rooms, 11 restaurants, and 94,000 square feet of casino. The Mirage was the first major Las Vegas casino to open in 15 years. The goal of the mega resort was to lure visitors to an all-inclusive hotel/casino with enough amenities to keep guests there the entire time, without venturing to other competitive properties on the Strip. Each new casino resort since then has broadened the definition of the all-inclusive resort, and each jurisdiction has adapted the idea to fit its natural attractions.

Gaming has adapted and changed to meet each competitive challenge. When the first modern-day floating casino set sail in 1991, it was the fourth gaming option to compete with the established land-based Nevada and Atlantic City casinos and the Native American casinos. It was a classic sellers market in the early 1990s. The supply was limited and the demand incredibly high. Nationally, gaming continues today in all states with the exception of Hawaii and Utah. In 2004, Pennsylvania approved as many as 61,000 slot machines at 14 venues statewide. That is more one-arm bandits than any other state, with the exception of Nevada. Many of the slot machines are designated for horse racing tracks for the continued growth of racinos. How will this new competition affect the Atlantic City market? A similar competitive situation is occurring in Ohio and Kentucky. Just as Pennsylvania saw revenue leaving the state to Atlantic City, Ohio and Kentucky are considering racinos to combat the floods of revenues going to riverboat gaming in other states. Casinos from the East to the West Coasts continue to renovate and reposition themselves so gamblers want to return to their venues. As an example, remember the Seminole Indian Tribe? It has teamed up with the Hard Rock Hotel Casino to lure more gamblers to its venue in Florida. In the spring of 2005, Steve Wynn opened a 2,700-room mega resort on the original site of the Desert Inn. He named the property the "Wynn."

Finally, if you wish to gamble, bet on sports, and play poker but do not want to leave your home, there is the Internet. However, there has been some controversy regarding playing on gaming websites. Many sites are located outside of the United States; so underage gamblers can possibly participate in these gambling sites. Another concern is that betting on the Internet is similar to playing a computer game, except that actual wagers are being placed! State governments have concerns regarding Internet gaming, because the state receives no revenues from that particular gambling activity. Historically, a gambling experience needed several participants; now you can experience it alone, inside or outside of your home. So what will be the future's next roll of the gaming dice?

Summary

Gambling has been part of the American and Native American cultures since precolonial times. As governments were being formed, gambling was either embraced or banned. As growth and development occurred throughout the country, so did gambling. Originally governments saw the benefit of taxation on gaming revenues yet could not control their own greed. As public sentiment against gambling increased, gambling still could not be stopped or banned. When government passed laws to stop or punish gamblers, organized crime took over the activity. As public opinion shifted toward accepting gambling, organized crime has taken a back seat to the gambling activity. Many state governments have seen the benefits of gambling: increased taxation revenues, tourism dollars, job creation, and infrastructure development and they embraced gaming in its present form as general entertainment. However, the question remains, how will casinos change further to meet their new challenges?

key terms

Sharpers	Racinos
Saw dust joints	Plenary Power
Corporate Gaming Act of 1967	Indian Gaming Regulatory Act (IGRA)
NIMBY	

review questions

1. Compare and contrast how gambling was introduced to early American settlers and to Native Americans during precolonial times.
2. What were some of the early colonial gambling laws?
3. What is the significance of the Crescent City House in New Orleans?
4. What is the relationship between the visitors to New Orleans in the 1800s and the miners in San Francisco?
5. How has the 1919 World Series affected baseball in the present day?
6. Why is Benjamin "Bugsy" Siegel considered a visionary in Las Vegas?
7. What events occurred during the 1940s, 1950s, and 1960s to cause the congressional investigation of gambling?
8. How was gambling finally approved for Atlantic City?
9. Why do Native Americans have gaming venues on their reservations?
10. What period of American history is the current rise of riverboat gaming attributed to?
11. What is a mega resort? Provide an example, describing its décor, motif, ambience, restaurants, and entertainment.
12. What does the future hold for gaming?

internet sites

Bally's
www.ballyac.com

Barona Valley Ranch
www.barona.com

Bellagio
www.bellagioresort.com

Borgata
www.theborgata.com

Caesars
www.caesars.com

Circus-Circus
www.circuscircus.com

Foxwoods
www.foxwoods.com

Harrahs'
www.harrahs.com

Hilton
www.hiltonac.com

Ho-Chunk Casino
www.ho-chunk.com

Luxor Hotel Casino
www.Luxor.com

Mandalay Bay
www.mandalaybay.com

Mirage
www.themirage.com

Mohegan Sun
www.mohegansun.com

Mystic Lake
www.mysticlake.com

Paris
www.paris-lv.com

Rio Hotel & Casino
www.playrio.com

Resorts
www.resortac.com

Sands
www.acsands.com

Tropicana
www.tropicana.net

Trumps Casinos
www.trumpmarina.com; www.trumpplaza.com; www.trumptaj.com

Venetian Hotel
www.venetian.com

Wynns
www.wynnlasvegas.com
www.library.ca.gov/crb/97/03/chapt2.html
http://govinfo.library.unt.edu/njisc/research/lotteries.html
www.americancasinoguide.com/Iowa.shtml

endnotes

1. Asbury, H. (1936) *The French Quarter*. New York: Alfred A. Knopf.
2. Devol, G. H. (1829) *Forty Years a Gambler on The Mississippi*. Bedford: Applewood Books.
3. Pileggi, N. (1995). *Casino Love and Honor in Las Vegas*. New York: Simon & Shuster.
4. Dombrink, J. & Thompson, W. N. (1990) *The Last Resort*. Reno: University of Nevada Press.
5. Indian Gaming Facts. (2005) NIGA. http://www.indiangaming.org/library/index.shtml. Accessed May 17, 2005.

references

Ash, B. (1998). Development of Gaming. Hashimoto, K., Fenich, G. & Kline, S.,

Bach, D. (2004). *The Automatic Millionaire*. New York: Broadway Books.

Bourie, S. (2004). *American Casino Guide*. FL: Casino Vacations.

Brokopp, J. G. (2004). The Magnificent Voyage of Riverboat Gambling, Casino Player 100–105.

Burns, K. (1994). "The Faith of 50 Million People" (*Baseball: A Film by Ken Burns*). The Baseball Film Project, Inc.

Fine, A. (2004). Now, "It's Pennsylvania's turn." *Casino Player*, 8.

Haley, J. (ed). (2004). *Gambling Examining Pop Culture*. Michigan: Greenhaven Press.

Hashimoto, K., Fenich, G., and Kline, S. (1998). *Casino Management Past, Present, Future*.Dubuque, Iowa: Kendall/Hunt.

Hicks, J. (ed). (1977). *Gamblers of the Old West*. Alexandria,Virginia: Time-Life Books.

Kilby, J., Fox, J., and Lucas A. (2005). *Casino Operations Management*. New Jersey: John Wiley.

Leventhal, (2001). *The World Series—An Illustrated Encyclopedia of the Fall Classic*. New York: Black Dog & Leventhal Publishing.

Nestor, B. (2004). "Native American Casinos & You." *Casino Player*, 82–88.

Vignette
The Impact of Native American Gaming

Marlene Sproul, Coeur D'Alene

The impact of Indian gaming is difficult at best to describe. The Coeur d'Alene Tribe sits nestled in North Idaho, just 30 minutes south of Coeur d'Alene, Idaho, and Spokane, Washington. Our tribe, with just 1,900 members, has suffered for generations with lack of jobs and inadequate education.

We were just out of reach, as 30 miles is a long way when there is no money to purchase fuel for transportation, and not even a vehicle to transport a person from work, little less school. It all seemed like a vicious cycle of alcohol abuse and unemployment. And the last thing anyone ever expected was for Indian gaming to have an impact on our lives like it did.

I was attending college in Coeur d'Alene, Idaho, and living on the reservation in Worley, Idaho. I always thought that in order for people to change there had to be either a religious or educational experience. Indian gaming brought change through economic relief. At the time, I didn't realize the impact economic relief would have on our tribe, and I don't think anyone else did either.

The first area to be impacted was employment. Employment was huge and people I never thought would work or quit drinking did quit drinking excessively and went to work. Our people took pride wearing their new uniforms and in having a job. Our people's spirits were high and the smiles on their faces when they went to the store to purchase groceries, place money in the tithing basket, or just socializing were apparent throughout the reservation.

This was an important aspect. It was good to see our people happy and prosperous. Now our people could dream and make their dreams reality. New cars were purchased and clothes and household items. Before Indian gaming, most of our people didn't own phones, little less computers. Now our people own phones and computers. Email is widely used as a form of communication. All this and more occurred with the onset of Indian gaming.

Our tribal leaders were able to place the revenue generated from Indian gaming back into our businesses. Our natural resources department was able to build a new facility and hire many people to look after "Mother Earth." As natives we believe our ancestors left us with a huge legacy, "to protect or be the caretakers of Mother Earth."

Revenue generated also went into other programs such as higher education, our elders program, land acquisition, tribal court, development of a communications department, tribal farm, tribal police department, offering our tribal employees a 401k program, and many more aspects I am not fully aware of.

Moreover, my point about the impact of Indian gaming being difficult to describe at best is to understand this one philosophy. Imagine having no hope for the future day after day. Knowing even if you are able to do well at school, there is no job. Knowing if you want to look for a job off the reservation there is no car to get you to work day after day. Knowing if you want a job, you must leave the reservation, your family, your home and venture out into a culture you don't feel comfortable in. Plus out into a culture that doesn't understand your way of life. Trapped like a bird in a cage, that is what our life was like before Indian gaming. Now we are free to fly.

4

Internal Control

9 Product: Games and Statistics

Robert C. Hannum, University of Denver

Learning Objectives

1. To identify the primary games offered in most casinos.

2. To explain how the mathematics governing the games generates revenues.

3. To identify the house advantage associated with the various games.

4. To differentiate among the several ways to express win rate.

5. To explain the role of volatility in casino operations.

6. To describe the role of mathematics in gaming regulation.

Chapter Outline

Introduction

This chapter discusses the various casino game products and shows how casinos make money from these games. The discussion includes a nontechnical overview of the necessary mathematics—basic probability, odds, expectation, and house advantage—as well as several related topics, including confusion about win rates, game volatility, player value and comp policies, casino pricing mistakes, and regulatory issues. Statistical advantages associated with the major games are also provided.

Overview of Casino Games

Some casino games are pure chance—no amount of skill or strategy can alter the odds.[1] Games of pure chance include roulette, craps, baccarat, keno, the big-six wheel of fortune, and slot machines. Of these, baccarat and craps offer the best **odds**,[2] with **house advantages** of 1.2 percent and less than 1 percent (assuming only pass/come with full odds), respectively. Roulette and slots cost the player more—house advantages of 5.3 percent for double-zero roulette and 5 percent to 10 percent for slots—while the wheel of fortune feeds the casino near 20 percent of the wagers, and keno is a veritable casino cash cow with average house advantage close to 30 percent (Table 9–1).

Games in which an element of skill can affect the house advantage include blackjack, video poker, and the four popular poker-based table games: Caribbean Stud poker (CSP), Let It Ride (LIR), Three Card poker (TCP), and Pai Gow poker (PGP). For the poker games, optimal strategy results in a house edge in the 3 percent to 5 percent range (CSP has the largest house edge, PGP the lowest, with LIR and TCP in between). For video poker, the statistical advantage varies depending on the particular machine, but generally this game can be very player friendly—a house edge less than 3 percent is not uncommon and some are less than 1 percent—if played with expert strategy.[3]

Blackjack, the most popular of all table games, offers the skilled player some of the best odds in the casino. The house advantage varies slightly depending on the rules and number of decks, but a player using basic strategy faces little or no disadvantage in

Table 9–1   House advantage for popular casino games

House Advantages for Popular Casino Games

Game	House Advantage
Roulette (double-zero US)	5.3%
Craps (pass/come)	1.4%
Craps (pass/come with double odds)	0.6%
Blackjack–average player	2.0%
Blackjack–6 decks, basic strategy*	0.5%
Blackjack–single deck, basic strategy*	0.0%
Baccarat (no tie bets)	1.2%
Caribbean Stud*	5.2%
Let It Ride*	3.5%
Three Card Poker*	3.4%
Pai Gow Poker (ante/play)*	2.5%
Slots	5%–10%
Video Poker*	0.5%–3%
Keno (average)	27.0%

*optimal strategy

a single-deck game and only a 0.5 percent house edge in the common six-deck game. Despite these numbers, the average player ends up giving the casino a 2 percent edge due to mistakes and deviations from basic strategy. Complete basic strategy tables can be found in many books, and many casino-hotel gift shops sell color-coded credit card–sized versions. Rule variations favorable to the player include using fewer decks, dealer stands on soft seventeen (worth 0.2 percent), doubling after splitting (0.14 percent), late surrender (worth 0.06 percent), and early surrender (uncommon, but worth 0.24 percent). However, if the dealer hits soft seventeen, it will cost you, as will any restrictions on when you can double down. Table 9–2 shows the house advantages for major casino wagers.

The sections that follow give further details about the major casino games and the basic mathematics underlying these games. The discussion is necessarily limited; readers wishing to delve deeper into the mathematics and its role in casino gaming are referred to Hannum and Cabot (2005), from which the following has been adapted.

Table 9–2 House advantages for major casino wagers

House Advantages for Major Casino Wagers

Game	Bet	HA
Baccarat	Banker (5 % commission)	1.06%
	Player	1.24%
Big Six Wheel	Average	19.84%
Blackjack	Card-counting	−1.00%
	Basic strategy	0.50%
	Average player	2.00%
	Poor player	4.00%
Caribbean Stud	Ante	5.22%
Casino War	Basic bet	2.88%
Craps	Any craps	11.11%
	Any seven	16.67%
	Big 6, Big 8	9.09%
	Buy (any)	4.76%
	C&E	11.11%
	Don't Pass/Don't Come	1.36%
	Don't Pass/Don't Come w/1 × odds	0.68%
	Don't Pass/Don't Come w/2 × odds	0.45%
	Don't Pass/Don't Come w/3 × odds	0.34%
	Don't Pass/Don't Come w/5 × odds	0.23%
	Don't Pass/Don't Come w/10 × odds	0.12%
	Don't Place 4 or 10	3.03%
	Don't Place 5 or 9	2.50%
	Don't Place 6 or 8	1.82%
	Field (2 or 12 pay double)	5.56%
	Field (2 or 12 pays triple)	2.78%
	Hard 4, Hard 10	11.11%
	Hard 6, Hard 8	9.09%
	Hop Bet–easy (14–1)	16.67%
	Hop Bet–easy (15–1)	11.11%
	Hop Bet–hard (29–1)	16.67%
	Hop Bet–hard (30–1)	13.89%
	Horn Bet (30–1 & 15–1)	12.50%
	Horn High–any (29–1 & 14–1)	16.67%
	Horn High 2, Horn High 12 (30–1 & 15–1)	12.78%
	Horn High 3, Horn High 11 (30–1 & 15–1)	12.22%

(continued)

Table 9–2   House Advantages for Major Casino Wagers (*Continued*)

House Advantages for Major Casino Wagers

Game	Bet	HA
	Lay 4 or 10	2.44%
	Lay 5 or 9	3.23%
	Lay 6 or 8	4.00%
	Pass/Come	1.41%
	Pass/Come w/1 × odds	0.85%
	Pass/Come w/2 × odds	0.61%
	Pass/Come w/3 × odds	0.47%
	Pass/Come w/5 × odds	0.33%
	Pass/Come w/10 × odds	0.18%
	Place 4 or 10	6.67%
	Place 5 or 9	4.00%
	Place 6 or 8	1.52%
	Three, Eleven (14–1)	16.67%
	Three, Eleven (15–1)	11.11%
	Two, Twelve (29–1)	16.67%
	Two, Twelve (30–1)	13.89%
Keno	Typical	27.00%
Let It Ride	Base bet	3.51%
Pai Gow Poker	Skilled player (non-banker)	2.54%
	Average player (non-banker)	2.84%
Red Dog	Basic bet (six decks)	2.80%
Roulette	Single-zero wheel (all bets)	2.70%
	Double-zero wheel (all bets except five-number)	5.26%
	Double-zero wheel (five-number bet)	7.89%
Sic Bo	Big/Small	2.78%
	One of a kind	7.87%
	7, 14	9.72%
	8, 13	12.50%
	10, 11	12.50%
	Any three of a kind	13.89%
	5, 16	13.89%
	4, 17	15.28%
	Three of a kind	16.20%
	Two-dice combination	16.67%
	6, 15	16.67%

(continued)

Table 9–2   House advantages for major casino wagers (*continued*)

House Advantages for Major Casino Wagers

Game	Bet	HA
	Two of a kind	18.52%
	9, 12	18.98%
Slots	Dollar slots (good)	4.00%
	Quarter slots (good)	5.00%
	Dollar slots (average)	6.00%
	Quarter slots (average)	8.00%
Sports Betting	Bet $11 to win $10	4.55%
Three Card Poker	Pair plus	2.32%
	Ante	3.37%
Video Poker	Selected machines	−0.50%

*House Advantages under typical conditions, expressed "per hand" and including ties, where appropriate. Optimal strategy assumed unless otherwise noted. Although the HA is constant for all bets at the roulette wheel (except for the 5-way), the payoffs do vary according to the bet (from even money on a color bet to 35–1 on a single number).

Summary of Major Casino Games

This section outlines the basic rules for many of the popular casino games.

Roulette

Roulette is a simple game to play: players merely try to guess which number will occur as the outcome of the spin of a ball around a numbered wheel (Figure 9–1). There are two types of wheels, the double-zero, common in the United States, and the single-zero, favored in Europe.

The double-zero wheel contains 38 pockets, numbered 1 through 36, 0, and 00. Of those numbered 1–36, 18 are red and 18 are black. The 0 and 00 are green. The single-zero wheel lacks the 00, and so has only 37 numbers. The game is played essentially the same regardless of which wheel is used, although the house advantage for the single-zero wheel is about half that of the double-zero game (2.7 percent vs. 5.3 percent). To play the game, players wager on a number, color, parity, or combination of numbers. Table 9–3 shows the types of bets available, with their payoffs and true odds for the double-zero game.

Traditionally, the dealer spins the wheel counterclockwise and releases a small ball clockwise on a track on the upper portion of the wheel. When the ball loses its momentum, it

Figure 9–1
Courtesy of the Isle of
Capri.

Table 9-3 Roulette—types of bets

Roulette (Double-Zero Wheel)

Type of Bet	True Odds	Payoff
Straight-up (1 number)	37 to 1	35 to 1
Split (2 numbers)	36 to 2	17 to 1
Street (3 numbers)	35 to 3	11 to 1
Corner (4 numbers)	34 to 4	8 to 1
Five-Number Bet (5 numbers)	33 to 5	6 to 1
Double Street or Line (6 numbers)	32 to 6	5 to 1
Dozens/Columns (12 numbers)	26 to 12	2 to 1
Red/Black/Odd/Even/High/Low (18 numbers)	20 to 18	1 to 1

drops, bounces, and settles into one of the numbered pockets. Players win or lose depending on whether the winning number was among those that they selected with their wagers. The casino makes money because the payoff odds are less than the true odds.

Craps

Craps is played by betting on the outcome of a roll of a pair of dice (Figure 9–2). The roll is determined as the sum of the values of the two dice thrown except for certain bets such as hardways, which depend on the particular value of the individual die. There are

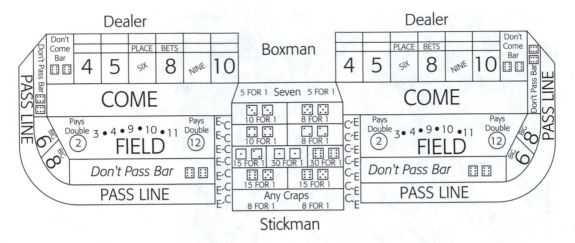

Figure 9–2 Craps layout.

a myriad of possible wagers that can be made, each with different odds, payoff, and house advantage.

The Pass Line.   When a game or new round of play begins, the roll (the total shown on the two dice thrown) is called the "come-out" roll. A bet on the pass line wins even money if the come-out roll is a 7 or 11 and loses if it is a 2, 3, or 12 (a roll of 2, 3, or 12 is called "craps"). If any other number is rolled, this number becomes the "point." Once a point is established, the pass wager is not resolved until the point is rolled again or a 7 is rolled. If the point is rolled a second time before a 7, the pass line wager wins even money. If a 7 occurs before the point is rolled a second time, the pass line wager loses. After a point is established, a bet on the pass line cannot be removed or reduced, although it may be increased. This latter move is unfavorable to the player, since the advantage on the pass line bet is on the come-out roll, and the odds are against the pass line bet once a point is established. This is also why the "put" bet, a wager on the pass line after a point is established, is unfavorable. The put bettor never has the benefit of the player-favorable come-out roll, and the mathematical advantage favors the casino after the point has been established.

Odds.   Odds can be taken after a point has been established on the pass line wager (odds can also be taken on "come," or given on "don't pass," and "don't come" after a point is established—these bets are discussed later). Like the pass line bet, if the point is rolled before a 7, the odds bet wins. If a 7 is rolled before the point, the odds bet loses. Unlike the pass line, which pays even money, a winning odds bet is paid according to the true odds. For example, suppose a $5 pass line bet is made and a 4 is thrown on the come-out roll. Odds may now be taken on the point 4. The amount of odds that can be taken varies depending on the casino, but for this example let's assume single odds are taken. This is an additional $5 bet that will win if a 4 is rolled before a 7 and lose if a 7 is rolled before a 4. Since there are six ways to roll a 7 and three ways to roll a 4, the true odds against winning this bet are 6 to 3 or 2 to 1. If the point is made (a 4 is rolled before a 7), the pass line will be paid $5 (even money), and the odds bet will be paid $10 (2 to 1): both payments in addition to the original bets. Because odds bets are paid according to the true odds, the expectation and house advantage are zero. The odds bet may be removed at any time. Come odds (see "Come Bet") are typically "off," or inactive, on a come-out roll, unless the bettor specifically asks that they be "on." Don't come odds are always "on."

Come Bet.   The come bet gives the player the opportunity to make what is essentially a pass line bet on any roll after a point is established. A come bet turns the next roll of the dice into a come-out roll that wins on a 7 or 11; loses on a 2, 3, or 12; and otherwise establishes a point that will win if the point number is rolled again before a 7 and will lose if a 7 is rolled before the point. Multiple come bets can be made, each establishing its own point and each paying off according to whether or not the point is made.

Don't Pass Bet.   The don't pass wager works the opposite of the pass line bet, except that don't pass bettors are barred from winning on a come-out roll of 12. The don't pass bet wins on a come-out roll of 2 or 3, loses on a 7 or 11, and ties on a 12. On point rolls, the don't pass wins if a 7 is rolled before the point and loses if the point is rolled before a 7. Like the pass line bet, odds can be given once a point is established. Odds on the don't pass line bet will win if a 7 rolls before the point and are paid at true odds—1 to 2 for the 4 or 10, 2 to 3 for the 5 or 9, and 5 to 6 for the 6 or 8. Don't pass odds bets can be removed or reduced after a point is established.

Don't Come Bet.   The don't come bet is essentially a don't pass bet made after a point has been established.

Place and Don't Place Bets.   A place bet on one of the point numbers, 4, 5, 6, 8, 9, or 10, is a bet that the number will roll before a 7. Payoffs are less than true odds, typically 9 to 5 for the numbers 4 and 10, 7 to 5 for the numbers 5 and 9, and 7 to 6 for the numbers 6 and 8. A don't place bet is the opposite of a place bet—it's a bet that a 7 will roll before the number. Like place bets, these wagers are paid off at less than true odds. The don't place on a 4 or 10 pays 5 to 11 (true odds are 1 to 2), a don't place on a 5 or 9 pays 5 to 8 (true odds 2 to 3), and a don't place on a 6 or 8 pays 4 to 5 (true odds 5 to 6).

Buy and Lay Bets.   Buy and lay bets are similar to the place and don't place bets except that the payoffs are at true odds, and a 5 percent commission is charged on the amount of a buy bet and on the possible winning amount of a lay bet.

Field Bet.   The field is a bet that the next roll will be a 2, 3, 4, 9, 10, 11, or 12. The payoff is typically 2 to 1 for 2 or 12, and even money for 3, 4, 9, 10, or 11. Although this wager covers 7 out of 11 numbers, the losing numbers (5, 6, 7, and 8) can be rolled in more ways.

Big 6 and Big 8.   The big 6 is a bet that the 6 will roll before a 7; the big 8 is that the 8 will roll before a 7. The big 6 and big 8, the place 6 and place 8, and the buy 6 and buy 8 are exactly the same wagers but with different payoffs, and hence different house advantages.

Hardways.   There are four hardway wagers: hard 4, hard 6, hard 8, and hard 10. A hardway is a wager that the selected number will roll with doubles (both die the same) before the number is rolled any other way or a 7 is rolled. For example, a hard 6 wins if 3–3 comes up before an easy 6 (1–5, 5–1, 2–4, or 4–2) or a 7. Payoffs are 7 to 1 for hard 4 and hard 10, and 9 to 1 for hard 6 and hard 8.

Any Craps.   Any craps is a one-roll bet that the next roll will be a 2, 3, or 12. If the next roll is not a 2, 3, or 12, the wager is lost. The payoff is 7 to 1.

Any Seven.   Another one-roll bet, any seven wins 4 to 1 if the next roll is a 7.

Craps and Eleven (C&E).   Craps and eleven (C&E) is a one-roll bet that the next roll will be a 2, 3, 11, or 12. Typical payoffs are 3 to 1 on the 2, 3, or 12, and 7 to 1 on the 11.

Two or Twelve.   These are two separate one-roll bets—a wager can be made that the next roll will be a 2 or a wager can be made that the next roll will be a 12. The payoff is typically 30 to 1 for each.

Three or Eleven.   Like the wagers on 2 or 12, these are two separate one-roll bets. Each typically pays 15 to 1.

Horn Bet.   The horn is a one-roll bet that the next roll will be 2, 3, 11, or 12. It is really just four separate bets on these four numbers, so the bet is made in multiples of four. The horn returns the usual payoffs for the individual winning number: typically 30 to 1 for the 2 and 12, and 15 to 1 for the 3 and 11. With these payoffs and four units wagered on the horn, the bet will net 27 units for a hit on 2 or 12, and 12 units for a hit on 3 or 11.

Horn High Bet.   The high horn is a horn bet made in multiples of five with the extra unit wagered on the "high" number designated by the bettor. For example, a $5 high twelve would put $1 each on the 2, 3, and 11, and $2 on the 12.

Hop Bet.   The hop is a one-roll bet that the next roll will be a certain combination. There are two types, an "easy" or two-way hop, such as 6–1, and a "hard" or one-way hop, such as 2–2. Typical payoffs are 15 to 1 for an easy hop and 30 to 1 for a hard hop.

Blackjack

Blackjack, or "21," is the most popular and largest revenue-generating casino table game (Figure 9–3). Blackjack's popularity stems from its simple play, the fact that the player to some extent can guide his or her own destiny, the (correct) perception that the game can be beaten, and the camaraderie among players in a friendly competition against the casino. The objective of blackjack is to beat the dealer by having a total higher than the dealer's without exceeding 21. The object is not, as some people think, to get as close to 21 as possible.

Cards 2 through 10 are worth their face value; face cards (jacks, queens and kings) are worth 10, and aces can be counted as either 1 or 11. Card suits are meaningless. In the discussion that follows, the term *ten* will be used to refer to any card—face card

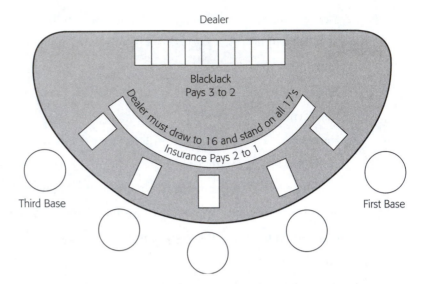

Figure 9–3 Blackjack layout.

or 10—that is a 10-valued card in blackjack. The value of a hand is the total of the values of the individual cards making up the hand. The name of the game is derived from the best possible hand, an ace-ten combination on the first two cards. This combination, called a *blackjack* or *natural*, totals 21 and is unbeatable. A dealer blackjack beats all player hands, even those with three or more cards totaling 21, except a player who also received a natural on the first two cards.

A *hard* hand is one that either does not contain an ace or if it does, the ace counts as 1. A *soft* hand is one that contains an ace counted as 11. For example, A–6 is a soft 17, A–2–3 is a soft 16, A–6–8 is a hard 15, and 9–7 is a hard 16. When a hand value exceeds 21, it is *busted*. Hands totaling 17 through 21 are called *pat* hands—generally players will stand pat with these totals. Hands with hard totals of 12 through 16 are known as *stiff* hands — these hands can be busted by drawing an additional card.

To begin the game, each player makes a bet, the dealer then deals each player a card, starting with the player on the dealer's left, and one card to him- or herself. This is repeated so that each player and the dealer have two cards. One of the dealer's cards is face up (up card) and the other is face down (hole card).

If the dealer's up card is an ace, he or she may offer the players *insurance*, an optional side bet on whether the dealer has a natural. Players may wager up to one-half their original bet. If the dealer has a natural (hole card is a ten), insurance bets are paid 2 to 1 and then the original hands are settled. If the dealer does not have a natural, insurance bets are lost and play of the hands proceeds as usual.

If the dealer's upcard is a ten, he will check the hole card to see if he or she has a natural before proceeding. If the dealer has a natural, all players' hands lose, except if a player also has a natural, in which case it's a *push* (tie) and that player neither wins nor loses. If the dealer does not have a natural, play then proceeds as usual.

If the dealer does not have a natural, then beginning with the player to the dealer's left, each player completes his or her hand by exercising one of the following options: *stand, hit, double down, split,* or (if offered) *surrender*.

A player may stand if satisfied with the original two-card total or may choose to hit by taking an additional card to try to improve the total. The player can take as many cards as he or she likes until the total exceeds 21 (called busting or breaking), or the player is satisfied with the total and stands. If the player has a natural (blackjack), he or she is immediately paid 3 to 2 on the initial bet. If the player busts, he or she automatically loses the wager.

The double down option allows the player to double the original wager in favorable situations. When this option is exercised, the player receives one, and only one, additional card. The hand is settled in the usual way with payouts or losses based on the new total wager. Most casinos allow the player to double down on any first two cards, although this can vary. Most double downs are played when the player has 9, 10, or 11. Restrictions on doubling down and their effect on the house advantage are discussed later in this section.

If the player's first two cards are equal in value, he or she may elect to split the pair and play two independent hands, each starting with one of the original two cards. The player will place an amount equal to the original wager to cover the second hand. Each hand is played as usual, except that split aces receive only one card each (and if this card is a ten, the total is 21 but it is not a natural). Rules on resplitting and doubling down after a split vary.

Surrender is an option offered by some casinos that allows the player, after seeing the first two cards and before taking any other action, to forfeit half the original wager rather than playing out the hand. When offered, surrender is almost always *late surrender*, which means it is an option only if the dealer does not have a natural.

Once all players have finished their hands, the dealer plays his or her own hand. The dealer has no options in playing the hand and must adhere to a fixed set of rules. These rules usually require the dealer to hit all hard totals of 16 or less and to stand on totals of 17 or more. In some casinos, notably those in downtown Las Vegas and northern Nevada, the dealer must hit a soft 17. If the dealer busts, all players remaining in the game (who did not bust or surrender) win and are paid even money regardless of their total, except that naturals are paid 3 to 2. If the dealer does not bust, the dealer's hand is compared with each of the remaining player's hands to resolve their bets. If the player's total exceeds the dealer's total, the player wins—again the payoff is even money for all hands except naturals. If the dealer's total is higher than the player's total, the player's wager is lost. If the totals are equal, the hand is a push (tie). Once all bets are resolved, the cards are cleared, new wagers are made, and the process begins again.

Baccarat

Although the results of consecutive hands in baccarat are mathematically dependent as in blackjack, it is not possible for the player to take advantage of this dependency, and baccarat is for all practical purposes a game of pure chance, unlike blackjack (Figure 9–4). In addition, it is a relatively easy game to play since hitting and drawing rules are fixed and no decisions are required (or even possible) once play begins. Players need only decide whether to bet on the *banker* or the *player* (there is also a *tie* bet).

Play proceeds as follows. After bets are made, two cards are dealt to each side (player and banker). All cards are community cards—there are no individual hands. Face cards and tens are worth zero, aces count as one, and all other cards are worth face value. The total for a hand is the sum of the values of the individual cards in the hand. If the hand totals more than 9, the left digit of the sum is disregarded.

A total of 8 or 9 on the first two cards is called a natural. If either side has a natural, the hand is over and wagers are resolved. If neither side has a natural, a fixed set of

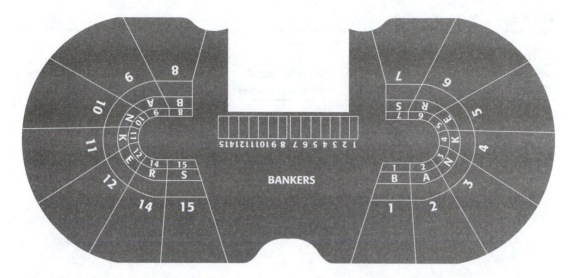

Figure 9–4 Full baccarat layout.

rules is applied to determine if either side takes a third card. Once the hands are complete, the side with the higher total wins. If the two sides have equal totals, player and banker bets are a push. The payoff on winning player and banker bets are even money, but a 5 percent commission is charged to banker wins. A winning tie bet pays 8 to 1.

Baccarat's hitting and standing rules are presented in Table 9–4. To read the table, start with the player's first two cards total in the left column and proceed to the right, column by column, to determine the drawing/standing rules.

As mentioned earlier, since the drawing rules are fixed, baccarat offers no opportunity for strategic decisions as blackjack does. Furthermore, although the game involves dependent trials—similar to blackjack—it has been shown that card-counting techniques are not effective in baccarat.

Caribbean Stud Poker

Caribbean Stud poker is played with a single standard deck of 52 cards and uses the usual five-card hand rankings in poker. Players make an **ante** bet before the cards are dealt and may also make an optional $1 progressive jackpot side bet. Each player is then dealt five cards face down. The dealer is also dealt five cards, one of which is face up.

Table 9–4   Baccarat drawing rules

*Baccarat Drawing Rules**

Player's Total (first two cards)	Player's Rule	Banker's Total (first two cards)	Player's 3rd card	Banker's Rule
0, 1, 2, 3, 4, 5		0, 1, 2	Anything	Draw
		3	1, 2, 3, 4, 5, 6, 7, 9, 0	Draw
			8	Stand
		4	2, 3, 4, 5, 6, 7	Draw
	Draw		1, 8, 9, 0	Stand
		5	4, 5, 6, 7	Draw
			1, 2, 3, 8, 9, 0	Stand
		6	6, 7	Draw
			1, 2, 3, 4, 5, 8, 9, 0	Stand
		7	Anything	Stand
6, 7	Stand	0, 1, 2, 3, 4, 5	–	Draw
		6, 7, 8, 9	–	Stand

*If either player or banker totals 8 or 9 on first two cards, no cards are drawn and hand is over.

Players evaluate their own cards and then either fold and forfeit the ante bet or call the dealer by placing an additional *call* bet equal to exactly twice the ante. The dealer then turns over his or her other four cards to make a five-card poker hand. If the dealer's hand is an ace-king or better, the dealer is said to qualify. If the dealer does not qualify, any player who made the call bet is paid even money on only his or her ante.

If the dealer qualifies, the value of his or her hand is compared to that of each player who made the call bet. If the dealer wins, the player loses both the call bet and the ante bet. If the player wins, he or she is paid even money on the ante bet, and the call bet is paid as shown in Table 9–5.

Let It Ride

Let It Ride is another poker-type game played with a single standard deck of 52 cards. Players place three bets of equal size before the cards are dealt. An optional bonus side bet of $1 may also be made. Each player is then dealt three cards and the dealer two cards, all face down. After examining the three cards, each player may take back one of

Table 9-5 Caribbean stud poker payoffs

Caribbean Stud Poker Payoffs

Hand	Call Bet Pays	Jackpot (typical)
Royal Flush	100 to 1	100%
Straight Flush	50 to 1	10%
Four of a Kind	20 to 1	$100
Full House	7 to 1	$75
Flush	5 to 1	$50
Straight	4 to 1	0
Three of a Kind	3 to 1	0
Two Pair	2 to 1	0
One Pair or less	1 to 1	0

the three bets, or "let it ride" and keep all three bets active. The dealer then turns over one of his or her two cards, which acts as the fourth card for each player. The players must again make the decision to either take back one of their bets (of the two or three that remain depending on their first decision) or let all remaining bets ride. The dealer then exposes the second community card and remaining wagers are resolved and paid according to Table 9–6.

Players are not playing against the dealer or other players. The player is simply trying (hoping) to get a good poker hand using his or her three cards and the dealer's two

Table 9-6 Let it ride payoffs

Let It Ride Payoffs

Hand	Payoff
Royal Flush	1,000 to 1
Straight Flush	200 to 1
Four of a Kind	50 to 1
Full House	11 to 1
Flush	8 to 1
Straight	5 to 1
Three of a Kind	3 to 1
Two Pair	2 to 1
Pair of Tens or better	1 to 1

community cards. A five-card hand with a pair of 10s or better wins at least even money on the remaining wagers. Although the players always starts with three units bet, they always have control of two of the three bets. Let It Ride also offers a $1 side bet similar to the jackpot bet in Caribbean Stud, although the Let It Ride "jackpot" payout for this bonus bet is not usually progressive.

Pai Gow Poker

Pai Gow poker uses 53 cards—a standard single deck plus one Joker. The Joker can be used to fill a straight or flush, otherwise it is an ace. After bets are placed, each player and the dealer are dealt seven cards, used to make a five-card hand and a two-card hand. The five-card hand must be of equal or higher rank than the two-card hand. Hand rankings are as follows: Five Aces, Royal Flush, Straight Flush (A–2–3–4–5 is highest), Four of a Kind, Full House, Flush, Straight (A–2–3–4–5 is second highest), Three of a Kind, Two Pair, One Pair, and High Card. Note that the highest-ranking hand is five aces, not the royal flush, and the second highest straight is (in most casinos) A–2–3–4–5.

One person is designated the banker. In the casino version of the game, the dealer usually acts as banker, although a player may be the banker. A player who acts as banker must be able to cover all bets at the table if all other players win.

Once all hands are set, the player's two hands are compared to the banker's two hands. If the player's five-card hand outranks the banker's five-card hand and the player's two-card hand outranks the banker's two-card hand, the player wins. If both of the banker's hands outrank both of the player's hands, the player loses. If one of the player's hands outranks the corresponding banker's hand and one of the banker's hands outranks the corresponding player's hand, it is a push. The payoff on winning hands is even money, but the casino takes a 5 percent commission on the winning bets.

Three Card Poker

Three Card poker is a relatively new poker-based game that has become popular because of its simplicity, fast action, and reasonably player-friendly house advantage (compared with other nontraditional games). The game is played with a single deck of 52 cards. Since, as the name implies, each player's hand is made up of only three cards, hand rankings are slightly different from the usual five-card poker rankings. Some types of hands that occur in five-card poker are not possible in three-card poker (four of a kind, full house, two pair), and the relative rankings of three of a kind, straights, and flushes are reversed: a three of a kind occurs less often and so is higher ranking than a straight, and a straight occurs less often and is better than a flush.

Each player and the dealer receive three cards. Players may wager on either one or both of two independent propositions: *ante/play* and *pair plus*.

If betting on the ante/play, the player places the ante wager and then decides to play or fold after examining his or her three cards. If the player folds, the ante wager is forfeited. If the player wishes to play, he or she places a second bet equal in size to the ante. The dealer then checks his or her three-card hand to see if it "qualifies" with a queen or better. If the dealer's hand does not qualify, the player wins even money for the ante wager and the play wager is returned. If the dealer does qualify, the player's hand is weighed against the dealer's hand. If the player's hand outranks the dealer's, the player wins even money on both the ante and play wagers. If the dealer's hand outranks the player's, the player loses both the ante and play wagers. If the player and dealer hands are equal in rank, it is a push.

Regardless of the outcome of the ante/play wager and regardless of whether the dealer qualifies, if the player has a straight or better, a bonus is paid on the ante wager (but not the play wager). This bonus pays 1 to 1 for a straight, 4 to 1 for three of a kind, and 5 to 1 for a straight flush. It is possible that the player loses the ante wager and play wager but wins the bonus. This would happen, for example, if the player has three of a kind and the dealer has a straight flush.

The pair plus wager is a bet on the value of the player's cards and is independent of the dealer's hand. If the pair plus wager is made and the player has a pair or better, he or she will win according to 1 to 1 for one pair, 4 to 1 for a flush, 6 to 1 for a straight, 30 to 1 for three of a kind, and 40 to 1 for a straight flush.

Slot Machines

Slot machines come in an incredible variety of models (Figure 9–5). The term *slots* is used today to refer to both traditional (but now computer controlled) reel-type machines and the plethora of new video games now on the market. In American casinos, slot machines

Figure 9–5
Courtesy of the Isle of Capri.

are more popular than table games. On average they produce 70 percent to 75 percent of the gaming revenues and typically fill 80 percent or more of the floor space. In 2004, approximately 750,000 slot machines were installed and operating in legal gaming establishments in the United States. Four types of slot machines are most popular: traditional spinning reel machines, video poker, multiline/multiplay video devices, and wide area progressives (*wide area* refers to machines that are linked together from many casinos; a *progressive* slot is one in which the jackpot becomes progressively larger as more and more coins are dropped into the machine). Most video games are either poker games or electronic versions of the traditional spinning reel machines. Other less popular video games are electronic versions of other casino games such as keno and blackjack. Video reel machines often are themed and can be based on subjects such as board games (Monopoly, Battleship), television shows (*Wheel of Fortune*), and rock and roll icons (Elvis).

Keno

Keno is played by choosing up to 10 out of the 20 numbers that are randomly drawn by computer from the numbers 1 through 80. Several types of keno tickets are available, depending on how many numbers the player marks, or selects, and the payoffs for how many of these selected numbers appear among the 20 drawn. The casino advantage on keno is large—25 percent to 35 percent depending on the type of ticket and payout schedule.

Basic Casino Math

At its core, the business of casino gaming is pretty simple. Casinos make money on their games because of the mathematics behind the games. As Nico Zographos, dealer-extraordinaire for the Greek Syndicate in Deauville, Cannes, and Monte Carlo in the 1920s observed about casino gaming: "There is no such thing as luck. It is all mathematics."[4]

Importance of Mathematics in Casino Gaming

It is not uncommon to hear someone ask whether the casino business is the gambling industry or the gaming industry. Critics of the gaming industry have long accused it of creating the name *gaming* to sound less offensive than the *gambling* industry. The term *gaming*, however, has been around for centuries and more accurately describes the operators' view of the industry because most often casino operators are not gambling. Instead, they rely on mathematical principles to assure that their establishments generate positive gross gaming revenues, sufficient to cover deductions such as bad debts, expenses, employees, taxes, and interest.

Many casino professionals fail to understand the basic mathematics of the games and their relationship to casino profitability. It is not enough to say that the casino makes money simply because it maintains a house advantage; given that products offered by casinos are games, managers must be able to identify the amount of that advantage or what aspect of the game created the advantage. In short, it is important to understand exactly why the games provide the expected revenues.

Mathematics should also overcome the dangers of superstitions, long a part of gambling on both sides of the table. Superstitions can lead to irrational decisions that may hurt casino profits. For example, believing that a particular dealer is unlucky against a particular (winning) player may lead to a decision to change dealers. The players, many of whom are superstitious themselves, may resent that the casino is trying to change their luck or, worse, that the new dealer is skilled in methods to "cool" the game.

Understanding the mathematics of a game also is important for the casino operator to ensure that the reasonable expectations of the players are met. For most persons, gambling is entertainment and provides an outlet for adult play. As an entertainment alternative, players may consider the value of the gambling experience. If the house advantage is too strong and the person loses money too quickly or has an exceptionally remote chance of winning, he or she may not value that casino entertainment experience. On the other hand, if a casino can entertain someone for an evening and provide a "complimentary" meal or drinks, he or she may want to repeat the experience, even over other entertainment options.

Since the casino industry is heavily regulated and some of the standards set forth by regulatory bodies involve mathematically related issues, casino managers should also understand the mathematical aspects relating to gaming regulation. Gaming regulation is principally dedicated to assuring that the games offered in the casino are fair and honest, and that players get paid if they win. Fairness is often expressed in the regulations as either requiring a minimum payback to the player or, in more extreme cases, as dictating the actual rules of the games offered.

Casino executives should understand the impact that changes in rules have on the payback to players to ensure that they meet regulatory standards. Equally important, casino executives should understand how government-mandated rules would impact their gaming revenues.

Probabilities and Odds

Probability represents the long run ratio of (number of times an outcome occurs) to (number of times experiment is conducted). *Odds* represents the long run ratio of (number of times an outcome does not occur) to (number of times an outcome occurs). If a card is randomly selected from a standard deck of 52 playing cards, the probability it is a spade is 1 in 4; the odds (against spade) are 3 to 1. The true odds of an event represent the payoff that would make the bet on that event fair. For example, a bet on a single number in double-zero roulette has probability of 1 in 38, so to break even in the long run a player would have to be paid 37 to 1 (the actual payoff is 35 to 1).

House Advantage

The fundamental reason that casino games make money for the casino is the house advantage. As one popular author put it, "A casino is a mathematics palace set up to separate players from their money. Every bet made in a casino has been calibrated within a fraction of its life to maximize profit while still giving the players the illusion that they have a chance."[5]

With a few notable exceptions, the house always wins—in the long run—because of the mathematical advantage the casino enjoys over the player. That is what Mario Puzo was referring to in his famous novel *Fools Die*, when his fictional casino boss character, Gronevelt, commented: "Percentages never lie. We built all these hotels on percentages. We stay rich on the percentage. You can lose faith in everything, religion and God, women and love, good and evil, war and peace. You name it. But the percentage will always stand fast."[6]

Puzo is, of course, right on the money about casino gaming. Without the **house edge**, casinos would not exist. This edge, coupled with the famous mathematical result called the *law of large numbers*, virtually guarantees the casino will win in the long run.

Players' chances of winning in a casino game and the rate at which they win or lose money depend on the game, the rules in effect for that game, and for some games, their level of skill. The amount of money players can expect to win or lose in the long run—if the bet is made over and over again—is called the players' wager **expectation**, or **expected value** (EV). When players' wager EV is negative, they will lose money in the long run. For a $5 bet on the color red in roulette, for example, the expectation is −$0.263. On the average, players will lose just over a quarter for each $5 bet on red.

When the wager EV is viewed from the casino's perspective (i.e., the negative of the player's expectation) and expressed as a percentage, you have the house advantage (HA). For the roulette example, the house advantage is 5.26 percent ($0.263 divided by $5). The formal calculations are as follows:

EV = (+5)(18/38) + (−5)(20/38) = −0.263.

HA = 0.263/5 = 5.26 percent.

The general formula for the expectation of a wager, of which this roulette calculation is an application, is given here:

> *Wager Expected Value (EV)*
>
> $EV = \Sigma \, (Net \, Pay_i \times P_i)$
>
> where *Net Pay$_i$* is the net payoff and *P$_i$* is the probability of *Net Pay$_i$*.

When the EV calculation is performed for a one-unit amount, the negative of the resulting value is the house edge. Here are the calculations for bets on a single-number in double-zero and single-zero roulette:

Single Number Bet, Double-zero Roulette:

EV = (+35)(1/38) + (−1)(37/38) = −0.053; HA = 5.3 percent.

Single Number Bet, Single-zero Roulette:

EV = (+35)(1/37) + (−1)(36/37) = −0.027; HA = 2.7 percent.

The house advantage represents the long-run percentage of the wagered money that will be retained by the casino. It is also called the house edge, the 'odds' (i.e., avoid games with bad odds), or just the 'percentage' (as in Mario Puzo's *Fools Die*). Although the house edge can be computed easily for some games—for example, roulette and craps—for others it requires more sophisticated mathematical analysis and/or computer simulations. Regardless of the method used to compute it, the house advantage represents the price to the player of playing the game.

Because this positive house edge exists for virtually all bets in a casino, gamblers are faced with an uphill and, in the long run, losing battle. There are some exceptions. The odds bet in craps has zero house edge (although this bet cannot be made without making a line bet, which itself is a negative expectation wager); a few video poker machines return greater than 100 percent if played with perfect strategy, and exceptional blackjack card counters (if permitted to play[7]), poker players, and sports bettors can make money playing their games. But these are small groups—very few have what it takes to win money in the long run at any of these games. Occasionally, the casino will offer a promotion that gives the astute player a positive expectation. These promotions are usually mistakes—sometimes casinos fail to check the math—and are terminated once the casino realizes the player has the edge. But by and large the player will lose money in the long run, and the house edge is a measure of how fast the money will be lost. A player betting in a game with a 4 percent house advantage will tend to lose money twice as fast as a player making bets with a 2 percent house edge. The trick to intelligent casino gambling—at least from the point of view of mathematical expectations—is to avoid the games and bets with the large house advantages.

Confusion About Win Rate

There are many types of percentages in gaming such as **win percentage**, theoretical win percentage, **hold percentage**, and house advantage. Sometimes casino bosses use these percentages interchangeably, as if they are just different names for the same thing. Admittedly, in some cases this is correct. House advantage is just another name for theoretical win percentage, and for slot machines, hold percentage is (in principle) equivalent to win percentage. But there are fundamental differences among these win rate measurements.

The house advantage—the all-important percentage that explains how casinos make money—is also called the house edge, the theoretical win percentage, and expected win percentage. In double-zero roulette, this figure is 5.3 percent. In the long run, the house will retain 5.3 percent of the money wagered. In the short term, of course, the actual win percentage will differ from the theoretical win percentage (the magnitude of this deviation can be predicted from statistical theory). The actual win percentage is just the (actual) win divided by the handle (*handle* is the total amount wagered). Because of the law of large numbers—or as some prefer to call it, the law of averages—as the number of trials gets larger, the actual win percentage should get closer to the theoretical win percentage.

Because handle can be difficult to measure for table games, performance is often measured by hold percentage (sometimes erroneously called win percentage). Hold percentage is equal to win divided by drop (*drop* is the total amount of the currency and chips in the table's drop box—a locked box affixed to the table—plus the value of credit instruments issued or redeemed at the table). In Nevada, this figure is about 24 percent for roulette. The hold percentage is affected by many factors; we will not delve into these or the associated management issues. Suffice it to say that the casino will *not* in the long term keep 24 percent of the money bet on the spins of roulette wheel (well, an honest casino will not).

To summarize: House advantage and theoretical win percentage are the same thing; hold percentage is win over drop; win percentage is win over handle. Win percentage approaches the house advantage as the number of plays increases, and hold percentage is equivalent to win percentage for slots but not table games:

- Hold percent = Win/Drop
- Win percent (actual) = Win/Handle
- HA = Theoretical Win percent = Limit (Actual Win percent) = Limit (Win/Handle)
- Hold Percentage ≠ House Edge

Furthermore, the house advantage is itself subject to varying interpretations. In Let It Ride poker, for example, the casino advantage is either 3.51 percent or 2.86 percent depending on whether the advantage is expressed with respect to the base bet or the average bet. Those familiar with the game know that the player begins with three equal base bets but may withdraw one or two of these initial units. The final amount put at risk, then, can be one (84.6 percent of the time assuming proper strategy), two (8.5 percent), or three units (6.9 percent), making the average bet size 1.224 units. In the long run, the casino will win 3.51 percent of the hands, which equates to 2.86 percent of the money wagered. So what's the house edge for Let It Ride? Some prefer to say 3.51 percent per hand, others 2.86 percent per unit wagered. No matter; either way, the bottom line is the same: assuming three $1 base bets, the casino can expect to earn 3.5¢ per hand (note that $1.224 \times 0.0286 = 0.035$).

The question of whether to use the base bet or average bet size also arises in Caribbean Stud poker (5.22 percent versus 2.56 percent), Three Card Poker (3.37 percent versus 2.01 percent), Casino War (2.88 percent versus 2.68 percent), and Red Dog (2.80 percent versus 2.37 percent).

For still other games, the house edge can be stated including or excluding ties. The prime examples here are the player (1.24 percent versus 1.37 percent) and banker (1.06 percent versus 1.17 percent) bets in baccarat, and the don't pass bet (1.36 percent versus 1.40 percent) in craps. Again, these are different views on the casino edge, but the expected revenue will not change.

That the house advantage can appear in different disguises might be unsettling. When properly computed and interpreted, however, regardless of which representation is chosen, the same truth (read: money) emerges: the expected win is the same.

Volatility and Risk

Risk in the gaming business depends on the house advantage, standard deviation, bet size, and length of play.

Statistical theory can be used to predict the magnitude of the difference between the actual win percentage and the theoretical win percentage for a given number of wagers. When observing the actual win percentage a player (or casino) may experience, how much variation from theoretical win can be expected? What is a normal fluctuation?

The basis for the analysis of such **volatility** questions is a statistical measure called the **standard deviation** (essentially the average deviation of all possible outcomes from the expected mean). Together with the central limit theorem (a form of the law of large numbers), the standard deviation (SD) can be used to determine confidence limits with the following volatility guidelines:

Volatility Guidelines
- *Only 5 percent of the time will outcomes be more than 2 SD's from expected outcome*
- *Almost never (0.3 percent) will outcomes be more than 3 SD's from expected outcome*

Obviously a key to using these guidelines is the value of the SD. Computing the SD value is beyond the scope of this book, but to get an idea behind confidence limits, consider a series of 1,000 pass line wagers in craps. Since each wager has a 1.4 percent house advantage, on average the player will be behind by 14 units. It can be shown (calculations omitted) that the wager standard deviation for a single pass line bet is 1.0, and for 1,000 wagers, the SD is 31.6. Applying the volatility guidelines, we can say that there is a 95 percent chance the player's actual win will be between 49 units ahead and 77 units behind, and almost certainly between 81 units ahead and 109 units behind.

A similar analysis for 1,000 single-number wagers on double-zero roulette (on average the player will be behind 53 units, wager SD = 5.8, 1,000 wager SD = 182.2) will yield 95 percent confidence limits on the player win of 311 units ahead and 417 units behind, with win almost certainly between 494 units ahead and 600 units behind.

Note that if the volatility analysis is done in terms of the *percentage* win (rather than the number of units or amount won), the confidence limits will converge to the house advantage as the number of wagers increases. This is the result of the law of large numbers—as the number of trials gets larger, the actual win percentage should get closer to the theoretical win percentage.

Casino Games and Odds

Table Games

The major table games include blackjack, craps, roulette, baccarat, Caribbean Stud poker, Let It Ride, Pai Gow poker, and Three Card poker.[8] As mentioned previously, the skill of the player affects the house advantage in several of these games (all except craps, roulette, and baccarat) and for these, the statistical advantage is usually reported assuming optimal strategy.

Blackjack is by far the most popular table game. In addition to the skill of the player, the house advantage for this game also depends on the game rules. For a typical game six-deck game,[9] optimal strategy—usually referred to as *basic strategy* for blackjack—results in a 0.5 percent house edge. Basic strategy is the player's strategy that maximizes his or her expectation, or average gain, playing one hand against a freshly shuffled pack, without keeping track of the cards. It is a complete set of decision rules that tells the player whether to hit, stand, double down, split, or surrender (if offered) depending only on the player's present cards and the dealer's upcard. It does not depend on other players' cards or previously played cards. Basic strategy was developed by analyzing all possible combinations of decisions and outcomes for a given set of player's cards and dealer's upcard. The decision resulting in the largest expected win (or smallest average loss) is the basic strategy decision. In the long run, a player who follows basic strategy perfectly will maximize his or her average gain or minimize average loss.

However, most blackjack players do not use basic strategy (or make mistakes when trying to do so), and for the average player the casino advantage is about 2 percent. A table showing representative figures for the changes in the house advantage resulting from some of the common rule variations in blackjack is shown in Table 9–7. The benchmark for the figures in this table is a single-deck game under old Las Vegas Strip rules—dealer stands on soft 17, double down on any first two cards but not after splits, split non-ace pairs up to four times, split aces receive only one card, no surrender—for which the house advantage is essentially zero. For each rule variation that is in effect in a given game, add the corresponding percentage from the table to the 0.00 percent

Table 9–7   Effect of common rule variations in blackjack

Effect of Common Rule Variations in Blackjack*

House Favorable	
Two decks	+0.32 %
Four decks	+0.48 %
Six decks	+0.54 %
Eight decks	+0.57 %
Dealer hits soft 17	+0.20 %
No soft doubling	+0.13 %
Double down only on 10 or 11	+0.26 %
No doubling on 9	+0.13 %
No doubling on 10	+0.52 %
Double down only on 11	+0.78 %
No re-splitting of pairs (non-aces)	+0.03 %
Dealer wins ties	+9.00 %
Blackjacks pay 6–5	+1.39 %
Blackjacks pay even money	+2.32 %
Player loses splits and double downs to dealer natural	+0.11 %
Player Favorable	
Double down on any number of cards	−0.24 %
Double down after splitting pairs	−0.14 %
Late surrender	−0.06 %
Early surrender	−0.62 %
Re-split Aces	−0.06 %
Draw to split Aces	−0.14 %
Blackjack pays 2–1	−2.32 %
Six card winner	−0.15 %
Player's 21 pushes dealer's 10-up blackjack	−0.16 %

*Percentages will vary slightly depending on the number of decks in play.

benchmark value to arrive at the approximate overall house advantage for the game. For example, a 6-deck game in which dealer stands on soft 17 and double down is allowed on 10 and 11 only, the house advantage is 0.54 percent + 0.26 percent = 0.80 percent. This same game with dealer hitting soft 17 would have a 1.00 percent house advantage.

For the other skill-based table games, the house advantages assuming optimal strategy are 5.2 percent for Caribbean Stud poker, 3.5 percent for Let It Ride, 3.4 percent for Three Card poker (ante bet), and 2.5 percent for Pai Gow poker. The house edge in baccarat is about 1.2 percent, and for double-zero roulette 5.3 percent. In craps the house advantage varies widely among the different wagers, but the primary pass-line bet carries a 1.4 percent house edge. Taking odds, which are free (there is no house edge on the odds bet), will lower the overall player disadvantage on the combined pass line plus odds to less than 1 percent, the precise figure depending on the amount of odds taken.[10] Odds can be taken in multiples of the original bet, the max being established by the casino.

Gaming Devices

As mentioned earlier, a great variety of gaming devices can be found in casinos today, from the traditional spinning reel machines, to video poker, multiline/multiplay video devices, and wide area progressives. The differences between traditional spinning reel machines and video reel machines are only in the way that the results are displayed to the player. Since traditional spinning reel machines are no longer mechanical but controlled by computer microchips like video reel machines, they also can be programmed for virtually any number of "stops," any hit frequency, and any house advantage within the limits of applicable regulations. Multiline/multiplay video devices are clearly becoming more popular, taking shares from the traditional spinning reel. These machines come in a wide variety of types depending on how the games pay winning players. Line games allow the player to activate additional pay lines by playing more coins. In a typical reel slot, for example, three horizontal lines and the diagonals might be activated to pay back with winning combinations. With today's video slots, many more pay lines can be activated. Multipliers pay for winning combinations on a single line only—usually the center horizontal line. Payback for additional coins is simply a multiple of the payback for a single coin. Multiline/multiplay video games combine both multipliers and line games.

The house advantage for slot machines is often referred to as the theoretical win percentage or theoretical hold percentage. The flip side of the house advantage, the proportion of wagered money returned to the player, is the **payback**, or **return, percentage**. For example, if a machine holds 5 percent (about average for Nevada slot machines), the payback percentage is 95 percent.

The theoretical hold percentage can be set to virtually any value with the computer program that controls the machine. Whatever this theoretical hold, the actual percentage will vary somewhat but will be close to the theoretical amount after a large number of plays. Assessing the likelihood of a certain difference between actual and theoretical win is possible because of the random selection of outcomes. The extent of the disparity between the actual and theoretical wins for slot machines can be assessed using techniques discussed in the volatility and risk section earlier in this chapter.

The hold percentage for slots in Nevada averages 6 percent to 8 percent depending on the particular type of machine and denomination. Higher denomination devices tend to have lower hold percentages. In jurisdictions other than Nevada, slots tend to have slightly larger hold percentages. Video poker, a game with an element of skill, can be very favorable for the player if the correct strategy is used. Under optimal strategy, the house edge on video poker tends to be in the low single digits, and some even have a negative house advantage, returning greater than 100 percent to the player.

Related Operations Issues

Player Value and Complimentaries

Using the house advantage, bet size, duration of play, and pace of the game, a casino can determine its **earning potential** from a certain player. This player earning potential (also called player value, player worth, or theoretical win) can be calculated by the formula:

$$Earning\ Potential = Average\ Bet \times Hours\ Played \times Decisions\ per\ Hour \times House\ Advantage$$

For example, suppose a baccarat player bets $500 per hand for 12 hours at 60 hands per hour. Using a house advantage of 1.2 percent, this player's worth to the casino is $4,320 ($500 \times 12 \times 60 \times .012$). A player who bets $500 per spin for 12 hours in double-zero roulette at 60 spins per hour would be worth about $19,000 ($500 \times 12 \times 60 \times .053$).

Many casinos set comp (complimentary) policies by giving the player back a set percentage of his or her earning potential. Although comp and rebate policies based on theoretical loss are the most popular, rebates on actual losses and dead chip programs are also used in some casinos. Some programs involve a mix of systems. The mathematics associated with these programs will not be addressed in this chapter.

Casino Pricing Mistakes

In an effort to entice players and increase business, casinos occasionally offer novel wagers, side bets, increased payoffs, or rule variations. These promotions have the effect of lowering the house advantage and the effective price of the game for the player. This is sound reasoning from a marketing standpoint but can be disastrous for the casino if care is not taken to ensure that the math behind the promotion is sound. One casino offered a baccarat commission on winning banker bets of only 2 percent instead of the usual 5 percent, resulting in a 0.32 percent player advantage. This is easy to see (using the well-known probabilities of winning and losing the banker bet):

$$EV = (+0.98)(.4462) + (-1)(.4586) = 0.0032; HA = -0.32 \text{ percent.}$$

A casino in Biloxi, Mississippi, gave players a 12.5 percent edge on Sic Bo, a game in which players bet on the outcome of the roll of three dice, when it offered 80 to 1 payoffs instead of the usual 60 to 1 for bets on (a total of) 4 and 17. Again, this is an easy calculation. Using the fact that the probability of rolling a total of 4 with three dice is 1/72 ($1/6 \times 1/6 \times 1/6 \times 3$), here are the expected values for both the usual and the promotional payoffs:

Usual 60 to 1 payoff: $EV = (+60)(1/72) + (-1)(71/72) = -0.153$; HA = 15.3 percent.
Promotional 80 to 1 payoff: $EV = (+80)(1/72) + (-1)(71/72) = +0.125$; HA = -12.5 percent.

(The same calculation applies for a total of 17.)

In other promotional gaffes, an Illinois riverboat casino lost a reported $200,000 in one day with its "2 to 1 Tuesdays" that paid players 2 to 1 (the usual payoff is 3 to 2) on blackjack naturals, a scheme that gave players a 2 percent advantage. Not to be outdone, a Native American casino in California paid 3 to 1 on naturals during its "happy hour," offered three times a day, two days a week for more than two weeks. This promotion gave the player a whopping 6 percent edge. A small Las Vegas casino offered a blackjack rule variation called the "Free Ride" in which players were given a free right-to-surrender token every time they received a natural. Proper use of the token led to a player edge of 1.3 percent, and the casino lost an estimated $17,000 in eight hours. Another major Las Vegas casino offered a "50/50 Split" blackjack side bet that allowed the player to stand on an initial holding of 12–16 and begin a new hand for equal stakes against the same dealer up card. Although the game marketers claimed the variation was to the advantage of the casino, it turned out that players who exercised the 50/50 Split only against dealer 2–6 had a 2 percent advantage. According to one pit boss, the casino suffered a $230,000 loss in three-and-a-half days. As one gaming expert put it, "I always find it amusing when these billion dollar casinos, and their official state gaming control agents, never think to hire a competent mathematician to analyze a new game for possible problems."

Gaming Regulations and Mathematics

Casino gaming is one of the most regulated industries in the world. Most gaming regulatory systems share common objectives: keep the games fair and honest and assure that players are paid accurately if they win. Fairness and honesty are different concepts. A casino can be honest but not fair. Honesty refers to whether the casino offers games whose chance elements are random. Fairness refers to the game advantage—how much of each dollar wagered should the casino be able to keep? A slot machine that holds, on average, 90 percent of every dollar bet is certainly not fair but could very well be honest (if the outcomes of each play are not predetermined in the casino's favor). Two major regulatory issues relating to fairness and honesty—ensuring random outcomes and controlling the house advantage—are inextricably tied to mathematics, and most regulatory bodies require some type of mathematical analysis to demonstrate game advantage and/or confirm that games outcomes are random. Such evidence can range from straightforward probability analyses to computer simulations and complex statistical studies. Requirements vary across jurisdictions, but it is not uncommon to see technical language in gaming regulations concerning specific statistical tests that must be performed, confidence limits that must be met, and other mathematical specifications and standards relating to game outcomes.

Summary

This chapter has discussed the various games found in many of today's casinos, the mathematics underlying these games, and the related issues of game pricing, player value and comps, and the role of mathematics in gaming regulation. Probability and statistics are the foundations of the gaming industry and the role of mathematics in all facets of casino operations cannot be overemphasized. From the assurance of revenues due to the game advantage, to the regulations regarding fairness and honesty, mathematics is an ever-present cog in the machinery of the gaming business. Honest games based on good math, with a positive house advantage, minimize the short-term risk and ensure the casino will make money in the long run. In the short term, fluctuations in both directions will occur. Players view these fluctuations as good luck or bad luck, depending on the direction, but mathematicians call them fluctuations. In the gaming business, there is no such thing as luck... it is all mathematics.

key terms

Ante	Odds
Earning potential	Payback percentage
Expectation	Probability
Expected value	Return percentage
Hold percentage	Standard deviation
House advantage	Volatility
House edge	Win percentage

review questions

1. Identify the primary games offered in most casinos.

2. Name three casino games that are pure chance and three that involve an element of skill.

3. Explain how the mathematics governing the games generates revenues.

4. Ignoring poker and sports betting, which games generally have the largest and which the smallest overall house advantages? (Name three of each.)

5. What is the difference between the expectation and house advantage of a wager?

6. What precisely does it mean to say that a wager has a house advantage of 2 percent?

7. Differentiate among the several ways to express win rate.

8. Explain the role of volatility in casino operations.

9. Describe the role of mathematics in gaming regulation.

internet sites

Urbino, a casino and gaming management site
    www.urbino.net

Institute for the Study of Gambling and Commercial Gaming, University of Nevada, Reno
    www.unr.edu/gaming

The Wizard of Odds, an excellent site for general game mathematics and odds
    www.wizardofodds.com

Blackjack (mainly) sites
    www.bjmath.com, www.bj21.com, www.advantageplayer.com

endnotes

1. There may, however, be various wagers available with different house advantages. In craps, for example, the pass line bet carries a 1.4 percent house advantage, while many of the proposition bets have larger house advantages—16.7 percent on the "any seven" bet, 11.1 percent on the "any craps" bet, 5.6 percent on the field, 9.1 percent on the "hard 6" and "hard 8," and 11.1 percent on the "hard 4" and "hard 10," to name a few.

2. The word *odds* is being used informally here to mean "house advantage," the long-run percentage of money wagered that is retained by the casino. The word *odds* is more often used in a slightly different (and perhaps more appropriate) way, the chances of an event not occurring relative to its occurring—that is, the odds against rolling a double-six with a pair of honest dice are 35 to 1. Both the concepts of odds and house advantage are discussed in more detail later in the chapter.

3. There are even a few video poker machines (e.g., the rare 9/7 Jacks or Better, as well as the full-pay versions of Deuces Wild, Joker Wild, Double Bonus, All-American Poker, Loose Deuces, and Deluxe Deuces) that return greater than 100 percent when played with optimal strategy.

4. Quoted in Spanier, D. (1994) *Inside the Gambler's Mind.* Las Vegas: University of Nevada Press.

5. Pileggi, N. (1995) *Casino*. New York: Simon & Schuster.

6. Puzo, M. (1976) *Fools Die*. New York: Signet.

7. Contrary to the belief of some, card counting is not illegal. In Nevada, the casino may bar a suspected card counter from playing blackjack—the player may be permitted to play games other than blackjack, such as slots or roulette, or the suspected counter may be required to leave the premises altogether. In New Jersey, casinos must allow suspected card counters to play blackjack but can take other countermeasures such as shuffling more often or "flat betting" the player (requiring the same bet size on each wager).

8. We are not including cardroom poker since it is not a house-banked game.

9. Dealer stands on soft 17, double down on any first two cards but not after splits, split non-ace pairs up to four times, split aces receive only one card, no surrender.

10. For example, on the combined pass-line plus odds wagers, taking double odds results in a 0.61 percent house edge, triple odds 0.47 percent, and 10 times odds 0.18 percent. With the 3/4/5× odds structure offered in many casinos, the house edge on the combined pass-line plus odds wagers is 0.37 percent.

references

Cabot, Anthony N. (1996). *Casino Gaming: Policy, Economics, and Regulation*. Las Vegas, NV: UNLV International Gaming Institute.

Cabot, Anthony N., and Hannum, Robert C. (2002). Gaming regulation and mathematics: A marriage of necessity. *John Marshall Law Review*, 35 (3), 333–358.

Eadington, William R., and Cornelius, Judy (eds.) (1992). *Gambling and Commercial Gaming: Essays in Business, Economics, Philosophy and Science*. Reno, NV: University of Nevada, Institute for the Study of Gambling and Commercial Gaming.

Eadington, William R., and Cornelius, Judy (eds.) (1999). *The Business of Gaming: Economic and Management Issues*. Reno, NV: University of Nevada, Institute for the Study of Gambling and Commercial Gaming.

Epstein, Richard A. (1995). *The Theory of Gambling and Statistical Logic*, rev. ed. San Diego, CA: Academic Press.

Feller, William (1968). *An Introduction to Probability Theory and Its Applications*, 3rd ed. New York: John Wiley.

Griffin, Peter A. (1999). *The Theory of Blackjack*, 6th ed. Las Vegas, NV: Huntington Press.

Griffin, Peter (1991). *Extra Stuff: Gambling Ramblings*. Las Vegas, NV: Huntington Press.

Hannum, Robert C., and Cabot, Anthony N. (2005). *Practical Casino Math*, 2nd ed. Reno, NV: University of Nevada, Institute for the Study of Gambling & Commercial Gaming.

Humble, Lance, and Cooper, Carl (1980). *The World's Greatest Blackjack Book*. New York: Doubleday.

Kilby, Jim, Fox, Jim, and Lucas, Anthony F. (2005). *Casino Operations Management*, 2nd ed., New York: John Wiley.

Levinson, Horace C. (1963). *Chance, Luck and Statistics*. Mineola, NY: Dover Publications.

Millman, Martin H. (1983). A statistical analysis of casino blackjack. *American Mathematical Monthly*, 90, 431–436.

Packel, Edward (1981). *The Mathematics of Games and Gambling*. Washington, D.C.: The Mathematical Association of America.

Thorp, Edward O. (1966). *Beat the Dealer*. New York: Vintage Books.

Thorp, Edward O. (1984). *The Mathematics of Gambling*. Hollywood, CA: Gambling Times.

Vancura, Olaf (1996). *Smart Casino Gambling*. San Diego, CA: Index Publishing Group.

Vancura, Olaf, Cornelius, Judy A., and Eadington, William R. (eds.) (2000). *Finding the Edge: Mathematical Analysis of Casino Games*. Reno, NV: University of Nevada, Institute for the Study of Gambling and Commercial Gaming.

Weaver, Warren (1982). *Lady Luck: The Theory of Probability*. New York: Dover Publications.

Wilson, Allan (1970). *The Casino Gambler's Guide*. New York: Harper & Row.

Vignette

Pachinko in Japan

"I Can Not Believe It, There Is Gambling Going on Here!"

Is it gambling, or isn't it? I suppose it all depends on the meaning of the word *is*.

Pachinko parlors are pervasive throughout Japan. More than 18,000 parlors house 4 million machines. These very popular machines produce net gambling revenues of more than $30 billion a year for their owners, which is approximately 70 percent of all gambling wins—by operators—in Japan. It is close to the wins of all U.S. gambling casinos, even though the U.S. population is twice that of Japan. Additionally, while the United States has about one slot machine for every 400 residents, Japan has one gaming machine for every 30 residents, and that makes for a lot of gambling.

But are the pachinko players gambling?

Pachinko machines are not authorized under any exceptions to Japan's antigambling laws. Lotteries, horse races, bicycle races, and motorcycle and motorboat

Figure 9–6 Pachinko.
This is an exterior shot of a typical Pachinko parlor.
Photo courtesy of Bill Thompson.

race gambling operations all have specific exemptions to these laws. Pachinko is instead loosely governed and even more loosely regulated by local and national police under Japanese "amusement" laws. The police and other officials close their eyes to the general gambling ban, as they maintain popular fictions about pachinko not really being gambling. *Gambling* is defined as an activity with "consideration," "chance," and "prizes." To understand the popular fictions about pachinko, we must first understand how the game operates.

First, while pachinko games used to be activated by inserting cash currency, they are now activated with a special debit card. The plastic card is purchased and used only at the pachinko parlor. The debit card allows the pachinko machine to give players a supply of balls. No money is placed into the machines—hence, in the popular fiction, there is really no "consideration."

Second, players twist a knob on the pachinko machine causing little metal balls the size of ball bearings to fly upward onto a vertical board having shoots and pins on it (Figure 9–6). The balls fall downward, and if they fall into certain areas, they activate spinning reels that determine if there are winnings. With any wins, a new supply of balls falls into a tray at the bottom of the machine board. The balls may be replayed by the player, or they may be exchanged for merchandise. Officials maintain that the twisting of the activating knob involves special "skills" allowing certain players to win. Ergo, pachinko does not involve "chance."

Finally, the pachinko player does not "win," that is, he or she does not win a money prize. Rather, the player can only win more balls. However, the player may use the balls for more games or may exchange them for merchandize prizes at the pachinko parlor. Each parlor has a gift area. The parlor may not give the player money for the balls. Hence, there is "no prize," the third element of the definition of gambling.

However, the players *are* playing for money. They can get the money by asking for special merchandise, specifically for a pretty plastic card that may have a chip of gold or silver on it. The player then takes the card outside of the parlor to a separate building. Sometimes the building is actually attached to the pachinko parlor. There the player puts the plastic card into a little window (that hides the people inside) and is given money for the plastic card. This exchange operation must be owned and operated by some party other than the owners of the pachinko parlor. This preserves the fiction that there are no money prizes with pachinko games.

These popular fictions exist so that no laws need to be passed in order to have legal pachinko games and also so that the police do not have to be concerned that any laws are being violated by the pachinko parlors. The pachinko parlors present many problems, but they are accepted by authorities for a variety of reasons, including the fact that their gambling product is desired by large numbers (albeit a minority) of the Japanese people. In addition, many retired police officer's are hired as security officers by pachinko parlors, and many former police own and operate many of the merchandise-money exchange businesses.

This whole arrangement gives pachinko a special quality that does not exist with other gambling games around the world. Players, who think that they have skills, maintain that they *always* win. In reality, there is no skill in the activity of twisting the machine knob. The balls may go upward in different speeds, but they fall in random fashion, and as they cause reels to spin, the spins randomly select winning plays. (Before the machines are played, some measure of skill may be used by experienced players who can detect machines that have more favorable distributions of pins and shoots on their boards).

But it is also true, although unlikely, that the players may actually always win. Indeed, a few machines are computerized and set to pay back players at rates in excess of 100 percent. That is, for 100 balls played, the machines may give back more than 100 balls, perhaps 110 balls on average. Used in replays, the winnings can allow a long period of play. However, this marginal player advantage is totally destroyed when the player initiates the exchange process. That process results in balls being exchanged for plastic cards that are exchanged for money. For example, the debit card may cost 400 yen in order to give the player 100 balls. If the player wins 110 balls and trades them first for a plastic card, and then again for cash money, he or she may receive 300 yen back. The catch is this—the "winning" player must exchange the balls. The pachinko parlors close before 11 p.m. each evening, and the balls may not be taken out of the parlors.

The pachinko system in Japan allows perpetually losing players (that is, players who daily lose money at play) to be "hooked" with the notion that they are winners, as they indeed often win more balls than they start with. In this way, the system can foster compulsive gambling traits among players. About 80 percent of the play in pachinko parlors is at the pachinko-type games.

There is another downside with the pachinko exchange system. Over the history of Japanese pachinko parlors, the exchange businesses have been controlled not only by former police officers, but also on occasion by members of the Yakusa, the Japanese organized crime families. This has given pachinko a bad name, and ironically, it has caused a strong move in the direction of actually labeling pachinko as gambling, and having a specific exceptions law to provide for regulation of the games. However, it is so much easier now for authorities to simply shrug their shoulders, and say, with a puzzled look on their faces, "What, is there gambling going on here?"

Figure 9—7

A Historical Note on Pachinko

Pachinko may be a funny sounding word, but actually it is derived from the sound—"pachin-pachin"—that is made by balls as they bounce down the face of the game board toward winning or losing positions. Pachinko has origins outside of Japan. Most researchers find beginnings of the game in the United States. The Corinthian game was played in Detroit in the early 1920s. This game was played with a board placed on an incline. Balls were shot up one side of the board and then fell downward onto circles of nails (arranged like Corinthian architecture) and bounced into winning slots or fell into a losing pool at the bottom.

The game developed in two different directions. In the United States, it developed into the popular pinball games found in recreation halls across the land, until computerized video games replaced them in the 1980s. The Corinthian game moved to Japan in the 1930s. The game board was placed into a vertical position to save space. Machines were also converted so that the balls could come out of the machine in increased volumes if winning placements were made.

The machine was very popular; however, the game was made illegal in 1937 after Japan began military actions in China and assumed a wartime posture. Plants making the games were converted into munitions factories. The government also did not want individuals to waste time at play, and many of the players were drafted for military service.

After the war, the machines were once again permitted. The government now encouraged play as the occupying armies used it as a means to distribute scarce goods such as cigarettes, soap, and chocolate to the public. In ensuing decades, the pachinko machines were refined. Shooting mechanisms enabled players to put more than 100 balls a minute into play. Pachinko machines incorporated new games within the game. Slot machine type reels were placed in the middle of the playing board. As balls went into winning areas, the reels spun, and enabled greater prizes to be won if symbols could be lined up in winning combinations.

A new variation of the game called Pachi-slo was also introduced. This game is essentially like the reel slot machines found in casinos all over the world. However, after the reels are activated, they may be individually stopped by the player pushing buttons. With special skill, the player is supposed to be able to line up symbols in winning patterns. However, the reels spin so fast that almost all winners claim their prizes through luck. While Pachinko wins are conveyed in

balls from the machine, Pachi-slo machines use tokens for play, and tokens come out for winners.

Only Japan has widespread commercialized Pachinko parlors. It is a fun experience to visit a Pachinko parlor and to play the game. The Pachinko games exist because of popular fictions, but then, everywhere gambling itself exists (either legal or illegal) is fraught with much ambiguity.

10 Product—Organization

Marilyn Riley, CTC, Inc.

Learning Objectives

1. To present an outline of the organizational structures within a casino.

2. To identify the relationships between casino departments.

3. To summarize the duties and responsibilities of casino departments and employees.

4. To investigate the importance of top customer service.

5. To discuss casino service management.

Chapter Outline

Introduction

This chapter identifies the organizational structures within a casino. It reviews the categorization of roles and responsibilities within each department and discusses the cooperation required by each department to complete assigned roles successfully. The reader should be able to recognize the main objective of departmental cooperation as providing courteous, safe, and consistent customer service to all casino customers.

Casino Organizational Structures and Amenities

The casino industry has grown rapidly over the past several years. As a result, it has changed in regard to policies, marketing strategies, procedures, technologies, and design. Casino organizational structures have also changed over the years and are now relatively identical from one casino to the next. Although casinos can range from an establishment with a handful of slot machines and no table games to a much larger property containing thousands of slot machines and multiple table games, the organizational structures have common elements.

As is evident from Figures 10–1 and 10–2, casino organizational structures can differ in size and design. Small casinos employ fewer employees and, in turn, fewer managers. Large casinos require more employees and more managers, including slot managers, table game managers, surveillance technical supervisors, and directors of surveillance and security. Small casinos may combine the duties and responsibilities of certain positions to fit their business needs. For example, many smaller casinos have combined slot and table games management positions and renamed the position "casino operations manager." Knowing each department and the positions held within each provides great insight into the organizational structure of a property. To understand the connection between departments and structures better, the following sections introduce each department with a brief overview of responsibilities and positions held within each.

Casino Managers

The general manager (GM) has many responsibilities but is basically accountable for the overall day-to-day operations of the entire casino. The GM oversees the daily operations of each department and is the person responsible for the casino's win percentages. Larger

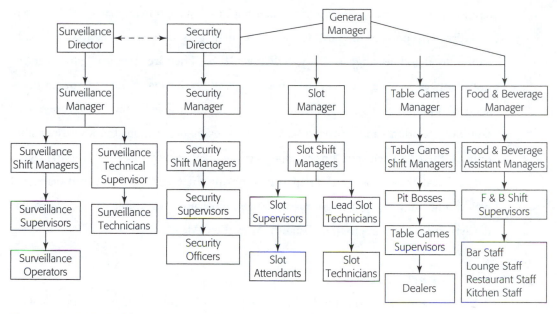

Figure 10–1 Typical Organizational Chart for a Large Casino

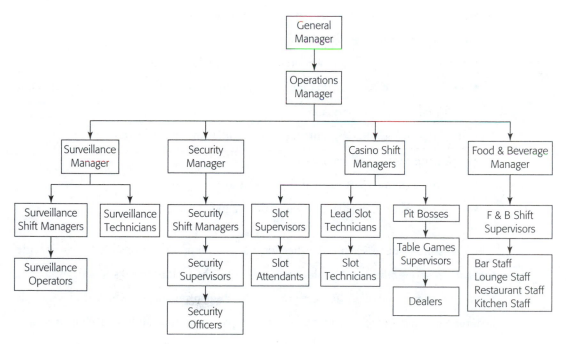

Figure 10–2 Typical Organizational Chart for a Small Casino

casinos may also include an operations manager or assistant general manager who assists and directly reports to the GM. Other casino managers are responsible for slots, table games, food and beverage, security, and surveillance. They are responsible for overseeing all aspects of their specific departments. Directly reporting to the department managers are the shift managers. The shift managers are responsible for the smooth operation, employee relations, and customer service of a specific department but are responsible only for their assigned shift. For example, a casino may employ three slot shift managers who are responsible for the slot department during their shift. The slot shift managers would report directly to the slot manager, who in turn is responsible for the entire slot department and reports to the assistant GM or the GM.

Slot Department

A slot manager is responsible for the direction and administration of controls with regard to personnel and operations within the department. The slot manager is specifically responsible for

- promoting outstanding customer and employee relations
- evaluating employees
- ensuring that department employees are trained properly
- monitoring the issuing of complimentary items to players from the department shift managers or supervisors
- ensuring that all department rules and regulations are followed
- reporting results and records
- making certain department discrepancies are completed
- ensuring that the department operations run smoothly

The slot shift managers report to the slot manager and are responsible for overseeing the same responsibilities as the slot manager, but only during their assigned shifts. The slot supervisor on the other hand, reports to the slot shift manager, whose duties include assigning the duties of all slot attendants, such as paying jackpots, filling machine **hoppers** and completing related paperwork, as well as ensuring that all duties are performed accurately. The slot supervisor also handles any complaints from the slot customers.

Slot attendants and slot technicians in general are the base line or hourly employees of the department and report to the department supervisors. The attendants are typically assigned zones on the casino floor by the slot supervisor. Each slot attendant is responsible for his or her zone during the shift. Slot attendants have numerous responsibilities within their zones. Some of these responsibilities include but are not limited to paying jackpots, monitoring zones for machines requiring hopper fills, assisting customers, completing slot paperwork when necessary, and making each customer's visit an enjoyable one. Although slot attendants monitor their zones and tend to payouts and patrons, the machines also need tending. A lead slot technician organizes slot machine moves, trains slot technicians, and assigns schedules to slot technicians. In addition to all these duties, a lead slot technician is responsible for all regular slot technician duties such as monitoring the slot machines, handling slot machine malfunctions, repairing and installing slot machines, removing slot machines, and providing top customer service.

Table Games

Reporting to the GM or assistant GM, a table games (TG) manager is responsible for the overall efficient operation of the table games department. He or she is also responsible for

- development and accurate implementation of department policies and procedures
- employee relations
- supplying quality customer service
- monitoring the issuing of complimentary items to customers from the department shift managers or pit managers
- assigning pit managers to a TG pit each shift
- training the staff
- completing evaluations of the department

The TG shift managers report to the TG manager and are responsible for overseeing the same responsibilities as the TG manager, but only during their assigned shifts. The **pit** managers or pit bosses report to the TG shift managers and are responsible for the operation of their assigned pits. The pit managers allocate dealers to specific games and tables and assign supervisors to their sections of tables within the pit. The assigning of tables and games for dealers or table sections for supervisors is not completed in advance but is completed throughout each shift.

The TG supervisors report to the pit manager and are responsible for monitoring the activity of the table games in their assigned sections to ensure game accuracy. The TG supervisors ensure that dealers follow proper guidelines. If a dealer must leave a table at any time before a replacement has been assigned, the TG supervisor will step in and take control of the game until another dealer can take over. TG supervisors also handle any TG customer complaints and discrepancies.

Dealers in general are the baseline hourly employees of the department and report to the supervisors of the department. The dealers deal pit games such as roulette, blackjack and Let it Ride. While dealing any game, the dealer is responsible to discretely report any customers they suspect of cheating or those who are simply acting in an inappropriate manner (dealer's judgement call) to the on-duty supervisor. Dealers are responsible to follow all game protection rules and follow strict policies and procedures. It is imperative that all dealers follow the same set of rules, such as picking up chips, exchanging customer money for chips, shuffling cards, delivering cards, and entering or leaving a table (clearing of hands for the cameras). The dealers are also responsible for enforcing minimum and maximum posted table limits (customer wagers). They must take care that they follow all required actions to ensure the games are running honestly. If dealers do not follow these procedures, they can easily be targeted by casino cheaters who will take advantage of their lack of attention, and the casino may unnecessarily lose profits. Not following guidelines can result in termination, as dealers who cannot stay focused are casino liabilities.

Casino Cage

The casino **cage** is referred to as the heart of the casino because it is responsible for all casino monies. The main function of the cage is to handle all cashiering functions. Whether performing cashiering functions within the service windows or exchanging cash and cash equivalents with the gaming floor, the cage at one point or another handles all incoming cash.

The cage manager reports to the GM or assistant GM and is responsible for managing all operations of the casino cage. The manager ensures the department is properly staffed, provides excellent customer service, and performs accurate accounting of all cage transactions. The manager is also responsible for department evaluations and reports. The cage shift managers report to the cage manager and have the same responsibilities as the manager, but only during their assigned shifts. The cage supervisors assign the cashier duties and with the manager are responsible for authorizing and overseeing these functions along with other large financial transactions. For example, cage supervisors and managers work closely with table game managers to complete approved lines of credit for high-limit table game players.

Cage cashiers report to the cage supervisors. Cashiers take care of many transactions during a shift and are assigned one cashier function per shift. For instance, a cage cashier could be assigned to perform in-house financial functions such as jackpot payouts and hopper fills from an employee-only cage window for one shift and could be assigned to work the main cage window and provide customers with their financial transaction needs on another shift. Cage cashiers exchange coin and chips for currency for all casino customers and are also responsible for the cash counting of jackpots, selected department tips, and nightly employee floats.

Security

Another department that performs many jobs is the security department. The main objective of this department is to ensure that employees, guests, and assets are safe. Employees of this department should be equipped with first aid training, as they oversee all accident reports within the casino. Security also acts as an escort for transporting cash and chips within the casino. This department *must* also take the initiative to ensure that no person enters the gaming area without being of legal age. Casino properties can face a large fine and have their gaming licenses suspended if any under-aged person enters or remains on the gaming floor.

The security director reports to the GM and is responsible for the overall security of the entire property, including casino assets, hotel possessions, external grounds, and customer and employee safety. The manager reports to the director and supervisors report to the manager. Each member of the management team receives extensive training on common casino crimes, hotel security, and gaming regulations and procedures.

Security officers are responsible for money transfers, including slot drops, table game fills, and credits. They are also responsible for handling disturbances, monitoring activity and access to restricted gaming and entertainment areas, escorting employees and patrons, reporting all policy violators and criminal activity, completing incident reports, and providing customer service. In addition, officers are responsible for patrolling the casino floor and grounds to ensure the security and safety of the guests, employees, and the cash and physical assets of the hotel and casino.

Surveillance

Regardless of the size of the casino property, there is one department that casinos cannot afford to dismiss, overlook, or underestimate. The surveillance department is one of the most important departments of the casino, as it ensures that the operations within the property are running smoothly and honestly. Surveillance departments have changed in size, equipment, and location over the years. In times past, surveillance departments consisted of a few untrained men. These men were required to observe employees and casino gamblers from a distance by walking the "catwalk" above the casino gaming floor. The surveillance department today is located in a secured area consisting of many television monitors. Employees are granted entry only with permission, and the area is not accessible to patrons of the casino. As a result, in well-run casinos, surveillance personnel are not allowed to fraternize with other casino employees. This is to protect the casino from security problems such as employee collusion. The rooms can be located anywhere in the casino but are usually not on the same level as the casino gaming area. Employees of surveillance departments today normally receive continuous training in order to be familiar with all casino activity. This includes procedures and policies of each and every department as well as knowledge of casino cheating, monitoring, reporting, written and verbal communication skills, and alert observation.

The surveillance department has gained a wide variety of modern technological devices over the past couple of decades as well. At one time, the surveillance persons were considered the department's equipment. Today, the department consists of highly technical monitoring equipment. Suspended cameras can observe every aspect of the casino floor. The cameras can zoom in on a table game and enlarge a serial number from currency. Television monitors are no longer displaying a black-and-white picture but may display a color picture better than those on the most expensive residential television systems.

The surveillance department includes surveillance camera operators, supervisors, managers, and directors. The director of surveillance is a salaried management position. He or she has many duties and vast responsibility. The director of surveillance is responsible for overseeing all staff activities. Hiring, training, evaluations, department promotions, dismissals, and employee disciplinary action reports must be considered and approved by the director. All personnel of this department are the responsibility of the director. In addition, the director of surveillance is normally expected to create, enforce, and make alterations to department policies and procedures when necessary. The director examines and recommends solutions for security, surveillance, and cheating within the property.

Reporting directly to the surveillance director, the surveillance manager is also responsible for the employees of this department. The manager is responsible for creating training programs, hiring employees, enforcing policies, offering suggestions for the department, completing daily reports, and the ordering and purchasing of supplies for the department. The shift managers have the same responsibilities as the manager but only during their assigned shifts. Managers work closely with the hourly employees of the department and make necessary recommendations to the director.

The surveillance supervisors report directly to the surveillance shift managers. The supervisors execute staff schedules and assign hourly employees with shift duties. Surveillance operators directly report to the surveillance supervisor. Supervisors are responsible for the facilitation of training new hires as department operators and all training outlined by the surveillance manager. Surveillance supervisors must also review security tapes for violations of federal, state, or local laws and assist with all related investigations. The surveillance operators are responsible for protecting casino assets. Operators conduct continuous surveillance of all areas of the casino via a closed circuit television (CCTV) system (Figure 10–3) and do not limit their surveillance to **crossroaders** (casino cheats) and games and slot players. In addition to monitoring property activities, officers are responsible for changing out machines when tapes are full and preparing daily logs and incident reports. The operators are not in charge of the maintenance of camera or department equipment. The surveillance manager also oversees duties performed by the surveillance technical supervisor, who is responsible for the inventory of CCTV equipment and supplies, scheduling of surveillance technicians and continuous training of upgraded systems. The surveillance technicians repair, update, and install all surveillance equipment.

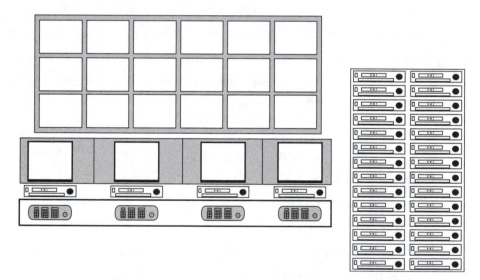

Figure 10–3 Diagram of Multiplex Screens, Monitors, and Video Storage for Surveillance
The 18 monitors in front can be focused on the main floor, pits, entry doors, and other valuable casino assets. You would find shift managers and operators seated at the four workstations. These monitors are used for close observations of casino assets and incidents. The **racks** of VCRs make it easy to switch out machines as tapes are filled so that there are no gaps in recording.

Departments Outside the Casino

Food and Beverage

The food and beverage department's responsibility is to attend to guests' requests for food and beverage. This department may include several fast food outlets, coffee shops, bars, lounges, dining areas, and several other restaurants. Food and beverage services provided by the casino are typically open the same hours as the casino operations area. If the casino operations are open 24 hours and 7 days a week, several of the food and beverage establishments may also be open 24 hours and 7 days a week to keep customers comfortable and to provide service to casino patrons. The establishments that remain open are chosen after careful consideration by management. For example, if patrons were utilizing the coffee shop continuously 24 hours a day, this site would remain open. If a particular restaurant was not being utilized after a certain time of day, management may close that establishment during periods when it was underutilized. Although many casino properties provide complimentary drinks and meals for some casino patrons during all hours of operation, the casino food and beverage department is a profit center for the casino property and can provide a large profit if managed well.

There are usually a variety of restaurants located in a casino, as the casino wants to attract a wide variety of customers (Figure 10–4). Once a casino catches the attention of a customer, it wants the customer to stay and take advantage of the services provided. Chances are that if a customer is hungry and the restaurant options do not appeal to the customer, the customer will leave and may not return to the game until another day. If the casino offers a variety in food selection, prices, and atmospheres, the customer will be more likely to continue playing in the gaming area after the meal.

Food and beverage managers and assistant managers have a considerable number of duties and responsibilities, including

- ensuring that equipment and surroundings meet both health and internal regulations
- directing and coordinating activities of high-volume food and beverage facilities
- ensuring that health policies are being followed by each departmental employee
- creating menus

Figure 10–4
Courtesy of Isle of Capri.

- arranging special events
- implementing department and property policies and procedures
- considering and maintaining the department budget
- implementing training programs
- completing and issuing employee evaluations

Food and beverage supervisors have many responsibilities as well. Supervisors are responsible for resolving guest complaints and interviewing, hiring, and training department staff. Supervisors must also ensure that policies are followed within all food establishments on the property. Supervisors take charge of a wide range of staff, including workers in coffee shops, fine dining restaurants, and staff cafeterias. Floor servers, cocktail servers, bartenders, banquet staff, chefs, bus persons, kitchen staff, and waitstaff all report to the supervisors of the department.

Lodging

The rooms in casino hotels vary dramatically depending on the type of customer the casino hopes to attract. In the past, interiors were designed to encourage the player to spend time in the casino. For example, when the Mirage first opened, the guest rooms were decorated with bold, bright floral colors. Bright colors tend to have an energizing effect on people. As a result, the colors tended to make people want to go to the casino rather than rest. However, now most casino hotel rooms are just like any other standard hotel room. But not all rooms are created equal. Like a traditional hotel, the more you spend on the room, the larger and more luxurious the setting. Of course in a casino hotel, the more you spend in the casino, the less you spend to obtain the more deluxe suites. The most luxurious suites or villas are not available to rent but are reserved for use for the casino's high rollers. In fact, high rollers or whales do not even have to check in at the front desk. They have their own special hosts who handle all aspects of their visit.

Traditionally, rooms and food and beverages were given as comps to people who spent money in the casino. It was a way to draw people to the casino and encourage them to stay longer. As a result, the expense of running these departments was written off as casino promotions. It was assumed that these departments would lose money and their expenses would be a line transfer to the casino marketing department. However, this caused tension between rooms division managers and casino marketing people. The rooms division manager was taught that a sold-out hotel was the optimal strategy. On the other hand, the casino marketing people always want to have a few rooms in reserve for special guests, such as the high rollers. This is especially troubling when, as we said earlier, the best suites are not available for rent by the hotel. Therefore, the hotel spends a great deal of money creating luxury suites and no hotel rental fees are generated to offset the expense on the hotel accounting side.

Entertainment and Recreation

Las Vegas showgirls are not a new phenomenon. Recollect, if you will, every Western film with a saloon scene. Invariably there is the card table and in the background the piano player with singers, dancers, or both. Entertainment has always been an integral part of a casino's atmosphere. Lounge shows change weekly, and big name entertainers and stage extravaganzas are brought in to match guests' interests: Frank Sinatra impersonators for the senior, retired set; Blood, Sweat, and Tears for the baby boomers;

and rap groups for the younger crowds. Entertainment can be an important comp because it draws people in for the show and then they might drop a few coins in the slots or play a couple of hands at the tables while they wait for the show to begin. In addition, they might come in early for dinner or stay late for some drinks and always the casino is tempting people to stay.

Like entertainment, recreational amenities also draw people to spend time in the resort complex. If people are staying at the hotel, they like to have the swimming pool, saunas, and workout areas. More and more casino resorts are offering spas for day trippers as well as vacation travelers. Many casinos offer bowling, ice skating, movie theatres, or dancing. Outside of the facilities on the Mississippi Gulf Coast, one can go sailing or deep-sea fishing or play a round of golf at exclusive courses.

Shopping is a great past time. Guests can buy presents for friends, celebrate winnings, or just wander around checking out the merchandise. Retail has long been a part of the grand hotel tradition, and every casino has some form of retail selling of souvenirs. Perhaps the most dramatic retail operation associated with a casino is the Forum shops at Caesars. This indoor shopping mall has become a must-visit attraction on the Las Vegas Strip. The unsuspecting traveler who enters the Forum from Las Vegas Boulevard is ultimately drawn into Caesars Palace casino because there are no other exits possible. The ceiling is painted and lighted to replicate a 24-hour day/night cycle every hour. There are two fountains with animated shows for free, provided you come at the right time. The storefronts capture an Italian Renaissance street scene. So, Caesars has successfully used retail as one differentiating strategy.

Currently, more casino resort hotels are realizing that as long as people spend money, it really does not matter which venue they use, so long as they spend. Different people come to the casinos for a variety of reasons. Some come for a meal, shopping, relaxing spa treatments, working out at the health club, watching shows, or even gambling. As a result, the current trend is for every department to be a profit center. The casino is still the biggest money maker, but now casino resorts have become entertainment megaplexes for locals and tourists. After all, at the end of the day, the money still goes into the same pocket.

Marketing

Another important department in the casino industry is the marketing department. Casino marketing strategies are the techniques that draw customers into a casino. Because of the price of gambling, a casino must use marketing strategies to convince customers that they are getting their money's worth. Some commonly used marketing strategies include free or reasonably priced entertainment, free beverages, and discount hotel accommodations. The goal is to attract as many customers as possible. Advertising with radio stations, television commercials, and newspaper articles makes it easy to reach a large audience. Using attractions such as celebrity performances and high-ticket sporting events will interest some audiences, while hosting dinner theatres and plays may attract others. The casino industry is unique when it comes to entertainment because it has to appeal to customers with a wide variety of interests, and not target a specific audience.

Like any business, casinos want their guests feel important to increase the chance of their returning. To do this, casinos offer customer players' club cards, which accumulate points (the more they play, the more points they gain); retail merchandise such as pens, cups, sweaters, hats; and even large prizes such as trips or cash draws. Casino hosts report people who spend a great deal of money to the marketing department, and its primary responsibility is to provide special attention to these guests, creating excellent customer service.

Customer Service: Making Sure the Guest is Happy

Why should a customer visit one casino rather than another nearby establishment? Many factors affect a customer's decision as to which casino to patronize. Although prices, locations, promotions, accommodations, and comps are all strategies to influence a customer's decision, customer service is one of the most important factors a customer uses to distinguish one casino from another. Customers want to be treated with respect and recognition while they are spending their money. Discount promotions are no longer enough to guarantee a returning customer. Today, that factor is customer service—a win-win situation. The customers win because they have an enjoyable experience, and the casino wins because the high quality of customer service results in a higher percentage of repeat business. The casino also wins because enthusiastic customers promote the property (free advertising).

How Casino Departments Work Together

To better understand the connection of the departments and structures, let's examine the processes of paying a slot machine jackpot. If one wanted to know which department is responsible for paying jackpots, the answer is often the slot department, but that answer would be only partially correct. Although the slot department is the first to initiate the jackpot payout, the process requires the assistance and cooperation of several departments.

The general procedure for paying a jackpot begins with a slot attendant identifying the jackpot and then greeting and congratulating the player. The slot attendant then fills out a request for the jackpot and takes the request to the cage employee services window (ES). The cage cashier is required to have the attendant and a security officer verify the request and all related paperwork and monies for accuracy. Both the slot attendant and the security officer will proceed to the winner and again verify the paperwork with the jackpot payout on the machine. Once verified, the slot attendant pays the winner. The security officer signs the paperwork and returns to the cage ES window to deliver the signed paperwork.

Game Protection

Let's take another look at the interaction and shared responsibilities of casino departments. Game protection is often thought to be the sole responsibility of the table games department. In essence, that is correct, but game protection is the responsibility of many more parties. One example of table game protection is the roulette dealer's hand motion over the table to signal "no more bets." To ensure top game protection, table game supervisors and dealers must continually watch the layout to ensure no bets are placed after this signal. The surveillance department also monitors this by observing the dealer's hand signals and watching for late betters. If the surveillance operators witness late bets being placed after the dealer signals over the layout, they will contact the pit boss who will inform the supervisor to watch more closely and direct the dealer to pass back any late or questionable bets to the customer.

Completing a table game **fill** is another example of a table game activity that requires assistance from multiple departments to ensure the protection of the games. When a roulette game requires a fill, the supervisor requests the financial transaction. Several parties are involved to ensure the best game protection. A security officer and cage cashier are notified. If a fill is requested, the security officer retrieves the chips from the employee cage cashier window after both parties have verified the request and determined that the amounts being delivered match the amounts requested. Once the security officer arrives, the pit boss verifies the chips with the paperwork and contacts a surveillance operator to monitor the transaction. The supervisor also verifies the request and chip amount. The chips are then placed on the table and broken down to be reverified for the surveillance operator and supervisor. Once all parties verify the chips, the dealer places the chips in a chip tray or bank. Once the chip addition has been completed, the security officer brings all signed paperwork back to the cage for accounting purposes.

It is necessary to have all departments working together to ensure that everyone is following procedures and guidelines to protect the casino assets. The layers of positions and departments work together to prevent casino cheats from stealing casino and customer assets. It is necessary to have all these parties involved in each process because casinos have large sums of available cash and chips. Dealers monitor the games, supervisors monitor the dealers, and the customers play. Pit managers monitor suspecting cheaters; security personnel monitors dealers, supervisors, and customers, while surveillance monitors everyone. A dealer cannot always deal a game and watch ten customers; a supervisor is responsible for monitoring more than one table at a time; the pit boss must monitor the entire pit; and finally someone needs to watch everyone and everything, which is why there is an **eye in the sky**.

Service Management: Making Sure the Employees Are Happy

We live in a society in which individuals are spending more and more of their time at their workplaces. With this in mind, it is important for organizations, including casinos, to evaluate the quality and type of work they supply for their employees. Employees no longer want to participate in passive work. Instead, workers want their opinions and thoughts valued.

With casinos always changing, and the number of properties around the world increasing, casinos need to reevaluate the objectives of their organizations. Many casinos realize that the first step to improving the quality of work for the dealers, cage cashier, security officer, or surveillance representative is to promote and enforce life-long learning within the organization that generates improved quality of work. What is lifelong learning and what can casinos do to promote and incorporate it? How can this benefit a casino and its workers? Education should be promoted through-out the workplace. Some businesses believe that the aim of lifelong learning is to provide employees with the skills they need to compete in today's paid workforce. However, in the casino industry, the goal of lifelong learning is that individuals acquire the knowledge they need to ensure a better life for themselves and their communities.

Casino management is also recognizing that the second step in improving the quality of work for employees is to create a democratic work environment. This system of organization could address and resolve many of the inequalities, injustices, and hin-drances to quality facing individuals and organizations. Conceivably, it encourages personal growth, creativity, and motivation, concurrently enhancing the workplace for all parties. This system also encourages workers to become part of the organization's direction through decision making. Policy then becomes a synergetic process benefiting the players. If a casino manager's focal point is a democratic casino property, communica-tive obstructions will eventually be obsolete.

For employees to view a casino property as a good workplace, managers need to work together to promote a cooperative society within the organization. It is impera-tive to understand that employees have opinions, thoughts, and ideas that need to be included in the decision-making process. Employees cannot be expected to show up for work and complete assigned duties without input. Managers need to learn that work-ers bring with them experience, knowledge, and skills that can benefit the company as a whole. As part of an organization promoting quality work, managers need to pro-mote an environment in which individuals can engage in discussion with management as well as with each other concerning the organization.

- Be current on members of your department.
- If an employee is unable to resolve a situation with a customer, it is the responsibility of the employee to direct the problem to a manager. Ensure the matter is handled in a friendly and courteous manner while respecting the employee who brought the situation to your attention.

- Provide tips, coaching, and feedback to each member of your department.
- Promote departmental employee training.
- Create employee recognition programs for employees who demonstrate quality customer service.

- Always remain approachable and communicative.
- Provide opportunities for your direct reports to voice their comments and concerns.
- Be accountable at all times.

Figure 10–5 Service Management Tips

It is essential for casinos to hear the concerns, comments, and thoughts of workers in order to think critically about the organization's goals and objectives. Workers need to be treated as equals to eliminate their feelings of isolation. By allowing all workers to participate in educational activities and eliminating power relations, workers are given the opportunity to grow and better themselves and the company.

It is evident that many workers are unhappy with the quality of work they are participating in. It is not solely the responsibility of the organization to conquer this problem. However, organizations must take the initiative. Creating high-quality jobs and workplaces is not an easy task, but there are steps that can be taken in order to achieve these goals. Understanding and promoting learning within the sphere of work and creating democratic working conditions for employees are imperative to beginning to achieve these goals (Figure 10–5).

Summary

This chapter has explored casino organizational structures. We began by introducing several casino departments and then outlining the major players and their responsibilities and duties within the casino. The chapter then focused on the relationships between these departments. We reviewed the process of a jackpot payout and analyzed some table game protection policies to show how one department interacts and depends on another department. We discussed departmental cooperation as being imperative in order to properly, effectively, and efficiently operate a successful property. In closing, the chapter explained the importance of service management.

key terms

Cage	Hopper
Crossroader	Pit
Eye in the sky (the eye)	Racks
Fill	

review questions

1. What are the main responsibilities of the surveillance department?

2. Why is customer service important?

3. Why is it important for casino managers and supervisors from separate departments to effectively communicate with one another?

4. What is the difference between the surveillance department and the security department?

5. What are the responsibilities of a security officer?

6. How can a casino manager promote lifelong learning within a casino?

7. Which departments are responsible for game protection?

8. List five marketing strategies used by casinos.

internet sites

The American Gaming Association
   http://www.americangaming.org/

Casino Surveillance News
   http://www.casinosurveillancenews.com/

Casino News from Casino Floor
   http://www.gamingfloor.com/

Alcohol and Gaming Commission of Ontario
   http://www.agco.on.ca/en/a.about/a2.orgstructure.html

Casinorecruiter. com
   http://www.navegantegroup.com/Executive_Search.html

Vignette

Interview with Thomas Kelly, Casino Surveillance Technician

To help us take a closer look into the organizational structure of the surveillance department and its relation to other casino departments, Thomas Kelly supplied some answers to gain a better understanding of this casino department. (Interview held September 6, 2004)

Riley: Thomas, what is your involvement in the casino industry and surveillance?

Kelly: I started working within the casino industry almost ten years ago as a surveillance operator. I have been with the same establishment during my entire casino career. Although the casino here in Nova Scotia is considered a smaller casino, I have traveled with my various positions and received training in places such as Las Vegas and Atlantic City. Although I started my career as a surveillance operator and advanced to a senior surveillance position, I currently hold a position of casino surveillance technician. Currently, I am also the owner of business called Inhome Alarms in which I am responsible for CCTV and security installation systems in residential and commercial properties.

Riley: The surveillance department works with several other departments. With which subdivisions do these departments work most closely?

Kelly: Surveillance works most closely with security, the cage, slot, and the table games departments. These departments are in constant contact with surveillance to better serve the guests and their needs. For example, the cage calls a surveillance operator or shift manager to review tapes for cage transaction errors, and table games calls with requests to view tapes on table payout errors. Security officers often call for coverage of incidents or accidents and representatives from the slot department contact members of the surveillance department to verify and record large jackpot payouts. Slots also contact the department when they enter a slot machine to complete duties such as a hopper fill.

Riley: Managers and directors are trained on many functions of each department within the casino. Are nonmanagement employees of one casino department required to train on various other departments?

Kelly: Well, surveillance operators have to have a fluent knowledge of each table game and the procedures and policies in order to be able to identify inaccurate pay-outs. Surveillance basically needs to know all department policy and procedures to be able to effectively monitor the casino floor for errors. Although it is not always a requirement, some employees are cross-trained to be able to perform duties in more than one department. For example, some casinos have employees who can work a shift as a dealer, another as a cage cashier, and another as a slot representative.

Riley: What procedures do surveillance operators follow when a casino cheat is detected?

Kelly: In surveillance when a cheat is detected a surveillance operator would notify the surveillance manager, security shift manager, and casino shift manager. The surveillance operator would cover the incident and obtain an identification of the suspect. The person caught cheating, depending on the seriousness of the situation, could be excluded from the establishment or detained and arrested by the local law enforcement.

Riley: Which departments have access to the actual surveillance room?

Kelly: Well, although the room is off limits to many casino employees, there are quite a few with access to the room as well. It is of course up to the discretion of the surveillance managers but in most casinos many department leads may enter the surveillance room for a vast number of reasons. General managers, directors of security, directors of casino operations, the cage director, slots managers, casino managers and shift managers, corporate investigators, surveillance technicians, members of human resource departments, and local gaming commission representatives usually visit the room.

Riley: As a previous casino surveillance operator, what do you feel is the most important information a surveillance operator should remember while on duty?

Kelly: That is a difficult question. It is important to remember the goals of the department. The main goal of this department is to *observe* the daily operations of the casino. The operators are to monitor the operations of table games, slot machines, and the cage and count rooms to observe suspicious activities such as theft and cheat at play. It is the surveillance department's responsibility to also *record* these situations and *report* this information to the proper departments and persons. Although this is important, I personally feel operators need to always remember that what they have been exposed to through the surveillance of the casino floor is to remain in the strictest of confidence and should only be discussed within the room or with upper management and never discussed with other employees or patrons.

Riley: Is there a department responsible for apprehending an alleged or bona fide criminal?

Kelly: The security department handles physical conflict on the casino property to ensure patrons safety, but the local police department will be called in if the situation escalates. The surveillance department would record the incident.

Riley: Do you think people speak of surveillance and security in an interchangeable manner and if so why do you think there is this confusion?

Kelly: This is a common occurrence. Again, surveillance's main tasks are to observe, record, and report situations. The security department handles all physical incidents. I believe casino patrons have been mislead through conversations in which uniformed security officers are monitoring screens. Many smaller businesses do hire security guards or officers to monitor CCTV monitors while on duty.

Riley: What are the responsibilities of a surveillance technician?

Kelly: A surveillance technician is in charge of installing, repairing, maintaining, and expanding the surveillance CCTV equipment. The technician is responsible for the update of all maintenance records for the CCTV system, the equipment inventory, and control of all external repair requirements. The technician is also responsible for the organization and general completion of all tasks with internal departments and external companies.

Riley: Although casino security officers are clearly visible at casino entertainment functions such as concerts and shows away from the casino floor, is it the sole responsibility of the security department to ensure the safety of the guests, entertainers, and employees?

Kelly: No. It is every employee's responsibility to ensure the safety of a guest. If there were a safety issue, surveillance and security would be informed of the situation. It is important for all casino staff members to be up to date on policies and procedures concerning workplace safety and many casinos offer this training to their staff.

Riley: Are there normally separate security and surveillance departments for the casino and hotel?

Kelly: I have not visited a property that has separate departments for the casino and the hotel. The surveillance department would monitor the casino floor and all company grounds, including hotel premises. Security for both properties would generally be combined as well with additional staff, of course. Some properties do have dual departments, however. For example, a casino/hotel property may consist of a casino property services department and a hotel housekeeping department in which the employees are not interchangeable.

Riley: Thank you for your time Mr. Kelly.

11 Pricing—Revenue Control

Steve Durham, The House Advantage

Learning Objectives

1. To understand the terms *drop*, *payouts*, and *hold*.

2. To differentiate between procedural, technological, and organizational controls.

3. To trace the flow of money from customers to the vault.

4. To list eight revenue control techniques.

5. To understand the use of hold percentage as a control device.

6. To understand how casinos' access to capital has changed since Nevada legalized gaming in 1931.

Chapter Outline

Introduction

Anyone who has patronized a casino knows that a lot of money changes hands. Customers slip $20 bills into slot machines (electronic gaming devices) or exchange cash for chips at the gaming tables. The money does not stay at the tables or in the machines. It is collected, counted, sorted, and recorded. The amount of money and its frequent movement present many opportunities for temptation to get the better of employees and guests alike. It is essential for casinos to control the flow of money in order to ensure their profitability. Government agencies charged with collecting taxes and regulating the integrity of gaming activities also have a vested interest in the accurate accounting of all revenue. The casino must implement and enforce an extensive web of mutually reinforcing controls to ensure that theft and embezzlement do not occur. This web of controls on the cash coming into the casino is called *revenue control*.

Vignette: John and Suzanne Visit a Las Vegas Casino

Let's follow John and Suzanne while they gamble at a casino in Las Vegas so we can see firsthand the controls placed on revenue. Our couple checked into the hotel this morning. They unpack but cannot wait to hit the casino. As they get off the elevator, they excitedly talk about which games they will play and where and when they will meet for dinner. John tells Suzanne that he is going to place a bet in the sportsbook before heading to the 21 tables. Suzanne says she is going to check out the bingo hall before finding her favorite slot machine. They agree to meet at 4:30 p.m. at the sports bar near the sportsbook.

John immediately heads to the sportsbook. He looks on the board and sees that his favorite team, the Tampa Bay Buccaneers, is favored to win in today's game. He walks up to the window to place his bet. He tells the sportsbook agent that he wants to bet $20 on the Buccaneers to win. The agent writes up the ticket by entering the information into a computer terminal. He accepts the $20 bill John hands him, places it in his drawer, and returns a copy of the ticket to John. John checks the ticket to be sure it is accurate and walks to the table games area.

John walks past several 21 tables until he finds one with a $5 limit and an open seat. He sits down and places a $100 bill on the table in front of him and asks for $5 chips.

The 21 dealer flattens the bill on the table top with the face up and calls out the denomination loudly so that the pit supervisor can hear. The dealer then removes approximately (twenty) $5 chips from the rack and creates a row of four stacks of five chips each. Any extra chips are returned to the rack. Each stack is touching the next stack. The dealer runs her finger across the top of each stack to be sure they all contain the same number of chips, then knocks over the one nearest to John to reveal five chips. The dealer then pushes the chips toward John who picks them up and places his initial bet in the circle in front of him. Next the dealer removes the paddle from the drop slot, places the bill flat across the slot, and then shoves the paddle back into the slot, forcing the bill into the **drop box**. The dealer then continues to deal the game (Figure 11–1).

When John or his fellow players lose a hand, the dealer collects the cards and the chips and places the chips in his or her rack. When the customers win a hand, the dealer removes chips from the rack, displays them next to the bet, and then collects the cards. Chips constantly move in and out of the rack. John settles into a rhythm as he watches his stack of chips rise and fall with his fortunes.

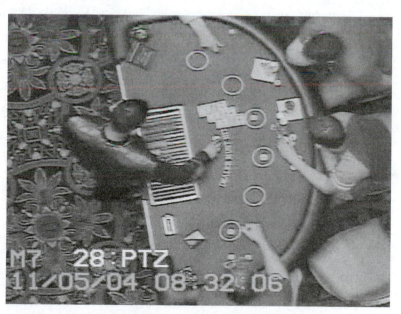

Figure 11–1 A 21 table layout with money/chip exchange. The customer in the upper right is buying $60 worth of chips. Courtesy of Steve Durham, The House Advantage.

Meanwhile, Suzanne has entered the bingo hall. She approaches the cashier window near the entrance. She asks to purchase a pack of paper. She lays her money on the counter while the cashier enters the sale into the computer terminal. The cashier gives Suzanne her change and the pack. Suzanne then finds a seat near a group of elderly women who are laughing and enjoying themselves. Suzanne brought her own dauber (felt marker) but notices that the women have several daubers in different colors as well as several troll dolls and other good luck totems. The caller soon begins. Suzanne does not win on the first two games but wins on the third game. She raises her hand and calls, "bingo!" A bingo attendant comes to her and confirms that she has marked the card correctly and verifies the win with the caller. The attendant brings the money to her and counts it out on the table in front of her. The elderly women are excited for Suzanne, and they start to chat. Suzanne socializes with them during the rest of the games.

Back at the 21 table, John is winning and has $155 in chips. It is break time for the dealer, and a new dealer comes up to her from behind. The new dealer taps her on the shoulder. The dealer finishes the hand, claps her hands once, holds them palms up to the ceiling, and leaves the table. The new dealer starts to deal a new hand.

Meanwhile, Suzanne finishes playing bingo and leaves the bingo hall. She wanders through the casino looking for her favorite slot machine, which is modeled after her favorite television game show, *Wheel of Fortune*. At last she finds several of them near the showroom. She sits down and removes a $20 bill from her purse. She inserts it into the slot, and the machine pulls it inside. After a few seconds, the machine comes alive and shows her **credits**. It is a nickel machine so it displays 400 credits. Suzanne chooses to play nine lines with a nickel bet on each line. The machine deducts the amount of the bet. She presses the "Spin" button and the reels move and the music plays. She does not win, so she repeats the bet. The machine deducts a like amount of credits and the reels spin. This time Suzanne wins a jackpot of five credits. Lights and sound signify the winning bet. The machine automatically credits Suzanne's total with the five credits. Suzanne continues to play.

Back at the 21 table, John and his fellow players are winning. The pit supervisor notices that the number of chips in the dealer's rack is getting low. He orders a **fill** from the cashier cage. Soon a security guard brings several plastic racks full of chips to John's table. The dealer stops play while the transaction occurs. The dealer counts the chips in the plastic racks and confirms that amount on the paperwork while the pit supervisor watches. The dealer also confirms that the table number and other information are correct. He signs the form and places the chips in the rack in the table. The pit supervisor signs the form. The entire time the security guard is watching to be sure all chips are accounted for and delivered. Once the chips are transferred, the security guard leaves and the dealer resumes the game.

Suzanne grows tired of playing the slot machine and goes to the sports bar near the sportsbook. It is only 3:30 p.m., so she sits down and orders a drink. The bartender mixes the drink, rings it into the computer, and places the drink and the ticket in front of Suzanne. As she pays the tab, Suzanne remembers she promised her mother that she would play keno using her mother's lucky numbers. Her mother had given Suzanne $20. She removes a keno ticket from the stand on the bar and writes an "X" across each chosen number. Moments later the keno runner walks by calling, "keno!" Suzanne hands him the ticket and the $20 bill. Since her numbers will remain the same, she plays a multigame bet. When the runner returns, he hands Suzanne a computerized copy of the ticket with the details of the bet. As Suzanne continues to sip on her drink and watch people, she also watches the keno board. On the fifth game, the ticket wins a small amount. Suzanne is happy for her mother and decides to pass the time by playing the poker machines embedded in the bar top. She inserts a $20 bill into the machine. It is a quarter machine, so she receives 80 credits. She decides to play three credits on each hand. She presses the "Deal" button and examines her cards. She holds three cards of the same suit and hopes for a flush. She presses the "Deal" button again but draws two cards from a different suit. She repeats the bet and continues to play.

At 4:30 p.m., John joins her. He excitedly tells her that he started with $100 but walked away with $255. He relates that the first dealer was okay, but the second dealer was "hot." He kept dealing John blackjacks and cards totaling 20. Suzanne told him she had won a little jackpot in bingo but had lost a few dollars on the slot machines. She also tells him that she placed a keno bet for her mother that so far had won a couple dollars.

The final game of the series will not be played until after 5:00 p.m. They decide to sit at the bar, have a drink, and people watch.

A keno runner passes John and Suzanne after the final game is played, and Suzanne calls her over. She tells the runner that her ticket won on the fifth game. The runner takes the ticket to the keno counter to verify the win. She returns to Suzanne and pays her the amount of the win. She smiles and leaves. John and Suzanne agree that they have had a good time so far and cannot wait to see the show later tonight after dinner in the steakhouse restaurant.

Terminology: Drop, Payouts, and Hold

The scenario described in this vignette is not out of the ordinary. As you can tell, there are many procedures for handling money and some are peculiar to the casino industry. The need to control the influx of money is paramount if a casino is to be profitable. But a casino must have rigidly enforced procedures to ensure the integrity of its gaming activity and to maintain the public's perception that it will get a fair deal from the casino. Before we enter into a discussion of revenue control, we need to define some basic terms used in the gaming industry. As you know, people go to casinos to gamble in order to possibly win money on their wagers. This is the start of the cash flow for a casino.

In our vignette, John and Suzanne gave money to the casino at several instances. When John placed the bet on the Buccaneers and gave the $100 bill to the 21 dealer, he generated revenue for the casino. When Suzanne purchased the bingo paper and inserted the $20 bill into the slot machine, she, too, generated revenue for the casino. The money that people use for the purpose of placing a bet is called the **drop**. This includes the money won from the casino. The name derives from the fact that historically most money gambled by customers was dropped into some sort of collection container. Even today, the money drops into a drop box at the gaming tables (Figure 11–2). Slot machines are still equipped to accept coins that drop into a bucket in the base of the machine. While the common term for this money is the *drop*, other games have words for it more closely related to their individual activities.

Figure 11–2 Picture of drop box from gaming table. Courtesy of Steve Durham, The House Advantage.

In keno it is called the *write*, in sportsbook, the *handle*, and in bingo, the *take*. Drop can also represent the amount of money a player is willing to risk. Increasingly, but not consistently, the term *revenue* is used across the board. It is important, therefore, for the student of casino management to know that drop and revenue refer to the money coming into the casino for the purposes of betting, or simply, the money wagered.

Obviously, sometimes customers win their bet. A jackpot is paid on the slot machine. A 21 player has a higher total than the dealer. A bingo player matches the game pattern first. When the casino pays the winning bet, it becomes part of **payouts**. Occasionally, it is referred to as a *paid out*. These terms are used interchangeably and refer to the money paid for winning wagers.

The final term to be explained is *win* or *hold*. These terms are used interchangeably and refer to the difference between drop (money wagered) and payouts (money paid for winning wagers). Quite literally, it is the money the casino holds onto after the gaming activity ceases. The money paid to customers who win must be deducted from the money wagered so that the casino knows how much it has in revenue to pay for expenses. The formula for win/hold is

Win/Hold = Drop − Payouts

A Paper Trail of Revenue

So let's look at the paper trail that is left when money changes hands in a casino. Remember when John placed the bet on the Buccaneers? The sportsbook agent entered the information into the computer and issued John a ticket. When the agent registered the transaction in the computer, he officially recorded the receipt of John's bet. John and the agent have a hard copy for their respective uses, and the computer has a digital record of the transaction. At the end of his shift, the agent will have to balance the computer's record of bets placed with his hard copies and cash on hand, much the same way cashiers or servers in a restaurant must balance to their computer readout. Similarly, when Suzanne purchased the bingo paper or the keno ticket, a hard copy and a digital record were created, and the casino employees must reconcile their hard copies with their digital accounts.

These hard copies and computer-stored information constitute the revenue in these gaming centers. Each dollar bet is logged and an accounting is made of actual bet activity. The sportsbook manager can look at drop, payouts, and hold by sporting event. Similarly, the bingo and keno managers know exactly what activity occurred in their departments during a specific period of time. In addition, each manager can look at the records for individual employees who handled money, and their accuracy or lack thereof will be clear.

However, the pit manager does not have such detailed information on his revenue or gambling activity. Remember when John asked for $5 chips for a $100 bill? The dealer did not issue a hard copy of the transaction. Neither did she create a digital record. Instead she made sure that the surveillance camera saw the transaction by displaying the bill on the table layout face up. She also made sure the pit supervisor was aware of the transaction with a large denomination by calling out the bill size loudly.

She went on to display that she was issuing the correct number of $5 chips by stacking, then knocking them over for the surveillance camera. Table games provide a challenge for revenue accounting. To be completely accurate, a casino should record each bet placed and each payout issued. However, this would slow the pace of play to a level that would discourage customers from playing, so the casino only approximately tracks drop and payouts.

The $100 bill John gave to the dealer was inserted into the drop box. All the drop boxes in a casino are collected on a regular basis and replaced with empty drop boxes. Some casinos are busy enough to require collecting drop boxes once a shift or every eight hours. Others are slower and collect them only once a day. Regardless, the least frequent interval for collecting drop boxes is once a day, in order to maintain control on revenue; any longer and too many employees can be traced to handling the same drop box. If funds are missing, it becomes difficult to identify the responsible employee. Once the drop boxes are collected, they are taken to the vault area. There they are opened and the contents counted. The money inside a drop box is recorded as the revenue for that table. While this does not include every transaction that occurred at that table, it is the money that generated those transactions.

Electronic gaming devices have a little different situation—both the actual and approximate transactions are recorded and used. Each transaction is recorded by a computer chip in the machine that constantly transmits the data to a mainframe computer. When Suzanne bet the nine credits and lost, it was recorded. When she bet the nine credits and won, it was recorded. An exact record of each bet and its outcome is created. However, the amount of money inserted into each machine is also recorded. The mainframe computer tracks the drop in this manner as well. When the drop is counted for a machine, the total can be compared to the digital record and any discrepancies recorded and investigated. Assuming the integrity of the computer system is maintained, the total recorded and the total counted should be identical.

Increasingly, casinos are converting to coinless machines. These machines accumulate credits as described in the scenario. When the customer decides to stop playing, he or she presses the "Cash Out" button and a ticket with a bar code is printed (Figure 11–3). The

Figure 11–3 Ticket cash out from a coinless machine. A ticket in, ticket out (TITO) machine will issue a voucher like this one instead of dispensing coins when a customer cashes out. TITO improves customer service and reduces costs.
Courtesy of Steve Durham, The House Advantage.

ticket is approximately the size of a bill and comes out of a slot on the front of the machine. The dollar amount of the cash out is printed on the ticket and encoded in the bar code. The customer can take the ticket to another machine and insert it into the bill validator slot just the same as currency. Or it can be taken to the cashier cage and converted to cash. The ticket is considered a pay out when it is issued from a machine and a drop when it is inserted into the next machine.

As you can see, electronic gaming devices have a dual system of revenue control, while keno, bingo, and the sportsbook have a single system. Table games must rely on nondocumented forms of control that constitute the many procedures peculiar to the pit. Surveillance and security also play a large role in maintaining revenue controls.

A Paper Trail of Paid Outs

We now know how drop is accounted for in the various gaming activities of a casino. Paid outs show a similar pattern. When a customer is paid a winning bet in keno, bingo, or the sportsbook, a hard copy and a digital record are created. The employee must balance his hard copies at the end of the shift with a computer printout showing all of his activity. Each transaction is recorded and accounted for.

Table games use an approximate measure for paid outs, as they did with revenue. Let's take a look again at our opening vignette. The pit supervisor ordered a fill, a request

Figure 11–4 Fill Slip. The fill slip machine will print a fill slip when a pit supervisor enters a request into his or her computer. Courtesy of Steve Durham, The House Advantage.

for more chips for a specific table (Figure 11–4). This was necessary because the dealer's rack of chips was getting low in inventory. The pit supervisor examined the rack, which is the slotted tray where the chips are stored on the table. The supervisor determined how much of each denomination chip was needed and completed a fill slip on the computer terminal located in the pit. The fill slip is an order form for chips. Most fill slips require the table number, the dollar amount of each chip denomination requested, several blanks for signatures, the date, and the time or shift. Other ancillary information may be required, depending upon the requirements of individual casinos or regulatory bodies. The computer immediately communicated to the cage at a window dedicated to employees only. A special window is set aside for employees to ensure quick processing of their requests. If an employee gambles off duty, he or she must use the guest windows.

At the window, the cashier took the fill slip and laid it flat on the counter face up so the surveillance cameras could see and record the request. The cashier then filled the order. The security guard assigned to fills also counted the number of chips issued and signed the fill slip. The cashier took a copy of the fill slip for her records in order to balance her bank at the end of the shift. The security guard took the other fill slip copy with the chips to the pit. There the security guard waited for the dealer to finish the hand in progress. Once the hand was done, play was interrupted and the dealer counted out the fill. After confirming the accuracy of the fill slip, the dealer signed the fill slip and inserted it into the drop box. She then placed the chips in her rack. The security guard then returned the empty chip racks to the cage.

Since the casino cannot document each paid out, it must rely on the fills for a proxy of the amount paid out. Clearly, a fill is required only when the number of chips moving into a dealer's rack is substantially less than the number of chips being paid out. If players are winning, that is, receiving a large quantity of paid outs, then the dealer's rack will need a fill. Consequently, fills are used to represent the paid outs.

Electronic gaming devices utilize both an actual record of paid outs and an approximate method as they do for tracking revenue. Each time Suzanne won on her slot machine, the machine would add to her credit balance. These additions were recorded via the computer chip in the machine on the mainframe computer as a paid out. The slot department manager can monitor each machine in the casino by printing reports off the computer. These reports show the drop, paid outs, and hold as well as actual amount bet and paid out.

Occasionally, electronic gaming devices require a fill like the gaming tables do, and the paperwork from the fill is recorded as a payout. Usually a fill is brought to the attention of an employee when a customer tries to cash out his or her credits, but the machine runs out of coins in its hopper. The machine stops issuing coins, lights begin to flash, and a computer notification is sent to a central location. An employee will arrive at the machine, verify a fill is needed, then go to the cashier cage to complete the paperwork and obtain a sack of coins. When he returns to the machine, he will open the front of the machine, empty the contents into the hopper, complete the paperwork, and close the machine, which will resume issuing coins.

In addition to fills, any hand payouts made on a machine are recorded as a paid out. A hand payout is required on a machine that pays out coins for jackpots but has run out of coins in the hopper to dispense or whose jackpot is over a preset limit. Again, the machine will automatically notify a slot department employee that a hand payout is needed. The employee will come to the machine, verify the amount of the hand payout, and go to the cashier cage to obtain the money. The employee will return with the money for the customer and complete the paperwork to document the transaction. Usually, the employee will complete a fill on the machine at the same time so that the next customer does not encounter the same situation.

Coinless electronic gaming devices, or "ticket in, ticket out," greatly reduce the need for fills and hand payouts. Since the customer receives a ticket for credits, no cash changes hands until the customer takes the ticket to the cashier cage or an ATM-like machine to exchange the ticket for cash. Of course, the cage has adequate inventories of cash to handle routine payouts. Just as keno, bingo, and the sportsbook track each paid out, the pit relies on an approximate form of tracking paid outs, while electronic gaming devices have a dual system. Regardless of the system, tracking paid outs is as important as tracking drop.

Cage Operations

So far we have looked at the flow of money in a casino from the customers' point of view and how it is documented by the casino. We have referred to the cashier cage, the drop process, and the vault area. But there is more to the story. Cage operations is the casino department primarily responsible for the control of money (Figure 11–5). The terminology varies somewhat from casino to casino, but whether the term is *cage*, *cashier*, or something else, it refers to the department that maintains the inventory of cash and cash equivalents in a casino. This department includes four distinct areas of the casino: cashier cages, soft count room, hard count room, and the vault. Each area has a separate manager who reports to the controller or a similarly titled financial executive. Each area has a separate manager so that there is a clear separation of duties and responsibilities and to maintain the integrity of funds. Since cash and cash equivalents are transferred among these areas, embezzlement could occur if one individual was ultimately responsible for sending and receiving funds between these areas. Frequently, however, there is a single manager for the hard count room, soft count room, and vault because these

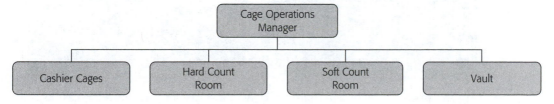

Figure 11–5 Typical Organizational Chart for the Cage Operations Department of a Casino.

areas often occupy a single space and utilize a single group of employees. The soft count room, the hard count room, and the vault are located in the back of the house away from the public. These areas contain large amounts of money and are highly secure. Only employees cleared to enter them may enter. Naturally, surveillance cameras are in abundance, and procedures are enforced strictly to avoid even a suspicion of theft.

The Cashier Cage

The cashier cages are located in central locations on the casino floor and are available for use by customers. If the casino is large, there will be more than one cashier cage to provide convenience to customers and employees. The cashier cage typically looks like an old time bank; employees stand behind individual windows that often have bars or some kind of barrier to prevent intrusion. There may be stanchions to create a single line so that the first person in line can go to the next available cashier. Numerous surveillance cameras are trained on the windows, on the area inside the cashier cage, and on the area outside the cashier cage. Cashier cages are also used by employees while on duty, as described in our opening scenario. When transacting casino business, they may use the special windows set aside to expedite their activity (Figure 11–6).

Customers go to the cashier cage for a number of reasons. They can exchange currency for chips or coins. Similarly, they can exchange chips, coins, or tickets from electronic gaming devices for currency. A customer can also cash a check at the cashier

Figure 11–6 Cashier Cage.Here is a view of the cashier cage from the casino side and from the inside. The cashier cage is similar to a bank.
Courtesy of Steve Durham, The House Advantage.

cage. Increasingly, casinos have ATMs or similar machines available in the casino for customers to withdraw cash directly from their bank accounts. The machine will issue a document that is similar to a check that the customer can take to the cashier cage to cash. The commercial service will bill the customer's credit card for the amount of the check plus a service fee. This improves the convenience and service for the customer and reduces the risk of bad checks (Figure 11–7).

The Drop Team

The count rooms and the vault are the processing and storage areas for all of the casino's cash and cash equivalents. Before we discuss these areas, an explanation of the drop team is required. The drop team's sole function is to collect the drop boxes, buckets, and the bill validators on the casino floor. The drop team is composed of cage employees. The number of employees will depend upon the number of drop boxes, buckets,

Figure 11–7 An ATM and a Cash Machine. ATMs are increasingly common in casinos for the convenience of the customers. The machine between these ATMs issues a check to customers after charging their credit card for the amount of the check.
Courtesy of Steve Durham, The House Advantage.

and bill validators to be collected. Regardless of the number of employees, there is always a security detail accompanying them to be sure no one tries to take the money. The system for performing the drop varies from casino to casino, but typically one employee is placed in charge to coordinate the activity. This "lead" will assign tasks to different employees on the team.

When the drop team empties the buckets of the electronic gaming devices, one employee will first unlock and open all the cabinets and the fronts of a bank of machines, which are hinged and swing open. Customers are asked to stand back while the drop team does this. Another employee will follow this one employee and remove the buckets while replacing them with an empty bucket. Each bucket must have a ticket that notes the machine number, date, shift, and initials and/or employee number of the individual removing it. Typically, these tickets are completed beforehand except for the initials and/or employee number. The employee removing the bucket will complete the ticket as he or she removes it. The full buckets are placed in a caged cart that can be secured with a lock when in transit to prevent theft. The buckets are stacked in a set sequence, usually following the slot sections of the casino floor (Figure 11–8).

At the same time the buckets are being removed, the bill validator is removed by another employee. This employee must insert a ticket similar to the one placed in the bucket into the bill validator, which is placed in the caged cart. A replacement bill validator is then inserted into the electronic gaming device. In some jurisdictions, each electronic gaming device has a log inside the body of the machine that must be completed whenever someone opens the machine. Before the cabinet and machines are closed and locked, an employee, usually the lead, will complete this form. Once all the buckets and bill validators in a bank of machines have been replaced and the cabinets and fronts are closed and locked, the drop team moves on to the next bank of machines and customers can resume playing. The drop team rolls through the casino until it has collected and replaced every drop box, bucket, and bill validator. If the casino is large enough, there may be more than one drop team to ensure the drop is completed in a timely fashion.

The drop team for the pit has a similar routine. The cart is caged and fitted with a lock. The team will walk through a pit and remove drop boxes from tables without

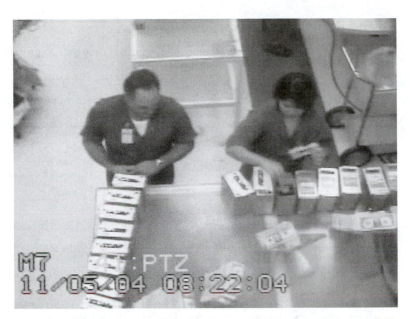

Figure 11–8 Drop Team in ActionThese employees are opening bill validators from electronic gaming devices. Notice the currency on the clear Plexiglas table.
Courtesy of Steve Durham, The House Advantage.

interrupting play. They will replace the drop box with an empty one. The drop boxes are stacked on the cart. Since the drop boxes are locked, there is no need for a ticket to be inserted. No one had access to the money inside so there is no need to identify who handled the money. If a question arises, the security guard and surveillance can determine what happened. Because the number of table games is much lower than the number of electronic gaming devices and because it is a simpler process, the drop does not take nearly as long in the pit as it does in the slot areas.

The revenue from keno, bingo, and the sportsbook arrives in the vault area through the banks of the individual employees. At the start of their shift, they pick up their banks. They count it down, confirm the accuracy of the paperwork, and sign their names. At the end of their shifts, they return with their banks, a computer printout of their activity, and a reconciliation showing they have accounted for all bets taken and winnings paid out. The employee accepting the bank confirms the accuracy of the paperwork before initialing it and relieving the gaming area employee of responsibility for the bank.

The Soft Count Room

Once the drop boxes are collected as described, they are taken to the vault area. This area can be configured in several ways. Sometimes the coin and currency count areas are separate rooms, often with a common entrance for security reasons. The currency count area is called the **soft count room**, and the coin count area is called the **hard count room**. Obviously, the names derive from the physical traits of the items being counted. Increasingly, though, the two rooms are combined because coinless electronic gaming devices have substantially reduced the number of coins circulating in a casino, and a single staff person in one room can process the volume efficiently. Although the rooms may be combined, they are still referred to separately.

The drop boxes from the pit and the bill validators from electronic gaming devices are taken to the soft count room because the contents of these drop boxes are nearly all currency and paper forms. Each drop box is identified by game type, table number, pit number, and shift. While the systems vary, typically the drop box from John's 21 table might read "BJ12, #6, DAY." This indicates that the drop box is from 21 table #12 in Pit 6 on day shift. This particular drop box will be used only on that table, in that pit, on the day shift. If a drop box is labeled differently from where and when it was taken, an investigation results to determine why procedure was violated. Any hint of variation from the proper procedure is cause for suspicion of theft. A team of employees counts the contents of all the drop boxes. As you can imagine, a Las Vegas Strip resort with a large pit would need to employ numerous counters. In larger facilities, though, machines count the bills and register the total automatically in the computer (Figure 11–9). The need for staff is reduced accordingly.

Soft count room employees will open one drop box at a time so the contents of drop boxes are not commingled. They will empty the contents onto a clear Plexiglas surface. The purpose of the clear surface is so that an employee cannot hide any money from the surveillance camera. They will arrange the money by denomination and count it twice. If the total is different, a third count is done. If problems persist in arriving at an accurate count, the supervisor is involved. Once a confirmed count is derived, the amount is entered into a computer terminal. In addition, the employee counts and logs the fill slips. He or she treats these as cash since they represent cash transactions.

Figure 11–9 This machine sorts and counts currency in large volumes. Modern casinos need this type of equipment in order to operate efficiently.
Courtesy of Steve Durham, The House Advantage.

Another term for forms that represent cash is *cash equivalent*. Since fill slips are considered cash, they are counted twice. If there is a discrepancy that the employee cannot reconcile, the supervisor becomes involved.

The employee also counts any credit slips. These are forms that perform the reverse function of a fill slip. If a dealer's rack is getting too full because customers are losing, the pit supervisor will order a credit. The pit supervisor will complete the credit slip on the computer that notifies the cage. A security guard is dispatched to the pit with the credit slip. Once he arrives, the pit supervisor removes the corresponding amount in chips. The dealer witnesses the removal and inserts her copy of the credit slip into the drop box. The security guard takes the chips and the credit slip to the cage. There, the cashier accepts the chips after verifying the amount and signing the credit slip. The chips and credit slip become part of the cashier's daily work.

Credit slips are rarely used. Although more people lose than win in a casino, they are simply returning the chips they bought from the dealer. In John's case, if he had lost his twenty $5 chips, they would have returned to the spot from which the dealer had taken them. The only time a credit slip is used is when a customer or customers walk up to a table with chips from another table and proceed to lose them. After the cash and cash equivalents are counted and verified, their totals are entered into the computer terminal. The table number, pit number, shift number, and soft count room employee are identified. The currency total is entered as drop or revenue. The fill slips total is entered as payouts. The credit slip total is entered as a reduction to payouts.

The Hard Count Room

The buckets from electronic gaming devices are taken to the hard count room because nearly all of their contents are coins. Like the soft count room, a team of employees counts the contents of the buckets. The number of employees depends on the number of buckets. Each employee takes a bucket to count. Each bucket is identified by the ticket placed in it by the drop team. The counter enters the information from the ticket into the computer terminal. Then the coins are dropped into a coin counting machine that automatically sorts, counts, and bags the coins. This amount is recorded by the computer as the drop for that machine for that drop period. The counter will also enter the fill slips and hand payouts into the computer so that they are assigned to the correct machine. Due to automation and the increasing use of coinless machines, the process of counting in the hard count room is fairly smooth and quick.

The Vault

After the money is counted in the hard and soft count rooms, it is transferred to the vault. This area is just as it sounds. Heavy secure doors, surveillance cameras, security guards, and extensive procedural controls are all in place to ensure the prevention of theft and embezzlement.

The vault employees treat the cash and cash equivalents like inventory. They must sign for and log all items received and issued. Nothing comes in or goes out without documentation showing a change in responsible party. Vault employees prepare the banks for the bartenders, cashiers, keno writers, bingo cashiers, and others. They follow guidelines set up by the casino that identify the total value of each bank and the breakdown by denomination. They count down the bank and create a document showing the total and the breakdown. When employees come to pick up their banks, they count it down to verify the total and the breakdown before signing for the bank and taking it to their workstations.

Similarly, vault employees receive the banks when the employee's shift is complete. As stated earlier, employees reconcile their activity as shown on their computer printout to their bank. Once they have completed that process, they present the paperwork and the bank to a vault employee. The vault employee verifies the accuracy of the work and accepts the bank by signing the paperwork. At that point, the employee is free to go because the vault has accepted the responsibility for the bank.

Controls in Place

In the opening vignette and the discussion up to this point, you have seen many controls. Some are procedural, some technology based, and others are organizational in nature. The following is a further discussion of some of the controls in the scenario.

Signatures

Numerous times, a signature or initials are required before cash or cash equivalents are exchanged. The purpose of a signature or set of initials is to provide a traceable line of responsibility for the items. In the event that a discrepancy is discovered, the signatures will narrow the number of employees possibly involved in the situation. Good employees quickly realizes that they do not accept responsibility without signing for cash or cash equivalents. They also quickly realize that they do not hand over cash or cash equivalents to anyone, not even the CEO, without getting a signature. It is their credibility and job on the line. Without that signature, they may be accused of theft if the funds disappear.

Separation of Duties

The concept of *separation of duties* is utilized in all industries. The concept rests on the belief that when more than one person is involved in a transaction, there is less likelihood of theft or collusion. Suppose the dealer were the one to request and execute the order for a fill. If he had access to the chips in the cage, he could take what he wanted and write down any amount. That would allow him to pocket part of his fill without any-one knowing for sure how much was taken and how much was placed on the gaming table. A better system separates the duties so that the pit supervisor, the security guard, the cashier, and the dealer are all involved. Not to mention, surveillance watches the whole process through its camera coverage. There is too much money and temptation in a casino to not institute a strict and thorough separation of duties.

Multiple Employee Involvement

Along with separation of duties, you probably noticed the number of employees involved in various activities in the scenario. The drop team has several members; the security guard, pit supervisor, dealer, and cashier are needed to complete a fill; and the count rooms have more than one person counting cash. It is a given of human nature that we are less likely to do something that would draw disapproval if others are around us. Imagine what would happen if only one employee counted all of the drop boxes. The surveillance department has the responsibility to watch all the activity in the casino. Particular attention is paid to transactions of high value.

Duplicate/Triplicate Forms

At several points in our opening vignette, forms were used to transfer responsibility for the funds. Each form had a few copies, so that different individuals could include it in their respective work for the day. The purpose of the multiple copies is not only to verify the transfer of responsibility, but also to confirm an exact description of the funds being transferred. These forms are used by the accounting staff to ensure that all funds are accurately accounted for.

Cash Countdowns

Whenever the responsibility for cash or cash equivalents is transferred, the receiving indi-vidual counts down the amount. This is to ensure that the receiving individual is actually receiving what the delivering individual claims to be delivering. The documentation used during the exchange is signed by both individuals to confirm that they agreed on the amount being exchanged.

Digital Trails

Whenever practicable, a digital record is made of a transaction. This provides a trail that should match the paper trail that is being created simultaneously by the hard copies of forms. Both trails are used when investigating any discrepancies to lead to the responsible party or parties. The digital trail is used to remind employees that there is a record of the transaction, regardless of what happens to the hard copies. While hard copies can be lost, a digital trail discourages even the temptation to steal or embezzle.

Man Trap

The man trap feature of the vault area was not described in our story, but it plays an important role in maintaining the security of that area. A man trap is a small anteroom at the entry into the vault or count rooms. The door into the man trap must be closed and locked before the door into the secure area can be unlocked and open. In this way, there is never any free access to the secure area. The entry to the man trap and the man trap itself are heavily covered with surveillance cameras and constantly monitored. The surveillance staff will quickly see if someone is trying to enter the secure area without authorization. In addition, surveillance can lock down the man trap so that neither door can be unlocked or opened. In that way, a suspect or suspects can be trapped inside until security or the police can arrive.

Supervisory Oversight

Finally, the oversight of supervisory personnel is essential to control. The pit supervisor watches the dealer to be sure she follows procedure. The cage supervisor watches the cashier. The drop team lead watches the drop team. Besides monitoring employee behavior toward customers and other employees, the supervisors are to keep a watchful eye to be sure employees strictly follow all procedures relating to cash handling.

Hold Percentage

The **hold percentage** is used by casino management as a control tool. Before we discuss it, we need to define what it is. Remember the formula for hold? We subtract payouts from drop to determine hold:

$$\text{Drop}$$
$$\underline{- \text{Payouts}}$$
$$\text{Hold}$$

Management expects payouts and hold to maintain a constant relationship with drop. The law of large numbers says that given enough trials, there is an expected pattern to outcomes. In a casino, the payout percentage is determined in advance. For example, an electronic gaming device may be set to pay out 97 percent of total bets placed. On average, customers can expect to walk away with $97 for every $100 they bet on that machine. Of course, results vary widely because the average is based on millions of bets. That is how someone can lose money quickly in a machine, but the next player wins a big jackpot after only a couple of handle pulls. However, the casino has the total record for each machine that reflects many bets placed by many customers.

To calculate the hold percentage, the hold dollar amount is divided by the drop dollar amount. For example, suppose during an eight-hour drop period, an electronic gaming device showed a drop of $800 and payouts of $560. The hold would be $240 ($800 – $560). By dividing $240 by $800, we see that the hold percentage on this machine is 30 percent as shown in column 1 of Table 11.1.

As you read earlier, the drop is the approximation of bets placed. The results using approximations for drop and payouts in the formula can vary significantly. Suppose this machine had paid out a large jackpot just before the drop team exchanged buckets. Its

Table 11–1 Variation in hold percentage by drop period

	Drop Period 1		Drop Period 2		Combined	
Drop	$800	100%	$800	100%	$1,600	100%
– Payouts	–560	70%	–760	95%	–1,320	83%
Hold	$240	30%	$40	5%	$280	17%

hopper is nearly empty. That means that a fill will be required shortly into the next drop period. Because fills are included in payouts, that fill will reduce the hold significantly in the drop period. The hold percentage will consequently be lower and could look something like column 2 in Table 11–1.

As you can see, the results are very different on the same drop on the same machine. Combining the two results would give a more accurate picture. Table 11–1 shows the combined result in column 3.

Analyzing results in this way is necessary when there are no records of actual betting activity such as in the pit. Pit managers look at hold percentage by individual gaming table to be sure controls are effective. Obviously, when the percentages are not what are expected, it is often hard to say whether someone is stealing or if there is just a natural, statistical variation. Because of this uncertainty, there are more controls on the pit operation than elsewhere. Besides the descriptions given so far, there were other examples in our opening vignette of procedural controls. One example occurred when the dealer left the table. She clapped her hands and showed them palm up. That was so that surveillance and the pit supervisor could be sure she was not leaving the table with a chip in her hand.

However, the slot department, keno, bingo, and the sportsbook track actual bets placed. This allows for a great deal of accuracy and control. For example, the machine described in our vignette also has a record of the actual bets placed and winnings paid. When Suzanne placed a bet of nine coins and lost, the computer chip in the machine recorded a $0.45 bet and no payouts. When she bet again and won five coins, it recorded a $0.45 bet and a payout of $0.25. It tracked every bet and its outcome. At the end of the drop period, it had an accurate picture of the activity on that machine. Table 11–2 represents the actual activity on the machine.

As you can see, the results are much more consistent from one period to the next. Management expects consistency and when it is missing, it raises alarms regarding controls. You will notice that the bets placed and the payouts in the actual record in Table 11–2 are much higher than in the system using approximations. Remember that the approximations are just the money collected in the buckets and bill validators, not each bet generated by that money. Every time Suzanne won, it increased the amount she could

Table 11–2 Actual Activity by Drop Period

	Drop Period 1		Drop Period 2		Combined	
Bets Placed	$7,100	100%	$2,230	100%	$9,330	100%
—Payouts	−6,860	97%	−2,190	98%	−9,050	97%
Hold	$240	3%	$40	2%	$280	3%

replay, thus increasing her total of bets placed. However, you will notice that the hold dollar amount is the same. Ultimately, the hold or win is the same whether each transaction is recorded or a proxy is used. The amount of money held by the casino at the end of the day is the money actually in the vault.

Obviously, casino management would prefer an actual accounting of every bet placed. This would remove any uncertainty related to the collection and recording of information. Fortunately, all gaming areas except the pit have this capability. However, until a system can be developed for the pit that tracks each bet but does not interfere with game pace, management will have to live with a system of approximations in controlling revenue in the pit.

Finances

We have examined the flow and control of revenue into a casino. Customers spend a tremendous amount of money. In order to be profitable, a casino must control this flow so that expenses can be met. However, there is another flow of funds into a casino. While casinos generate generous profits, their needs are also large. Few casinos can expand without some form of outside financing. Depending upon the organization, sources for this funding can be stock markets, investors, or government entities. But not all these sources of capital have been available to the gaming industry during its history.

Access to Capital

Access to capital has changed tremendously over the past 70 years of casino gaming. Initially, there was no access to the regular capital markets of Wall Street or banks. Gambling had a negative reputation. It was viewed as a vice and a sin and ran counter to the moral norms of the country. There also was a question of legitimacy: Could someone who ran a casino be trusted to pay back a loan?

When Nevada legalized casino gambling in 1931, gambling already existed in the saloons and back rooms of the dusty towns in the Nevada desert. The law was intended to recognize this reality and regulate the activity. The hope of the lawmakers was that tourism would grow and tax collections would increase. There was little need on the part of existing operations for capital. The purchase of additional table games or slot machines was funded by profits. However, nonresidents hoping to take advantage of the nation's only legal gaming jurisdiction needed capital to open their gaming operations.

The story of Bill Harrah, founder of what is called today Harrah's Entertainment, is typical. He opened a bingo parlor with his father on Virginia Street in Reno, Nevada, in 1937. They had moved from Southern California where they had also operated a bingo parlor. Bill and his father saw the wide-open opportunity Nevada offered. No financial institution would lend money for such a venture. They financed the Reno operation completely themselves by selling the California parlor.

The unsavory reputation of gaming was only reinforced when organized crime entered Las Vegas after World War II. To the casual observer, this was definitive proof that gambling was a vice. External funding remained virtually nonexistent. In Las Vegas, Benjamin "Bugsy" Siegel envisioned large casinos with gambling, showrooms, hotels, pools, restaurants, and golf courses. He built the Flamingo four miles outside of Las Vegas. The Flamingo required $6 million, an unheard of sum at that time. Like Bill Harrah, Siegel was self-funded. He obtained backing from his organized crime family. Other organized crime families then moved into Las Vegas. They had the financial resources to build the huge resorts needed to compete with the Flamingo. They either used their own internal funds or raided the Teamster's Union's Pension Fund. Essentially, no outside sources were used to fund these projects.

However, in the 1950s, the state of Nevada began to see that it had a problem with organized crime running the casinos in Las Vegas. The original regulations required owners of casinos to go through a licensing process that included a background check. At first this was a cursory process because most "casino owners" were bar owners who wanted to put a couple of slot machines and tables in their bar. The state was happy to have any economic activity to provide jobs for residents. However, pressure from the federal government and a concern that organized crime was not reporting all revenues for tax purposes moved the state to create new regulatory rules and bodies. Over a 20-year period, organized crime was evicted from Las Vegas.

However, the market had changed and large casinos were needed to compete. Individuals interested in opening a new casino rarely had the resources to do so. Banks and more traditional sources of funding shied away from casinos because of gambling's unsavory reputation. Howard Hughes purchased many of the casinos formerly owned by organized crime families, but no new construction was attempted. In response, Nevada changed the law and made it legal for a corporation to be licensed. Instead of the individual owner, the key members of management and those individuals with a significant investment in the corporation would need to pass the licensing process. This change opened up new possibilities. As the number of casino operators grew, they incorporated to enhance their wealth and to limit their liability. And as a corporation, they could issue shares to the public, thus tapping a large source of funding. Bill Harrah did just that and in the early 1970s, Harrah's became the first strictly gaming company to be listed on the New York Stock Exchange.

In the past three decades, the casino market has grown remarkably. The ability of casinos to obtain external financing was critical in their ability to expand, open new casinos, and acquire already existing properties. Today, mergers in the Nevada market are quickly consolidating the industry. These megacorporations command a great deal of respect on Wall Street and among the investing public. They have operations all over the country and in foreign countries. This legitimacy did not occur solely because gambling was tightly regulated. Over the course of the past 50 years, gambling has gone from a generally perceived vice to just another vacation or entertainment option. It seems families talk about going to Las Vegas as much as they talk about going to Disneyland. While Nevada's tight regulation of the industry has been a key to this shift in perception, there are other factors involved.

Casino gaming has expanded beyond Nevada. All but two states have some form of gaming, and 28 states have casinos. There are more than 300 Native American casinos scattered among 27 states. These casinos are typically small and largely located in rural areas. With greater availability, there has been greater acceptance of gambling. The baby-boom generation also tends to have a more relaxed moral code than the World War II generation. As the baby-boom generation came of age and became the dominant force in the economy, their attitudes influenced the marketplace through the forces of supply and demand.

Another factor in this growth is that prosperity in the United States has generally increased the amount of disposable income. Gambling and vacations are discretionary expenditures. If a consumer has enough money only for the basics of life, he or she will not spend money on a vacation or gambling. However, the vast majority of Americans go on vacation and have extra money to spend at a local casino.

The glamour of casinos is also alluring. Beginning with the Rat Pack and Hollywood stars who visited and performed in Las Vegas, the image of casino gambling transformed from a dirty, back-room affair into an exciting escape from every day life. The casinos still offer first-rate entertainment but have added to their image with full service, themed mega resorts. For example in Las Vegas, the Venetian has canals and gondolas woven among shops and a replica of St. Mark's Square on the second floor; New York–New York has a downsized replica of the New York City skyline as its façade; the Luxor is a huge dark glass pyramid. The excitement generated by the amenities, lights, and action draws customers from all over the world, and this glamour has rubbed off on all casinos.

As the perception of casino gaming has changed, the access to capital has also changed. It is not uncommon for casinos to obtain funds from public markets in stocks and bonds. In fact, they have typically outperformed the market as a whole over the past several years. Investors find them very attractive because they are consistently profitable and well-run organizations. The future access to capital will depend upon several factors. First is the continued success of both the individual company seeking funds and the overall casino industry. Prospects for growth and profits must exist for people to invest. Second is the continued stability in the legality of gaming. If a trend toward recriminalizing gambling appears, it could make public sources of funds nervous. Third, regulatory bodies must ensure criminal elements are not reintroduced into the industry. The first hint of financial malfeasance will affect the guilty and the innocent alike. And fourth, there must be a continued social acceptance of gambling as just another form of entertainment. A shift in the public's moral attitude would negatively impact the prospects of casinos.

Financing Expansion: Equity vs. Debt

The debate on whether equity or debt should be used to finance expansions and acquisitions is ongoing. The characteristics of the individual firm as well the nature of the industry and market will dictate the answer. In general terms, equity allows greater financial flexibility. Equity financing also gives up some control, dilutes partners/owners percentages by increasing the number of owners, and while debt financing is a fixed payment, it does come to an end, while equity financing is an investment by the equity partners who expect continual dividends for as long as the entity (casino) exists, or until they sell their ownership. All of this assumes the equity was raised as stock sales. Debt financing includes principal plus interest payments that must be repaid at regular intervals. The interest portion of the payment becomes an expense that is deducted from profits, thus affecting the profitability of the operation. Equity on the other hand need not be repaid, nor is there a mandatory interest payment, but investors do not invest without an expectation of a return, usually at rates higher than the interest on a loan, depending on risk. Dividends are issued in lieu of interest, but the amount and timing are at the discretion of the organization, subject, of course, to market expectations. Dividends are a cash flow item only and are not deducted from profits until after taxes are paid.

However, equity raises other issues, primarily control. Large corporations issue many thousands of shares. Initially, these shares are held in large part by the founding entrepreneur. Over time, though, these are typically purchased by a large number of investors. Although institutional investors will buy large blocks of shares, it is rare to have any sizeable amount of shares in one person's or organization's control. However, the possibility exists that one or several shareholders can agree to cooperate to influence the organization. This influence is exerted on the board of directors and not on the daily activities of the company. Even though the influence is indirect, it can complicate management's efforts to run the business.

Naturally, casino companies face these same challenges. The decision of whether to seek equity or debt is weighed seriously. Equity has been the option of choice for most casino companies because of its relative low cost and the amount of funds that can be raised easily. However, as the economy and the environment in which casinos operate change, other factors may lead casinos to favor debt options.

Conclusion

As we have seen, the fun and excitement of a casino that attract tourists such as Suzanne and John are built on an interlocking web of controls to assure that revenue is properly accounted for. Some of the controls are observable by customers, such as the handclap of the dealer or the computerized keno ticket receipt. Other controls are not so obvious. Not all surveillance cameras are apparent and back of the house areas such as the vault area are strictly off limits for customers. However, all of these controls are necessary to ensure the integrity of the casino. This integrity is important to guests so that they are assured of receiving a fair deal by the casino. It is also important to the regulatory bodies so that the proper amount of tax is collected. And certainly, it is important to local governments that use gambling as a tourist attraction to generate economic activity and jobs.

Most monetary controls used in gambling activities account for the effort of each transaction. This allows for tracing any discrepancies to one employee or just a few employees. However, in the pit, operational concerns overrule the need for exact records. An approximation of drop and payouts is used to represent the gambling activity. Regardless of these approximations, the hold is still the money in the vault at the end of the day.

The casino industry is an extremely profitable industry and has always attracted eager participants. Unfortunately, that has included organized crime figures. Nevada and the industry worldwide have done an effective job of eliminating this element. Today, major casino companies can seek equity funding through the major stock exchanges like any other reputable industry. The future growth of casino gaming is not guaranteed, but the outlook is positive.

key terms

Credit	Hard count room
Drop	Hold percentage
Drop box	Payouts
Fill	Soft count room

review questions

1. Why do table games use an approximation for bets placed and paid outs and other gaming areas use the actual figures?

2. What are the formulas for hold and hold percentage?

3. How do coinless electronic gaming devices impact a casino's controls and labor?

4. Define the term *separation of duties* and give an example from a casino setting.

5. List and describe the factors that led to the acceptance of gaming as merely a form of entertainment.

6. Explain how hold percentage is used as a control tool.

internet sites

National Indian Gaming Association
   www.indiangaming.org

American Gaming Association
   www.americangaming.org

Harrah's Entertainment, Inc.
   www.harrahs.com

Nevada State Gaming Control Board
   http://gaming.nv.gov/about_board.htm

National Indian Gaming Commission
   http://www.nigc.gov/nigc/documents/regulations/Sec542.jsp

references

Shook, Robert L. *Jackpot: Harrah's Secrets for Winning Customer Loyalty*. (New York: John Wiley, 2003).

Scarne, J. *Scarne's New Complete Guide to Gambling*. (New York: Simon & Schuster, 1986).

12 Pricing: Comps and Credit

Jeff L. Voyles, MGM Grand

Learning Objectives

1. To understand the importance of a quality promotional club of a casino.

2. To recognize the benefits of a competitive casino industry.

3. To understand the differences in comp distribution among table games and slots.

4. To learn how to price the product.

5. To recognize the risks involved with comps in a casino.

6. To understand the importance of rewarding customer loyalty.

7. To identify comp abuse by players and employees.

8. To recognize a player's worth to the casino.

9. To learn to utilize casino credit as a marketing tool.

Chapter Outline

Introduction

The purpose of this chapter is to identify the significance of a solid price structure and a quality comp and credit program for a casino. There are three distinct sections in this chapter, one devoted to casino pricing, the second discussing casino complimentaries and player ratings, and the final section discussing casino credit. This chapter enables the reader to recognize the expected earning potential of a player and to make the proper decisions to keep the customer returning. The comps, pricing, and credit sections of this chapter will aid the reader in charting a promotional plan to maintain a customer base favorable to the culture of the gaming company and its jurisdiction. Moreover, gaming history has laid the foundation for new jurisdictions, while providing a unique outline for gaming operations and management. Gaming history has also afforded an opportunity to study and research trends and patterns associated with this rapidly growing industry.

Pricing

Casino *pricing* is represented by the **house advantage**. Basically, a game's house advantage is the price the player is charged to play the game. The price can change according to jurisdiction, regulations, game rules, level of competition, or, simply, the different areas of the casino. The price of a game can be very deceiving for most gamblers. Casinos are not required to advertise the house advantage in most jurisdictions in the United States. Other gaming jurisdictions around the world may require the casino to post odds of winning and house advantages associated with the games offered.

Fairness

It is the responsibility of gaming regulators and casino operators to offer a fair game with reasonable house advantages. Casinos must be careful not to exploit the inexperience of a gambler through strong house percentages. Is it good management to use the highest house advantage? Should players be made aware of what they are being charged to play? What is management willing to exchange for offering lower house advantages, and more popular playing rules and conditions? The answers to these questions may lie in governmental regulations in the form of higher tax structures, tighter regulations, and more restrictions on playing rules. Pricing games can be complicated, not only for the player, but also for casino management. Management needs to offer the right price mix to attract and maintain a flow of loyal guests without taking unfair advantage of the customers.

This is exactly why casino management is able to manipulate a house advantage and not experience disagreement from the player. The smallest change in procedure may yield a casino millions of dollars and virtually go unnoticed by the average gambler. Each of these changes adds a small percentage to the house advantage. For example, changes in blackjack that favor the casino may include requiring the dealer to hit soft 17 (using the ace as the value of one), which adds 0.20 percent to the house advantage; using multiple decks, which adds 0.50 percent, to the house advantage; not allowing pairs to be resplit (non-aces), which adds 0.03 percent to the house advantage; and only allowing doubling on 10 or 11, which adds 0.26 percent to the house advantage.

For example, casinos in Nevada began to offer single-deck blackjack at a natural blackjack payoff of 6 to 5 instead of 3 to 2. This simple change in a blackjack payout gives the casino a significant increase in house advantage of 1.39 percent. Casinos also have options to offer different pay tables on a variety of games. The versions of stud poker vary drastically in house advantage with different pay tables game developers offer. Casino management must decide what pay table or house rule best fits the style of game and the players.

Through maximum price structuring, casinos are able to protect uninformed gamblers from losing too much money or underestimating the price they are paying for their overall gaming experience. Casino managers must find a balance that allows players to extend their time played, enjoy their experience, and permit the casino to make a profit. Regulations most often allow for a broad range of payback percentages, thus allowing the casino to fluctuate house advantages throughout the casino floor. Casino guests have the disadvantage of not being able immediately to compare the prices or theoretical house advantages and to make an educated decision of which casino to visit or which game to play. This type of comparison would require research that most players are reluctant to pursue.

Casino Complimentaries and Player Ratings

The gaming business has long recognized the gambler as the casino's most valuable asset. A casino chooses to acknowledge the worth of a player through a complimentary system that rewards players for their time spent gambling. By definition, a *complimentary* is something given free, or as a gift, and is often simply known as a "comp." A casino complimentary is a reflection of this definition as it strives to maintain a balance between profit and customer reward.

A complimentary in a casino is a marketing tool that has become essential to remaining competitive in the gaming business. Never before has the gaming business been so competitive and challenging, thus creating a need for a creative and effective marketing department. This current state of competition has driven casinos to design and develop a complimentary system that rewards and encourages patrons to gamble and revisit a gaming property, while maintaining an adequate level of earnings for the casino.

The casino must plan and prepare for guests' requests in order to accommodate them efficiently and fairly. Planning and preparing will allow a casino to focus on satisfying the guests while anticipating their needs. A thorough analysis of a player's gambling session

Figure 12–1 Calypso's Restaurant.
Courtesy of Isle of Capri Casino Resort.

through a player rating will be the deciding factor in granting or denying a customer a complimentary.

History

Early casino complimentaries represented a more flexible, subjective approach to offering free or discounted rooms, food, and beverage. Most casinos offered complimentaries to their *known* guests with little research or rationale. Past casino gambling and player ratings were much different experiences than one would witness today. It was more common to have an informal approach that did not include searching for theoretical values, or a player's immediate worth. This approach was subjective in nature with little concern for every gambling detail. Complimentaries were granted on a handshake with hopes that the players would return to risk their money. To this day, there are people who adhere to the old ways of doing things and see them as a *better* way of doing business. However, this approach has proven to be inconsistent, unprofitable, and unreliable, as the gaming industry has evolved into a corporate force capable of measuring and calculating the smallest of expenses. Competition in the 1980s forced casinos to develop more innovative ways to attract and keep customers.

Figure 12–2
Courtesy of Isle of Capri Casino Resort, Biloxi. Exterior hotel.

Gaming corporations soon realized the importance of analyzing a player's betting action and determining the player's worth. These new corporate philosophies and strategic approaches changed the way one manages a gaming organization. The gaming industry has refocused the strategy and purpose of complimentary systems to satisfy the demands of shareholders and positively affect the bottom line, while also accommodating the player. Monitoring and interpreting a player's rating have become necessary processes to ensure an effective marketing program and complimentary arrangement. This process has placed the responsibility to examine the play of every qualified player with the casino **floor supervisor**. This development has also given the floor supervisor the authority to issue complimentaries when deemed appropriate. This newfound responsibility added a fresh dimension to the level of customer service expected by casino guests. Moreover, it has raised the awareness of the power of marketing and complimentaries and the overall effect they have on the guest's experience.

Modern management techniques have kept the gaming industry in a pattern of sustained growth. Gaming is on a path of adopting, securing, and encouraging new techniques that have proven successful in many different business settings. The idea that gaming is *too* unique of an industry to implement modern management theories has begun to lose momentum. The future of gaming management will soon change the way that both society and academics view the industry by improving the way we examine and scrutinize a player's value and how gaming managers operate on a daily basis. The process begins by identifying a customer's gambling session, rating his or her action and then analyzing his or her playing habits, all while recognizing how the interactions of the employees relate to a more satisfied guest.

Player Ratings

A **player rating** is a process by which a table game floor supervisor monitors the gambling routine of a patron, or by which a gaming device monitors a player's action through a computerized rating system. The data produced are used in determining the value of a player. This value is recognized by the casino and rewarded with a complimentary. It is essential to the success of a marketing program that qualified guests are recognized through a personalized rating card and given complimentary privileges when earned.

Players should experience their rated play as consistent, fair, and reasonable. In addition, a casino's rating policy and procedure must be dependable to ensure that patrons receive a reliable and accurate evaluation of their play. The accuracy of the player rating has tremendous effects on the theoretical win. The theoretical win is only as good as the estimated figures presented. When the theoretical percentages are less than accurate, the decisions being made from these numbers will be inaccurate as well.

Casino operations and casino marketing must coordinate to maintain a steady and profitable flow of rated players. A casino depends on the abilities of these departments to utilize player ratings and complimentaries as a tool to capture the interest of the players, thus developing strong relationships and repeat customers.

Table Game Ratings

Some guests may eventually meet the requirements (average bet, length of play) to be considered a rated player as their betting increases. Floor supervisors should acknowledge the players' potential and begin rating them with a nameless **rating slip**. Once guests have met the required betting limits, the floor supervisor greets them and asks if they would care to be rated. Timing is everything! Floor supervisors should know when to approach a guest when gambling; casinos breed superstition, and losing guests can be challenging. It is much easier to have a nameless rating with the information input, ready for a name to be added, than to recall hours of gambling when players request to be rated for the previous play.

As the play continues, the floor supervisor may add comments about the style of play, game pace, and anything suspicious that should be noted. At the conclusion of the play, the floor supervisor will close out the rating by calculating the average bet, record the time played, total amount in or out, and the win or loss. The floor supervisor would then apply his or her signature and employee number to the rating slip.

The rating slip is then given to the pit clerk and the information is put in to the computer to be calculated and assessed. If there was a significant win or loss, or surveillance was observing the play, the pit manager may want to review the conclusion of play before submitting the slip. After the rating slip is submitted, the computer calculates the conclusions of all guest plays, and a cumulative history of the player's gambling

Figure 12–3
Courtesy of Isle of Capri
Casino Resort.

sessions is available for review. This information can be used to decide whether a complimentary is appropriate, or if a guest has been overcomped and requires more play to increase his or her comp value. If a guest's action does not merit a comp at the time, a comp can still be issued if the player's past action is indicative of potential future play.

What qualifies a player to be rated? *Qualifying* indicates that a player has made consecutive wagers that meet a certain criterion set by the casino that assures that the casino receives a sufficient theoretical win over a period of time. This criterion could range from a table game bet of $5 in a smaller casino to a $25 or higher average bet in a larger casino operation. Such a determination will vary from casino to casino. These requirements are necessary to assure the casino of the expected profits needed to provide complimentaries and overcome operating expenses.

The qualifying process begins with a casino floor supervisor observing the guest's initial play. Once the floor supervisor has determined that the player qualifies to be rated, the supervisor obtains the rating card and records the player's name, card number, seat number, time play started, first bet, description of the player, type of initial buy-in (i.e., cash, cheques, or credit), and name of game and table number. If a guest does not have a personalized rating card and qualifies to be rated, the floor supervisor should ask if the guest would like to receive a new rating card. If the guest agrees, then a driver's license or government-issued identification is required.

If a table game player requests to be rated, but does not qualify, the floor supervisor should politely ask if the guest is familiar with the rating system. If the response is "yes," and the player insists, on being rated, then the floor supervisor should continue to rate him or her, knowing that the guest is aware of the player rating policy and the required average bet. A comment should be noted on the rating slip that the guest was made aware of the rating policy. If the guest is not familiar with the player rating policy, then the floor supervisor should clearly explain the policy and allow him or her to make the decision of whether or not to meet the required betting levels. If a player qualifies to be a rated player but refuses to be rated, the floor supervisor may begin rating them under the title "refused name" to keep track of cheques or chips that may be acquired by the unrated player.

Floor supervisors must also remember that, depending upon the game the player chooses to play, the average bet will be recorded differently for various games. For example, a blackjack player will produce an average bet based upon his or her initial bet, not including double downs or splits. A dice player may be rated on the odds bet but be expected to generate a higher average bet to qualify for comps. Most casinos do not rate the odds bet as part of the average bet in craps, thus resulting in a lower average bet requirement by the casino. A Three Card Poker player should be rated on the Pair Plus bet, the Ante bet, and half of the Play bet. A Let It Ride poker player should be rated on the first bet and half of the second bet. The rating requirements are established by the casinos and reflect the amount a casino can recognize as a qualified profitable bet after rewarding complimentaries. To accurately evaluate the value of a player, these variables must not go unnoticed by management.

Casino Expected Win/Theoretical Win.

An important aspect of a player rating is the average bet and length of play. These two areas of data will help determine the player's worth by calculating the theoretical win, which represents what the casino *expects* to win from the player on a particular game, thus determining what the casino can offer the player in complimentaries. For example, if a guest plays $100 on red on a single-zero roulette with a house advantage of 2.70 percent and a black number hits, the player's *actual loss* is $100, but the casino can expect to make $2.70. The challenges begin when a player expects the casino to consider the loss as $100, and not $2.70. Unfortunately, many players are not familiar with the mathematics behind the casino games and struggle with understanding the difference between an actual loss and a theoretical loss.

A theoretical win is the expected win by the casino throughout a significant length of play. The longer the gambling session, the closer the actual win will be to the theoretical win. The **central limit theorem** states that over a large number of independent trials, the casino will see a normal probability distribution. This is important when analyzing playing sessions of various gamblers. This normal distribution, or bell curve, allows the casino to examine how long it will take to achieve the expected value from the actual casino win. A theoretical win or expected win is calculated using the following formula:

House Advantage × Game Pace × Average Bet × Duration = Theoretical Win

For example:

(Single "0" roulette) 2.7 percent × 3.75 × $200 × 60 = $1215.00 (theoretical win)

Because the customer in our previous example feels the effects of losing $100 and not the house advantage of 2.70 percent, or $2.70, casinos need to understand more thoroughly the reactions of those losing, and how they perceive their losses. This can be difficult for the customer because the money is a tangible loss, but the experience is not, thus resulting in mixed feelings, and sometimes uncontrollable emotions.

Computerized Systems

Computer systems are designed to provide a constant source of information that can be accessed for review at any time. Computers have streamlined the management process by integrating software programs capable of analyzing business transactions, managing credit, player tracking, auditing, accounting, and many other functions allowing the casino to reach higher levels of efficiency.

Most newly constructed casinos and some existing ones have experienced the benefits of technology with player ratings. Casinos have begun to incorporate digital ratings that are conveniently positioned on every table game. The player's card is swiped through the computer; the player is immediately identified, and the rating begins. The floor supervisor has more time to protect the games, generate accurate ratings, and provide a higher level of customer service.

There are also tables equipped with monitoring systems for players to rate themselves. This is accomplished by players simply inserting their player's card in the slot designated for the seat on the table game. These "smart tables" will begin reading the players' card and the cheques they use in the designated betting area. As technology such as this becomes more affordable, it will continue to play a major role in developing a more dependable and accurate description of specific player gambling practices.

The future of complimentaries will rely greatly on the advancement of technology. Convenience, accuracy, and efficiency are critical to staying competitive and profitable in the gaming industry. Although technologies are available, casino managers must be willing to invest in them in order to see the benefits. Modern technology will be the key ingredient to functioning at a competitive level in the gaming industry.

The casino industry is also becoming more interested in players self-comping, possibly through a computerized kiosk system, thus eliminating the labor costs associated with the comping process. This process may appeal to certain guests but will probably never replace the human element necessary to service the customer. Casinos must find a balance between the use of too much technology and the personal attention that some customers require.

Challenges and Concerns

Casinos must rely on a tremendous amount of labor from a table games department for evaluating and inputting the data necessary for a casino to administer complimentaries. Accurately monitoring the playing habits of multiple players can prove to be very challenging, often resulting in player complaints and unsatisfied guests.

Players sometimes take advantage of understaffing and busy periods to increase their time played and the amounts of their average bets. This is accomplished by playing with slow dealers, taking long breaks from play while leaving money to reserve a spot on the table, or playing only on crowded tables that reduce the number of hands played per hour. This ultimately reduces the casino's earning potential.

Customers may also experience frustration if they are new to a gaming property. If a customer has extensive play at other casinos and decides to play somewhere new, he or she may not receive similar personal attention. A player's gambling history is extremely important to evaluating a player's potential value. If a guest is an unknown player to the casino and asks for a complimentary, he or she may be placed on a *qualifying basis* status and instructed to room charge all in-house activities. The player will be evaluated, and complimentaries distributed at the conclusion of his or her stay. The casino may also contact previous casinos and request the player's history. This can be accomplished if the casino has established a relationship with other marketing departments. To meet a new guest's expectations, the casino must do everything possible to assess a player's worth, while building his or her trust; that means being honest and fair about what you can offer.

Players may also acquire multiple player's cards to distribute among friends or family. It is important that the casino identify how many cards have been printed for the player. This information is available in the computer as additional cards are printed. The distribution of multiple cards can generate hours of play from different players under the same name. Casinos may opt to see photo identification first before printing another card. This identification may then be scanned into the computer to attach to the player's file.

Casinos must be cautious when requesting information from a player. Is it appropriate to ask a player for a social security number or email address? Do guests feel comfortable supplying this information? What if a player asks not to receive promotional mail? These are all fair and legitimate questions that casinos must carefully address, as it is extremely important to maintain player confidentiality. Moreover, casinos that have effective rating systems capable of analyzing and tracking a player's worth, and retaining them as guests without violating their privacy, will maintain a competitive advantage.

Advantage Players

Casinos may experience abuse of complimentaries by what the casino industry refers to as an **advantage player**. Advantage players have sophisticated skill levels that may reduce and sometimes eliminate the casino's house advantage by exploiting certain

Figure 12–4 Harrah's New Orleans, Louisiana. Courtesy of Harrah's Entertainment, Inc.

opportunities. Advantage players will utilize any legal approach necessary to gain an advantage in a game. This may include exploiting mechanical flaws in gaming equipment, sloppy shuffling, the biases of a roulette wheel, weak casino procedures, or their knowledge of holecards. There is nothing illegal in taking advantage of these particular situations in a casino. Advantage players may significantly decrease or eliminate a casino's expected profits. An advantage player is able to accrue a larger average bet, accumulate a significant amount of playing time, and reduce his or her risk of losing by playing only when there is an advantage. This type of play usually results in an extremely high comp value if the player chooses to be rated.

Some advantage players will take the alternative route by not requesting to be rated because they value their anonymity and longevity as a player more than receiving complimentaries. It is the responsibility of pit personnel, surveillance, and the marketing department to recognize this type of player behavior to ensure that the casino earns what is expected and distributes complimentaries fairly, while maintaining the integrity of the game.

Casino managers must also become familiar with what is a normal theoretical expectation of all games and recognize when a player's action falls outside the normal standard deviation. The *standard deviation* tells how much deviation can be expected when large numbers of independent trials (wagers) are experienced. An unusual winning streak may be the sign of advantage play, illegal activity, or just good luck. It is the casino management's responsibility to evaluate and decide which of these has taken place. Remember, the casino is in business to make money, not force players to leave.

Human Error

Human error will also continue to be a concern of casino player ratings. Errors in player ratings create inconsistencies, which most often result in disagreements with players. The information inputted by the employee may be inaccurate simply because of the overwhelming volume of rated players, a lack of equipment, lack of training, or inefficient staffing. These errors can significantly affect a player's rating, thus resulting in low comp values and frustrated customers.

False Ratings

What is a false rating? A **false rating** represents a gambling session that never took place. A pit clerk, pit manager, floor supervisor, or anyone who has the authority to generate player rating slips may create false ratings. False ratings are created to generate an artificial theoretical win, ultimately resulting in complimentary shows, meals, rooms, or major discounts throughout the casino property without the player having to gamble. False ratings can be entered with relative ease because of the large number of rated players an employee is responsible for, therefore allowing the false rating to go unnoticed.

Inflated Ratings

Other occasions may involve an actual player's rating being inflated by an employee in order for the employee to use complimentaries from the guest's account. An **inflated rating** is a rating that actually took place, but it reveals larger average bets and longer time played than actually happened. This, too, is very difficult to monitor and prevent. Management must be aware of how people are behaving inside of work and socially outside of work. There may be obvious signs that the inflating of ratings is taking place. Employees may comment on how good a show was or how the service was at a particular restaurant. If the shows and restaurants are on the same property, and the employees seem to dine and entertain themselves much too often, this may be considered suspicious activity.

In addition, guests are sometimes very generous when offering their comps to other guests or employees. The acceptance of player comps by an employee requires prior approval by management. In some incidents, players may not know that their accounts are being used for someone else's benefit. Players most often are not notified if their accounts are being used for comp privileges outside of their approval. This happens much too often, as certain players who seldom ask for complimentaries are targeted for the use of their earned value.

Once again, this type of behavior is extremely difficult to identify because of the sheer volume of players and complimentaries distributed. Management must be aware of conversations and behaviors recognized as unusual or abnormal. If given the space, individuals will eventually convict themselves by becoming too relaxed. Management must remain vigilant about watching and securing the ratings to help prevent these episodes from happening. There is currently no system of checks and balances to assist in preventing this from occurring. The watchful eyes of the pit clerk manager, casino manager, and other supervisors are the casino's last line of defense.

It has also become common for gaming companies to pursue multiple jurisdictions through national and international mergers and acquisitions to help diversify their revenues. This ultimately means operating within many different socioeconomic conditions and with different calibers of players. It is vital to the success of a gaming company to identify its market and adjust the complimentary system to fit its specific region. For example, the complimentary system in Biloxi, Mississippi, may be less stringent than that in a casino in Las Vegas, Nevada. A major Las Vegas casino may have more to offer a player but also have more expenses. Casinos must inform guests of their policies and procedures so the guest's expectations are met without uncertainty or inconsistencies.

Figure 12–5
Courtesy of Isle of Capri
Casino Resort.

Slot Ratings

Slot marketing efforts are critical to the success of a gaming organization. Slot machines offer a gaming atmosphere that encourages higher gross handles (total amount wagered), volumes of players, lower costs, more game variety, and less risk than a table game may offer (Figure 12–5). The marketing efforts of a casino are dependent upon the jurisdiction. Each jurisdiction may have demands that are unique to its location. For example, in Las Vegas, Nevada, the local casinos identify certain demographics that anticipate a larger available selection of video poker. The local population is known to be more sophisticated gamblers, thus demanding games with lower house expectancies. In Macau, China, the demand is quite the opposite from that in American-based casinos. The casino floors in Macau are populated with more table games than slot machines. The culture has dictated this particular type of casino floor layout. A society will accept many forms of gaming, as long as they correspond with its culture and expectations.

A slot data tracking system outperforms all data collection efforts seen in the table games department. Table games have had to rely on human efforts to generate their data.

As mentioned earlier, these figures have proven to be particularly inaccurate for table games. Unfortunately, the table games department depends on these data because nothing else is readily available.

The slot department must identify a data tracking system that accommodates its marketing and operational demands. Slot departments today require more from a system because of the elevated expectations of corporate management, player demands, and rapid industry growth. Technology has afforded casinos the opportunity to collect vital performance data from the slot machine, while tracking pertinent player information for the marketing department. This highly integrated software monitors the performance of the machine by tracking the gaming revenue, while assuring that the machine achieves its intended potential. Technology has slowly reduced the human element of data tracking by offering fully computerized systems capable of accepting data, analyzing data, and measuring slot performance, while also monitoring slot players and their action.

A slot customer is evaluated in generally the same way that a table games player is analyzed; guests are evaluated for the potential value they bring to the casino. For a guest to be rated on a slot machine, the guest must place his or her card in the slot designated for player tracking. The player tracking system will monitor and record all action on the machine at the time of play. The evaluation of the data is critical to identifying the value of the guest. Each guest generates a comp value or earning potential, which allows a casino to offer complementaries based upon the player's action. Similar to those for a table games player, the comps for a slot player can include rooms, food, beverage, shows, and many other amenities. A slot player's performance and reward system has expanded to allow a more flexible redemption program. A slot player now has the option to choose certain gifts that match the equivalent of his or her comp value. Some casinos even have a shopping spree once a year for slot players who have not redeemed all of their earned complimentaries.

The primary supply of data used to evaluate the players and award comps is revealed through the player tracking system. Much like a table game player playing on a low house advantage game such as blackjack (basic strategy, +0.50 percent), a slot player is also evaluated for the type of games played. If a player chooses to play a machine with a high hit frequency (number of winning hands) and high hold percentage (amount the casino wins), the player will accumulate a higher comp value.

The slot department must also be aware of the slot mix distributed throughout the casino floor. Casinos may use lower pricing (house advantage) or higher more frequent paybacks (amount returned to player) as a marketing tool to allure players. This has proven in some jurisdictions to be too narrow a marketing focus to compensate for the low house advantages or high paybacks advertised. It is customers' perceptions of the game that will keep them coming back. If the slot mix is strategically dispersed, and players experience longer play and more frequent hits, they will return. Achieving this balance is the difficult part. If the price of playing a slot machine is too high, customers will begin to realize that they are getting little entertainment value for their dollar. The planning and design of a slot floor take careful analysis of the slot models and player expectations. Technology has afforded the slot departments the tools and ability to monitor both, with impressive results.

Players' Group

In the early 1980s the slot club movement began. This concept was designed to reward slot players for frequently visiting the casino and eventually included the table games department as part of a new marketing campaign. A **players' group** includes all of the players who sign up to have their play tracked and evaluated through table games or slots in order to receive promotions, rebates, and complimentaries. Every casino has a unique name attached to its players' group, as well as a distinctive players' card design that represents the specific company. This card is presented to the table game floor supervisor or inserted into the slot machine to begin the player rating process. A players' group allows the casino to create and maintain a large database of players for marketing purposes. Casinos will often attract players to their casinos through players' group sign-up incentives. These incentives may include a discounted room, free buffet, or points toward future complimentaries.

The effectiveness of a casino player's group is only as good as the player ratings generated. The strength of a casino company today is how well it manages the database of players it has created often through a data-mining effort. The cost of managing and maintaining a database of players is increasing. Casinos continue to struggle to find ways to be more efficient and profitable. Today, casinos face the ongoing task of strengthening and expanding their player databases, while recognizing player trends and patterns of behavior. From the complex algorithms used in data mining, to the handshakes by a casino host, every effort is used to attract the optimal player to the property and keep that person there.

As a result of the overwhelming competitiveness of gaming, casinos must continue to reinvent the way they present themselves to customers and how they respond to their needs. One way to do this is to continue to make the players' group processes player-friendly and convenient. Casinos may permit player rating cards to be linked together as one account if the players are married or are significant others residing at the same address. This has allowed players to establish a stronger comp value as their player ratings are combined to establish one account. Casinos may also allow players to apply for and receive player's cards in the table game pits, as well as players' group locations throughout the casino. Casinos may also present a player's card to the guest upon check-in to the hotel. Casinos must make it convenient for new members to obtain player's cards in order to maintain a steady player development program.

Gaming companies can also make efforts to connect multiple properties to one player's card, while allowing accumulated comp values to be used at any of their locations. Mega gaming mergers have made this particular change necessary for casinos to remain competitive in the expanding gaming market. The merging of compter databases from multiple locations can be difficult as gaming companies attempt to become seamless in appearance. Customer service must remain a priority during a company merger or database consolidation. The database consolidation efforts of gaming companies can prove to be ineffective if customers are inconvenienced or unrecognized.

Casino Credit

Casino credit is closely associated and coordinated with the complimentary systems that casinos use to attract players to the property, which is why we discuss it in relationship to player ratings discussed earlier in this chapter. Casino credit is an amenity that has drastically increased the popularity of gambling in a casino. Casinos can stimulate the volume of play by allowing guests to play from their credit lines. Casino credit is a dominant and lucrative amenity for gaming, providing billions of dollars of credit to players, thus inducing and facilitating increased play.

Types of Credit

Casino credit comes in many different forms, the most common being a casino-issued counter-check, or **marker**. Check cashing also represents credit in a variety of ways, from personal checks and payroll checks, to cashier's checks and traveler's checks. These are all considered forms of credit since the casino has risked the chance of the responsible party not honoring the check.

A certain caliber of players may access their credit line by using a **rim card**. A rim card is a document used on a table game by the floor supervisor or pit manager to track the credit transactions of a high-profile player who requests multiple credit transactions throughout his or her play, thus eliminating the need for a player to sign multiple documents throughout the gambling session. The rim card is a matter of convenience for the player.

Rim transactions are also available if players prefer to make a **call bet** if they proceed to lose at a rapid pace. Call bets are verbal requests to make a specific bet without placing a gaming cheque or generating a marker. The dealer simply places a *lammer*, or button representing the amount requested on the specific bet when instructed by the floor supervisor. The rim card balance of the transaction is complete when the player redeems the amount owed by means of gaming cheques, cash, or a marker.

Casinos may also allow guests to deposit **front money** and draw from the deposit by signing a counter check, or marker, against the balance of the deposit. When applying for credit, a player can also request a permanent or temporary credit line. A permanent credit line is one that will be available for the player each time he or she visits the casino. A temporary credit line may be available for one visit only, expiring once the guest has left the casino or after a designated period.

Credit Process

The credit process begins when the player fills out a credit application, much like consumer credit is generated. Credit applications are now offered in an online format for convenience and more efficient processing. The casino credit department then reviews the application and the amount of credit requested. If credit is approved, the customer must sign a signature card that represents the legal signature of the guest who will sign the markers to access the account. The guest with the established credit line is the only person eligible to use the account, and it is to be used for gambling purposes only.

An eligible player may request a credit line ranging from $2,500 up to 1 million or more. The amount is determined by evaluating many different factors, including the amount of credit already established at other casinos, the guest's credit score, bank balances, past delinquent accounts, or a history of slow pay. Each gaming jurisdiction has different policies, procedures, and regulations. Regardless of the jurisdiction, it is critical that the casino establishes and observes all regulatory requirements and procedures involving credit.

Credit Distribution

In table games, the floor supervisor is responsible for verifying that the player has credit available before distributing gaming cheques to the guest. Once the floor supervisor has verified that the credit is available, he or she will instruct the dealer to give the player the designated amount of cheques. The player is then asked to sign the marker. Once the marker is signed, it is given to the pit clerk to match the signature against a digital signature in the computer. If the signature matches, then the marker is filed for possible redemption or cage deposit at the end of the night. The floor supervisor and dealer must also initial a portion of the marker that has the player's name, amount of the marker, table number, and time the marker was generated. This slip is then put into the drop box on the game. A table card on the game is also signed by the floor supervisor and dealer and put back on the game table, which concludes the issuance of the marker. In Nevada, if a player wishes to redeem the marker, he or she has the option of using cash or cheques and may complete this transaction at the table game if the marker has not been transferred to the cashier at the end of the night.

Credit Extension

What happens when a player loses the credit line and wants to continue playing? A casino marketing executive must first evaluate how the player lost the credit line in order to grant a credit extension. The credit extension is coded as a TTO, meaning "this trip only." Casino hosts are able to grant or extend credit to a guest if they are authorized to do so. The evaluation may begin by first asking how much of an extension the player is requesting. How fast did the player lose the money, at what game, and under what conditions? Was the player intoxicated? Was the player giving friends and family members cheques? Does he or she appear to be irresponsible when gambling, for example, playing the entire credit line in one or two hands of blackjack? It is the responsibility of the marketing executive to determine whether the player is fit to continue or should refrain from gambling for a moment to reevaluate his or her situation.

Credit Hold

The casino reserves the right to put a hold on a credit line if it deems necessary. The reasons may include a player winning and preferring to use credit to gamble instead of the winnings. The casino can require that the guest use casino credit only after the guest's front money or winnings are exhausted. A player may also have long periods of time between visits, which requires a player check-in at the cashier and new signature card to be signed to release the hold on the account. A player may also have bad debt from slow pay or no pay from previous trips. Some players may also attempt to obtain the credit and use the money for shopping, sport betting, or other non–gaming related activities.

If a patron cashes out an entire credit line with one marker, the host should be notified immediately in order to investigate the reason why, and to track the guest's gambling habits for the trip. Cashing out a credit line may appear attractive to some players because they receive money interest free for up to 30 days with little or no risk. It is the responsibility of management to recognize these behaviors immediately to prevent further abuse of the credit system.

Collections

Credit collections are an essential part of any business that extends credit to its guests or clients. Casino credit departments must evaluate how and when they will attempt to collect a gambling debt. The applicant can designate how he or she will pay the balance of a gambling debt at the time the application is completed. A statement may be prepared and sent to the guest's address requesting payment within 30 days. The guest may elect to make a payment outside the property in 30 days. The guest may also request not to receive a statement and pay within 30 days. The guest may also pay by check or other means at the conclusion of his or her stay.

Collection agencies may also provide a third-party collection service for gambling debts. Casinos may choose to use a collection agency after all options have been unsuccessfully attempted. If the collection agency is successful in collecting the debt, the agency will be paid a percentage of the amount owed. Casinos may offer special arrangements for guests who have difficulty paying their debts. For example, if a casino fails to collect a debt, it will be charged against earnings as a bad debt expense. The write-off must be presented and approved by the executive level, and only at that time can it be considered irretrievable, or written off.

Summary

Although participating in gambling activities is a voluntary decision, the conditions by which a player makes those decisions is controlled by the casino. The rules of the games are carefully written to ensure a casino's profitability. Understanding the pricing or house advantage is critical for consumers to make good financial decisions and for casinos to generate revenue. However, most consumers are more concerned about the types and amount of comps they will receive, and not the conditions under which they are playing. Understanding these different components allows the casino to recognize the expected earning potential of a player. It is this earning potential that marketing departments use as the basis of their efforts to develop a database of existing and potential players. Casinos must utilize the tools they have, from technology to casino credit, in order to attract profitable players and create a competitive advantage necessary to survive in the competitive world of casino gaming.

key terms

Advantage player
Call bet
Central limit theorem
False rating
Floor Supervisor
Front Money
House Advantage

Inflated Rating
Marker
Player rating
Player's group
Rating slip
Rim cards

review questions

1. What is the price a gambler pays to play?

2. Is everyone who gambles entitled to a comp? Why or why not?

3. Are table games and slot players rated the same? Why or why not?

4. Is it possible to rate two players on the same account? Why or why not?

5. What is advantage play?

6. Does an advantage player deserve comps? Why or why not?

7. Can players exclude themselves from comps? Why or why not?

8. How must a player qualify to be rated when gambling?

9. Can a player with casino credit use this money to place sport bets? Why or why not?

10. What does TTO mean?

11. What constitutes a credit instrument?

12. What is a marker?

internet sites

Urbino
www.urbino.net

Advantage player
www.advantageplayer.com

American Gaming Association
www.americangaming.org

Gaming Today
www.gamingtoday.com

Gaming Floor
    www.gamingfloor.com

UNLV gaming
    http://gaming.unlv.edu/

BJ Math
    www.bjmath.com

Casino Enterprise Management
    www.casinoenterprisemanagement.com

Casino Magazine
    www.casinomagazine.com

Conjelco
    http://conjelco.com

references

Cabot, A.N. (1996). *Casino Gaming: Policy, Economics, and Regulation*. Las Vegas: UNLV, International Gaming Institute.

Cabot, A.N., & Kelly, J.M., (2003). *Casino Credit and Collections*. Reno: The Institute for the Study of Gambling & Commercial Gaming.

Griffin, P.A. (1999). *The Theory of Blackjack*, 6th ed. Las Vegas: Huntington Press.

Hannum, R.C., & Cabot, A.N., (2001). Practical Casino Math. Reno: The Institute for the Study of Gambling & Commercial Gaming.

Kilby, J., & Fox, J. (1998). *Casino Operations Management*. New York: John Wiley Pub.

Lehman, R. (2002). Slot Operations: The Myth and The Math. Reno: The Institute for the Study of Gambling & Commercial Gaming.

13 Location and Transportation

Chang Lee, New Mexico State University

Learning Objectives

1. To understand the effect of location and transportation on the growth of the casino industry.

2. To introduce the categories of casino locations and their significance.

3. To explore the relationship between casinos and neighboring attractions.

4. To understand the importance of the various types of transportation in determining a casino's market.

Chapter Outline

Introduction

Gaming is a proven tourist attraction. As a result of the growth of casinos, gaming has become more widespread in the United States, and most states have legalized casino gaming in one form or another. What has taken place in Las Vegas and Atlantic City over the past few decades has been repeated on a smaller scale in new gaming jurisdictions throughout the country. The business of casino tourism is increasing in many parts of the world. In the United States, casinos have been introduced to Native American reservations and small towns to enhance local economies. Their development has spread after Native American reservations in Connecticut and South Dakota proved their potential economic values. Casinos bring visitors to the region and also prompt visitors drawn to neighboring attractions to stay longer. This increases the number of times tourist dollars are turned over in the local economy.

Casino gaming has rapidly spread throughout the country because of two significant developments: the Indian Gaming Regulatory Act of 1988 and the legalization of modern riverboat gambling in 1989. Along with these two significant developments, the improvement of accessibility made going to casinos an activity that more and more people enjoyed. Consumers' propensity to gamble is influenced by their proximity to a gaming facility and the availability of convenient transportation. Most of the U.S. population is within an easy day's drive of a casino. This chapter discusses transportation's role in casino development.

Accessibility

"Build it, and people will come" is not always true in the current casino industry. This might have been true prior to the late 1970s when casino facilities were primarily found in the Las Vegas area. People traveled to these casinos even when they were not convenient because there were no other places to gamble. This situation has changed because more and more casinos with convenient access have opened throughout the country. People tend to visit areas that provide multiple attractions, and the development of convenient transportation encourages people to visit areas that were not previously appealing because of their inaccessibility. Casinos are designed in such a manner

Figure 13–1 Wynn Casino, Las Vegas, in the final stages of building. Courtesy of George G. Fenich.

as to maximize the economic potential of the facility and a surrounding area. The issue of placement concerns all the decisions involved in getting the right product to the target markets. A product, especially a casino, is not much good to travelers if it is not available when and where it is wanted. Casinos approach their target markets differently based on their level of accessibility.

The gaming industry has been spread out across the country from two mega gaming cities, Las Vegas and Atlantic City. Many communities have seen casinos as one source that generates revenue and brings in travelers' dollars. However, the casino is not the only destination that attracts visitors to an area. Casinos have also been developed within areas that have provided other tourist attractions. For example, casinos have been established in Deadwood, South Dakota, a small town in the heart of the Black Hills, where established tourist attractions such as national parks and monuments already exist.

Casino Locations

Casinos are located in both metropolitan areas such as Las Vegas, Tunica, and Atlantic City, as well as in rural or suburban areas such as Silver City, Deadwood, and Black Hawk. They all may be accessible by most means of transportation; however, some of them may not be as convenient as others. As an example, Deadwood, is located in the heart of the Black Hills, about 400 miles away from any large hub airport. Even though there is a regional airport 50 miles away from Deadwood, the majority of customers still drive, because the regional airport is inconveniently located. Travelers from metropolitan areas such as New York City or Los Angeles need to stop over at other hub airports before actually getting to Deadwood. Also, casinos on most Native American reservations are inconvenient for air travelers because of their isolated locations and limited transportation infrastructure. For instance, Prairie Casino, on the Pine Ridge Sioux Indian Reservation, has only one main highway for access. On the other hand, since Las Vegas and Tunica are a few miles away from large or medium hub airports, they may only require transit directly from those airports.

Casino locations can be categorized by distance or by type of market. Casino locations categorized by distance can be broken into two types according to the distance of travel from home. The first are local or regional casinos, such as riverboat casinos or small town casinos in the Midwest that mainly serve travelers from a particular region. The second are nonlocal casinos, such as those in Las Vegas, Atlantic City, or Reno that mainly serve long-distance travelers. Casino locations that are categorized by type of market can be divided into three categories: the convenience market, the transit market, and the pleasure market. The convenience market falls in the local or regional casino category, and the transit market and the pleasure market fall in the nonlocal casino category.

Location by Distance

In general, local casinos are those that mainly serve people traveling less than 100 miles from home, and nonlocal or tourist casinos as those that mainly serve people who travel at least 100 miles from home. Casinos in Las Vegas can be categorized as nonlocal casinos, while casinos in small towns or on Native American reservations could be categorized as local casinos since they draw a majority of visitors from the legal region. Because of their limited market, local casinos are established within areas that do provide other tourist attractions. Casinos in Native American reservations and small towns in the Midwest provide cultural or nature-related activities for local visitors.

For visitors on the East Coast of the United States, the bulk of casinos are along the Jersey shore in Atlantic City, and in Native American casinos in other inland communities. The Mississippi and Missouri Rivers are home to an increasing number of riverboat casinos, and midwesterners are becoming regular visitors to these riverboat casinos. Small town casinos in South Dakota and Colorado became popular destinations for visitors to the Rockies in Colorado and to the Black Hills in South Dakota. The fact that there are more casinos in more varied locations has resulted in a drop in the percentage of overall casino revenues from casinos in Atlantic City and Las Vegas. In 1991, revenues from casinos in these two cities accounted for 80.2 percent of total casino revenue in the United States. By 1998, they accounted for only 38 percent of total casino revenue.[1] However, as more people began to gamble, these numbers began to grow again as the population accepted gaming as a new recreational activity and as a vacation choice. This helps to illustrate that gaming has spread throughout the entire nation, except Hawaii and Utah, which are the only two states that prohibit all forms of gambling.

Location by Type of Market

There are three categories of casino location by type of market. **Convenience markets** are located within easy driving distance from major urban areas but are not convenient by air. Many Native American casinos in California and Minnesota are examples of the convenience markets. **Pleasure markets** may require long-distance travel; they are convenient by air but not located within easy driving distance from a major urban area. Casinos in pleasure markets provide more than gambling facilities; they also can provide lodging and restaurants. Casinos in Atlantic City, Tunica, or Las Vegas fall in this category. **Transit markets** are located between the pleasure markets and the convenience markets. This market has no other facilities, nor does it have easy access for air travelers. Transit markets do not tend to focus on one specific potential market; instead, they focus on markets that have multiple characteristics. Visitors in this type of market are not gambling oriented but are there for other activities. The casino is a supplementary activity for them. Casinos in South Dakota, Colorado, Iowa, and North Dakota or on many Native American reservations can fall in this category.

Table 13-1 Characteristics of types of casino markets

Transit Markets	Convenience Markets	Pleasure Markets
• Tend not to be traveler's only destination • Consist of small of medium size casinos because of a lack of mass travelers • Tend to be sensitive to seasons—more traffic during the peak season • Tend to have natural attractions such as national or state parks or other cultural attractions • Tend to have limited lodging facilities • Tend to be located in rural areas • Tend to have accessibility limited to ground transportation	• Travel destinations • Consist of small, medium, or large casinos because of more mass travelers • Tend to not be sensitive to seasons • Tend to have more activities/amenities • Tend to have limited lodging facilities • Tend to be located in urban or suburban areas close to metropolitan areas • Tend to have easy accessibility by ground transportation, but not air transportation	• Travel destinations • Consist of large casinos • Tend to be somewhat sensitive to the seasons • Tend to have more amenities and activities besides gaming • Tend to have natural and human-made attractions • Tend to have various lodging facilities for various markets • Tend to have more luxurious lodging facilities • Tend to be located in urban or suburban areas • Tend to have easy accessibility by both ground and air transportation

Since gaming has become more acceptable as a leisure or recreational activity in American society, more people tend to travel to casinos. It is clear that there are more auto travelers in the convenience markets compared to other markets. There are also fewer air travelers in the transit market compared to pleasure markets because of the lack of air transportation. Another reason may be that travelers in the transit market tend to visit multiple places during their trips. Travelers in the pleasure market need to spend more money for their trips than those in other markets because of the need for long-distance travel, lodging, and food and beverages. Characteristics in each category are summarized in Table 13-1.

Transportation and Casinos

In earlier years, people traveled by horses or by foot. Then, railroads and waterways became popular for long-distance travelers, and then the automobile was introduced. The locations of hotels then shifted from along rivers or stagecoach routes to towns with train stations. Communities on the routes with new infrastructure and communities with lodging facilities were able to attract more travelers and settlers. Hotels were built close to train stations or waterway landings. With the increasing numbers of people coming to the communities, they began to need more entertainment activities along with their hotel development. As lodging facilities were built for travelers and residents, they also became gathering places. As hotels became more social places, other amenities such as casinos and bars were needed to attract travelers. Gambling then began to be offered in these hotels.

Today, people travel using many different modes of transportation such as automobile, bus, train, or airplane. As people tend to have more disposable income and time, the tourism industry further develops, and additional demands will be made on transportation systems. In general, the factors influencing travelers' choices of transportation are a combination of the length of the trip, the number of people in the group, and the amount of disposable time and income they have for travel. In order to meet the demands of travelers, transportation accessibility is a key factor for casinos to consider. There is no doubt that gaming generates travel; however, casinos need to identify ways to attract potential travelers who have limited time in order to be better positioned in the very competitive tourism communities.

It is interesting to note the differences in types of tourists and their modes of transportation when comparing the accessibility of casinos. There are casinos that can be accessed by multiple modes of transportation, while others are not as easily accessible. Major casinos in metropolitan areas such as Las Vegas, Tunica, Atlantic City, or Foxwoods

Figure 13–2

have convenient accessibility by ground and air transportation. In contrast, casinos on many Native American reservations and in casino towns in the Midwest are accessible only by bus or automobile.

The casino product has been spread out to all segments of the market. It has been estimated that there is a casino within 300 miles of any urban area in the United States. With casinos, as well as other forms of tourism development, transportation is an important concern, especially in rural areas. Communities that provide casinos as a major travel product also provide convenient multiple transportation modes, while communities that provide casinos as a supplementary travel product provide a more limited transportation mode. The result is more nonlocal casino users in communities with specific casino-oriented areas, and more local casino users in communities with smaller casino-supported areas.

Modes of Transportation

As the casino industry grows and people travel more to experience exciting new environments using increasing amounts of disposable income and time, the preferred types of transportation have shifted from less expensive to faster and more convenient. As the tourism industry becomes more globalized, people look for travel destinations that meet their expectation, from natural sites to cities that provide multiple attractions. Air travel dominates long-distance and middle-distance tourism, while the automobile dominates short-distance tourism. It is important to understand that the foundation of tourism is people, transportation, and destination. Destinations that provide multiple transportation modes have an advantage of attracting more visitors compared to areas that provide limited transportation modes.

There are a variety of ways that people can travel between multiple destinations, and many theories have been developed about how people select modes of transportation. People select transportation modes by considering availability, frequency, cost, speed, and comfort. Destinations that provide transportation modes that move passengers quickly, comfortably, and frequently for a low price are generally better positioned in the marketplace. The availability of multiple transportation options highly affects people's destination choices along with many other factors. These factors include affordability, length of travel time, convenience, and whether or not the mode of transport is well marketed. Today, people can choose among three major modes of transportation: water, ground, and air. The majority of travelers still use ground transportation, even if the number of air travelers has rapidly increased.

Water Transportation

As Americans extended the frontiers of the nation in a relatively short period of time, from the shores of the Great Lakes to the north, to the Mississippi in the west, and to the Gulf of Mexico in the south, transportation was supplemented by the extensive use of the many miles of natural waterways. Transportation developed along the waterways, which provided easy and fast access to casinos. As early as the first decade of the nineteenth century, water traffic through New Orleans had developed in the towns and settlements along the Ohio and Mississippi Rivers. The introduction of the steamboat on inland rivers in the early 1800s marked the beginning of important traffic by packet boats. As transportation developed along the waterways, gaming activities became a part of the amenities on passenger riverboats along the Mississippi and Ohio Rivers.

Before the first steamship was designed, water transportation had been used for exploration, commerce, transportation, and some leisure travel. The types of water transportation then consisted of transoceanic liners and riverboats. Today, the ship is no longer an important mode of passenger transportation except in ferry service. Water transportation became less popular compared to ground transportation when the railroad and automobiles were introduced. Just as the automobile led to the decreased use of the train, the introduction of commercial air services added to the decreased use of ships as passenger transportation. Today, cruising by water is more of a tourist attraction in and of itself than a mode of transportation.

Ground Transportation

Rail transportation was the major mode of travel in the United States until 1920. As the Hosmer Report in 1958 indicated, its role became limited because its infrastructure did not advance as did that of the highway infrastructure. However, the current development of high-speed trains will improve the role of rail in regions that are connected to highly populated areas. Trains have been perceived as slow in reaching destinations, relatively inflexible with regard to departure and arrival times, and high in cost. When the automobile began to make inroads in the 1920s and 1930s, the railways began to lose their market share. Roadside accommodations and services became far more important to automobile travelers than accommodations in city centers.

The majority of travelers in most developed countries travel in automobiles. Since the introduction of the automobile in the late 1800s, public acceptance of the automobile in the United States has been so great that it was the major cause of the decline of passenger train travel. Since the U.S. Interstate Highway System started in 1954, about 90 percent of U.S. cities with populations larger than 50,000 are serviced by interstate highways. The convenience of the automobile has minimized the importance of other modes of transportation.

The automobiles and buses provided accessibility for travelers to many areas that they could not reach by other transportation modes. They allowed people to travel from the Atlantic Coast to the Pacific Coast. People started to travel more and for longer distances, stopping several places on their journeys. Casino developments were heavily

Figure 13–3 Atlantic City, noted for its proximity to major East Coast cities, found it needed a transportation center for all the different types of vehicles. Here, as you drive into Atlantic City, the sides of the highway are lined with linear parking lots for cars. You can then get picked up by mass transport and taken to the transportation center. Photo courtesy of George G. Fenich.

influenced by the development of ground transportation. As an example, Las Vegas started as a small desert railroad town, the first settlement traced to 1829. This small town became the casino capital of the world after it legalized gambling in 1931. Casino gambling grew rapidly there after WWII, along with the development of transportation and accommodation facilities. On the other hand, bus transportation was used by Atlantic City to develop the market along the northeast corridor. Chartered buses allowed people to relax and sleep before and after the casino visit, easing the burden of driving for long hours. However, the automobile is still the dominating mode of passenger transportation, even after the introduction of air transportation. Shifting the development of transportation from waterways to railroads, and then to the highways and airways, changed the development of casinos from water-based to land-based.

Air Transportation

The first flight by the Wright brothers in Kitty Hawk, North Carolina, in 1903 was in a machine that flew only about 40 yards. After that, air transportation was developed mainly for military, freight, and mail purposes. It is important to understand that early planes were no faster than trains over the same routes and were much less reliable. Since there was no incentive for the airlines to carry passengers, U.S. airlines counted on the government's mail contracts to survive. The modern airline industry was established in 1930 with four major airlines: United, American, Eastern, and TWA. Air transportation took on an important transportation role as the number of international and intercontinental travelers increased. Since the U.S. airline industry was deregulated in 1978, airlines were forced to reduce prices to attract travelers; however, this caused a lack of air services for small communities.

Air transportation is particularly important for the current casino gaming industry, as the market has expanded to include business travelers. Many casinos especially in Las Vegas, are equipped with meeting facilities to attract an increasing number of conventions. In the transportation industry, the more people fly, the more flights can be offered, and the more prices can be lowered. Also, the more competition there is among the airlines, the lower the price will be for their customers.

Air traffic hubs are designated as geographic areas based on the percentage of total passengers enplaned in that area. A hub may have more than one airport in it. This definition of hub should not be confused with the definition used by the airlines in describing their "hub-spoke" route structure. Where there are hub airports, it is easier for travelers to make a long-distance trip to a casino.

Importance of Location and Transportation in Casinos

Destination choice is not as simple as judging transportation options; it is more about how much money and time people have. Location is important in choosing transportation modes; if the trip is a long distance, people tend to fly; if it is a short distance, people drive. Destinations that provide accessible transportation infrastructure for travelers are in a better position to attract potential travelers. In general, visitors who travel long distances to casinos require overnight accommodations in the region, which brings in additional dollars to the community. Visitors who travel short distances to casinos are generally people from the region, or **day-trippers**, and may not require places to stay. These day-trippers may bring business to the casino but not necessarily to other businesses in the community.

Casinos that are located in metropolitan areas such as Atlantic City and Las Vegas are more likely to provide sufficient transportation infrastructure, including interstate

Figure 13–4 Rio All-Suite Hotel & Casino, Las Vegas, Nevada. Courtesy of Harrah's Entertainment, Inc.

highways, major airports, and scheduled air services. Casinos in the areas that have a multifaceted transportation infrastructure also have stronger marketing advantages compared to the ones in rural areas. Long-distance travelers tend not to make trips to rural casinos unless those casinos are located on the way to their destinations or have popular attractions in surrounding areas. This indicates that each casino should specifically target its marketing for either short-distance, local, or regional travelers; long-distance travelers; or transit travelers who visit casinos on the way to their final destinations.

People go to every corner of the world to fulfill their desires. They drive hours and hours or they fly long distances to casinos, not only for gambling but also for other activities or attractions. Las Vegas, Atlantic City, Tunica, and Foxwood are all located near major hub airports. Since casino gambling was legalized in Las Vegas, the state of Nevada has brought in millions of visitors from every corner of the world. Las Vegas is a fully developed tourist destination, served by 60 major airlines. McCarron International Airport averages more than 800 flights daily, which bring millions of visitors to the city, including 4 million international visitors. Laughlin, Nevada, was a town with a population of 95 that introduced casino gambling in late 1960. While visitors from all over the world visit Las Vegas, Laughlin now attracts nearby prosperous visitors coming from surrounding states. Compared to Las Vegas, the majority of visitors to Laughlin are vacationers who use ground transportation modes such as recreation vehicles, charter buses, or personal automobiles. Laughlin's proximity to Las Vegas has led to further economic benefits for the entire area.

Atlantic City is another example of the advantages of a multifaceted transportation system. The city provides multiple tourism products along with a well-developed transportation system with convenient accessibility for nearby residents. The city is also located a short distance from other populated areas, such as New York and Baltimore. Atlantic City has been a tourism destination since its founding in the 1850s. It was once a premier resort city with resort hotels catering to middle- and upper-middle-class Americans. With the introduction of the automobile and the improvement of highway infrastructures and lodging developments, Atlantic City experienced a decline in visitors until casino gaming was introduced. Atlantic City has since successfully promoted short-duration motor coach tours to increase the number of casino travelers.

Since casinos have been developed in almost all regions in the United States, people now can visit casinos to gamble regardless of their location. Because of the rapid development of casinos in other areas, Las Vegas's and Atlantic City's market shares have been divided with casinos in other regions. Smaller communities and casinos in areas that do not provide other tourist attractions may have to struggle to survive in the highly competitive casino market. Casinos with other tourist attractions and casinos in populous communities such as Las Vegas can be better positioned for development.

Casino Travelers

The sole purpose for visiting casinos has long been gambling, but this has become less true in recent years. Previously, people who liked to gamble had to visit sites such as Las Vegas because of a lack of casino facilities in their home areas. Now, with gambling legalized in most states, people can visit casinos simply by driving a few hours. Because of the easy access to casinos, people tend to visit destinations that provide more than just casinos.

People tend to make longer trips as long as they are convenient, and sufficient transportation infrastructure is provided. There are various air services that offer relatively low-cost travel from cities around hub airports to destination cities. The increasing number of business-related travelers to casinos allows casinos near major airports to take advantage of this convenient accessibility. The lower air ticket price to these areas attracts more travelers, including business travelers. For example, the more business travelers (for conventions) fly to Las Vegas, the more flights are offered, the more competition, and the lower the airfare prices.

Casinos can fall into more than one defined market, such as casinos in Colorado that can be in both transit and convenient markets because of their location. People traveling a long distance to visit the Rockies may see communities with casinos such as Central City, Black Hawk, or Cripple Creek as having other activities besides viewing nature scenes and historical sites. It is difficult, if not impossible, to identify which specific market each casino community serves because casino communities in general do not fall in only one market. In the United States, even with an increasing number of air travelers, auto travelers make up more than 70 percent of total travelers. These auto travelers are generally exposed to some form of casino on the way to their destinations.

Table 13–2 Adults who gambled in a casino

	2001	**2002**	**2003**
United States adult population (age 21+)	196.9 million	197.1 million	205.6 million
Casino gamblers	53.2 million	51.2 million	53.4 million
Casino participation rate	27%	26%	26%
Average trip frequency	5.7 trips/year	5.8 trips/year	5.8 trips/year
Casino trips	303.3 million	297.2 million	310 million

Source: Harrah's Entertainment, Inc. /NFO WorldGroup, Inc. /U.S. Census Bureau.

As Table 13–2 illustrates, studies performed by Harrah's Entertainment show that the number of gamblers has increased from 51.2 million in 2002 to 53.4 million in 2003. The U.S. Census shows that the U.S. adult population increased from 196.9 million in 2001 to 205.6 million in 2003. As the United States adult population increases, there are also increasing numbers of casino gamblers. The number of gambling trips in the United States is likely to increase as new casinos open near major markets. More than 30 states generated more than 2 million casino trips in the last two years. On average, gamblers visit casinos about once every two months.

Casino Feeder States

Since there are casinos in almost every state, casinos have become a major part of leisure activity in the United States. A Harrah's survey (Table 13–3) found that a majority of Americans' casino trips in the last three years were taken by gamblers residing in the

Table 13–3 Top ten casino feeder states

2001	**2002**	**2003**
California	California	California
Illinois	Nevada	Illinois
Nevada	New York	Nevada
New York	Illinois	New York
Michigan	New Jersey	Michigan
Texas	Michigan	New Jersey
New Jersey	Texas	Texas
Louisiana	Louisiana	Louisiana
Missouri	Missouri	Florida
Pennsylvania	Arizona	Missouri

Source: Harrah's Entertainment, Inc. / NFO WorldGroup/U.S. Census Bureau.

major casino feeder states: California, Illinois, Nevada, New York, Michigan, Texas, New Jersey, Louisiana, Missouri, Arizona, Florida, and Pennsylvania. As there is a convenient transportation infrastructure between California and Nevada, 17 percent of casino trips originated in California alone.

A Harrah's study shows that visitors to casinos are usually residents of neighboring areas (or states). For example, as Table 13–4 indicates, residents in Alabama visit the Gulf Coast and Native American reservations in Mississippi, while residents in Iowa and Nebraska visit the Iowa and South Dakota Indian reservations, in Quad cities and Council Bluff, and in Iowa riverboats. Destinations that provide multiple mega casinos and other activities are still favorite destinations for visitors across the nation. Las Vegas is easily accessible from all communities in the United States through its airport, while the access to Deadwood or riverboat casinos in Iowa is generally limited to the surrounding communities. Communities that do not have convenient transportation infrastructure such as major hub airports or do not provide multiple mega casino facilities tend to only attract people from neighboring states.

Table 13–4   Casino destinations by state of origin

State	Casino Destination
Alabama	Gulf Cost, Indian reservations, Tunica
Arizona	Arizona Indian, Las Vegas, Laughlin
Arkansas	Shreveport, Bossier City, Tunica
California	Las Vegas, California Indian
Colorado	Colorado, Las Vegas
Connecticut	Atlantic City, Connecticut Indian, Las Vegas
Delaware	Atlantic City, Delaware, Las Vegas
Florida	Cruise Ship, Florida Indian, Gulf Coast, Las Vegas
Georgia	Cherokee, NC, Gulf Coast, Las Vegas
Idaho	Idaho Indian, Las Vegas, other Nevada
Illinois	Chicago area, Las Vegas, St Louis
Indiana	Chicago area, Las Vegas, Southern IL
Iowa	Iowa Indian, riverboats, Quad Cities/Council Bluffs
Kansas	Kansas City, MO; Kansas Indian; Las Vegas

(*continued*)

Table 13–4   Casino destinations by state of origin (*continued*)

State	Casino Destination
Kentucky	Southern IL, Tunica
Louisiana	Gulf Coast, MS; Lake Charles; New Orleans; Shreveport/Bossier City
Maine*	N/A
Maryland	Atlantic City, Delaware
Massachusetts	Connecticut Indian, Rhode Island
Michigan	Detroit/Windsor, Michigan
Minnesota	Las Vegas, Minnesota Indian
Mississippi	Gulf Coast, MS, Tunica, Vicksburg
Missouri	Kansas City, MO; St. Louis
Montana*	N/A
Nebraska	Quad Cities/Council Bluffs, South Dakota Indian
Nevada	Las Vegas, Reno
New Hampshire	Atlantic City, Connecticut Indian
New Jersey	Atlantic City, Las Vegas
New Mexico	Las Vegas, New Mexico Indian
New York	Atlantic City, Connecticut
North Carolina	Atlantic City, Cherokee, NC
North Dakota	Minnesota Indian, North Dakota Indian
Ohio	Detroit/Windsor, Las Vegas, Southern IL, West Virginia
Oklahoma	Las Vegas, Oklahoma Indian, Tunica
Oregon	Las Vegas, Oregon Indian
Pennsylvania	Atlantic City, West Virginia
Rhode Island	Connecticut Indian, Rhodes Island
South Carolina	Cherokee, NC; Las Vegas
South Dakota	North Dakota Indian, South Dakota Indian
Tennessee	Cherokee, NC; Southern IL; Tunica
Texas	Lake Charles, Las Vegas, Shreveport/Bossier City
Utah	Las Vegas
Vermont*	N/A
Virginia	Atlantic City, Las Vegas, West Virginia
Washington	Las Vegas, Washington Indian
West Virginia	Las Vegas, West Virginia
Wisconsin	Las Vegas, Wisconsin Indian
Wyoming	

Source: Harrah's Entertainment, Inc. / NFO WorldGroup/US Census Bureau.

* Samples are too small

Table 13–5   Casino participation rates by region

Year	West Region (12 states)	North Central Region (11 states)	Northeast Region (13 states)	South Region (12 states)
	Washington (28%),	North Dakota (31%),	Maine (12%)	Oklahoma (16%),
	Oregon (28%),	South Dakota (32%),	New Hampshire (20%),	Texas (21%),
	California (38%),	Kansas (26%),	Massachusetts (31%),	Arkansas (22%),
	Nevada (40%),	Minnesota (34%),	New York (27%),	Louisiana (39%),
	Montana (18%),	Wisconsin (29%),	New Jersey (36%),	Mississippi (35%),
	Idaho (25%),	Iowa (26%),	Connecticut (40%),	Alabama (20%),
	Wyoming (17%),	Missouri (30%),	Rhode Island (36%),	Tennessee (20%),
	Utah (27%),	Illinois (28%),	Maryland (17%),	Florida (17%),
	Colorado (34%),	Michigan (32%),	Delaware (28%),	Georgia (13%),
	Arizona (41%),	Ohio (19%),	Vermont (9%),	South Carolina (8%),
	New Mexico (32%),	Indiana (22%)	West Virginia (7%),	North Carolina (8%),
	Nebraska (35%)		Virginia (12%),	Kentucky (19%)
			Pennsylvania (21%)	
2002	35%	29%	27%	19%
2003	35%	27%	27%	18%

Source: Harrah's Entertainment, Inc. / NFO WorldGroup/U.S. Census Bureau.

Dividing the country into census regions, the Western region has the highest gambling participation rate. The rate in the North Central region where commercial or Native American gambling is available is second. Many states in the Northeast and South census regions had participation rates below the national average of 26 percent. States that have participation rates below the national averages are states that have fewer casinos than states that rate above the national average. States that rated higher than 35 percent in the year 2003, such as Nevada, Arizona, and Mississippi, have or are close to having multiple casino facilities. As Table 13–5 indicates, many areas of the country are undersupplied by casino gambling opportunities, and many residents are required to travel significant distances, often across state lines, to visit a casino. For example, people from Massachusetts, Connecticut, and Rhode Island may have convenient access to casinos in Connecticut, while people from Maine, New Hampshire, Vermont, and West Virginia do not.

Summary

Significant comparisons can be made between areas that have convenient transportation and those that do not. Las Vegas and Atlantic City have major international airports and convenient interstate highways. Their casinos attract potential travelers in multiple markets, such as adult and youth markets, and theme park markets along with entertainment markets. Casinos on Native American reservations and rural casinos with a limited stake, such as those in South Dakota or Colorado, are inconvenient to access. These casinos attract potential travelers with alternative tourism products such as natural or historic tourism. People visiting casinos in this category consider the casino as a secondary purpose unless they are day-trippers from the local areas. It has been said that the consumer's propensity to gamble is influenced by how close the gambling facility is to them. Areas that are located in densely populated areas, which are more likely to provide advanced transportation infrastructure, may attract day-trippers whose destinations are casino facilities that also provide other activities such as shopping. These areas also focus on mass tourism that brings visitors from multiple markets. Areas that do not provide advanced transportation infrastructure attract alternative tourism that focuses on a single market. Therefore, location is one of the most important factors in any business. It impacts on the business's potential market and its characteristics. As Goodman described, people are attracted to close shopping places; gaming facilities attract people from local areas; and people tend to choose the nearest gaming centers that meet their expectations, unless they use casinos as their vacation destinations.[2] In the selection of casinos as travel destinations, decisions are based on destination type, cost, safety, seasonality and accessibility[3]

As casinos are introduced in many states as land-based casinos, race tracks, dockside casinos, or riverboat casinos, the impact of gaming on tourism and the local economy is very evident. Given the level of its current growth, it is safe to predict that gaming will continue to play a role in tourism and economic development. Rural areas around the world are facing everything from decreasing populations to changes in government policy on agriculture and a general lack of economic resources. In many of these places, tourism has been seen as a solution, a way of rejuvenating rural economies and providing a new future. The development of casinos has become an economic option regardless of the state of the surrounding area. The development of casinos will continue, not only in the United States but also in other countries.

key terms

Convenience markets	Pleasure markets
Day-trippers	Transit markets

review questions

1. What are the three markets that casinos can be divided into? List three characteristics of each.

2. Why are local casinos established within the areas that provide other tourist attractions?

3. What factor has resulted in a drop in the percentage of overall casino revenues from casinos in Atlantic City and Las Vegas?

4. In which market is there more auto travel than in other markets?

5. Which factors influence travelers' choices of transportation?

6. Which type of people do communities without convenient transportation infrastructure tend to attract?

internet sites

Conjelco
   http://conjelco.com/faq/casino.html

Gaming Observer
   http://www.gamingobserver.com

Indian Country
   http://www.indiancountry.com/content.cfm?id=1028048151

University of Massachusetts
   http://www.umassd.edu/communications/articles/showarticles.cfm?a_key=394

endnotes

1. McQueen, P. (1998, September). North America gaming at a glance. *International Gaming & Wagering Business*, pp. 48–60.

2. Goodman, L. R. (1995). Market analysis of reservation-based gaming: A North Dakota case study. *Economic Development Review*, 13 (4), 16–18.

3. Morrison, A. M., Braunlich, C. G., Liping, A. C., and O'Leary, J. T. (1996). A profile of the casino resort vacationer. *Journal of Travel Research*, 35, 55–61; Qu, H, and Li, I. (1997). The characteristics and satisfaction of Mainland Chinese visitors to Hong Kong. *Journal of Travel Research*, 35, 37–41.

14 Promotions

Kathryn Hashimoto, East Carolina University

Learning Objectives

1. To introduce the four major promotional techniques.

2. To understand integrated marketing communications.

3. To explain the difference between "push" and "pull" strategies.

4. To provide an understanding of personal sales, sales promotion, public relations, and advertising.

5. To introduce aspects that need to be considered when creating advertisements.

6. To understand how direct marketing fits with the effective options casinos use to reach their customers.

Chapter Outline

Introduction

Promotions are the links that a casino uses to communicate with the outside world. Promotions can be personal interactions or group techniques designed to communicate a message to a large audience. There are four major promotional techniques: personal sales, sales promotion, public relations or publicity, and advertising. The best campaigns integrate and coordinate these communication channels so that there is one clear consistent message about the organization and its products. This is referred to as **integrated marketing communications (IMC)**. IMC can result in a synergistic strategy in that the sum of the parts is greater than the whole.

In the IMC strategy, several factors determine which of these promotional elements to use and when.

- First, the nature of the offering is important. The offer of a dinner for two at the casino restaurant is not appropriate for a mass audience, but a personal invitation by a casino host or a direct mail piece would be.

- Second, whether to use a push or pull strategy should be determined. A **push strategy** tries to push the offer or package through the players' club or casino host to the player. The casino wants its employees to make the offer and sell the product. On the other hand, in a **pull strategy**, the players learn of an offer and they go to the casino to obtain the deal. In this strategy, the players are the ones who pull the offer from the casino.

- Third, it is important to understand where in the buyer readiness stage the potential clients are. Are they new to casinos? Are they new to your particular casino? Are they new to the players' club? Are they new to the casino's hosts or an old hand at the casino? In each of these cases, a different strategy and offer should be made.

For example, if you are looking for someone new to casinos, you might want to have a friend extend an invitation to spend some time at the casino. In this push strategy, an offer can be made to a regular player to invite 10 of his or her best friends to a party at the casino. These friends are asked to fill out a players' club card while they are at the casino. This pushes the offer through the casino and obtains new players who might be interested in gambling now that they have been exposed to the casino. This strategy obtains new customers who are influenced by their friend who does the selling. On the other hand, a pull strategy would be to send out an offer for a comped pair of tickets to a concert in order to have the clients come to the casino and ask for their tickets. The clients are the ones who make the move toward the casino. Since it is hard to identify new gamblers, this offer might be a better follow-up offer to the invitees from the previous party. They have been to the casino and gambled a bit, and the pull strategy now encourages them to return.

In this scenario, the personal selling or face-to-face contact was conducted by the regular player instead of a casino employee. A casino host attended the party to make sure everything was going smoothly and passed out sales promotions, such as key chains, decks of cards, or T-shirts. These are short-term items that will remind the guests about the fun they had at the casino.

Personal Sales

Personal sales are most effective with a well-trained staff, but they are also the most expensive and labor intensive of the four promotional techniques. Personal sales are a one-on-one interaction in which a trained salesperson communicates with a single client. This technique requires a person who knows the product and is sensitive to the buyer's needs and can judge verbal communication as well as nuances in body language to create the most effective timing and exchange. To some degree, a superb salesperson is born; he or she instinctively knows the right thing to say at the right time and can automatically sense a client's moods (Figure 14–1).

Personal sales are frequently used in the casino environment. It used to be that the dealers were expected to "dummy up and deal" for security reasons. However, now dealers can have conversations with the guests at the table. A likeable or lucky dealer can draw a gambler back to the casino. In addition, pit bosses and floor people also spend time getting to know their clientele. As an example, a regular blackjack player, Don, goes back to the same casino because he likes the dealers and supervisors. When

Figure 14–1 Personal selling is a constant requirement of all employees in a service operation.

he walks in, everyone says "Hi Don!" He plays strictly by the same rules, and dealers who know his habits can often anticipate his actions. Don prides himself on the fact that the dealers know him and can almost play his hands for him, and sometimes they do because he is so predictable. So, getting to know the customer personally can be a very effective sales tool.

Casino hosts are employees who are hired to anticipate and expedite a high roller's needs. Typically, they organize special, individual comps. Sometimes they can make the first move in a push strategy by inviting a high roller to celebrate an event, such as a birthday or anniversary at the casino. At other times, a high roller may call the host to have a party arranged for him or her in a pull strategy. Hosts arrange suites and/or reservations for dining. They can make sure a favorite wine or food is readily available in the room. For example, in Atlantic City there was once a high roller who was so captivated by Batman that he demanded that the hotel recreate the bat cave for his room. Because he was such a good customer with an extremely high credit limit, it complied. Some casino hosts become so close to the high rollers that they become very good friends and are invited on trips unrelated to the casino property.

Group Sales

Group sales refer to selling to an individual or small group of people who represent a larger association. It is personal selling in that the salesperson is promoting the casino to an individual. However, there are different decision-making processes that occur with a group. Mainly, the individual does not make the purchase decision but rather gathers information to pass on to the larger group that makes a consensus decision. This makes the process for influencing the purchase harder because there are so many people in the decision process. Destinations may offer a "fam" or familiarization trip to a small group of influencers. Fam trips are invitations to stay and eat for free for specific dates. This allows the decision makers time to see the facilities and attractions so that they can get first-hand information on the casino. This positive experience may help sway people to write a contract to bring their meeting or convention to the site.

The casino industry has always relied on gamblers for its business. In the past, the gaming industry created themes for people to fantasize about their dreams. These fantasy themes, such as pirate's treasures or Egyptian pyramids filled with gold, elicited images that included top-notch entertainment, inexpensive buffet meals, comp rooms, and people who gamble all night while sleeping all day. This is entirely different from the habits of convention/meeting attendees. The attendees are in meetings all day, want a nice dinner, and are not particularly price conscious about rooms. Therefore, one would expect the casino and convention industries to operate in totally different areas. This was the case until the mid-1990s.

Casino destinations were attractive to meeting planners because there were a large number of rooms, name entertainers, and things to do while meetings were not in session. Historically, however, casino operators did not want the meeting/convention traveler because of the widely held belief that a casino could be successful only if it derived all its revenue from the casino floor. Given the tradition of giving comps to patrons, the operators rationalized that they did not want patrons who gambled little and spent their days in meetings rather than on the casino floor. Everything the casino did was based on the perception that visitors must be involved in gambling for most of their visit. "I have actually been told in so many words, 'We don't need your business'; says Debbie Hubler, National Cattlemen's Beef Association."[1]

In the early 1990s, Las Vegas and Atlantic City were joined by riverboats and Native American casinos. Competition increased. As marketers looked for new gambling segments to tap, innovators found meetings and conventions. They realized that these attendees had larger pocketbooks and were not as sensitive to rates as were leisure travelers. Thus, casino hotels could charge attendees a higher room rate and counteract the lower gaming activities with their higher spending on food and beverage, entertainment, and shopping. Unlike the leisure gambler, conventions/meeting attendees would spend money on full-priced food and beverage. The convention/meeting sponsor would pay for banquets, receptions, coffee breaks, and more. And, the exhibitors at trade shows would spend huge amounts entertaining attendees/clients at hospitality suites, elaborate dinners, and receptions. The average convention delegate spends $968 in the community during the convention, while convention sponsors spend an additional $73 per delegate for a total of $1,041.[2] The casino corporations determined that conventions/meetings could generate more, in the aggregate, than the average gambler.

In addition, conventions/meetings are a good source of business for casinos because they complement, not compete with, the leisure gambler. Gamblers prefer to frequent casinos on weekends, holidays, and summer periods, just like most leisure travelers. By contrast, conventions/meetings rarely start their program before Monday and prefer to finish activities by Thursday so their attendees can be at home with families on the weekends. The same holds true for holidays and summers: most groups do not meet then. As a result, conventions/meetings fit nicely with the ebb and flow of casino clientele. As a result, the casino industry is embracing the convention industry and constructing facilities to meet the needs of the convention and meetings attendee.

In contrast to personal sales, the other three promotional techniques communicate to large numbers of people at the same time.

Sales Promotion

The **sales promotion** is a reminder designed to quickly get the casino's name out to groups of people. This short-term strategy can draw traffic into the casino for a specified period of time and reminds people about the casino. There are several objectives for a sales promotion. Some promotions, such as drink, entertainment, or food discounts, are used to create immediate foot traffic in the casino. Once the people are in the casino, other promotions such as hourly drawings and double jackpot payoffs are designed to get a gambler to stay longer. To get patrons to play table games, promotions can include bonus pay on certain blackjack hands or coupons that can be used in place of cash on table bets. To get customers to play the machines, free pulls or prizes tend to dominate the market. However, sales promotions can be used for other attractions as well. At the Mills Casino Hotel in North Bend, Oregon, management imprinted an original Native American artwork by Peggy O'Neal on the front of the hotel room key cards.[3] On the back was the message "Original prints are available in the General Store." This promotion encouraged guests to stop at the store to buy Native American goods.

A classic example of a sales promotion is the bus programs that were created by Atlantic City to encourage the millions of potential guests along the densely populated

Figure 14–2 At the annual G2E—Global Gaming Expo, T-shirts and small reminder items are given away to remind attendees about the company.
Photo courtesy of George G. Fenich.

Northeast Corridor to take a chance on the casinos. The programs were designed to be affordable to help people get to the casino without driving a long distance. They were designed as social events with food, beverages, and entertainment to keep the people happy. When they got off the bus, they typically received a comped buffet and some tokens. When they got tired, it was time to get back on the bus and rest on the return trip. In the beginning, the casinos gave $20 in tokens to each bus passenger, and as a rule, patrons spent the $20 plus another $60 of their own money. This made the bus promotion worthwhile for the casino. However, as competition for bus passengers increased, the offers became more expensive, and some casinos almost went bankrupt because they spent more than they earned.

Another big sales promotion is the tournament. A tournament can introduce inexperienced gamblers to the fun and excitement of the games and give them the opportunity to meet new people. A tournament also generates additional gaming revenue and creates positive publicity for the casino. Finally, it expands the number of new members in the casino's player database.

For people who spend a lot of money at the casino, there are very special promotions. In 1961 a casino stockholder flew some wealthy friends from Florida to Las Vegas and the casino hotel paid for everything. While they stayed at the hotel, the casino recorded its biggest drop during their gambling spree. As a result, the casino began to experiment with this type of promotion, now called a **junket**. By 1970, most Strip hotels had adopted junkets as a viable form of sales promotion. Junkets are completely comped, invited trips that are linked to special events such as boxing matches, PGA golf tournaments, or other high-profile events. While everything is paid for by the casino, it is expected that the gamblers will, in turn, spend equal amounts of time in the casino gambling.

Another promotion, at the Sands Regency Hotel Casino in Reno allowed guests to swipe their player's cards daily in order to receive a guaranteed daily prize.[4] Also, the swipes allowed them to accumulate game pieces toward a big cash price. Further, they gave the guests a chance at an instant $1 million prize and an invitation to the end of the month "Joker Poker" guest party. The objective of the promotion was to encourage casino customers to come in more often, stay longer, and feel as if they obtained value while spending money. The 3,000 swipes a day at the guest kiosk, along with a double-digit increase in coin-in levels indicated that the promotion achieved its goals. These short-term strategies for generating quick responses can be very lucrative sales promotions.

Public Relations or Publicity

Public relations (PR) are promotional techniques that attempt to inform people of activities or create perceptions without controlling the message or media. The goals of a publicity campaign can be to highlight individual properties, create images for owners/operators, emphasize possible locations, or remind people about products or services. These can be in the form of press releases announcing new games, jackpot winners, or changes in leadership—anything that goes through the media. Some announcements are simply faxes sent to media; others are announced at a press conference; and still others are accentuated with food, drink, and important dignitaries present. However, although the message is freely given to the media, the press can write anything it wants about the event, or nothing at all. For example, an announcement of a new poker room can be written as a front-page story for a local casino newspaper, a page 10 story in a daily newspaper, or not at all for the radio or television depending on the news editor's viewpoint.

An example of a special publicity campaign is Las Vegas' 1946 "Hometown Art" campaign. The town publicist directed photographers to take pictures of attractive couples and families visiting the various resorts, especially when they were outdoors enjoying the sun and recreational activities. These photographs, along with short stories about the tourists and Las Vegas, were sent to the society editors of the tourists' hometown newspapers. This gave Las Vegas a positive reception in the local papers and created a more personal image. In another interesting publicity effort, the Sahara in the 1950s and 1960s created a professional journal for American barbers that was placed in barbershop magazine racks throughout the country. Along the same lines, the Sahara also created a national magazine for bellhops, which featured the winner of the magazine's bellman of the year contest. The Sahara estimated that 20 percent of the new customers who registered at the hotel were referred by bellhops in other cities.

Figure 14–3 Trade shows with beautiful women and cartoon characters attracting clients are a long-standing tradition for publicity. Photo courtesy of George G. Fenich.

According to Barreca and Callahan,

> [The] best way to understand the value of your media coverage is to track it over time. Monitor the tone of the coverage, check whether your key messages are being communicated, evaluate the share compared to your competitors and plot this information in tandem with other variables like business levels or coin-in. You will begin to see trends that your PR department's work with local food critic resulted in covers in your restaurants. Or you may see how a string of negative editorials about the odds occurred in tandem with a drop in your coin-in. There's also value in the stories that don't run.[5]

Understanding these relationships can help evaluate where to spend the PR budget. For example, if you notice that increased revenue runs parallel to media exposure, then you could decide media relations need attention. Public relations efforts must be carefully planned, controlled, and analyzed for results. It is easy to spend money on ineffective campaigns if you do not track their effects.

Advertising

Advertising is a controlled process. The casino creates the message and expects the media to communicate it exactly. The casino also pays for the timing and placement of the message. In this way, the public sees, hears, feels, touches, and smells exactly what the casino wants it to.

The Three Objectives of Advertising

There are three major objectives to choose for an advertisement: to inform, persuade, or remind. Do you want to tell people about a *new offer* or *product*? Or do you want to inform *new people* about your products? For example, when tourists arrive in Las Vegas, they usually have a place to stay. However, they may not know what their entertainment options are or where they want to eat. Therefore, the billboards between the airport and the Strip are filled with dining and entertainment attractions[6] to inform visitors.

Perhaps visitors already know about the casino, so now you need to persuade them to come again or come more often. After examining headlines to attract clients to a casino, John Romero named the worst persuasive advertising lines in casino marketing.[7] See if you agree with his analysis.

1. *Call your host for details.* Romero claims that this is a lazy tactic. Hosts should be phoning clients, not the other way around.
2. *Management reserves rights to . . .* Guests already know that you are trying to weasel out of any bad things that can happen during the offer and absolve themselves of all blame.
3. *Unique.* Casinos claim all manner of things are unique, including the décor, the buildings, even the service. "Show me a hotel where the guests sleep outside and I'll show you a unique hotel."

4. *Player development executive.*

> You've just become a rated player at a big casino and one day you get a letter from someone who identifies herself as a player development executive. You giggle at first thinking "Oh, gosh they sent me an internal memo by mistake." There it is in black and white, they want to "develop" you. But you don't want to be "developed," it sounds like a plot to get the rest of your money.

5. *This offer is nontransferable.*

> Did I miss something? Was there a big scandal with customers rushing out to find friends to take their places? I doubt it. My guess is that some casino slipped this line into an invitation 35–40 years ago and because it sounds so logical, the others fell in line. In December, some joints would welcome anybody.

6. *This card is the property of the ABC Casino and must be returned on request.* Did you ever hear of any casino, anywhere asking a slot club member to return his card?

7. *"Relax and unwind."*

> Nobody goes to a casino to relax. Relax is what you do when you get home after a brutal day at the office, when you go to a casino you want to raise hell, see shows, and win a bundle. Any attempt by casinos to make customers behave otherwise is—let's be kind—misguided.

So what do you think? Do you agree with Romero's commentary or do you have different ideas?

The third objective of advertising is to remind people that the casino is still at the same location and they should return for a visit because they have not for a while. Casinos that cater to the local crowd carefully place billboards along the travel routes of their known players (Figure 14–4). They use billboards to announce local promotions and to keep event-oriented messages at the front of the players' minds while keeping the casino's name awareness. Billboards or outdoor advertising is usually the last form of advertising cut from the budget. Because market-penetration strategies are less expensive

Figure 14–4 Billboards are great ways to remind people about activities going on at the casinos.

and can be innovative, especially with new technologies of lights, movement, and videos, they are easy to implement.

Aspects of Creating Advertising

When creating advertisements, consider *attention*, *interest*, *desire*, and *action*—**AIDA**. An advertisement should gain a client's attention. Once you have gained a person's attention, the best way to provide the information is **KISS** (keep it simple, stupid), so that it can effectively pique interest in the product. Typically, you have only five seconds before people move on through the newspaper or magazine. In that time, you have to let them know what your product is and why they should buy it. Therefore, making the message as simple as possible is important in getting the message across. If you have targeted the audience correctly, knowledge about the product should create a desire to take an action. This action can be, for example, picking up the phone and calling or buying the product.

The final decision is which media to use for the advertisement. Part of this decision is to understand reach and frequency. **Reach** refers to how many people actually use the medium. For example, how many people listen to WWOZ radio at 8:00 in the morning on their way to work, or watch Channel 2 on television on Tuesday at 6:00 in the morning? In the 1950s and 1960s, an advertiser could use two TV stations in a market and reach everybody in that market. Then there were three stations per market. Now cable and satellite stations have emerged, and there may be at least 60 stations and hundreds of channels in a market. This division of channel reach and the increased quality of lesser known channels has resulted in the need for careful selection of stations and a true understanding of the target market. The same trend has occurred in radio. Most major markets used to have only a handful of radio stations; the average city today has 38 radio stations that most people hear only when they are driving. No advertiser can realistically afford to use 38 radio stations.

In addition, **frequency** refers to how often people do something. For example, one of the positive aspects of a billboard is that many people probably drive past the same billboard every day to work or school and back again. In the 1960s and 1970s, Northern Nevada casinos depended primarily on automobile traffic. Therefore, Harrah's created a highly successful billboard campaign by buying highway billboard space in a 500-mile radius leading into Reno and Lake Tahoe. As a rule, people need about five to six exposures before they truly begin to be aware of an ad. Therefore, a billboard is an attractive option because it has great frequency and repetition. Selecting the target audience and determining what it is doing at a particular time of day can also determine what media will be most successful in getting the message out.

On the other hand, with a website, it may be easier evaluate responses by asking people to sign in to measure reach and frequency. As Lou Ragg, MGM Grand senior manager for Internet operations notes, MGM staff members update information on the site easily and quickly: "Consumers don't want to go to a site that has the same information that was on it a month or six months ago. We are changing it daily. You can always go to the MGM website and see something fresh, something new."[8] Glen Christenson, executive vice president and chief financial officer for Station Casinos, says that his company caters to local residents. Since most of these residents are computer literate, the firm has found that the website is a quick, easy, and effective way to communicate with them. In addition, Station Casinos send out emails to inform regulars about upcoming events and invite them to those events.[9] Using email is a relatively inexpensive method of advertising. David Norton, Harrah's vice president of Loyalty Marketing, agrees that the Internet is a new channel that can be fun. However, the best aspect of a website is its self-service functionality. For example, whenever someone wants to know about Harrah's, he or she can instantly check out the website at a convenient time.[10]

However, creating and developing advertisements is a relatively new issue for the gaming industry. On June 25, 1948, the federal government enacted 18 USC 1304, which strictly forbade any radio or television station from broadcasting any information concerning gambling or gaming. Therefore, casinos could advertise their food or hotels, but there could be no mention of people playing cards, dice, or slot machines. In fact, in 1984, the Casino Control Commission added additional constraints that made the federal laws even stronger. Product offerings had to be generic in nature, which made competing against another casino virtually impossible. Therefore, the advertising strategies kept the tone and style of the advertisements geared toward entertainment. Casino advertisements were filled with elegant men, pretty women in scant outfits, lots of lights, and lots of glamour.

Finally, in 1999, the Greater New Orleans Broadcasting Association challenged the ruling, and on June 14, 1999, the regulation was declared unconstitutional. Now casinos can show their true creativity by developing advertising campaigns like any other business. However according to David Van Kalsbeek, MGM Grand senior vice president of Sales/Marketing, that isn't as easy as it sounds:

> Think about driving down the Strip: you've got your cab tops, your wrapped bus, your TV and magazine inside the cab. You're passing billboards, neon messages, and LCD displays with 30-second live video. Which one are you going to pick out? If you are looking at your ad agency to tell you what and how to communicate with your customers, you've got a big problem. What today's casino marketer is up against are not restraints of legality but the limits of creativity.[11]

There are many aspects of advertising to consider. It is an expensive project, so it is important to know your target so that you can create the right message with the right media at the right time.

Direct Marketing

The traditional four types of promotions have begun to merge. Combinations of these promotions offer better, more effective options to reach the customers. **Direct marketing** develops interactive communications with the casino's best customers. It begins by building and maintaining a collection of personal information about players who enter the casino, as well as potential players.

Direct response advertising asks a reader, viewer, or listener to provide feedback directly to the casino. For example, a casino might immediately send new players a guest satisfaction survey when they return home. In this fashion, the casino can discern a player's likes and dislikes about the casino experience. It is then possible to change the negative aspects of the casino and enhance the positive ones. Furthermore, offering a free gift or a chance to win a lottery for returning the survey enhances the chance for additional encounters with the gambler and obtains valuable information for the casino. Sometimes, telemarketing can be used to sell or prospect a potential guest by telephone, to answer specific phone inquiries, or to provide sales-related services. If a guest has requested information, a telephone call is a nice personal touch. However, many people feel trapped by sales calls on the phone, especially when they disrupt meals or quiet times.

Direct mail allows an inexpensive bulk mailing to be sent to a target audience and possibly increase traffic in the casino. There are three elements to a direct mail campaign: the database, the offer, and the packaging. It has been suggested that 60 percent of the success of a direct mail piece is the quality of the database and the selection of criteria to target the appropriate audience. Obviously the offer is important, but it needs to be matched to the specific interests of the targeted person. For example, if I am a vegetarian, I am not going to be interested in a dinner for two at the steakhouse. Finally, it may be surprising to learn that the packaging or the appearance of the mailer is important. How do you pique someone's curiosity enough to even open the envelope and read the offer rather than immediately throwing it in the trashcan?

Along with direct mail and direct response is the less expensive communication strategy of Internet ads and email. However, according to Romero,

The latest online surveys show that Internet ads and email have grown steadily less effective in the past 3 years (1999–2002). In the beginning of large volume casino direct mail (mid-1980s), customers were delighted to receive a personal letter from a casino general manager. Response exceeded expectations. But as a flood of casino mail came crashing across America, delight and curiosity waned. Casinos learned the medium was definitely not the message. Now the same thing is happening online. The clock-through rates for email, even those messages sent to prospects and customers, who opt in has plummeted from 5.4 percent in 1999 to a current 1.8 percent ... the reason for the downtrend is no secret. Privacy advocates have blunted what little existed online so advertisers try to reach everyone. ... The Wall Street Journal forecasts 430 billion email advertisements this year and 960 billion by 2006... Once your customers and prospects group you in with the spammers, it's over.[12]

To cut through some of this advertising clutter, here are some pointers that have worked:

- Pretest the offer using a sample clientele from the database paired with a particular package before sending it to everyone. Using a small sample first allows you to see whether the offer is interesting before spending money on a full-blown campaign.
- AIDA. Remember the acronym from earlier? First you need to attract people's attention so that you can gain their interest and fan their desire so they will take action. To do this, casinos should
  - Gain potential customers' attention by asking a provocative question.
  - Keep potential customers' interest by using letters to create the personal touch. Letters seem to be more effective than postcards.
  - Keep the rules of etiquette by using words such as *please* and *thank you*.
  - Use phrases such as "There is no obligation" or "no salesperson will call." They are stress relievers.
  - Emphasize the benefits of the offer, not the features. What will it do for them? This will fan their desire.

- Close the sale with a "limited time" or a deadline. People tend to procrastinate. Even if it is a good offer and they like it, the envelope might sit on their desk for "when they get to it." Time limits create a sense of urgency to take action.

Direct marketing campaigns rely on using a good database and segmenting the population of gamblers into smaller units that have some aspect in common. These commonalities could be something simple such as having the same birthday or anniversary. However, it is easy to get lazy and do the same thing for everyone. All casinos offer free food and hotel rooms. A possible conversation might point out the problems. Two couples were sitting at a table in the casino; obviously they had just driven over together. "What offers do you have?" says Joe. "I have a free room at Casino A but it's not a suite so we all can't stay for free," says Sally. "That's okay," replies Tony, "I have an offer for a suite at Casino B." "Ok. So it's settled where to stay. Now where can we eat?" Offers are easily duplicated by competitors, so players can be inundated with a number of offers. In this case, we have trained the players' club members to be careful shoppers. They have learned that by pooling their resources, they can stay, eat, and be entertained for almost nothing. However, what is the point of the players' club? It is to build brand loyalty, but here it is clear that the exact opposite has occurred. We have trained the players to go for the best offer rather than to be loyal to the brand.

Personalizing the offers is critical, especially with gamblers who spend a lot of time and money at the casino. An old saying in research is, "If you want to know what your guests are thinking … ask them." Because these guests come often, an offer for another buffet may not be attractive. In fact, one regular customer said that the standard offers were offensive. In effect, he felt that the casino was sending a message that it did not care enough about him and his money to personalize the offer. He said that he knows all the dealers and floor people at the casino and talks to them on a regular basis. Therefore he suggested, "Why can't the floor person simply ask me what I want?"

Another regular guest on the Gulf Coast said he is not interested in the food or hotel offers since he lives a half hour away. So, when asked, "Is there something we can do for you?" he replied, "Yes. Occasionally I have some friends who want to get together, socialize and gamble. So it would be great if on those occasions, I could call up my host and ask for comps for my friends." This gives you more guests in your database, more people gambling at your tables… sounds like a winner!

As with any communication, designing the message, selecting the appropriate media, and paying attention to details are important. Keep in mind that the best sales are done face to face when tone, facial expression, body language, and words can all be used to evaluate the client's responses and quickly react to any negatives. All the senses can be brought to bear to evaluate the response so that the message can be instantly tailored to persuade specific buyers. Phone calls keep the tone and words, but the nonverbal communication is gone. This means you can't see someone frown at your words or roll his or her eyes. Some research suggests that more than 70 percent of communication is found in the nonverbal gestures. Finally, email messages are only words with nothing else to back up the meaning. This makes it easy to misinterpret them. Therefore, it is important to clearly state your message. There is no room for subtleties or sarcasm. Clearly state your needs, including when you need a response. For example, many people tend to abbreviate their email messages into alphabet soup, "What R U up 2?" In an advertisement or sales pitch, when the sender does not use proper grammar, capitalization, and punctuations, he or she looks sloppy, unorganized, and even irresponsible. So, for a coherent, clear promotional message, you need to spell out the information so that everyone can understand. When you reply, answer all the questions and preempt additional questions. Take a moment to organize your thoughts and think before sending an email.

Summary

In celebration of Customer Service Month, Gold Dust West, a local Reno casino, combined all the different marketing media into a success IMP.[13] It began with a direct mail piece introducing locals to Customer Service Month and offered free dessert during the month. Club members could double their cash back points on specific days of the month, which would become all month if they filled out the guest survey attached to the direct mail offering and returned it to the casino. In addition, they could enter the "Worth a Million" drawings by voting for their favorite employees for 10,000 cash points toward the drawings each time they entered. To reinforce the Customer Service Month theme, advertisements in the newspaper and TV showed real employees with the slogan, "Service. How the West was won" and "You're still the one." To involve the public more, anonymous customers were selected to look for the 40 best employees to be honored with cash awards in a public recognition ceremony. Finally, a direct mail piece thanked everyone for participating and invited customers to donate food for the local food drive to receive an entry for the biggest Christmas Stocking giveaway.

When a holistic campaign is created that integrates all the different media, it reinforces the messages into a whole that is greater than the sum of its parts. When the four types of promotions are integrated into one strategy, the effects can be spectacular. Integrated marketing communications is a way to think about the project as a whole and then to decide which promotion or combination of promotional ideas is the most effective.

key terms

Advertising
AIDA
Casino host
Direct marketing
Integrated marketing communications
    (IMC)
Junket
KISS

Promotions
Public Relations
Pull Strategies
Push Strategies
Reach
Frequency
Sales promotion

review questions

1. List the four major promotional techniques.
2. When using the IMC strategy, what are some factors that determine which promotional elements to use and when they should be used?
3. Which promotion is the most effective with a well-trained staff but also the most expensive and labor intensive? Support your answer.

4. Which three promotional techniques communicate to large numbers of people at the same time?

5. What are the three major objectives in preparing an advertisement?

6. In a direct mail piece, which methods can be used to pique someone's curiosity enough to open the envelope and to read the offer?

internet sites

Integrated marketing communications (IMC)
    http://www.entarga.com/mktgplan/imc.htm

The Direct Marketing Association
    http://www.the-dma.org/

Public relations for Casinos
    http://www.casinocitytimes.com/news/article.cfm?contentID=153481

Synergistic strategy and online casinos
    http://www.cardplayer.com/poker_magazine/archives/?a_id=14333

Push and pull marketing strategies
    http://www.tutor2u.net/business/marketing/promotion_pushpull.asp

endnotes

1. Finney, M. I. (1997). High stakes relationships: Casinos and conventions. *Association Management*, 49(3), 64–66.
2. Hanson, B. (2002 November). Slow to recover, with meetings a priority market. *Convene*, 19–40.
3. Conrad, D. (2005). The good, the bad, and the unique. *Casino Journal*, 18(8), 19–24.
4. Shemeligian, B. (2003). Getting the word out: Tribes respond to media attacks with new PR campaign. *Casino Journal*, 16(4), 32–35.
5. Barreca, M., and Callahan, K. (2006). Communicating effectively. *Casino Journal*, 19(7), 35–36.
6. Plume, J. (2002). The writing on the wall. *Casino Journal*, 15(6), 30–31.
7. Romero, J. (2002). Dirty dozen of marketing lines. *IGWB* 23(6), 40.
8. Green, M. (2000). Finally wired. *IGWB*, 21(8), 38.
9. Ibid.
10. Ibid.
11. McKee, D. (2002). Broadened appeal. *Casino Journal*, 15(7), 29.
12. Romero, J. (2002). To sell online, get back to basics. *IGWB*, 23(9), 79–80.
13. Conrad, D. (2004). A near-perfect casino promotion. *Casino Journal*, 17(5), 38.

Vignette

An Early Harrah's Advertising Campaign: Harrah's Entertainment Treasure Hunt Promotion

Tracy Locke, Advertising

Overview

Founded in 1938, Harrah's Entertainment, Inc (HET), owns or manages through various subsidiaries 23 properties in 13 states and is the only national gaming brand. Harrah's Entertainment is focused on building loyalty and value with its target customers through a unique combination of great service, excellent products, unsurpassed distribution, operational excellence, and technology leadership. Harrah's Entertainment is the most recognized and respected name in the casino industry.

Harrah's brand essence is exuberantly alive. Harrah's focuses advertisements and promotions on the gaming experience: the adrenaline rush, potential to hit it big, and entertainment value. Harrah's "Oh Yeah!" experiential positioning focuses on those feelings of gaming versus a competitor focus on property amenities. In an environment in which consumers can literally walk next door to a competitor, differentiation is necessary. Harrah's uses large-scale national promotions to set it apart from the competition.

The competitive landscape for Harrah's properties includes Ameristar Casinos (in Kansas City and Council Bluffs), Caesar's Entertainment (Reno, Atlantic City, Las Vegas, and Tunica), and heavyweights such MGM Mirage Mandalay Resort Group (in Las Vegas). Each competitor's market share varies by local markets.

Harrah's properties execute several local, property-specific promotions a year. The opportunity was to create the largest (HET) national brand promotion that all properties could support. Since each of Harrah's markets has different needs, based on location, consumer traffic, budgets, and so on Treasure Hunt 2004 (Figure 14–5) needed to be totally customizable for each market, while enticing new customers and rewarding loyal gamers, as well.

To capitalize on the Harrah's customer mindset, three insights were identified that helped bring Treasure Hunt 2004 to fruition. The element of adventure is

Figure 14–5 Poster for the Harrah's Treasure Hunt Campaign

inherent in the risk-taking mindset of a gamer. The search for hidden treasure has always been a compelling consumer storyline, and gamers have high interest and propensity for travel. With these insights in mind, Treasure Hunt 2004 was born.

Promotion Objectives

- Generate at least $13 million in revenue
- Include 135,000 promotional participants
- Acquire 15,000 new customers

Promotion Description

The promotional time period for Treasure Hunt 2004 was March 1–May 6. The budget totaled $5.4 million. Consumer prizes included $1 million buried in the Las Vegas desert, trips for finalists to Las Vegas, and cash and prizes both online and at local Harrah's properties. The promotion was supported by TV, Radio, Print, Direct Mail, Internet, email blasts, Outdoor, point of purchase (POP), and PR.

Concept

Win a Million in the Mojave! Get to Harrah's today and pick-up an official gold coin game piece for two ways to win—instantly or match-n-win. You could win cash, prizes or a spot in the exclusive $1 million Treasure Hunt in Las Vegas on May 6th. In the Las Vegas desert, all finalists will receive maps that will lead them to hidden treasure chests—including the $1 million treasure. But you must have a Total Rewards card to play—sign-up during the promotional period to receive your first gold coin and an official Treasure Hunter Kit to get in on the action. Only at Harrah's!

Methods for Winning

The Treasure Hunt Promotion had several ways to win: gold coin game piece, online promotion, and property drawings. The gold coin game piece had two components, collect and win and instant win. When consumers signed up for the Harrah's loyalty program, Total Rewards, they received a game piece. The more the consumers played, they could earn additional "lucky coins." If their game piece number was called out in weekly property drawings, they won cash and prizes. Via match and win, consumers could also save their gold coins for a chance at the property-level grand prize, a trip to Las Vegas, for the culminating event. The second component of the game piece was instant win. The game piece had a perforated tear-off section that awarded cash and prizes instantly.

The second way to win was online at Harrahs.com. On the Harrah's website was a link to the Treasure Hunt promotional page, where consumers could play four different Treasure Hunt–themed custom games. The four games were "Dig It!" "Search for Treasure!" "Unlock the Chest," and "Desert Illusion!" Each online game ran for two weeks during the eight-week promotion. A grand prize was awarded from online for the culminating event.

Customers had the chance at winning their share of millions in cash and prizes through property-specific drawings and events as well.

Las Vegas Treasure Hunt

All of the events and drawings culminated in the search for $1 million in the Mojave Desert. Four participants from each property (plus one guest) won an all-expense paid trip to Las Vegas to search for $1 million. One winner from the instant-win method and two winners from the grand prize drawing method were chosen at each property.

Throughout the Treasure Hunt weekend, finalists were treated to several special events. There was a welcome reception with hors d'oeuvres and cocktails, live bingo, a magician, and photo opportunities with the Treasure Hunt Girls.

Tears came to the eyes of the winner as she opened a scroll revealing she had won the $1 million grand prize.

"I kept telling my husband, 'you never know' and then I saw a one and all those zeros after it and I couldn't believe it. I just couldn't believe it."

Performance Results

Harrah's accomplished all national objectives:

- GGR (gross gaming revenue) was $19,589,039.
- There were more than 300,000 promotion participants
- A total of 29,390 new customers exceeded acquisition goal by 100 percent.

Conclusion

The Treasure Hunt promotion was the largest promotion in Harrah's history. Customers, new and old, enjoyed the promotion mechanisms and events. Harrah's continues to be upheld as the premier name in gaming.

Figure 14–6 Print Advertisement for the Harrah's Treasure Hunt Campaign

5
Future

Chapter 15
Future of Gaming

15 Future of Gaming

Chris Roberts, University of Massachusetts

Learning Objectives

1. To describe the changing cycles of gaming throughout history.

2. To identify and understand the conditions that have radically changed from the onset of gaming through contemporary times.

3. To provide an understanding of the social and economic conditions of the gaming industry that exist at the present time.

4. To explore the physical structure of casinos and the three ways it differs from the structure in the past.

5. To present an overview of the future of the gaming industry.

Chapter Outline

Introduction

The gaming industry is said to be in the third wave of its cyclical life. There are those who predict that this wave will end in the full prohibition of gambling by 2029. This chapter argues that this third wave will not end in full prohibition. Interest and participation in gaming may dissipate to low levels, but gaming will never completely disappear. There are simply too many jobs, dollars, and customers involved in the industry. Two key factors, the Internet and sports betting, will especially help to ensure that society retains legalized gaming as a permanent feature.

The Changing Cycles of Gaming in History

A broadly accepted maxim is that history repeats itself. I. Nelson Rose embraces this view in his article "The Rise and Fall of the Third Wave."[1] Rose theorizes that gaming has a cyclical life. Governments need money, so they look to gaming to supply it. As the popularity of gaming increases, the levels of addiction, crime, and other social problems also increase, until the population cries out for deregulation, and gaming is outlawed. Rose suggests that the 1990s were the middle period of the third wave of a 70-year gaming cycle in the United States. Rose and others forecast this third wave will end with a complete ban on legalized gaming by the year 2029.

However, there are many dramatic differences in the social and economic conditions of the late twentieth and early twenty-first centuries that suggest history will not repeat in this case. Key among these differences are the physical structures of the gaming facilities, the tendency for entire communities to support gaming, the large numbers of workers in the gaming industry, the immense sums of capital invested, the broad economic and public policy impact of gaming in terms of taxes and jobs, and the rise in popularity of Internet gaming and professional sports. These differences encompass significant aspects of contemporary life. Because of the integration of gaming into contemporary society as a whole, its removal is neither desired nor prudent. This chapter argues that the third 70-year cycle of gaming in America will not end in prohibition. Rather, the third wave will ebb and flow naturally along with other industries in the marketplace.

The Different Conditions

Gaming is pervasive throughout the country. Currently, 48 states allow some form of gaming (including state-operated lotteries), and 27 states permit some form of casino operations, which result in more than 445 commercial casino choices for gamblers. Gaming supporters claim that there is a casino within 300 miles of every American's residence. There has never been such popular support for gaming—the majority of the American population believes that gaming is a form of recreation, not the "evil incarnate" of the past, and they do visit the casinos.

There are at least six different social and economic conditions today that suggest that this current third wave of gaming popularity in the United States will not end with a significant decline in gaming levels. These conditions are the physical structures, the human resources, the types of capital investment and ownership, the economic impact of gaming, the rise of the Internet and professional sports betting, and the nature of contemporary culture. Many of these conditions are significant for issues of size or volume or for their high degree of acceptance and integration into daily lifestyles.

Figure 15–1 Luxor Las Vegas.
Photo courtesy of George G. Fenich

Physical Structures

The present physical conditions of the gaming industry differ in three ways from those of the past. First, whole communities have developed around gaming enterprises. Second, the typical casino itself has grown from an intimate boutique into a very large hall. Finally, the casino has become integrated with several other industries in the delivery of the gaming product. Most commonly, these other products include hotels, restaurants, and retail shops.

A key difference between current patterns and those of the past is the emergence of entire communities revolving around, and in support of, gaming. Las Vegas, Reno, and Atlantic City in the United States and Macau in China are well-known examples of entire cities devoted primarily to the casino industry. Tupelo, Mississippi, and Deadwood, South Dakota, as well as many other Nevada towns are smaller less well-known examples. These cities were languishing with high unemployment rates and no new job prospects. Gaming provided the economic basis for these cities to grow and prosper. The casinos became the reason for tourists to flock to these cities and spend money on hotels, restaurants, and tourist attractions. These communities have come to depend on the casinos for their livelihoods.

Anyone who has visited Las Vegas recently can easily attest to the emergence of the casino as a mega resort. The largest hotel in the world is the MGM Grand in Las Vegas. It is a mega casino with more than 5,000 hotel rooms. There are currently 25 mega casinos with more than 1,500 hotel rooms in Las Vegas.[2] These resorts dwarf the traditional resort hotels located in other areas. Another example of a large casino is Foxwoods, which is the largest casino in the world. Located in southeastern Connecticut, it has more than 7,400 slot machines and 338 table games and employs more than 11,000 people. Seven miles away is the Mohegan Sun casino, which is just slightly smaller than Foxwoods, having "only" 6,200 slot machines and extensive meeting and convention facilities. These vast operations are quite a bit larger than most other businesses and are about the size of local shopping malls. Their size is important to drawing people to the site and making them want to stay for more than a day. This requires better infrastructure, and more local businesses and communities are benefiting from these improved operations.

While not all casinos are mega resorts, most are large facilities designed to offer a wide array of simultaneous gaming opportunities. Many nonhotel casinos in Las Vegas boast of having 200, 400, and 500 slot machines.[3] Riverboat casinos often accommodate hundreds of customers. Smaller, boutique-style casinos are often found where gaming is restricted to older buildings. As an example, in Colorado old mining towns such as Cripple Creek, Black Hawk, and Central City have small boutique casinos located in buildings dating from the beginning of the twentieth century.[4]

However, the modern casino typically offers more than just slots and table games. Today, many casinos offer a variety of food and beverage services, hotel rooms, entertainment, meetings and convention space, and retail shops. The mega casinos often offer eight or more different restaurants within the same property. At the extreme end of the scale is Foxwoods with 25 distinct restaurants, and Mohegan Sun with 29 food outlets. These amenities typically are used as loss leaders to draw guests to the casino. However, now casinos realize that as long as people spend money, it does not matter which venue draws them. So, entertainment, shopping, and meetings/convention spaces have become profit centers and have expanded to attract guests on their own. These services have become fused into one broad recreation concept in the mind of the gaming customer.

Human Resources

Casinos today employ hundreds, if not thousands, of workers at each facility. As is typical of a service industry, the labor component is a significant portion of the total operation. A 1996 assessment of the impact of casinos found that U.S. casinos employed more than 284,000 people.[5] By 2004, that number had increased to more than 350,000 people.[6] As gaming facilities expand to include more and more recreation opportunities for people, these numbers should continue to increase, giving more locals a chance to have a job and improved opportunities to relax and have fun.

Jobs in casinos are also desirable. The Mirage Hotel and Casino (Las Vegas) spent two years analyzing the labor pool to determine if it would support the first mega casino. While it did determine that the local labor pool would be sufficient, the hotel was surprised at the volume of applicants. More than 57,000 people applied for the 5,300 new positions.[7] Mitchell Ettis, who was senior vice president for marketing at the time, reported that the Mohegan Sun Casino in Connecticut used a nearby football stadium to handle the crowd of applicants during its initial hiring phase.[8] This is in stark contrast to the small saloon casinos of the nineteenth century that might have employed fewer than thirty workers. In addition, today's managers and workers are generally honest, upstanding citizens, and not the stereotypical mobsters of yesteryear. Being an employee of a casino is like any other job in terms of respectability, and, as a result, casinos typically treat their employees very well with good pay scales and benefits.

Capital Investment and Ownership

The sums of capital committed to the gaming industry today are staggering for any industry. For example, the construction costs for the Bellagio were in excess of $1.3 billion, and the full costs for the 6,000-room Venetian have been estimated at over $2.3 billion. As a result, casinos bring in not only jobs, but major capital investments to the communities in which they exist. This results in more tax burden being placed on businesses rather than residents.

However, a sole entrepreneur typically cannot provide such sums of capital. As the industry has shifted from small, single-owner casinos to large, corporate organizations, casinos have become publicly held enterprises with their stock openly traded in the major exchanges. There are so many active gaming corporations that the investment

Figure 15–2 Existing exterior photo along with an artist rendering our expansion. About 400 new hotel rooms opened in May 2005. Thank you for your interest in the Isle of Capri Casino Resort in Biloxi. (February 2005) Courtesy of Isle of Capri Casino Resort.

community has created the GAX, a gaming index to track its relative performance. Now millions of people, rather than a few, are owners of casinos.

Publicly held ownership has resulted in professional, corporate management. Teams of specialized managers have replaced the casino manager as the sole decision maker with skills in marketing, human resources, finance, and so on. In large part, this trend of corporate ownership and more professional management has helped the industry transition from images of sin, sex, and the mafia to those of modern entertainment destinations that are safe, clean, and fun for individuals and families.

Economic Impact

The economic impact of the gaming industry is felt on both the local and national levels. In 1999, the industry had gross gaming revenues exceeding $20 billion. This revenue reflects more spending than on all other forms of entertainment combined (including theatre, movies, sports, and prerecorded music sales), and it continues to increase.[9] In 2004, gross gaming revenues had grown to $29 billion—a significant impact in just five years.[10] A recent study by International Gaming Technologies, the world's largest slot machine manufacturer, found that state and local areas have improved their overall economic situation after allowing casino gambling. For example, newspaper reports show that Foxwoods pays the state of Connecticut a percentage of its *monthly* slots revenue in the range of $50 to 60 million, which results in more than $500 million each year.[11] In 1994, New Jersey reported that the casino industry spent more than $1.4 billion buying goods and services within the state.[12] Indirect spending in related industries further increased these totals. This is called the **multiplier effect**. In the years since, spending has continued to increase.

In general, in the states allowing gaming, employment percentages have increased, and the additional tax dollars are being used for education and infrastructure enhancements.[13] The levels of employment are not easily dismissed. According to a 1996 Arthur Anderson study, there were more than 284,000 workers in the gaming industry, and for every $1 million in casino revenues, 13 direct jobs were created. As noted previously, that number had grown to more than 350,000 workers in 2004. The 2004 payroll and state taxes across the United States contributed about $12 billion in wages and $4.7 billion in direct gaming taxes, a 9 percent increase over 2003.[14] While some economic expectations have not been completely met (such as in Atlantic City and on some Native American reservations), the total economic impact of the gaming industry is significant and cannot easily be subtracted from the general economy.

The Rise of the Internet and Professional Sports Betting

Perhaps one of the most notable creations of the information age is the Internet. It has linked customers and sellers in ways unimaginable 15 years ago. Gambling is no exception; it can be easily found on this vast electronic medium. A quick search of the web results in access to more than 1,800 vibrant virtual casinos. Although gambling over the Internet is considered illegal in the United States, various government entities find themselves powerless to reasonably enforce the law—yet many continue to search for effective enforcement methods.[15] The reality is that on the Internet there are too many players, and even if a government could identify a player's computer terminal by the use of an electronic trace, it is difficult to prove who actually operated the terminal and conducted the gambling transaction. Therefore, it is unlikely that Internet gaming can be effectively controlled by national governments.

Figure 15–3 Jockeys drive toward the finish at Tampa Bay Downs, Florida.

Most providers of Internet gaming avoid U.S. legal concerns by basing their virtual casino operations in other nations, such as Antigua and Barbuda, that do support this industry. There are still other issues with Internet gambling, such as the method of collection of bets and the payment of winnings and the determination of the true identity and age of a bettor. However, given the worldwide use of the web, these issues are primarily market concerns and will be more successfully resolved in the marketplace rather than by legislation. This Internet gambling market segment alone is expected to grow to over $18 billion by 2010.[16] In any event, the presence of the virtual casino on the Internet has been established, is aggressively growing, and has become a viable alternative to physically visiting a land-based or riverboat casino.

This era has also seen the incredible rise in popularity of professional sports. Given the advancements in communication and entertainment (TV, cable, satellites, etc.), these professional sports are viewed on an almost continual basis. Accompanying this interest in professional sports is the rise of sports betting. Although Nevada is the only state to legalize sports betting in the U.S., the process of betting on sporting outcomes replicates itself daily in offices, car pools, and neighborhoods. Betting on sports has become a common feature of many people's lives. Daily newspaper sport sections regularly cite the odds of winning given to various competitions by well-known professional gamblers. Casinos outside of Nevada often provide areas for customers to contemplate sports bets even though the casino does not take the bet. The size of the underground economy in private (and illegal) sports betting is virtually incalculable. Therefore, sports betting has significantly increased the level of acceptance of gambling.

The Nature of Contemporary Culture

Certain activities move in and out of public favor. The consumption of alcohol, the uses of recreational drugs, and gambling are frequent targets of social concern. In the United States, the early twentieth century experienced a complete prohibition on gaming. Then, at the end of the same century, gaming was widespread and popular. Even state governments now offer lotteries and other games of chance. This message sent by government approval of gaming is not lost on its citizens. Citizens generally believe that gambling is socially acceptable as long as minors are reasonably protected from it. In addition to government approval, the widespread geographic availability of gambling strongly contributes to the high levels of the social acceptance of gaming.

The present social acceptance of gaming may certainly reverse itself just as it has done in previous times. What is different, though, is that the modern era has been transformed by the social upheavals of the late 1960s and the early 1970s. Perspectives have been dramatically altered and definitions of acceptable behavior have radically changed as the internationalism of commerce and society in general increases. Not only are large firms operating across borders with ease, even nations are forming strategic alliances to foster markets (for example, the European Union and NAFTA). Information flows quickly and in vast quantities over the airwaves and satellites. Goods and people move easily around the globe in a wide range of jet aircraft with little or no border restraints, such as customs and immigration services. As a result, people are more accepting of different ideas, beliefs, and values. More of the public says that even though gambling is not right for them, other people should be able to gamble. This is contrary to traditional opinions that said "If I believe that gambling is immoral, no one should be allowed to bet." Ideas of what is socially acceptable for everyone have broadened.

While this expansive attitude toward gambling has developed, it has also become increasingly difficult for governments to prohibit people from gambling. If a given jurisdiction bans gaming, it is very easy for customers to travel to another area that permits it. Examples of this abound within the United States. Massachusetts legislators estimate that $600 million to $1 billion leaves its state for the casinos in Connecticut every year.[17] Also, parking lots of Nevada casinos along the Utah/Nevada border are filled with cars with Utah license plates.

Finally, society's fear of gambling addiction is waning as our understanding of it develops, and the methods to treat it mature. Gaming addiction appears to occur among the general population at about the same 3 percent rate as does alcohol addiction. The 12-step programs used for alcohol addiction have also proved useful for gaming addictions. The prevalence of casinos does make gambling more readily available, and hence more accessible to addictive personalities. However, people who have addictive problems usually also have more than one addictive problem (for example, with gambling and drinking). Arguments for and against gaming continue today.[18] However, addictive personalities will find risky outlets for their behaviors whether or not casinos are nearby. In sum, society has made advances in its understanding of gaming addiction and views it as an important issue, but not one requiring a full prohibition. In addition, as casinos develop, they realize that gaming addiction also impacts their businesses. Therefore, they have adopted vital, progressive programs to work with employees and guests who have identified themselves as problem gamblers.

The Rise of Native American Gaming

Another contemporary condition affecting the third wave of gaming popularity is the rise of Native American gaming establishments. Native American gaming has become a mainstay of reservation life for many tribes—and for their non–Native American

Figure 15–4 Exterior picture of Kewadin Indian Casino, Sault Saint Marie, Michigan.

customers. Foxwoods, the largest casino in the world, is operated by and for the Mashantucket Pequot Tribe. Mohegan Sun, seven miles away and the second largest casino, is operated by Sun International for the Mohegan Indian Tribe. From California and Arizona to Florida and New England, many Native American tribes are offering a vast array of gaming options. These casinos have become important vehicles of economic development and employment for the tribal members. They have made possible the improvement of the quality of tribal life and the expansion of recreational and business opportunities for the surrounding regions. However, it should be noted that not all Native American tribes have casinos on the scale of Foxwoods and Mohegan Sun. Because reservations are quite often located far away from city centers, some casinos are small operations with small profits. Some have gone under. In addition, there are many reservations that do not have casinos and generally believe that gaming is immoral and/or inappropriate for their cultural beliefs.

Conclusion

This chapter identified at least six conditions that have radically changed from when gaming began until contemporary times: the physical structures of gaming, human resources, capital investment and ownership, the economic impact of gaming, the rise of the Internet and professional sports, and cultural attitudes in general. Many of these conditions are significant because of their size or volume or for their degree of acceptance and integration into the daily lifestyles of the average American. Because of these changes, it is possible that Rose and others who theorized that gaming always cycles into deregulation might want to revise their opinions. Casinos are taking the social problems seriously and are dealing with them by taking positive, aggressive action. The American public is becoming sensitive to the changes in their lives as gaming and the resultant expanded shopping, entertainment, and restaurants increase the recreational options available to them. Taxes of gaming enterprises are now a sizeable part of many government budgetary requirements, and, without it, these governments would find it hard to scale back their spending. All in all, America has adopted gaming and casinos, and it may be difficult to cut it out from our lives.

The Future Forecast

The future forecast for gaming is one of continued institutionalization. The gaming industry will suffer the usual ebb-and-flow cycles that all industries experience. The international dimension of modern commerce—especially the travel industry—will ensure a steady supply of customers. Further, governments have come to rely upon the tax revenues of lotteries and casinos as well as the increases in local employment. Rather than face the daunting prospect of lost revenues and unemployment, states will continue to support the casino industry. Any proposed gaming regulation will be crafted with care, as it will directly impact state coffers.

Undoubtedly, there will be some areas of withdrawal from the gaming industry. As scandals emerge, there will be a call for a reduction or distancing from gaming. State lotteries may be adjusted or eliminated, and casinos may be more tightly controlled. Riverboat casinos may be banned from certain ports or states. The concept of **NIMBY** (*not in my b*ackyard) will certainly continue as an argument against the industry.

However, with entire communities supporting gaming, it is unlikely there would ever be a complete withdrawal. Las Vegas, Reno, and Atlantic City have all developed other commerce to sustain themselves without the gaming industry. If there is any general reduction in gaming across the country, these specialized communities will continue to operate. Gaming may, at the very least, become a geographic niche service as it was from the 1930s through the 1970s.

Gambling in virtual casinos on the Internet will not disappear but instead will expand. Governments cannot completely control the operation or the content of the web. Therefore, gambling in virtual casinos will continue to be widely available regardless of any lack of land-based casinos and any government regulation.

In conclusion, the third wave of gambling will not end in full prohibition by 2029 or any future year. It may dissipate to low levels of interest and use by society, but it will never completely disappear. The levels of social acceptance may oscillate, but with softer peaks and valleys. There are simply too many jobs, dollars, international competitors, and customers involved.

In addition to the quantity impact, gaming products are too widely available in the electronic world. Moreover, sports betting will be a parallel part of professional sports as long as teams compete. These two key factors, the Internet and sports betting, will help ensure that society permanently retains legalized gaming.

key terms

Multiplier effect   NIMBY

review questions

1. What are the two key factors that will especially help to ensure that society retains legalized gaming?

2. List the key social and economic conditions today that suggest that the popularity of gaming in the United States will not end with a significant decline.

3. What are the three ways that the physical conditions of the gaming industry today differ from those in the past?

4. What is the largest hotel in the world? What is the largest casino in the world?

5. Although gambling over the Internet is illegal in the United States, why are government entities powerless to enforce the law?

6. What does the modern casino typically offer in addition to gambling?

7. Which two factors strongly contribute to the high levels of the social acceptance of gaming?

8. Who are the owners of the Foxwoods Casino?

internet sites

Mega resorts
    http://www.gamingobserver.com/news_pi.html

International gaming technologies
    http://www.igt.com/Home/default.asp?pid=1&bhcp=1

Indirect spending in casinos
    http://www.wisc.edu/urpl/people/marcouiller/projects/clearinghouse/Destination%20Tourism.htm

The economic impact of casino gambling in Louisiana
    http://www.business.uno.edu/dber/gambling1998/EconR.pdf

endnotes

1. Rose, I. N. (1996). The rise and fall of the third wave: Gambling will be outlawed in forty years. In *Casino Management for the 90's*, K. Hashimoto, S. F. Kline and G. Fenich (eds.). Dubuque, IA: Kendall Hunt, pp. 491–501.

2. Roberts, C., and Fladmoe-Lindquist, K. (2004). Hypercompetition and mega-casinos. Unpublished manuscript, University of Massachusetts, Department of Hotel, Restaurant and Travel Administration.

3. Lasvegas.com. (2005). Hotel-casino guide. http://lasvegas.com/travel/hotels.

4. Hashimoto, K. (1998). Cripple Creek, Colorado. In *Casino Management: Past·Present·Future*, K. Hashimoto, S. F. Kline, and G. Fenich (eds.). Dubuque, IA: Kendall Hunt, p. 11.

5. Arthur Anderson LLP. (1996). *Casino Gambling in America: The Economic Impacts*. Washington, DC: American Gaming Association.

6. Annual Survey Shows More American Visiting Casinos. American Gaming Association. http://www.americangaming.org (accessed in 11/16/2005).

7. Elder, R. W. (1990). Opening the Mirage: The human-resources challenge. *Cornell HRA Quarterly*, 31(2), 24–31.

8. Ettis, M. (1997). Personal comments given during a private casino tour to a student group at the Mohegan Sun Casino, Ledyard, CT.

9. Fetto, J. (2002, September). Off the map: The legal gambling industry grows in popularity. *American Demographics*, 2; Sylvester, K. (1992). Casinomania. In *Casino Management: Past·Present·Future*, K. Hashimoto, S. F. Kline, and G. Fenich (eds.). Dubuque, IA: Kendall Hunt, pp. 428–432.

10. Annual Survey Shows More American Visiting Casinos. American Gaming Association. http://www.americangaming.org (accessed in 11/16/2005).

11. Foxwoods pays $58 million in July. (1998, September 10). *Daily Hampshire Gazette*, p. B1.

12. Heneghan, D. (1994, March 20). Casinos generate more than $1b in state economy. Atlantic Free Press, p. A1.

13. Michael Evans Group. (1996). *A Study of the Economic Impact of the Gaming Industry Through 2005*. Reno: I.G.T.

14. Annual Survey Shows More American Visiting Casinos. American Gaming Association. http://www.americangaming.org (accessed in 11/16/2005).

15. Kay, J. (2004). Department of Justice defends crackdown on Internet gambling. *Miami Business Review*; Rose, I. N. Court Rules Internet Gambling Is Not Illegal. *Casino City Times*. http://rose.casinocitytimes.com/articles/963.html (accessed in 11/15/2005).

16. Associated Press. Internet Gambling: Global "Trade"?. *CBS News.com: SciTech*. http://www.cbsnews.com/stories/2004/11/03/tech/main653492.shtml (accessed in 11/15/2005.)

17. Reilly opposes casino gambling. (1999, March 17). Associated Press (Boston).

18. Ibid.

Glossary

Action problem gambler—A person who gambles to achieve a rush that ultimately proves problematic. This individual develops a destructive affinity for the excitement of the game and seeks a "high" from it. These individuals tend to be associated with action-oriented games such as craps or sports wagering.

Advantage player—An individual who has sophisticated skill levels that may reduce and sometimes eliminate the casino's house advantage by exploiting certain opportunities. Advantage players will utilize any legal approach necessary to gain an advantage in a game. This may include exploiting things such as mechanical flaws in gaming equipment, sloppy shuffling, the biases of a roulette wheel, weak casino procedures, or their knowledge of holecards.

Advertising—Any paid, nonpersonal communication transmitted through mass media by an identified sponsor.

AGA—American Gaming Association.

AIDA—Acronym for attention, interest, desire, action. It describes the functions that advertisements need to obtain: get attention, gain interest, and create desire to cause action.

Ante—In a card game, a wager placed before the first card is dealt.

Bank Secrecy Act—The Currency and Foreign Transactions Reporting Act, also known as the Bank Secrecy Act (BSA) or Title 31, was established in 1970 to fight money laundering and other crimes involving currency. The act was initially created with an exclusive focus on banking institutions and required reports to be filed on anyone who completed a cash transaction involving $10,000 or more.

Cage—Location of the casino cashier; operates like a bank.

Call bet—A verbal wager that is made known by players and is illegal in New Jersey.

Cannibalization—One organization's brand takes customers away from one or more of the same company's other brands.

Casino host—A casino employee who provides a personal service link between the casino and premium players.

Central limit theorem—The statistical rule that as the sample size is increased, the sampling distribution approaches the normal distribution form and serves as the basis for craps.

Cognitive dissonance—Once a person makes the decision, the post purchase evaluation whereby the person asks whether or not it was the right decision.

Commercial casino gaming—A casino that operates in a state that has made it legal to operate casinos in accordance with certain rules and regulations established in that particular state.

Comps—Short for "complimentary goods or services" given to players and can apply to things as low cost as drinks to full room, beverage, and transportation costs. They are a marketing tool used to attract players to a certain casino.

Compulsive gamblers—People who may live by gambling; however, they more likely live *for* gambling, continuing to gamble obsessively even as losses mount. For these bettors, gambling is not a rational process, and typically they may steal to support their habit, create family crises, and have high job insecurity.

Consumer behavior—The study of why, who, what, where, and how people make purchase decisions.

Consumer surplus—If players are able to purchase gambling services more cheaply than before, they will be better off to that extent.

Convenience markets—Consumers located within easy driving distance from major urban areas, but not convenient by air.

Corporate culture—The personality of an organization. Governs how people relate to one another and their jobs: the overall feel or style of a company.

Corporate Gaming Act of 1969—The state of Nevada allowed publicly traded corporations to have Nevada subsidiaries that could be licensed for casino ownership in the name of the principal stockholders—not all of the stockholders.

Cost-benefit analysis—Whenever governments contemplate introducing any new policy or changing any existing one, they try to weigh the advantages against the disadvantages. They then compare possible advantages with the advantages and disadvantages of the other courses of action they might otherwise take. When this practice is systematically engaged in by governments or firms (and when it involves putting dollar values to all potential costs and benefits) it is called "cost-benefit analysis."

Credit—(1) The custom in casinos that allows gamblers to bet without money so long as they agree to repay all losses they might incur; (2) in accounting, an entry on the right side of an account.

Crossroader—Cheats who specialize in swindling the casino from the outside.

Day-trippers—A market segment that can drive to the property and return home again the same day.

Direct marketing—The process of attempting to reach the market directly through such media as mail and telephone.

Discretionary income—Individual's or family's money that is left over after paying taxes and buying necessities.

Displacement—Whatever types of economic advantage governments seek from liberalizing gambling laws, they need to be aware of the fact that if customers start spending money on gambling, they will stop spending it on something else.

Disruptive technologies—New technological advances, such as the Internet, disrupt the status quo of prior established product and service offerings.

Drop—Total amount of cash plus markers, during a given time frame. Can be at a table, on a shift, or in entire casino.

Drop Box—Box locked to the underside of a gaming table where the dealer deposits all currency, markers, and drop slips.

Earning potential—Earning potential = average bet × hours played × decisions per hour × house advantage. Also called player value, player worth, or theoretical win.

Escape problem gambler—A person who gambles not so much to feel great, but rather to feel nothing. They wish to anesthetize or "escape" from their problems through their gambling, a behavior that should be discouraged.

Expectation or expected value—The mean value of a variable in repeated samplings or trials, for example, gamblers' calculations of how much they could expect to win or lose in a fair game, in the long run, with a bet of a certain size.

Export earnings—In respect to commercial gambling, a jurisdiction benefits economically as people come into the jurisdiction because of gambling and spend money that they otherwise would spend elsewhere.

External forces—Cannot be controlled by the industry, but have great impact on the way a casino does business. These forces are the economic environment, the social environment, cultural/corporate and technological environment, the political environment, the legal environment, the buying behaviors of guests, and the historical/competitive environment.

Externality—Exists when the production or consumption of a good directly affects businesses or consumers not involved in buying and selling it and when those spillover effects are not fully reflected in market prices.

Eye in the sky (the eye)—Electronic surveillance equipment suspended from the ceiling and tied into a central observation point.

Facial recognition programs—Can zoom in on a person, identify him or her, and determine whether surveillance should be concerned.

False rating—A rating that represents a gambling session that never took place. A pit clerk, pit manager, floor supervisor, or anyone who has the authority to generate player rating slips may create false ratings.

Fill—Bringing additional checks from the cage to the table to replenish the dealer's bankroll.

Floor supervisor—Supervisor of the gaming tables who is responsible for keeping the racks full, attends to any problems at the tables, supervises the dealers, and watches for irregularities.

Frequency—The number of times an individual or household is exposed to an advertising message over a certain period of time.

Front money—Funds put forth by a player to establish credit in a casino.

Gambling—According to Webster's dictionary, gambling is "to play or game for money; anything involving a like risk or uncertainty." In this book, gambling discussions are restricted to legal forms of gambling performed in a specially designated facility called a "casino" or "house."

Gambling Devices Act—Establishes procedures for manufacturing and shipping gaming equipment in interstate commerce throughout the United States. The act prevents the shipment of gaming devices into jurisdictions where the machines are not legal under state law. The act also requires that manufacturers and distributors of gambling devices keep detailed records of machines they sell or service.

Gambling privilege taxes—Governments sometimes seek to capture abnormal profits by means of a special tax on gambling.

Hard count—Counting of hard money (coins). The process of counting the coins and tokens removed from the slot machine drop buckets through the use of a weight scale or coin counter. The hard count is performed by designated count personnel, also known as a count team, in a secured room that is monitored by surveillance cameras.

Hard count room—The secured room used to weigh, wrap, record, and verify the contents of the slot drop buckets. The hard count room can also act as a storage facility for the casino cage.

Hold percentage—The amount of money won by the casino expressed as a percentage of the amount of money or credit exchanged for gaming chips (the drop).

Hopper—Inside part of a slot machine that holds the money.

House—A synonym for casino, casino employees, casino's funds or bank.

House advantage—Mathematical winning edge that the casino gives itself by manipulating the rules of the games to ensure profitability.

House edge—When the EV calculation is performed for a 1-unit amount, the negative of the resulting value.

Import substitutions—To prevent gambling dollars from going abroad.

Infantilize—To treat like a young child.

Indian Gaming Regulatory Act—This federal law outlines procedures whereby federally recognized Native American tribes can operate casino gaming. The law divides the types of gaming that Native American tribes can operate into Class I, Class II, and Class III gaming.

Inflated rating—A rating that actually took place but reveals larger average bets and longer time played than actually happened.

Integrated marketing communications (IMC)—Campaigns that integrate and coordinate all of the communication channels so that there is one clear consistent message about the organization and its products.

Internal core attitudes—The psychological make-up of an individual filters the external information and blends it with his or her personality. This covers initial exposure, motivation, ability, perception, and opportunity to create a judgment.

Internal forces—Tangible and intangible factors that exist within the organization and are under its control. Forces that mold the casinos: product, organization, pricing, location and transportation, and promotions.

Junket—A form of comp in which a group of people who are known and rated gamblers are brought to the casino on an all-inclusive trip paid for by the casino and are expected to participate in a given level of casino action.

KISS—An advertising acronym for "keep it simple, stupid." Because people have a short attention span for advertisements, it is important to keep the message simple so that it can be understood quickly.

Leakage—The phenomena when parts of the tourist dollar are exported outside the local economy, such as when the dollar is sent to the corporate offices.

Lotteries—In gaming, a randomized drawing from a pool, usually of sold tickets.

Marker—An I.O.U. or credit extended to a player.

Multiplier effects—In regional economics, a term used to denote the change in an induced variable (GNP, money supply, tourism spending) per unit change in an external variable (government spending, tax rates, building a casino).

NIMBY—*not in my backyard.*

Occupational gamblers—Gamblers who believe that their skills will enable them to make money by gambling.

Odds—Ratio or probability that one event will happen over another.

One armed bandits—Synonym for slot machines.

Pathological gambling—Originally based upon the clinical experiences of Dr. Custer, the DSM criteria have evolved into a list of ten items, and an individual who satisfies five of the criteria is diagnosed with pathological gambling (see Table 3–2).

Payback Percentage—The flip side of the house advantage or the proportion of wagered money returned to the player.

Payout—In casinos, customer's winnings.

Permissivist—In the democratic jurisdictions that consider how much casino gambling the law should permit and what additional regulations should be applied, opinions will typically differ among politicians and the general public. At one end of the spectrum will be the champions of a permissive libertarian position who stress the role of government as restricted only to preventing citizens from harming others. This philosophy promotes that government should not be concerned with preventing people from doing things that may be harmful to themselves, nor compelling them to do things that others think would be good for them—even if the others are right.

Pit—In the casino layout, a single grouping of adjacent table games.

Players' club—The casinos have developed a way of tracking each player so the casino can offer comps to get gamblers into the system.

Player rating—A process by which a table game floor supervisor monitors the gambling routine of a patron, or by which a gaming device monitors a player's action through a computerized rating system.

Pleasure markets—Include consumers who may require long-distance travel; they are convenient by air, but not located within easy driving distance from a major urban area. Casinos in pleasure markets provide more than gambling facilities; they also can provide lodging facilities and restaurants.

Plenary power—Full, complete, power.

Probability—The likelihood that a particular event or relationship will occur; the proportion of tries that are successful; out of all possible outcomes, the proportionate expectation of a given outcome.

Probity—Honesty.

Problem gambling—The official psychological term for problem gambling is *pathological gambling*.

Promotions—A strategic marketing process to coordinate seller-initiated efforts to set up channels of information and persuasion to sell services or to promote an idea.

Protectivist—Person who believes that governments ought to enforce the moral rules that are accepted by the majority of the community. Such a person may also believe that governments must enforce adherence to particular moral and religious rules that they deem to be essential to spiritual well-being.

Psychographics—A consumer's personality, lifestyle, values, and attitudes.

Public relations—A marketing communications term that refers to the press coverage or other disseminated information that is not paid directly to the media and is not controlled by the corporation.

Pull strategies—Customers create demand by going to the retailer and asking for the product. For example, the players learn of an offer and they go to the casino to obtain the deal.

Push strategies—A business tries to push a product through different channels to reach the customer. For example, one that tries to push the offer or package through the players' club or casino host to the player.

Racinos—A facility that mixes dog or horse track activity with casino-type activities such as slots.

Racks—A piece of equipment for the tables; a rectangular metal tray that contains the table checks and silver and lies flat in the middle of table next to the dealer.

Radio frequency identification device (RFID)—Used in employee uniforms and on valuable pieces of equipment, allows items to be tracked.

Rating slip—(1) A sheet that indicates a player's activity for comps; (2) a record of a dealer's performance.

Reach—The number or percentage of different individuals who tune in, listen to, read, or interact with the media over a specific time period.

Recreational gamblers—A person who views gambling as a leisure time pursuit.

Regression analysis—The equation indicates the nature and closeness of the relationship between two or more variables, specifically, the extent to which you can predict some by knowing others.

Responsible gambling—Strategies employed by the gaming entertainment industry to mitigate pathological and underage gambling, including prevention, education, and awareness programs for employees, customers, and local communities.

Return percentage or payback percentage—The flip side of the house advantage or the proportion of wagered money returned to the player.

Rim cards—A document used on a table game by the floor supervisor or pit manager to track the credit transactions of a high-profile player who requests multiple credit transactions throughout his or her play, thus, eliminating the need for a player to sign multiple documents throughout the gambling session.

Sales promotion—A paid marketing communication that stimulates short-term consumer purchases.

Saw dust joints—Casinos that resembled the old Wild West with cowboys and loose rules; low-budget or low-roller casinos.

Sharpers—A card cheat or superior player who takes advantage of novices.

Social cost—The costs to society of compulsive gambling: bailout costs, unrecoverable loans, strain on public services, unpaid debts, bankruptcies, industry cannibalization, and higher insurance premiums resulting from pathological gambler-caused fraud. All of these cost are externalized onto the public.

Soft count—Counting the value of paper money, such as dollar bills, cheques, markers, and so on.

Soft count room—The location where the drop boxes are stored prior to the soft count and where the actual counting of the drop box contents takes place. This is a highly secured area under constant video surveillance monitoring.

Standard deviation—A measure of the average amount the scores in a distribution deviate from the mean.

Transit markets—Located between the pleasure markets and the convenience markets. This market has no other facilities or easy access for air travelers. Transit markets do not tend to focus on one specific potential market; instead, they focus on markets that have multiple characteristics.

U.S. Patriot Act—Permits financial institutions, upon providing notice to the U. S. Department of the Treasury, to share information with one another to identify and report to the federal government any activities that may involve money laundering or terrorist activity.

Vacuum florescent display (VFD)—Displays the game information, attract sequences, and diagnostic errors; also sets up messages.

Variable reinforcement schedule—Skinner developed schedules of reinforcement to show how animals behave when rewards are programmed. In his experiments, he used a variable reinforcement schedule, which means that rewards were given at totally random times.

Volatility—Normal fluctuations.

Wagering tax—A fee assessed by the state on gaming revenue generated by the casino operator.

Whales—Big bettors; for example, a gambler with a credit line in excess of $50,000.

Win percentage—The amount of each dollar wagered that is won or held by the house before operating expenses and other costs have been paid and does not represent profit.

Index